PRESIDENTIAL ELECTIONS SINCE 1789

SECOND EDITION

CONGRESSIONAL QUARTERLY

1414 22ND STREET, N.W., WASHINGTON, D.C. 20037

Congressional Quarterly Inc.

Congressional Quarterly Inc., an editorial research service and publishing company, serves clients in the fields of news, education, business and government. It combines specific coverage of Congress, government and politics by Congressional Quarterly with the more general subject range of an affiliated service, Editorial Research Reports.

Congressional Quarterly was founded in 1945 by Henrietta and Nelson Poynter. Its basic periodical publication was and still is the CQ *Weekly Report,* mailed to clients every Saturday. A cumulative index is published quarterly.

The CQ *Almanac,* a compendium of legislation for one session of Congress, is published every spring. *Congress and the Nation* is published every four years as a record of government for one presidential term.

Congressional Quarterly also publishes paperback books on public affairs. These include the twice-yearly *Guide to Current American Government* and such recent titles as *Urban America: Policies and Problems; Taxes, Jobs and Inflation* and *U.S. Defense Policy: Weapons, Strategy and Commitments.*

CQ Direct Research is a consulting service which performs contract research and maintains a reference library and query desk for the convenience of clients.

Editorial Research Reports covers subjects beyond the specialized scope of Congressional Quarterly. It publishes reference material on foreign affairs, business, education, cultural affairs, national security, science and other topics of news interest. Service to clients includes a 6,000-word report four times a month bound and indexed semiannually. Editorial Research Reports publishes paperback books in its fields of coverage. Founded in 1923, the service merged with Congressional Quarterly in 1956.

Book Department Editor: Patricia Ann O'Connor.

Major Contributor: Warden Moxley.

Contributors: Robert A. Diamond, Matt Pinkus, Mark Bedner, James R. Berger, Linda Cumbo, Edna Frazier, Robert E. Healy, Mary Neumann, Elizabeth Wehr.

Production Manager: I.D. Fuller. **Assistant Production Manager:** Maceo Mayo.

Cover Photo: From the Smithsonian Institution

Library of Congress Cataloging in Publication Data

Congressional Quarterly, Inc.
    Presidential elections since 1789.

    Includes bibliographies and indexes.
    1. Presidents — United States — Election —
Statistics.   I. Title.

JK524.C65 1979   329´.023´73   78-31928
ISBN 0-87187-145-9

Table of Contents

Introduction

Since 1789 Americans have gone to the polls 48 times to elect a president. The history of these elections has been the subject of countless volumes, monographs, dissertations and articles in academic journals. Nevertheless, it is difficult to find a single book which comprehensively and succinctly covers the basic facts and figures on the electoral college, popular returns, presidential primaries, nominations of minor party candidates and biographical data on presidential candidates.

Presidential Elections Since 1789, first published in 1975, contains within the pages of a single book an enormous range of information on American presidential elections which has been widely scattered in numerous sources not readily available to the general reader or researcher. It includes data on popular vote returns for president, obtained from the Historical Archive of the Inter-University Consortium for Political Research (ICPR) at the University of Michigan. Congressional Quarterly has updated this material and added data on the 1976 presidential election to produce a second edition of this comprehensive reference book.

The first section of the book deals with the constitutional origins and historical development of the electoral college, the uniquely American system of electing presidents. The section details complex and little-known methods used in the various states through the first third of the 19th century to choose presidential electors, recounts historical anomalies in the functioning of the electoral college and gives reasons why a state's electoral votes have frequently been divided among several candidates. It covers the two occasions when a president was elected by the House of Representatives, explains procedures for counting and challenging electoral votes in Congress and describes the famous Tilden-Hayes contest in 1877. The section concludes with a discussion of instances of presidential disability and the ratification of the 25th Amendment to the Constitution.

The second section contains maps and tables displaying all presidential electoral college results since 1789. Footnotes indicate instances of splits of states' electoral votes, disputed elections and other anomalies referring the reader to the appropriate page of the introductory section on the electoral college for a fuller explanation. Vice presidential electoral votes appear at the end of this section; each instance where the vice presidential candidate received a different number of electoral college votes than the presidential candidate of his party is explained in a footnote.

The popular vote returns for president up through 1972 were obtained from ICPR. The 1976 figures were compiled by Congressional Quarterly from the final, official reports of the secretaries of state and the District of Columbia Board of Elections. The ICPR data were compiled as part of a 10-year research project involving more than 100 scholars and archivists throughout the United States. Prior to publication of the first edition of this book, these data were available only on computer tape. Here, the material is presented in a readily readable format displaying the national plurality of the leading popular vote candidate, state-by-state breakdowns of votes, percentages and pluralities and national vote totals and percentages for each candidate. The scope of this material can best be appreciated by noting that the figures in the returns range from the record high of 47,170,179 votes cast for Richard M. Nixon in 1972 to the single vote cast for Andrew Gump in Iowa in 1924.

The comprehensive list of party nominees since 1831, the first year national nominating conventions were held, includes nominations of minor candidates — some of whom did not even receive popular votes. For example, on page 116 can be found the nominations in 1872 by the People's Party of the first woman candidate for president, Victoria Claflin Woodhull, and the first black candidate for vice president, Frederick Douglass.

The section on presidential primaries is introduced with a useful historical narrative on the origins and development of primaries together with a bibliography of supplementary sources. This is followed by tables of primary election returns since 1912, the first year presidential preference primaries were held, through the primaries of 1976.

The Biographical Directory of presidential and vice presidential candidates gathers information from a variety of sources and concisely presents significant data on 206 candidates since 1789. The General Index provides quick access to information contained throughout this book and is also itself a source of information. For example, the index entry for Herbert C. Hoover indicates that Hoover received votes in presidential primaries in the years 1920, 1928, 1932, 1936 and 1940 and was a presidential nominee in 1928 and 1932.

Presidents and Vice Presidents of the United States

President and Political Party	Born	Died	Age at inauguration	Native of—	Elected from—	Term of Service	Vice President
George Washington (F)*	1732	1799	57	Va.	Va.	April 30, 1789-March 4, 1793	John Adams
George Washington (F)			61			March 4, 1793-March 4, 1797	John Adams
John Adams (F)	1735	1826	61	Mass.	Mass.	March 4, 1797-March 4, 1801	Thomas Jefferson
Thomas Jefferson (D-R)	1743	1826	57	Va.	Va.	March 4, 1801-March 4, 1805	Aaron Burr
Thomas Jefferson (D-R)			61			March 4, 1805-March 4, 1809	George Clinton
James Madison (D-R)	1751	1836	57	Va.	Va.	March 4, 1809-March 4, 1813	George Clinton
James Madison (D-R)			61			March 4, 1813-March 4, 1817	Elbridge Gerry
James Monroe (D-R)	1758	1831	58	Va.	Va.	March 4, 1817-March 4, 1821	Daniel D. Tompkins
James Monroe (D-R)			62			March 4, 1821-March 4, 1825	Daniel D. Tompkins
John Q. Adams (N-R)	1767	1848	57	Mass.	Mass.	March 4, 1825-March 4, 1829	John C. Calhoun
Andrew Jackson (D)	1767	1845	61	S.C.	Tenn.	March 4, 1829-March 4, 1833	John C. Calhoun
Andrew Jackson (D)			65			March 4, 1833-March 4, 1837	Martin Van Buren
Martin Van Buren (D)	1782	1862	54	N.Y.	N.Y.	March 4, 1837-March 4, 1841	Richard M. Johnson
W. H. Harrison (W)	1773	1841	68	Va.	Ohio	March 4, 1841-April 4, 1841	John Tyler
John Tyler (W)	1790	1862	51	Va.	Va.	April 6, 1841-March 4, 1845	
James K. Polk (D)	1795	1849	49	N.C.	Tenn.	March 4, 1845-March 4, 1849	George M. Dallas
Zachary Taylor (W)	1784	1850	64	Va.	La.	March 4, 1849-July 9, 1850	Millard Fillmore
Millard Fillmore (W)	1800	1874	50	N.Y.	N.Y.	July 10, 1850-March 4, 1853	
Franklin Pierce (D)	1804	1869	48	N.H.	N.H.	March 4, 1853-March 4, 1857	William R. King
James Buchanan (D)	1791	1868	65	Pa.	Pa.	March 4, 1857-March 4, 1861	John C. Breckinridge
Abraham Lincoln (R)	1809	1865	52	Ky.	Ill.	March 4, 1861-March 4, 1865	Hannibal Hamlin
Abraham Lincoln (R)			56			March 4, 1865-April 15, 1865	Andrew Johnson
Andrew Johnson (R)	1808	1875	56	N.C.	Tenn.	April 15, 1865-March 4, 1869	
Ulysses S. Grant (R)	1822	1885	46	Ohio	Ill.	March 4, 1869-March 4, 1873	Schuyler Colfax
Ulysses S. Grant (R)			50			March 4, 1873-March 4, 1877	Henry Wilson
Rutherford B. Hayes (R)	1822	1893	54	Ohio	Ohio	March 4, 1877-March 4, 1881	William A. Wheeler
James A. Garfield (R)	1831	1881	49	Ohio	Ohio	March 4, 1881-Sept. 19, 1881	Chester A. Arthur
Chester A. Arthur (R)	1830	1886	50	Vt.	N.Y.	Sept. 20, 1881-March 4, 1885	
Grover Cleveland (D)	1837	1908	47	N.J.	N.Y.	March 4, 1885-March 4, 1889	Thomas A. Hendricks
Benjamin Harrison (R)	1833	1901	55	Ohio	Ind.	March 4, 1889-March 4, 1893	Levi P. Morton
Grover Cleveland (D)	1837	1908	55			March 4, 1893-March 4, 1897	Adlai E. Stevenson
William McKinley (R)	1843	1901	54	Ohio	Ohio	March 4, 1897-March 4, 1901	Garret A. Hobart
William McKinley (R)			58			March 4, 1901-Sept. 14, 1901	Theodore Roosevelt
Theodore Roosevelt (R)	1858	1919	42	N.Y.	N.Y.	Sept. 14, 1901-March 4, 1905	
Theodore Roosevelt (R)			46			March 4, 1905-March 4, 1909	Charles W. Fairbanks
William H. Taft (R)	1857	1930	51	Ohio	Ohio	March 4, 1909-March 4, 1913	James S. Sherman
Woodrow Wilson (D)	1856	1924	56	Va.	N.J.	March 4, 1913-March 4, 1917	Thomas R. Marshall
Woodrow Wilson (D)			60			March 4, 1917-March 4, 1921	Thomas R. Marshall
Warren G. Harding (R)	1865	1923	55	Ohio	Ohio	March 4, 1921-Aug. 2, 1923	Calvin Coolidge
Calvin Coolidge (R)	1872	1933	51	Vt.	Mass.	Aug. 3, 1923-March 4, 1925	
Calvin Coolidge (R)			52			March 4, 1925-March 4, 1929	Charles G. Dawes
Herbert Hoover (R)	1874	1964	54	Iowa	Calif.	March 4, 1929-March 4, 1933	Charles Curtis
Franklin D. Roosevelt (D)	1882	1945	51	N.Y.	N.Y.	March 4, 1933-Jan. 20, 1937	John N. Garner
Franklin D. Roosevelt (D)			55			Jan. 20, 1937-Jan. 20, 1941	John N. Garner
Franklin D. Roosevelt (D)			59			Jan. 20, 1941-Jan. 20, 1945	Henry A. Wallace
Franklin D. Roosevelt (D)			63			Jan. 20, 1945-April 12, 1945	Harry S Truman
Harry S Truman (D)	1884	1972	60	Mo.	Mo.	April 12, 1945-Jan. 20, 1949	
Harry S Truman (D)			64			Jan. 20, 1949-Jan. 20, 1953	Alben W. Barkley
Dwight D. Eisenhower (R)	1890	1969	62	Texas	N.Y.	Jan. 20, 1953-Jan. 20, 1957	Richard M. Nixon
Dwight D. Eisenhower (R)			66		Pa.	Jan. 20, 1957-Jan. 20, 1961	Richard M. Nixon
John F. Kennedy (D)	1917	1963	43	Mass.	Mass.	Jan. 20, 1961-Nov. 22, 1963	Lyndon B. Johnson
Lyndon B. Johnson (D)	1908	1973	55	Texas	Texas	Nov. 22, 1963-Jan. 20, 1965	
Lyndon B. Johnson (D)			56			Jan. 20, 1965-Jan. 20, 1969	Hubert H. Humphrey
Richard M. Nixon (R)	1913		56	Calif.	N.Y.	Jan. 20, 1969-Jan. 20, 1973	Spiro T. Agnew
Richard M. Nixon (R)			60		Calif.	Jan. 20, 1973-Aug. 9, 1974	Spiro T. Agnew
							Gerald R. Ford
Gerald R. Ford (R)	1913		61	Neb.	Mich.	Aug. 9, 1974-Jan. 20, 1977	Nelson A. Rockefeller
Jimmy Carter (D)	1924		52	Ga.	Ga.	Jan. 20, 1977-	Walter F. Mondale

*Key to abbreviations: (D) Democrat, (D-R) Democrat-Republican, (F) Federalist, (N-R) National Republican, (R) Republican, (W) Whig

SOURCE: Joseph Nathan Kane, *Facts About the President,* revised edition, 1976

Presidential Elections and the Electoral College

For almost two centuries, Americans have been electing their presidents through a unique method called the electoral college. Conceived by the Founding Fathers as a compromise between electing presidents by Congress or by direct popular vote, the system has continued to function even while the nation has undergone radical transformation from an agricultural seaboard nation to a world power.

Under the electoral college system, each state is entitled to electoral votes equal in number to its congressional delegation — i.e., the number of representatives from the state, plus two more for the state's two senators. Whichever party receives a plurality of the popular vote in a state usually wins that state's electoral votes. However, there have been numerous exceptions to that rule, including choosing of electors by district, statewide votes for each individual elector and selection of electors by state legislatures.

Constitutional Background

The method of selecting a president was the subject of long debate at the Constitutional Convention of 1787. Several plans were proposed and rejected before a compromise solution, which was modified only slightly in later years, was adopted. (Article II, Section I, Clause 2).

Facing the convention when it convened May 25 was the question of whether the chief executive should be chosen by direct popular election, by the Congress, by state legislatures or by intermediate electors. Direct election was opposed, because it was generally felt that the people lacked sufficient knowledge of the character and qualifications of possible candidates to make an intelligent choice. Many delegates also feared that the people of the various states would be unlikely to agree on a single person, usually casting their votes for favorite-son candidates well-known to them.

The possibility of giving Congress the power to choose the president also received consideration. However, this plan was rejected, largely because of fear that it would jeopardize the principle of executive independence. Similarly, a plan favored by many delegates, to let state legislatures choose the president, was turned down because it was feared that the president might feel so indebted to the states as to allow them to encroach on federal authority.

Unable to agree on a plan, the convention on Aug. 31 appointed a "Committee of 11" to propose a solution to the problem. The committee on Sept. 4 suggested a compromise under which each state would appoint presidential electors equal to the total number of its representatives and senators. The electors, chosen in a manner set forth by each state legislature, would meet in their own states and each cast votes for two persons. The votes would be counted in Congress, with the candidate receiving a majority elected president and the second-highest candidate becoming vice president.

No distinction was made between ballots for president and vice president. The development of national political parties and the nomination of tickets for president and vice president caused confusion in the electoral system. All the electors of one party would tend to cast ballots for their two party nominees. But with no distinction between the presidential and vice presidential nominees, the danger arose of a tie vote between the two. This actually happened in 1800, leading to a change in the original electoral system with the 12th Amendment.

The committee plan constituted a great concession to the less populous states, since they were assured of three

Sources

Petersen, Svend. *A Statistical History of the American Presidential Elections.* New York: Frederick Ungar, 1968.

Schlesinger, Arthur M. Jr., ed. *History of American Presidential Elections.* 4 vols. New York: McGraw-Hill, 1971.

Stanwood, Edward. *A History of the Presidency, 1788-1916.* 2 vols. Boston: Houghton Mifflin, Vol. 1, 1889; Vol. 2, 1916.

U.S. Bureau of the Census. *Historical Statistics of the United States, Colonial Times to 1957.* Washington, D.C.: U.S. Government Printing Office, 1960.

votes (two for their two senators and at least one for their representative) however small their populations might be. The plan also left important powers with the states by giving complete discretion to state legislatures to determine the method of choosing electors.

Only one provision of the committee's plan aroused serious opposition — that giving the Senate the right to decide presidential elections in which no candidate received a majority of electoral votes. Some delegates feared that the Senate, which already had been given treaty ratification powers and the responsibility to "advise and consent" to all important executive appointments, might become too powerful. Therefore, a counterproposal was made and accepted to let the House decide in instances when the electors failed to give a majority of their votes to a single candidate. The interests of the small states were preserved by giving each state's delegation only one vote in the House on roll calls to elect a president.

The system adopted by the Constitutional Convention was a compromise born out of problems involved in diverse state voting requirements, the slavery problem, big- versus small-state rivalries and the complexities of the balance of power among different branches of the government. It also was apparently as close to a direct popular election as the men who wrote the Constitution thought possible and appropriate at the time.

The 12th Amendment

Only once since ratification of the Constitution has an amendment been adopted which substantially altered the method of electing the president. In the 1800 presidential election, the Democratic-Republican electors inadvertently caused a tie in the electoral college by casting equal numbers of votes for Thomas Jefferson, whom they wished to be elected president, and Aaron Burr, whom they wished to elect vice president. The election was thrown into the House of Representatives and 36 ballots were required before Jefferson was finally elected president. The 12th Amendment, ratified in 1804, sought to prevent a recurrence of this incident by providing that the electors should vote separately for president and vice president. *(Amendment text, box, p. 3)*

Other changes in the system evolved over the years. The authors of the Constitution, for example, had intended that each state should choose its most distinguished citizens as electors and that they would deliberate and vote as individuals in electing the president. But, as strong political parties began to appear, the electors came to be chosen merely as representatives of the parties; independent voting by electors disappeared almost entirely.

Methods of Choosing Electors

1789-1796

In the early years, states chose a mixture of ways to select presidential electors. For the first presidential election, in 1789, four states held direct popular elections to choose their electors: Pennsylvania and Maryland (at large) and Virginia and Delaware (by district). In five states — Connecticut, Georgia, New Jersey, New York and South Carolina — the state legislatures were to make the choice.

Two states, New Hampshire and Massachusetts, adopted a combination of the legislative and popular methods. New Hampshire held a statewide popular vote for presidential electors with the stipulation that any elector would have to win a majority of the popular vote to be elected; otherwise, the legislature would choose.

In Massachusetts, the arrangement was for the people in each congressional district to vote for the two persons they wanted to be presidential electors. From the two persons in each district having the highest number of votes, the legislature, by joint ballot of both houses, was to choose one. In addition, the legislature was to choose two additional electors at large.

In a dispute between the two houses of the state legislature in New York, that state failed to choose electors. The state Senate insisted on full equality with the Assembly (lower house); that is, the Senate wanted each house to take a separate ballot and to resolve any differences between them by agreement rather than by having one house impose its will on the other. The assembly, on the other hand, wanted a joint ballot, on which the lower house's larger numbers would prevail, or it was willing to divide the electors with the Senate. The failure to compromise cost the state its vote in the first presidential election.

The 12th and 13th states — North Carolina and Rhode Island — had not ratified the Constitution by the time the electors were chosen, and so they did not participate.

Generally similar arrangements prevailed for the election of 1792. Massachusetts, while continuing the system of choosing electors by district, changed the system somewhat to provide for automatic election of any candidate for elector who received a majority of the popular vote. New Hampshire continued the system of popular election at large, but substituted a popular runoff election in place of legislative choice, if no candidate received a majority of the popular vote.

Besides Massachusetts and New Hampshire, electors were chosen in 1792 by popular vote in Maryland and Pennsylvania (at large) and Virginia and Kentucky (by district). Legislatures chose electors in Connecticut, Delaware, Georgia, New Jersey, New York, North Carolina, Rhode Island, South Carolina and Vermont.

By 1796, several changes had occurred. New Hampshire switched back to legislative choice for those electors who failed to receive a majority of the popular vote. Tennessee entered the Union (1796) with a unique system for choosing presidential electors — the state legislature appointed three persons in each county, who in turn chose the presidential electors. Massachusetts retained the system used in 1792. Other states chose their electors as follows: popular vote, at large: Georgia, Pennsylvania; popular vote, by district: Kentucky, Maryland, North Carolina, Virginia; state legislature: Connecticut, Delaware, New Jersey, New York, Rhode Island, South Carolina, Vermont.

Political Parties and Electors: 1800

With the rise of political parties, political manipulation of the system of choosing electors became evident by 1800. Massachusetts switched from popular voting to legislative selection of electors because of recent successes by the Democratic-Republican party in that state. The Federalist party, still in firm control of the legislature, sought to secure the state's entire electoral vote for its presidential candidate, native son John Adams. New Hampshire did likewise.

Nor were the Democratic-Republicans innocent of this kind of political maneuver. In Virginia, where that party was in control, the legislature changed the system for

Constitutional Provisions for Selection of the President

Article II

Section I. The executive Power shall be vested in a President of the United States of America. He shall hold his Office during the Term of four Years, and, together with the Vice President, chosen for the same term, be elected, as follows.

Each State shall appoint, in such Manner as the Legislature thereof may direct, a Number of Electors, equal to the whole Number of Senators and Representatives to which the State may be entitled in the Congress: but no Senator or Representative, or Person holding an Office of Trust or Profit under the United States, shall be appointed an Elector.

[The Electors shall meet in their respective States, and vote by Ballot for two Persons, of whom one at least shall not be an Inhabitant of the same State with themselves. And they shall make a List of all the Persons voted for, and of the Number of Votes for each; which List they shall sign and certify, and transmit sealed to the Seat of the Government of the United States, directed to the President of the Senate. The President of the Senate shall, in the Presence of the Senate and House of Representatives, open all the Certificates, and the Votes shall then be counted. The Person having the greatest Number of Votes shall be the President, if such Number be a Majority of the whole Number of Electors appointed; and if there be more than one who have such Majority, and have an equal Number of Votes, then the House of Representatives shall immediately chuse by Ballot one of them for President; and if no Person have a Majority, then from the five highest on the List the said House shall in like Manner chuse the President. But in chusing the President, the Votes shall be taken by States, the Representation from each State having one Vote; a quorum for this Purpose shall consist of a Member or Members from two thirds of the States, and a Majority of all the States shall be necessary to a Choice. In every Case, after the Choice of the President, the Person having the greatest Number of Votes of the Electors shall be the Vice President. But if there should remain two or more who have equal Votes, the Senate shall chuse from them by Ballot the Vice-President.]*

The Congress may determine the Time of chusing the Electors, and the Day on which they shall give their Votes; which Day shall be the same throughout the United States.

No person except a natural born Citizen, or a Citizen of the United States, at the time of the Adoption of this Constitution, shall be eligible to the Office of President; neither shall any Person be eligible to that Office who shall not have attained to the Age of thirty five Years, and been fourteen Years a Resident within the United States.

Amendment XII *(Ratified July 27, 1804)*

The Electors shall meet in their respective states and vote by ballot for President and Vice-President, one of whom, at least, shall not be an inhabitant of the same state with themselves; they shall name in their ballots the person voted for as President, and in distinct ballots the person voted for as Vice-President, and they shall make distinct lists of all persons voted for as President, and of all persons voted for as Vice-President, and of the number of votes for each, which lists they shall sign and certify, and transmit sealed to the seat of the government of the United States, directed to the President of the Senate; ...The person having the greatest number of votes for President, shall be the President, if such number be a majority of the whole number of Electors appointed; and if no person have such majority, then from the persons having the highest numbers not exceeding three on the list of those voted for as President, the House of Representatives shall choose immediately, by ballot, the President. But in choosing the President, the votes shall be taken by states, the representation from each state having one vote; a quorum for this purpose shall consist of a member or members from two-thirds of the states, and a majority of all the states shall be necessary to a choice. [And if the House of Representatives shall not choose a President whenever the right of choice shall devolve upon them, before the fourth day of March next following, then the Vice-President shall act as President, as in the case of the death or other constitutional disability of the President. —]† The person having the greatest number of votes as Vice-President, shall be the Vice-President, if such number be a majority of the whole number of Electors appointed, and if no person have a majority, then from the two highest numbers on the list, the Senate shall choose the Vice-President; a quorum for the purpose shall consist of two-thirds of the whole number of Senators, and a majority of the whole number shall be necessary to a choice. But no person constitutionally ineligible to the office of President shall be eligible to that of Vice-President of the United States.

Amendment XX *(Ratified January 23, 1933)*

Section 1. The terms of the President and Vice President shall end at noon on the 20th day of January . . . .

Section 3. If, at the time fixed for the beginning of the term of the President, the President elect shall have died, the Vice President elect shall become President. If a President shall not have been chosen before the time fixed for the beginning of his term, or if the President elect shall have failed to qualify, then the Vice President elect shall act as President until a President shall have qualified; and the Congress may by law provide for the case wherein neither a President elect nor a Vice President elect shall have qualified, declaring who shall then act as President, or the manner in which one who is to act shall be selected, and such person shall act accordingly until a President or Vice President shall have qualified.

Section 4. The Congress may by law provide for the case of the death of any of the persons from whom the House of Representatives may choose a President whenever the right of choice shall have devolved upon them, and for the case of the death of any of the persons from whom the Senate may choose a Vice President whenever the right of choice shall have devolved upon them.

* Superseded by the 12th Amendment.
† Changed to Jan. 20 by the 20th Amendment, ratified in 1933.

choosing electors from districts to a statewide at-large ballot. That way, the expected statewide Democratic-Republican majority could overcome Federalist control in some districts and result in a unanimous vote for Democratic-Republican presidential candidate Thomas Jefferson.

In Pennsylvania, the two houses of the state legislature could not agree on legislation providing for popular ballots, the system used in the first three elections, so the legislature itself chose the electors, dividing them between the parties.

In other changes in 1800, Rhode Island switched to popular election and Georgia changed to legislative election. The 16 states thus used the following methods of choosing presidential electors in 1800:

● By popular vote: Kentucky, Maryland, North Carolina (by district); Rhode Island, Virginia (at large).

● By the legislature: Connecticut, Delaware, Georgia, Massachusetts, New Hampshire, New Jersey, New York, Pennsylvania, South Carolina, Tennessee (indirectly, as in 1796), Vermont.

Trend to Winner-Take-All System

For the next third of a century, the states moved slowly but inexorably toward a standard system of choosing presidential electors — the statewide, winner-take-all popular ballot. The development of political parties resulted in the adoption of party slates of electors pledged to vote for the parties' presidential candidates. Each party organization saw a statewide ballot as being in its best interest, with the hope of sweeping in all its electors and preventing the opposition group from capitalizing on local areas of strength (which could result in winning only part of the electoral vote under the districting system).

From 1804 to 1832, there were three basic methods used by the states in choosing presidential electors — popular vote, at large; popular vote, by district and election by the state legislature. The following list shows the changing methods of choosing presidential electors for each state from 1804 to 1832:

1804

Popular vote, at large: New Hampshire, New Jersey, Ohio, Pennsylvania, Rhode Island, Virginia.

Popular vote, by district: Kentucky, Maryland, Massachusetts, North Carolina.

State legislature: Connecticut, Delaware, Georgia, New York, South Carolina, Tennessee, Vermont.

1808

Popular vote, at large: New Hampshire, New Jersey, Ohio, Pennsylvania, Rhode Island, Virginia.

Popular vote, by district: Kentucky, Maryland, North Carolina, Tennessee.

State legislature: Connecticut, Delaware, Georgia, Massachusetts, New York, South Carolina, Vermont.

1812

Popular vote, at large: New Hampshire, Ohio, Pennsylvania, Rhode Island, Virginia.

Popular vote, by district: Kentucky, Maryland, Massachusetts, Tennessee.

State legislature: Connecticut, Delaware, Georgia, Louisiana, New Jersey, New York, North Carolina, South Carolina, Vermont.

Methods of Selecting Electors: Sources

Information on the methods of selecting presidential electors for the period 1789-1836 appears in several sources, and the sources in a number of instances are in conflict. Among the sources are *Historical Statistics of the United States, Colonial Times to 1957*, prepared by the Bureau of the Census with the cooperation of the Social Science Research Council, published by the U.S. Government Printing Office, Washington, D.C., 1960; Edward Stanwood's *A History of the Presidency, 1788-1916*, Vol. I (Houghton Mifflin, Boston, 1889); Svend Petersen's *A Statistical History of the American Presidential Elections* (Frederick Ungar, New York, 1968); and Neil R. Peirce's *The People's President: the Electoral College in American History and the Direct Vote Alternative* (Simon & Schuster, New York, 1968).

Congressional Quarterly used the Census Bureau's *Historical Statistics of the United States* as its basic source. The chart on p. 681 of *Historical Statistics* presented the most detailed information of all the sources on the various methods used for choosing electors.

1816

Popular vote, at large: New Hampshire, New Jersey, North Carolina, Ohio, Pennsylvania, Rhode Island, Virginia.

Popular vote, by district: Kentucky, Maryland, Tennessee.

State legislature: Connecticut, Delaware, Georgia, Indiana, Louisiana, Massachusetts, New York, South Carolina, Vermont.

1820

Popular vote, at large: Connecticut, Mississippi, New Hampshire, New Jersey, North Carolina, Ohio, Pennsylvania, Rhode Island, Virginia.

Popular vote, by district: Illinois, Kentucky, Maine, Maryland, Massachusetts, Tennessee.

State legislature: Alabama, Delaware, Georgia, Indiana, Louisiana, Missouri, New York, South Carolina, Vermont.

1824

Popular vote, at large: Alabama, Connecticut, Indiana, Massachusetts, Mississippi, New Hampshire, New Jersey, North Carolina, Ohio, Pennsylvania, Rhode Island, Virginia.

Popular vote, by district: Illinois, Kentucky, Maine, Maryland, Missouri, Tennessee.

State legislature: Delaware, Georgia, Louisiana, New York, South Carolina, Vermont.

1828

Popular vote, at large: Alabama, Connecticut, Georgia, Illinois, Indiana, Kentucky, Louisiana, Massachusetts, Mississippi, Missouri, New Hampshire, New Jersey, North Carolina, Ohio, Pennsylvania, Rhode Island, Vermont, Virginia.

Popular vote, by district: Maine, Maryland, New York, Tennessee.

State legislature: Delaware, South Carolina.

1832

Popular vote, at large: All states except Maryland and South Carolina.

Popular vote, by district: Maryland.

State legislature: South Carolina.

By 1836, Maryland switched to the system of choosing its electors statewide, by popular vote. This left only South Carolina selecting its electors through the state legislature. The state continued this practice through the election of 1860; only after the Civil War was popular voting for presidential electors instituted in South Carolina.

Exception to Winner-Take-All System

Thus, since 1836 the statewide, winner-take-all popular vote for electors has been the almost universal practice. Exceptions include the following:

Massachusetts, 1848. Three slates of electors ran — Whig, Democratic and Free Soil — none of which received a majority of the popular vote. Under the law then in force, the state legislature was to choose in such a case. It chose the Whig electors.

Florida, 1868. The state legislature chose the electors.

Colorado, 1876. The state legislature chose the electors, because the state had just been admitted to the Union, had held state elections in August and did not want to go to the trouble and expense of holding a popular vote for the presidential election so soon thereafter.

Michigan, 1892. Republicans had been predominant in the state since the 1850s. However, in 1890 the Democrats managed to gain control of the legislature and the governorship. They promptly enacted a districting system of choosing presidential electors in the expectation that the Democrats could carry some districts and thus win some electoral votes in 1892. The result confirmed their expectations, with the Republicans winning nine and the Democrats five electoral votes that year. But the Republicans soon regained control of the state and re-enacted the at-large system for the 1896 election.

Maine, 1972. In 1969, the Maine legislature enacted a district system for choosing presidential electors. Two of the state's four electors were selected on the basis of the statewide vote, while the other two were determined by which party carried each of the state's two congressional districts. The system is still in force.

Historical Anomalies

Three Whig Candidates: 1836

The complicated and indirect system of electing the president has led to anomalies from time to time. In 1836, for example, the Whigs sought to take advantage of the electoral system by running different presidential candidates in different parts of the country. William Henry Harrison ran in most of New England, the mid-Atlantic states and the Midwest; Daniel Webster ran in Massachusetts; Hugh White of Tennessee ran in the South.

The theory was that each candidate could capture electoral votes for the Whig Party in the region where he was strongest. Then the Whig electors could combine on one candidate or, alternatively, throw the election into the House, whichever seemed to their advantage. However, the scheme did not work, because Martin Van Buren, the Democratic nominee, captured a majority of the electoral vote.

Death of Greeley: 1872

Another quirk in the system surfaced in 1872. The Democratic presidential nominee, Horace Greeley, died between the popular vote and the meeting of the presidential electors. Thus the Democratic electors had no party nominee to vote for, and each was left to his own judgment. Forty-two of the 66 Democratic electors chose to vote for the Democratic governor-elect of Indiana, Thomas Hendricks. The rest of the electors split their votes among three other politicians: 18 for B. Gratz Brown of Missouri, the Democratic vice presidential nominee; two for Charles J. Jenkins of Georgia, and one for David Davis of Illinois. Three Georgia electors insisted on casting their votes for Greeley, but Congress refused to count them.

Popular Votes and Electoral Votes

The provision that the electoral college, not the people directly, is to choose the president has led to three presidents assuming the office even though they ran behind their opponents in the popular vote. In two of these instances — Republican Rutherford B. Hayes in 1876 and Republican Benjamin Harrison in 1888 — the winning candidate carried a number of key states by close margins, while losing other states by wide margins. In the third instance — Democratic-Republican John Quincy Adams in 1824 — the House chose the new president after no candidate had achieved a majority in the electoral college.

Election by Congress

Congress under the Constitution has two key responsibilities relating to the election of the president and vice president. First, it is directed to receive and in joint session count the electoral votes certified by the states. Second, if no candidate has a majority of the electoral vote, the House of Representatives must elect the president and the Senate the vice president.

Although many of the framers of the Constitution apparently thought that most elections would be decided by Congress, the House actually has chosen a president only twice, in 1801 and 1825. But a number of campaigns have been deliberately designed to throw elections into the House, where each state has one vote and a majority of states is needed to elect.

In modern times the formal counting of electoral votes has been largely a ceremonial function, but the congressional role can be decisive when votes are contested. The pre-eminent example is the Hayes-Tilden contest of 1876, when congressional decisions on disputed electoral votes from four states gave the election to Republican Rutherford B. Hayes despite the fact that Democrat Samuel J. Tilden had a majority of the popular vote. *(Tilden-Hayes election, p. 11)*

From the beginning, the constitutional provisions governing the selection of the president have had few defenders, and many efforts at electoral college reform have been undertaken. Although prospects for reform seemed favorable after the close 1968 presidential election, the 91st Congress (1969-71) did not take final action on a proposed constitutional amendment that would have provided for direct popular election of the president and eliminated the existing provision for contingent election by the House. Reform legislation was reintroduced in the Senate during the 94th Congress (1975-77) and the 95th Congress (1977-79).

In addition to its role in electing the president, Congress bears responsibility in the related areas of presidential succession and disability. The 20th Amendment empowers

Splitting of States' Electoral College...

Throughout the history of presidential elections, there have been numerous cases where a state's electoral votes have been divided between two candidates. The split electoral votes occurred for a variety of reasons.

Electoral Vote Splits, 1789-1836

Splits of a state's electoral votes cast for president before 1836 occurred for these reasons:

● For the first four presidential elections (1789-1800) held under Article II, section 1 of the Constitution, each elector cast two votes without designating which vote was for president and which for vice president. As a result, electoral votes for each state were often scattered among several candidates. The 12th Amendment, ratified in 1804, required electors to vote separately for president and vice president.

● The district system of choosing electors, in which different candidates each could carry several districts. This system is the explanation for the split electoral votes in Maryland in 1804, 1808, 1812, 1824, 1828 and 1832; North Carolina in 1808; Illinois in 1824; Maine in 1828, and New York in 1828.

● The selection of electors by the legislatures of some states. This system sometimes led to party factionalism or political deals that resulted in the choice of electors loyal to more than one candidate. This was the cause for the division of electoral votes in New York in 1808 and 1824, Delaware in 1824 and Louisiana in 1824.

● The vote of an individual elector for someone other than his party's candidate. This happened in New Hampshire in 1820 when one Democratic-Republican elector voted for John Quincy Adams instead of the party nominee, James Monroe.

Voting for Individual Electors

By 1836, all states with the exception of South Carolina, which selected its electors by the state legislature until after the Civil War, had established a system of statewide popular election of electors. The new system limited the frequency of electoral vote splits. Nevertheless, a few states still, on occasion, divided their electoral votes among different presidential candidates. This occurred because of the practice of listing on the ballot the names of all electors and allowing voters to cross off the names of any particular electors they did not like, or, alternatively, requiring voters to vote for each individual elector. In a close election, electors of different parties sometimes were chosen. An example occurred in California in 1880, when one Democratic elector ran behind the Republican thus:

Winning Votes	Party	Losing Electors	Party
80,443	Democratic	80,282	Republican
80,426	Democratic	80,252	Republican
80,420	Democratic	80,242	Republican
80,413	Democratic	80,228	Republican
80,348	Republican	79,885	Democratic

Other similar occurrences include the following:

New Jersey, 1860. Four Republican and three Douglas Democratic electors won.

California, 1892. Eight Democratic electors and one Republican won.

North Dakota, 1892. Two Fusionists (Democrats and Populists) and one Republican won. One of the

---

Congress to decide what to do if the president-elect and the vice president-elect both fail to qualify by the date prescribed for commencement of their terms; it also gives Congress authority to settle problems arising from the death of candidates in cases where the election devolves upon Congress. Under the 25th Amendment, Congress has ultimate responsibility for resolving disputes over presidential disability. It also must confirm presidential nominations to fill a vacancy in the vice presidency. *(Constitutional provisions, p. 3)*

Jefferson-Burr Deadlock

The election of 1800 was the first in which the contingent election procedures of the Constitution were put to the test and the president was elected by the House.

The Federalists, a declining but still potent political force, nominated John Adams for a second term and chose Charles Cotesworth Pinckney as his running mate. A Democratic-Republican congressional caucus chose Vice President Thomas Jefferson for president and Aaron Burr, who had been instrumental in winning the New York legislature for the Democratic-Republicans earlier in 1800, for vice president.

The electors met in each state on Dec. 4, and the results gradually became known throughout the country: Jefferson and Burr, 73 electoral votes each; Adams, 65; Pinckney, 64; John Jay, 1. The Federalists had lost, but

because the Democratic-Republicans had neglected to withhold one electoral vote from Burr, their presidential and vice presidential candidates were tied and the election was thrown into the House.

The lame-duck Congress, with a partisan Federalist majority, was still in office for the electoral count, and the possibilities for intrigue were only too apparent. After toying with and rejecting a proposal to block any election until March 4, when Adams' term expired, the Federalists decided to throw their support to Burr and thus elect a relatively pliant politician over a man they considered a "dangerous radical." Alexander Hamilton opposed this move. "I trust the Federalists will not finally be so mad as to vote for Burr," he wrote. "I speak with intimate and accurate knowledge of his character. His elevation can only promote the purposes of the desperate and the profligate. If there be a man in the world I ought to hate, it is Jefferson. With Burr I have always been personally well. But the public good must be paramount to every private consideration."

On Feb. 11, 1801, Congress met in joint session — with Jefferson, the outgoing vice president, in the chair — to count the electoral vote. This ritual ended, the House retired to its own chamber to elect a president. When the House met, it became apparent that the advice of Hamilton had been rejected. A majority of Federalists in the House insisted on backing Burr over Jefferson, the man they

...Votes: Numerous Historical Cases

Fusion electors voted for Democrat Grover Cleveland and the other voted for Populist James B. Weaver, while the Republican elector voted for Benjamin Harrison, thus splitting the state's electoral vote three ways.

Ohio, 1892. Twenty-two Republicans and one Democratic elector won.

Oregon, 1892. Three Republicans and one Populist with Democratic support won.

California, 1896. Eight Republicans and one Democratic elector won.

Kentucky, 1896. Twelve Republicans and one Democratic elector won.

Maryland, 1904. Seven Democratic electors and one Republican won.

Maryland, 1908. Six Democratic and two Republican electors won.

California, 1912. Eleven Progressive and two Democratic electors won.

West Virginia, 1916. Seven Republicans and one Democratic elector won.

The increasing use of voting machines and straight-ticket voting — where the pull of a lever or the marking of an "X" results in automatically casting a vote for every elector — led to the decline in split electoral votes.

'Faithless Electors'

Yet another cause for occasional splits in a state's electoral vote is the so-called 'faithless elector.' Legally, no elector is bound to vote for any particular candidate; he may cast his ballot for whom he chooses. But in reality, electors are almost always faithful to the candidate of the party with which they are affiliated.

However, sometimes in American political history an elector has broken ranks to vote for a candidate other than his party's. In 1796, a Pennsylvania Federalist elector voted for Democratic-Republican Thomas Jefferson instead of Federalist John Adams. And some historians and political scientists claim that three Democratic-Republican electors voted for Adams. However, the fluidity of political party lines at that early date, and the well-known personal friendship between Adams and at least one of the electors, makes the claim of their being "faithless electors" one of continuing controversy. In 1820, a New Hampshire Democratic-Republican elector voted for John Quincy Adams instead of the party nominee, James Monroe.

There was no further occurrence until 1948, when Preston Parks, a Truman elector in Tennessee, voted for Gov. Strom Thurmond of South Carolina, the States Rights Democratic Party (Dixiecrat) presidential nominee. Since then, there have been the following additional instances:

● In 1956, when W.F. Turner, a Stevenson elector in Alabama, voted for a local judge, Walter E. Jones.

● In 1960, when Henry D. Irwin, a Nixon elector in Oklahoma, voted for Sen. Harry F. Byrd (D Va.).

● In 1968, when Dr. Lloyd W. Bailey, a Nixon elector in North Carolina, voted for George C. Wallace, the American Independent Party candidate.

● In 1972, when Roger L. MacBride, a Nixon elector in Virginia, voted for John Hospers, the Libertarian Party candidate.

● In 1976, when Mike Padden, a Ford elector in the state of Washington, voted for former Gov. Ronald Reagan of California.

despised more. Indeed, if Burr had given clear assurances that he would run the country as a Federalist, he might have been elected. But Burr was unwilling to make those assurances; and, as one chronicler put it, "No one knows whether it was honor or a wretched indecision which gagged Burr's lips."

In all, there were 106 members of the House at the time, 58 Federalists and 48 Democratic-Republicans. If the ballots had been cast per capita, Burr would have been elected, but the Constitution provided that each state should cast a single vote and that a majority of states was necessary for election.

On the first ballot, Jefferson received the votes of eight states, one short of a majority of the 16 states then in the union. Six states backed Burr, while the representatives of Vermont and Maryland were equally divided, so they lost their votes. By midnight of the first day of voting, 19 ballots had been taken, and the deadlock remained.

In all, 36 ballots were taken before the House came to a decision on Feb. 17. Predictably, there were men who sought to exploit the situation for personal gain. Jefferson wrote: "Many attempts have been made to obtain terms and promises from me. I have declared to them unequivocally that I would not receive the Government on capitulation; that I would not go in with my hands tied."

The impasse was finally broken when Vermont and Maryland switched to support of Jefferson. Delaware and

South Carolina also withdrew their support from Burr by casting blank ballots. The final vote: 10 states for Jefferson, four (all in New England) for Burr. Thus Jefferson became president, and Burr, under the Constitution as it then stood, automatically became vice president.

Federalist James A. Bayard of Delaware, who had played a key role in breaking the deadlock, wrote to Hamilton: "The means existed of electing Burr, but this required his cooperation. By deceiving one man (a great blockhead) and tempting two (not incorruptible), he might have secured a majority of the states. He will never have another chance of being president of the United States; and the little use he has made of the one which has occurred gives me but an humble opinion of the talents of an unprincipled man."

The Jefferson-Burr contest clearly illustrated the dangers of the double-balloting system established by the original Constitution, and pressure began to build for an amendment requiring separate votes for president and vice president. Congress approved the 12th Amendment in December 1803, and the states — acting with unexpected speed — ratified it in time for the 1804 election.

John Quincy Adams Election

The only other time a president was elected by the House of Representatives was in 1825. There were many contenders for the presidency in the 1824 election, but four predominated: John Quincy Adams, Henry Clay, William H. Crawford and Andrew Jackson. Crawford, secretary of the treasury under Monroe, was the early front-runner, but his candidacy faltered after he suffered an incapacitating illness in 1823.

When the electoral votes were counted, Jackson had 99, Adams 84, Crawford 41 and Clay 37. With 18 of the 24 states choosing their electors by popular vote, Jackson also led in the popular voting, although the significance of the popular vote was open to challenge. Under the 12th Amendment, the names of the three top contenders — Jackson, Adams and the ailing Crawford — were placed before the House. Clay's support was vital to either of the two front-runners.

From the start, Clay apparently intended to support Adams as the lesser of two evils. But before the House voted, a great scandal erupted. A Philadelphia newspaper printed an anonymous letter alleging that Clay had agreed to support Adams in return for being made secretary of state. The letter alleged also that Clay would have been willing to make the same deal with Jackson. Clay immediately denied the charge and pronounced the writer of the letter "a base and infamous character, a dastard and a liar." But Jackson believed the charges and found his suspicions vindicated when Adams, after the election, did appoint Clay as secretary of state. "Was there ever witnessed such a bare-faced corruption in any country before?" Jackson wrote to a friend.

When the House met to vote, Adams was supported by the six New England states and New York and, in large part through Clay's backing, by Maryland, Ohio, Kentucky, Illinois, Missouri and Louisiana. Thus a majority of 13 delegations voted for him — the bare minimum he needed for election, since there were 24 states in the union at the time. The election was accomplished on the first ballot, but Adams took office under a cloud from which his administration never recovered.

Jackson's successful 1828 campaign made much of his contention that the House of Representatives had thwarted the will of the people by denying him the presidency in 1825 even though he had been the leader in popular and electoral votes.

On only one occasion has the Senate chosen the vice president. That was in 1837, when Van Buren was elected president with 170 of the 294 electoral votes while his vice presidential running mate, Richard M. Johnson, received only 147 electoral votes — one less than a majority. This discrepancy occurred because Van Buren electors from Virginia boycotted Johnson, reportedly in protest against his social behavior. The Senate elected Johnson, 33-16, over Francis Granger of New York, the runner-up in the electoral vote for vice president.

Threat of Election by House

Although only two presidential elections actually have been decided by the House, a number of others — including those of 1836, 1856, 1860, 1892, 1948, 1960 and 1968 — could have been thrown into the House by only a small shift in the popular vote.

The threat of House election was most clearly evident in 1968, when Democrat George C. Wallace of Alabama ran as a strong third-party candidate. Wallace frequently asserted that he could win an outright majority in the electoral college by the addition of key midwestern and mountain states to his hoped-for base in the Deep South and border states. In reality, the Wallace campaign had a

narrower goal: to win the balance of power in electoral college voting, thus depriving either major party of the clear electoral majority required for election. Wallace made it clear that he would then expect one of the major party candidates to make concessions in return for enough votes from Wallace electors to win the election. Wallace indicated that he expected the election to be settled in the electoral college and not in the House of Representatives. At the end of the campaign it was disclosed that Wallace had obtained written affidavits from all of his electors in which they promised to vote for Wallace "or whomsoever he may direct" in the electoral college.

In response to the Wallace challenge, both major party candidates, Republican Richard M. Nixon and Democrat Hubert H. Humphrey, maintained that they would refuse to bargain with Wallace for his electoral votes. Nixon asserted that the House, if the decision rested there, should elect the popular-vote winner. Humphrey said the representatives should select "the president they believe would be best for the country." Bipartisan efforts to obtain advance agreements from House candidates to vote for the national popular-vote winner if the election should go to the House ended in failure. Neither Nixon nor Humphrey replied to suggestions that they pledge before the election to swing enough electoral votes to the popular-vote winner to assure his election without help from Wallace.

In the end, Wallace received only 13.5 per cent of the popular vote and 46 electoral votes (including the vote of one Republican defector), all from southern states. He failed to win the balance of power in the electoral college which he had hoped to use to wring policy concessions from one of the major-party candidates. If Wallace had won a few border states, or if a few thousand more Democratic votes had been cast in northern states barely carried by Nixon, thus reducing Nixon's electoral vote below 270, Wallace would have been in a position to bargain off his electoral votes or to throw the election into the House for final settlement.

The near success of the Wallace strategy provided dramatic impetus for electoral reform efforts in the 91st Congress.

Counting the Electoral Vote

Congress has mandated a variety of dates for the casting of popular votes, the meeting of the electors to cast ballots in the various states and the official counting of the electoral votes before both houses of Congress.

The Continental Congress made the provisions for the first election. On Sept. 13, 1788, the Congress directed that each state choose its electors on the first Wednesday in January 1789. It further directed these electors to cast their ballots on the first Wednesday in February 1789.

In 1792, the 2nd Congress passed legislation setting up a permanent calendar for choosing electors. Allowing some flexibility in dates, the law directed that states choose their electors within the 34 days preceding the first Wednesday in December of each presidential election year. Then the electors would meet in their various states and cast their ballots on the first Wednesday in December. On the second Wednesday of the following February, the votes were to be opened and counted before a joint session of Congress. Provision also was made for a special presidential election in case of the removal, death, resignation or disability of both the president and vice president.

Presidential Election by the House

The following rules, reprinted from Hinds' Precedents of the House of Representatives, were adopted by the House in 1825 for use in deciding the presidential election of 1824. They would provide a precedent for any future House election of a president, although the House could change them at will.

1. In the event of its appearing, on opening all the certificates, and counting the votes given by the electors of the several States for President, that no person has a majority of the votes of the whole number of electors appointed, the same shall be entered on the Journals of this House.

2. The roll of the House shall then be called by States; and, on its appearing that a Member or Members from two-thirds of the States are present, the House shall immediately proceed, by ballot, to choose a President from the persons having the highest numbers, not exceeding three, on the list of those voted for as President; and, in case neither of those persons shall receive the votes of a majority of all the states on the first ballot, the House shall continue to ballot for a President, without interruption by other business, until a President be chosen.

3. The doors of the Hall shall be closed during the balloting, except against the Members of the Senate, stenographers, and the officers of the House.

4. From the commencement of the balloting until an election is made no proposition to adjourn shall be received, unless on the motion of one State, seconded by another State, and the question shall be decided by States. The same rule shall be observed in regard to any motion to change the usual hour for the meeting of the House.

5. In balloting the following mode shall be observed, to wit:

The Representatives of each State shall be arranged and seated together, beginning with the seats at the right hand of the Speaker's chair, with the Members from the State of Maine; thence, proceeding with the Members from the States, in the order the States are usually named for receiving petitions* around the Hall of the House, until all are seated.

A ballot box shall be provided for each State.

The Representatives of each State shall, in the first instance, ballot among themselves, in order to ascertain the vote of their State; and they may, if necessary, appoint tellers of their ballots.

After the vote of each State is ascertained, duplicates thereof shall be made out; and in case any one of the persons from whom the choice is to be made shall receive a majority of the votes given, on any one balloting by the Representatives of a State, the name of that person shall be written on each of the duplicates; and in case the votes so given shall be divided so that neither of said persons shall have a majority of the whole number of votes given by such State, on any one balloting, then the word "divided" shall be written on each duplicate.

After the delegation from each State shall have ascertained the vote of their State, the Clerk shall name the States in the order they are usually named for receiving petitions; and as the name of each is called the Sergeant-at-Arms shall present to the delegation of each two ballot boxes, in each of which shall be deposited, by some Representative of the State, one of the duplicates made as aforesaid of the vote of said State, in the presence and subject to the examination of all the Members from said State then present; and where there is more than one Representative from a State, the duplicates shall not both be deposited by the same person.

When the votes of the States are thus all taken in, the Sergeant-at-Arms shall carry one of said ballot boxes to one table and the other to a separate and distinct table.

One person from each State represented in the balloting shall be appointed by the Representatives to tell off said ballots; but, in case the Representatives fail to appoint a teller, the Speaker shall appoint.

The said tellers shall divide themselves into two sets, as nearly equal in number as can be, and one of the said sets of tellers shall proceed to count the votes in one of said boxes, and the other set the votes in the other box.

When the votes are counted by the different sets of tellers, the result shall be reported to the House; and if the reports agree, the same shall be accepted as the true votes of the States; but if the reports disagree, the States shall proceed, in the same manner as before, to a new ballot.

6. All questions arising after the balloting commences, requiring the decision of the House, which shall be decided by the House, voting per capita, to be incidental to the power of choosing a President, shall be decided by States without debate; and in case of an equal division of the votes of States, the question shall be lost.

7. When either of the persons from whom the choice is to be made shall have received a majority of all the States, the Speaker shall declare the same, and that that person is elected President of the United States.

8. The result shall be immediately communicated to the Senate by message, and a committee of three persons shall be appointed to inform the President of the United States and the President-elect of said election.

On February 9, 1825, the election of John Quincy Adams took place in accordance with these rules.

* Petitions are no longer introduced in this way. This old procedure of calling the states beginning with Maine proceeded through the original 13 states and then through the remaining states in the order of their admission to the Union.

Under this system, states chose presidential electors at various times. For instance, in 1840 the popular balloting for electors began in Pennsylvania and Ohio on Oct. 30 and ended in North Carolina on Nov. 12. South Carolina, the only state still choosing presidential electors through the state legislature, appointed its electors on Nov. 26.

Congress modified the system in 1845, providing that each state choose its electors on the same day — the Tuesday next after the first Monday in November —a provision that still remains in force. Otherwise, the days for casting and counting the electoral votes remained the same.

The next change occurred in 1887, when Congress

Law for Counting Electoral Votes in Congress

Following is the complete text of Title 3, section 15 of the U.S. Code, enacted originally in 1887, governing the counting of electoral votes in Congress:

Congress shall be in session on the sixth day of January succeeding every meeting of the electors. The Senate and House of Representatives shall meet in the Hall of the House of Representatives at the hour of 1 o'clock in the afternoon on that day, and the President of the Senate shall be their presiding officer. Two tellers shall be previously appointed on the part of the Senate and two on the part of the House of Representatives, to whom shall be handed, as they are opened by the President of the Senate, all the certificates and papers purporting to be certificates of the electoral votes, which certificates and papers shall be opened, presented, and acted upon in the alphabetical order of the States, beginning with the letter A; and said tellers, having then read the same in the presence and hearing of the two Houses, shall make a list of the votes as they shall appear from the said certificates; and the votes having been ascertained and counted according to the rules in this subchapter provided, the result of the same shall be delivered to the President of the Senate, who shall thereupon announce the state of the vote, which announcement shall be deemed a sufficient declaration of the persons, if any, elected President and Vice President of the United States, and, together with a list of the votes, be entered on the Journals of the two Houses. Upon such reading of any such certificate or paper, the President of the Senate shall call for objections, if any. Every objection shall be made in writing, and shall state clearly and concisely, and without argument, the ground thereof, and shall be signed by at least one Senator and one Member of the House of Representatives before the same shall be received. When all objections so made to any vote or paper from a State shall have been received and read, the Senate shall thereupon withdraw, and such objections shall be submitted to the Senate for its decision; and the Speaker of the House of Representatives shall, in like manner, submit such objections to the House of Representatives for its decision; and no electoral vote or votes from any State which shall have been regularly given by electors whose appointment has been lawfully certified to according to section 6* of this title from which but one return has been received shall be rejected, but the two Houses concurrently may reject the vote or votes when they agree that such vote or votes have not been so regularly given by electors whose appointment has been so certified. If more than one return or paper purporting to be a return from a State shall have been received by the President of the Senate, those votes, and those only, shall be counted which shall have been regularly given by the electors who are shown by the determination mentioned in section 5† of this title to have been appointed, if the determination in said section provided for shall have been made, or by such successors or substitutes, in case of a vacancy in the board of electors so ascertained, as have been appointed to fill such vacancy in the mode provided by the laws of the State; but in case there shall arise the question which of two or more of such State authorities determining what electors have been appointed, as mentioned in section 5 of this title, is the lawful tribunal of such State, the votes regularly given of those electors, and those only, of such State shall be counted whose title as electors the two Houses, acting separately, shall concurrently decide is supported by the decision of such State so authorized by its law; and in such case of more than one return or paper purporting to be a return from a State, if there shall have been no such determination of the question in the State aforesaid, then those votes, and those only, shall be counted which the two Houses shall concurrently decide were cast by lawful electors appointed in accordance with the laws of the State, unless the two Houses, acting separately, shall concurrently decide such votes not to be the lawful votes of the legally appointed electors of such State. But if the two Houses shall disagree in respect of the counting of such votes, then, and in that case, the votes of the electors whose appointment shall have been certified by the executive of the State, under the seal thereof, shall be counted. When the two Houses have voted, they shall immediately again meet, and the presiding officer shall then announce the decision of the questions submitted. No votes or papers from any other State shall be acted upon until the objections previously made to the votes or papers from any State shall have been finally disposed of.

* Section 6 provides for certification of votes by electors by state Governors.
† Section 5 provides that if state law specifies a method for resolving disputes concerning the vote for Presidential electors, Congress must respect any determination so made by a state.

provided that electors were to meet and cast their ballots on the second Monday in January instead of the first Wednesday in December. Congress also dropped the provision for a special presidential election.

In 1934, Congress again revised the law. The new arrangements, still in force, directed the electors to meet on the first Monday after the second Wednesday in December. The ballots are opened and counted before Congress on Jan. 6 (the next day if Jan. 6 falls on a Sunday).

The Constitution states: "The President of the Senate shall, in the presence of the Senate and House of Representatives, open all the certificates, and the votes shall then be counted." It gives no guidance on disputed ballots.

Before counting the electoral votes in 1865, Congress

adopted the 22nd Joint Rule, which provided that no electoral votes objected to in joint session could be counted except by the concurrent votes of both the Senate and House. The rule was pushed by congressional Republicans to ensure rejection of the electoral votes from the newly reconstructed states of Louisiana and Tennessee. Under this rule, Congress in 1873 also threw out the electoral votes of Louisiana and Arkansas and three from Georgia.

However, the rule lapsed at the beginning of 1876, when the Senate refused to readopt it because the House was in Democratic control. Thus, following the 1876 election, when it became apparent that for the first time the outcome of an election would be determined by decisions on disputed electoral votes, Congress had no rules to guide it.

Hayes-Tilden Contest

The 1876 campaign pitted Republican Rutherford B. Hayes against Democrat Samuel J. Tilden. Early election-night returns indicated that Tilden had been elected. He had won the swing states of Indiana, New York, Connecticut and New Jersey; those states plus his expected southern support would give him the election. However, by the following morning it became apparent that if the Republicans could hold South Carolina, Florida and Louisiana, Hayes would be elected with 185 electoral votes to 184 for Tilden. But if a single elector in any of these states voted for Tilden, he would throw the election to the Democrats. Tilden led in the popular-vote count by more than a quarter million votes.

The situation was much the same in each of the three contested states. Historian Eugene H. Roseboom described it as follows: "The Republicans controlled the state governments and the election machinery, had relied upon the Negro masses for votes, and had practiced frauds as in the past. The Democrats used threats, intimidation, and even violence when necessary, to keep Negroes from the polls; and where they were in a position to do so they resorted to fraud also. The firm determination of the whites to overthrow carpetbag rule contributed to make a full and fair vote impossible; carpetbag hold on the state governments made a fair count impossible. Radical reconstruction was reaping its final harvest."

Both parties pursued the votes of the three states with a fine disregard for propriety or legality, and in the end double sets of elector returns were sent to Congress from all three. Oregon also sent two sets of returns. Although Hayes carried that state, the Democratic governor discovered that one of the Hayes electors was a postmaster and therefore ineligible to be an elector under the Constitution, so he certified the election of the top-polling Democratic elector. However, the Republican electors met, received the resignation of their ineligible colleague, then reappointed him to the vacancy since he had in the meantime resigned his postmastership.

Had the 22nd Joint Rule remained in effect, the Democratic House of Representatives could have objected to any of Hayes' disputed votes. But since the rule had lapsed, Congress had to find some new method of resolving electoral disputes. A joint committee was created to work out a plan, and the resulting Electoral Commission Law was approved by large majorities and signed into law Jan. 29, 1877 — only a few days before the date scheduled for counting the electoral votes.

The law, which applied only to the 1876 electoral vote count, established a 15-member electoral commission which was to have final authority over disputed electoral votes, unless both houses of Congress agreed to overrule it. The commission was to consist of five senators, five representatives and five Supreme Court justices. Each chamber was to select its own members of the commission, with the understanding that the majority party would have three members and the minority two. Four justices, two from each party, were named in the bill, and these four were to select the fifth. It was expected that they would choose Justice David Davis, who was considered a political independent, but he disqualified himself when the Illinois legislature named him to a seat in the Senate. Justice Joseph P. Bradley, a Republican, then was named to the 15th seat on the commission. The Democrats supported his selection, because they considered him the most independent of the remaining justices, all of whom were Republi-

cans. However, he was to vote with the Republicans on every dispute and thus assure the victory of Hayes.

The electoral vote count began in Congress Feb. 1 (moved up from the second Wednesday in February for this one election), and the proceedings continued until March 2. States were called in alphabetical order, and as each disputed state was reached, objections were raised to both the Hayes and Tilden electors. The question was then referred to the electoral commission, which in every case voted 8-7 for Hayes. In each case, the Democratic House rejected the commission's decision, but the Republican Senate upheld it, so the decision stood.

As the count went on, Democrats in the House threatened to launch a filibuster to block resumption of joint sessions so that the count could not be completed before inauguration day. The threat was never carried out, because of an agreement reached between the Hayes forces and southern conservatives. The southerners agreed to let the electoral count continue without obstruction. In return Hayes agreed that, as president, he would withdraw federal troops from the South, end Reconstruction and make other concessions. The southerners, for their part, pledged to respect Negro rights, a pledge they did not carry out.

Thus, at 4 a.m. March 2, 1877, the president of the Senate was able to announce that Hayes had been elected president with 185 electoral votes, as against 184 for Tilden. Later that day Hayes arrived in Washington. The next evening he took the oath of office privately at the White House, because March 4 fell on a Sunday. His formal inauguration followed on Monday. The country acquiesced. Thus ended a crisis that could have resulted in civil war.

Not until 1887 did Congress enact permanent legislation on the handling of disputed electoral votes. The Electoral Count Act of that year gave each state final authority in determining the legality of its choice of electors and required a concurrent majority of both the Senate and House to reject any electoral votes. It also established procedures for counting electoral votes in Congress.

Application of 1887 Law in 1969

The procedures relating to disputed electoral votes were utilized for the first time after the election of 1968. When Congress met in joint session Jan. 6, 1969, to count the electoral votes, Sen. Edmund S. Muskie (D Maine) and Rep. James G. O'Hara (D Mich.), joined by six other senators and 37 other representatives, filed a written objection to the vote cast by a North Carolina elector, Dr. Lloyd W. Bailey of Rocky Mount, who had been elected as a Republican but chose to vote for George C. Wallace and Curtis LeMay, the presidential and vice presidential candidates of the American Indepedent Party, instead of Republicans Richard M. Nixon and Spiro T. Agnew.

Acting under the 1887 law, Muskie and O'Hara objected to Bailey's vote on the grounds that it was "not properly given" because a plurality of the popular votes in North Carolina were cast for Nixon-Agnew and the state's voters had chosen electors to vote for Nixon and Agnew only. Muskie and O'Hara asked that Bailey's vote not be counted at all by Congress.

The 1887 statute, incorporated in the U.S. Code, Title 3, Section 15, stipulated that "no electoral vote or votes from any state which shall have been regularly given by electors whose appointment has been lawfully certified . . . from which but one return has been received shall be rejected, but the two Houses concurrently may reject the vote or votes when they agree that such vote or votes have not been so regularly given by electors whose appointment has been so certified." The statute did not define the term "regularly given," although at the time of its adoption chief concern centered on problems of dual sets of electoral vote returns from a state, votes cast on an improper day or votes disputed because of uncertainty about whether a state lawfully was in the union on the day that the electoral vote was cast. *(Text of law, p. 10)*

The 1887 statute provided that if written objection to any state's vote was received from at least one member of both the Senate and House, the two legislative bodies were to retire immediately to separate sessions, debate for two hours with a five-minute limitation on speeches, and that each chamber was to decide the issue by vote before resuming the joint session. The statute made clear that both the Senate and House had to reject a challenged electoral vote (or votes) for such action to prevail.

At the Jan. 6 joint session, in the House chamber with Senate President Pro Tempore Richard B. Russell, D-Ga., presiding, the counting of the electoral vote proceeded smoothly through the alphabetical order of states until the North Carolina result was announced, at which time O'Hara rose to announce filing of the complaint. The two houses then proceeded to separate sessions, at the end of which the Senate, by a 33-58 roll-call vote, and the House, by a 170-228 roll-call vote, refused to sustain the challenge to Bailey's vote. The two houses then reassembled in joint session at which the results of the separate deliberations were announced and the count of the electoral vote by state proceeded without event. At the conclusion, Russell announced the vote and declared Nixon and Agnew elected.

Although Congress did not sustain the challenge to Bailey's vote, the case of the "faithless" elector led to increased pressure for electoral reform.

Reform Proposals

Since Jan. 6, 1797, when Rep. William L. Smith, S.C., introduced in Congress the first proposed constitutional amendment for reform of the electoral college system, hardly a session of Congress has passed without the introduction of one or more resolutions of this nature. But only one — the 12th Amendment, ratified in 1804 — ever has been approved.

In recent years, public interest in a change in the electoral college system was spurred by the close 1960 and 1968 elections, by a series of Supreme Court rulings relating to apportionment and districting and by introduction of unpledged elector systems in the southern states.

House Approval of Amendment

Early in 1969, President Nixon asked Congress to take prompt action on electoral college reform. He said he would support any plan that would eliminate individual electors and distribute among the presidential candidates the electoral vote of every state and the District of Columbia in a manner more closely approximating the popular vote.

Later that year the House approved, 338-70, a resolution proposing a constitutional amendment to eliminate the electoral college and to provide instead for direct popular election of the president and vice president. The measure set a minimum of 40 percent of the popular vote as sufficient for election and provided for a runoff election between the two top candidates for the presidency if no candidate received 40 percent. Under this plan the House of Representatives could no longer be called upon to select a

25th Amendment
(Ratified Feb. 10, 1967)

Section 1. In case of the removal of the President from office or of his death or resignation, the Vice President shall become President.

Section 2. Whenever there is a vacancy in the office of the Vice President, the President shall nominate a Vice President who shall take office upon confirmation by a majority vote of both Houses of Congress.

Section 3. Whenever the President transmits to the President pro tempore of the Senate and the Speaker of the House of Representatives his written declaration that he is unable to discharge the powers and duties of his office, and until he transmits to them a written declaration to the contrary, such powers and duties shall be discharged by the Vice President as Acting President.

Section 4. Whenever the Vice President and a majority of either the principal officers of the executive departments or of such other body as Congress may by law provide, transmit to the President pro tempore of the Senate and the Speaker of the House of Representatives their written declaration that the President is unable to discharge the powers and duties of his office, the Vice President shall immediately assume the powers and duties of the office as Acting President.

Thereafter, when the President transmits to the President pro tempore of the Senate and the Speaker of the House of Representatives his written declaration that no inability exists, he shall resume the powers and duties of his office unless the Vice President and a majority of either the principal officers of the executive departments or of such other body as Congress may by law provide, transmit within four days to the President pro tempore of the Senate and the Speaker of the House of Representatives their written declaration that the President is unable to discharge the powers and duties of his office. Thereupon Congress shall decide the issue, assembling within forty-eight hours for that purpose if not in session. If the Congress, within twenty-one days after receipt of the latter written declaration, or, if Congress is not in session, within twenty-one days after Congress is required to assemble, determines by two-thirds vote of both houses that the President is unable to discharge the powers and duties of his office, the Vice President shall continue to discharge the same as Acting President; otherwise, the President shall resume the powers and duties of his office.

president. The proposed amendment also authorized Congress to provide a method of filling vacancies caused by the death, resignation or inability of presidential nominees before the election and a method of filling post-election vacancies caused by the death of the president-elect or vice president-elect.

Nixon, who previously had favored a proportional plan of allocating each state's electoral votes, endorsed the House resolution and urged the Senate to adopt it. To become effective, the proposed amendment had to be approved by a two-thirds majority in both the Senate and House and be ratified by the legislatures of three-fourths of the states.

When the proposal reached the Senate floor in September 1970, small-state and southern senators succeeded in blocking final action on it. The resolution was laid aside Oct. 5, after two unsuccessful efforts to cut off debate by invoking cloture.

Carter Endorsement of Plan

Another major effort to eliminate the electoral college occurred in 1977, when President Carter included such a proposal in his election reform package, unveiled March 22.

Carter endorsed the amendment approved by the House in 1969, to replace the electoral college with direct popular election of the president and vice president, and provide for a runoff if no candidate received at least 40 percent of the vote. Because the Senate was again seen as the major stumbling block, the House waited to see what the Senate would do before beginning any deliberation of its own.

After several months of deadlock, the Senate Judiciary Committee approved Sept. 15 the direct presidential election plan by a vote of 9 to 8. But Senate opponents of the measure promised another filibuster and the Senate leadership decided it could not spare the time or effort to try to break it. The measure was never brought to the floor and died when the 95th Congress adjourned in 1978.

On Jan. 15, 1979, the opening day of the 96th Congress, Sen. Birch Bayh (D) of Indiana began another effort to abolish the electoral college through a constitutional amendment. In putting off action in the previous Congress, Senate leaders had agreed to try for early action in the 96th.

Presidential Disability

A decade of congressional concern over the question of presidential disability was eased in 1967 by ratification of the 25th Amendment to the Constitution. The amendment for the first time provided for continuity in carrying out the functions of the presidency in the event of presidential disability and for filling a vacancy in the vice presidency.

Congressional consideration of the problem of presidential disability had been prompted by President Eisenhower's heart attack in 1955. The ambiguity of the language of the disability clause (Article II, Section 1, Clause 5) of the Constitution had provoked occasional debate ever since the Constitutional Convention of 1787. But it had never been decided how far the term "disability" extended or who would be the judge of it.

Clause 5 provided that Congress should decide who was to succeed to the presidency in the event that both the president and the vice president died, resigned or became disabled. Congress enacted succession laws three times. By the Act of March 1, 1792, it provided for succession (after the vice president) of the president pro tempore of the Senate, then of the House Speaker; if those offices were vacant, states were to send electors to Washington to choose a new president.

That law stood until passage of the Presidential Succession Act of Jan. 19, 1886, which changed the line of succession to run from the vice president to the secretary of state, secretary of the treasury and so on through the Cabinet in order of rank. Sixty-one years later, the Act of July 18, 1947 (still in force), placed the Speaker of the House and the president pro tempore of the Senate ahead of Cabinet officers in succession after the vice president.

Before ratification of the 25th Amendment in 1967, no procedures had been laid down to govern situations arising in the event of presidential incapacity or of a vacancy in the office of vice president. Two presidents had had serious disabilities — James A. Garfield, shot in 1881 and confined to his bed until he died 2-1/2 months later, and Woodrow Wilson, who suffered a stroke in 1919. In each case the vice president did not assume any duties of the presidency for fear he would appear to be usurping the powers of that office. As for a vice presidential vacancy, the United States has been without a vice president 18 times for a total of 40 years through 1978, after the elected vice president succeeded to the presidency, died or resigned.

Ratification of the 25th Amendment established procedures that clarified these areas of uncertainty in the Constitution. The amendment provided that the vice president should become acting president under either one of two circumstances. If the president informed Congress that he was unable to perform his duties, the vice president would become acting president until the president could resume his responsibilities.

If the vice president and a majority of the Cabinet, or another body designated by Congress, found the president to be incapacitated, the vice president would become acting president until the president informed Congress that his disability had ended. Congress was given 21 days to resolve any dispute over the president's disability; a two-thirds vote of both chambers was required to overrule the president's declaration that he was no longer incapacitated.

Whenever a vacancy occurred in the office of vice president, either by death, succession to the presidency or resignation, the president was to nominate a vice president, and the nomination was to be confirmed by a majority vote of both houses of Congress.

The proposed 25th Amendment was approved by the Senate and House in 1965. It took effect Feb. 10, 1967, after ratification by 38 states. *(Text, box, p. 12)*

Within only eight years, the power of the president to appoint a new vice president under the terms of the 25th Amendment was used twice. In 1973, when Vice President Agnew resigned, President Nixon nominated Gerald R. Ford as the new vice president. Ford was confirmed by both houses of Congress and sworn in Dec. 6, 1973. On Nixon's resignation Aug. 9, 1974, Ford succeeded to the presidency, becoming the first unelected president in American history. President Ford chose as his new vice president former Gov. Nelson A. Rockefeller of New York, who was sworn in Dec. 19, 1974.

With both the president and vice president holding office through appointment rather than election, members of Congress and the public expressed concern about the power of a president to, in effect, appoint his own successor. Accordingly, Sen. John O. Pastore, D-R.I., introduced a proposed constitutional amendment on Feb. 3, 1975, to provide for a special national election for president with more than one year remaining in a presidential term. Hearings were held before the Senate Judiciary Subcommittee on Constitutional Amendments but no action was taken.

—By Warden Moxley

Bibliography
Books and Reports

Abels, Jules. *The Degeneration of Our Presidential Elections: A History and Analysis of An American Institution in Trouble.* New York: Macmillan, 1938.

_____. *Out of the Jaws of Victory.* New York: Holt Rinehart, 1959.

Aly, Bower, ed. *Presidential Elections*. 2 vols. Columbia, Mo.: Lucas Brothers, 1949.

Bagby, Wesley. *The Road to Normalcy: The Presidential Campaign and Election of 1920*. Baltimore: Johns Hopkins Press, 1962.

Bean, Louis. *Ballot Behavior: A Study of Presidential Elections*. Washington, D.C.: American Council on Public Affairs, 1940.

Beman, L. T. *Abolishment of the Electoral College*. New York: H. W. Wilson, 1926.

Best, Judith. *The Case Against Direct Election of the President: A Defense of the Electoral College*. Ithaca, N.Y.: Cornell University Press, 1975.

Bickel, Alexander M. *The New Age of Political Reform: The Electoral College, the Convention and the Party System*. New York: Harper & Row, 1968.

_____. *Reform and Continuity: The Electoral College, the Convention and the Party System*. New York: Harper & Row, 1971.

Burnham, Walter D. *Presidential Ballots, 1836-1892*. Baltimore: Johns Hopkins Press, 1955.

Burrill, Richard L. *Controversy Over the Presidential Electoral System*. Palo Alto, Calif.: R&E Research Associates Inc., 1975.

Byrne, Gary C. and Marx, Paul. *The Great American Convention: A Political History of Presidential Elections*. Palo Alto, Calif.: Pacific Books, 1977.

Clancy, Herbert J. *Presidential Election of 1880*. Chicago: Loyola University Press, 1958.

Coleman, Charles H. *The Presidential Election of 1868*. St. Clair Shores, Michigan: Scholarly Press, 1933.

Cummings, Milton C. *The National Election of 1964*. Washington, D.C.: Brookings Institution, 1966.

Daniels, Walter M., ed. *Presidential Election Reforms*. New York: H. W. Wilson, 1953.

David, Paul T., ed. *The Presidential Election and Transition, 1960-1961*. Washington, D.C.: Brookings Institution, 1961.

"Electing the President: A Report of the Commission on Electoral Reform." Chicago: American Bar Association, 1967.

Ewing, Cortez, A. M. *Presidential Elections from Abraham Lincoln to Franklin Roosevelt*. Norman, Okla.: University of Oklahoma Press, 1940.

Gammon, Samuel R. *The Presidential Election of 1832*. Westport, Conn.: Greenwood Press, 1922.

Gunderson, Robert G. *The Log Cabin Campaign*. Lexington, Ky.: University of Kentucky Press, 1957.

Haworth, Paul L. *The Hayes-Tilden Disputed Presidential Election of 1876*. Cleveland: Burrows Brothers, 1906.

Hoyt, Edwin P. *Jumbos and Jackasses: A Popular History of the Political Wars*. Garden City, N.Y.: Doubleday, 1960.

Jones, Stanley L. *The Presidential Election of 1896*. Madison, Wis.: University of Wisconsin Press, 1964.

Keech, William R. and Matthews, Donald R. *The Party's Choice: With an Epilogue on the 1976 Nominations*. Washington, D.C.: Brookings Institution, 1976.

Knoles, George H. *The Presidential Campaign and Election of 1892*. Stanford, Calif.: Stanford University Press, 1942.

Lamb, Karl A. *Campaign Decision Making: The Presidential Election of 1964*. Belmont, Calif.: Wadsworth, 1968.

Longley, Lawrence D. *The Politics of Electoral College Reform*. New Haven, Conn.: Yale University Press, 1972.

MacBride, Roger L. *The American Electoral College*. Caldwell, Idaho: Caxton Printers, 1953.

Maisel, Louis and Cooper, Joseph, eds. *The Impact of the Electoral Process*. Beverly Hills, Calif.: Sage Publications, 1977.

Martin, Ralph G. *Front Runner, Dark Horse*. Garden City, N.Y.: Doubleday, 1960.

Michener, James A. *Presidential Lottery: The Reckless Gamble in Our Electoral System*. New York: Random House, 1969.

Moos, Malcolm. *Politics, Presidents and Coattails*. Baltimore: Johns Hopkins Press, 1952.

Ogden, Daniel. *Electing the President, 1964*. San Francisco: Chandler, 1964.

O'Neil, Charles A. *The American Electoral System*. New York: Putnam, 1887.

Peel, Roy V. *The 1928 Campaign: An Analysis*. New York: Smith, 1931.

_____. *The 1932 Campaign: An Analysis*. New York: Farrar & Rinehart, 1935.

Peirce, Neal. *The People's President: The Electoral College and the Emerging Consensus for a Direct Vote*. New York: Simon & Schuster, 1968.

Petersen, Svend. *A Statistical History of the American Presidential Elections*. New York: Frederick Ungar, 1968.

Polsby, Nelson. *Presidential Elections: Strategies of American Electoral Politics*. New York: Scribner, 1964.

Pomper, Marlene M., ed. *The Election of 1976: Reports and Interpretations*. New York: David McKay, 1977.

"Report of the Committee on Federal Legislation: Proposed Constitutional Amendment Abolishing the Electoral College and Making Other Changes in the Election of the President and Vice-President." New York: Association of the Bar of the City of New York, 1969.

Robinson, Edgar E. *The Presidential Vote, 1896-1932*. New York: Octagon Books, 1970.

_____. *They Voted for Roosevelt: The Presidential Vote, 1932-1944*. Stanford, Calif.: Stanford University Press, 1947.

Roseboom, Eugene H. *A History of Presidential Elections*. New York: Macmillan, 1957.

Runyon, John H. *Source Book of American Presidential Campaign and Election Statistics, 1948-1968*. New York: Frederick Ungar, 1971.

Sayre, Wallace S. *Voting for President: The Electoral College and the American Political System*. Washington, D.C.: Brookings Institution, 1970.

Scammon, Richard M., ed. *America at the Polls: A Handbook of American Presidential Election Statistics 1920-1964*. Pittsburgh: University of Pittsburgh Press, 1965.

_____. *America Votes: A Handbook of Contemporary Election Statistics*. Washington, D.C.: Congressional Quarterly, 1956-1977.

Schlesinger, Arthur M. Jr., ed. *The Coming to Power: Critical Presidential Elections in American History*. New York: McGraw-Hill, 1972.

_____, ed. *History of American Presidential Elections*. 4 vols. New York: McGraw-Hill, 1971.

Stanwood, Edward. *A History of the Presidency, 1788-1916*. 2 vols. Boston: Houghton Mifflin, 1889, 1916.

Thomas, Charles. *The 1956 Presidential Campaign*. Washington, D.C.: Brookings Institution, 1960.

Weston, Florence. *The Presidential Election of 1828*. Washington, D.C.: Ruddick Press, 1938.

Witcover, Jules. *Marathon: The Pursuit of the Presidency, 1972-1976*. New York: Viking Press, 1977.

White, Theodore H., *The Making of the President, 1960*. New York: Atheneum Publishers, 1961.

_____. *The Making of the President, 1964*. New York: Atheneum Publishers, 1965.

_____. *The Making of the President, 1968*. New York: Atheneum Publishers, 1969.

_____. *The Making of the President, 1972*. New York: Atheneum Publishers, 1973.

"Who Should Elect the President?" Washington, D.C.: League of Women Voters, 1969.

Wilmerding, Lucius Jr. *The Electoral College*. New Brunswick, N.J.: Rutgers University Press, 1958.

Yarnell, Allen, *Democrats and Progressives: The 1948 Presidential Election as a Test of Postwar Liberalism*. Berkeley, Calif.: University of California Press, 1974.

Yunker, John H. and Longley, Lawrence D. *The Electoral College: Its Bases Newly Measured for the 1960s and 1970s*. Beverly Hills, Calif.: Sage Publications, 1976.

Zeidenstein, Harvey. *Direct Election of the President*. Lexington, Mass.: D. C. Heath, 1973.

Articles

"American Presidential Elections." *Current History,* October 1964, pp. 193-235.

"Anatomy of a Carter Victory." *Gallup Opinion Index,* December 1976.

Bayh, Birch. "Electing a President: The Case for Direct Popular Election." *Harvard Journal on Legislation,* January 1969, pp. 1-12.

_____, and Allen, James B. "Should We Have Direct Election of Our Presidents?" *American Legion Magazine,* October 1977, pp. 22-23.

Bernardo, C. Joseph. "The Presidential Election of 1888." *New York World,* June 25, 1888, p. 224.

Blaine, J. G. "Presidential Election of 1892." *North American Review,* November 1892, pp. 513-25.

Branch, L. C. "Making a President in the Electoral College, 1880." *Overland,* November 1896, pp. 551-556.

Brewer, F. M. "Modernization of the Presidential Election." *Editorial Research Reports,* Oct. 12, 1949, Vol. II, pp. 651-668.

Brown, E. S. "Presidential Election of 1824-25." *Political Science Quarterly,* September 1925, pp. 384-403.

Bryan, William J. "Election of 1900." *North American Review,* December 1900, pp. 788-801.

Burns, James M. "A New Course for the Electoral College." *New York Times Magazine,* Dec. 18, 1960, p. 28.

Courtney, L. H. C. "Recent Presidential Elections." *Nineteenth Century,* January 1897, pp. 1-16.

Crabites, P. "American Presidential Elections," *Nineteenth Century,* November 1924, pp. 719-726.

"Direct Election of the President." *National Review,* Feb. 4, 1977, pp. 135-136.

Eshelman, Edwin D. "Congress and Electoral Reform: An Analysis of Proposals for Changing Our Method of Selecting a President." *Christian Century,* Feb. 5, 1969, pp. 178-181.

Feerick, John D. "The Electoral College: Why It Ought to Be Abolished." *Fordham Law Review,* October 1968, p. 43.

Freund, Paul A. "Direct Election of the President: Issues and Answers." *American Bar Association Journal,* August 1970, p. 733.

Gardner, J. W. "Should the Presidential Electoral System be Abolished?" *Independent,* Jan. 27, 1910, pp. 191-195.

Goldman, Ralph M. "Hubert Humphrey's S. J. Res. 152: A Proposal for Electoral College Reform." *Midwest Journal of Political Science,* February 1958, pp. 89-96.

Gossett, William T. "Direct Popular Election of the President." *American Bar Association Journal,* March 1970, p. 230.

Huddle, F. P. "Electoral College: Historical Review and Proposals for Reforms." *Editorial Research Reports,* Aug. 18, 1944, Vol. II, pp. 99-114.

Kallenback, J. E. "Recent Proposals to Reform the Electoral College System." *American Political Science Review,* October 1936, pp. 924-929.

Lechner, Alfred J. "Direct Election of the President: The Final Step in the Constitutional Evolution of the Right to Vote." *Notre Dame Lawyer,* October 1971, pp. 122-152.

McLean, S. J. "Presidential Election of 1908." *Quarterly Review,* October 1908, pp. 448-475.

McPherson, J. M. "Grant or Greeley? The Abolitionist Dilemma in the Election of 1872." *American Historical Review,* October 1965, pp. 43-61.

Miller, Arthur H. "Partisanship Reinstated? A Comparison of the 1972 and 1976 U.S. Presidential Elections." *British Journal of Political Science,* April 1978, pp. 129-152.

Plattner, Marc F. "Electoral College Reform." *American Spectator,* June/July 1978, pp. 22-23.

"Public Would Eliminate the Electoral College: Move Supported by Most Groups." *Gallup Opinion Index,* April 1977, pp. 10-12.

"The 1968 American Presidential Election." *External Affairs Review,* November 1968, pp. 3-11.

Ogburn, W. F. "A Measurement of the Factors in the Presidential Election of 1928." *Social Forces,* December 1929, pp. 175-183.

Peck, H. T. "Election of 1896." *Bookman,* December 1905, pp. 334-358.

Pomper, Gerald M. "The 1972 Presidential Election in the USA." *International Problems,* July 1972, pp. 44-54.

_____. "The Southern 'Free-Elector Plan'," *Southwestern Social Science Quarterly,* June 1964, pp. 16-25.

"Presidential Election of 1928." *Congressional Digest,* August 1928, pp. 219-250.

"Proposals to Change the Method of Electing the President: A Pro and Con Discussion on the Various Proposals for Change." *Congressional Digest,* November 1967, pp. 257-288.

"Proposed Abolition of the Electoral College: A Pro and Con Discussion." *Congressional Digest,* March 1941, pp. 67-96.

Shogan, R. "1948 Election." *American Heritage,* June 1968, pp. 22-31.

Sievers, H. J. "Reform of the Electoral College." *America,* Nov. 16, 1968, p. 465.

Silva, Ruth C. "Lodge-Gossett Resolution: A Critical Analysis." *American Political Science Review,* March 1950, p. 92.

_____. "Reform of the Electoral College." *Review of Politics,* July 1952, p. 397.

Smolka, Richard G. "Possible Consequences of Direct Election of the President." *State Government,* Summer 1977, pp. 134-140.

Steinberg, Lawrence B. "There's Another Move to Put the Electoral College Out of Business." *National Journal,* Oct. 8, 1977, pp. 1574-1576.

Strong, Donald S. "The Presidential Election in the South, 1952," *Journal of Politics,* August 1955, pp. 343-389.

Wechsler, Herbert, "The Lodge-Gossett Plan." *Fortune,* June 1949, pp. 138-146.

_____. "Presidential Elections and the Constitution: A Comment on Proposed Amendment." *American Bar Association Journal,* March 1949.

Wells, David I. "Electing the President: How Should It Be Done?" *National Civic Review,* May 1977, pp. 230-234.

West, H. L. "Elction of 1904." *Forum,* July 1903, pp. 3-15.

Wicker, T. "Abolishing the Electoral College." *Current,* January 1977, pp. 3-4.

Williams, Philip and Wilson, Graham K. "The 1976 Election and the American Political System." *Political Studies,* June 1977, pp. 182-200.

Wilmerding, Lucius Jr. "Reform of the Electoral System." *Political Science Quarterly,* Vol. 64, 1949, pp. 1-23.

Electoral Votes

Sources

Electoral votes cast for presidential candidates were listed in the *Senate Manual,* Washington, D.C., U.S. Government Printing Office, 1977, pp. 891-933.

Total electoral votes for each state were compiled from a chart of each apportionment of the House of Representatives, published in the *Biographical Directory of the American Congress,* Washington, D.C., U.S. Government Printing Office, 1971, p. 47. Article II, Section 1 of the Constitution gives each state a number of electors equal to the number of senators and representatives to which it is entitled.

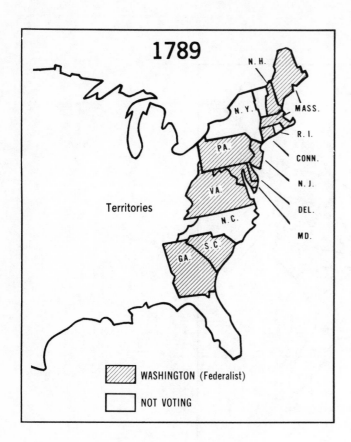

1789

Territories

WASHINGTON (Federalist)

NOT VOTING

Electoral Votes 1789-1800

Under Article II, section 1 of the Constitution, each presidential elector had two votes and was required to cast each vote for a different person. The person receiving the highest number of votes from a majority of electors was elected president; the person receiving the second highest total became vice president. Since there were 69 electors in 1789, Washington's 69 votes constituted a unanimous election. After ratification of the 12th Amendment in 1804, electors were required to designate which of their two votes was for president and which was for vice president. The electoral college tables on pages 19 to 22 show *all* electoral votes cast in the elections of 1789, 1792, 1796 and 1800; the charts for 1804 and thereafter show electoral votes cast only for president. For electoral vote totals for vice president, see table page 62.

States	Electoral Votes [6]	Washington	Adams	Jay	Harrison	Rutledge	Hancock	Clinton	Huntington	Milton	Armstrong	Lincoln	Telfair
Connecticut[1]	(14)	7	5	-	-	-	-	-	2	-	-	-	-
Delaware	(6)	3	-	3	-	-	-	-	-	-	-	-	-
Georgia[1]	(10)	5	-	-	-	-	-	-	-	2	1	1	1
Maryland[2]	(16)	6	-	-	6	-	-	-	-	-	-	-	-
Massachusetts	(20)	10	10	-	-	-	-	-	-	-	-	-	-
New Hampshire	(10)	5	5	-	-	-	-	-	-	-	-	-	-
New Jersey[1]	(12)	6	1	5	-	-	-	-	-	-	-	-	-
New York[3]	(16)	-	-	-	-	-	-	-	-	-	-	-	-
North Carolina[4]	(14)	-	-	-	-	-	-	-	-	-	-	-	-
Pennsylvania[1]	(20)	10	8	-	-	-	2	-	-	-	-	-	-
Rhode Island[4]	(6)	-	-	-	-	-	-	-	-	-	-	-	-
South Carolina[1]	(14)	7	-	-	-	6	1	-	-	-	-	-	-
Virginia[5]	(24)	10	5	1	-	-	1	3	-	-	-	-	-
Totals	(182)	69	34	9	6	6	4	3	2	2	1	1	1

1. For explanation of split electoral votes, see p. 6.
2. Two Maryland electors did not vote.
3. Not voting. For explanation, see p. 2.
4. Not voting because had not yet ratified Constitution.
5. Two Virginia electors did not vote. For explanation of split electoral votes, see p. 6.
6. Two votes for each elector, see text above.

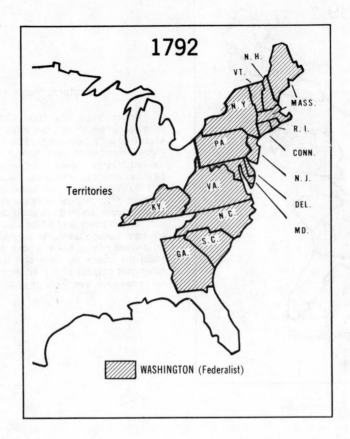

1792

WASHINGTON (Federalist)

States	Electoral Votes [3]	Washington	Adams	Clinton	Jefferson	Burr
Connecticut	(18)	9	9	-	-	-
Delaware	(6)	3	3	-	-	-
Georgia	(8)	4	-	4	-	-
Kentucky	(8)	4	-	-	4	-
Maryland[1]	(20)	8	8	-	-	-
Massachusetts	(32)	16	16	-	-	-
New Hampshire	(12)	6	6	-	-	-
New Jersey	(14)	7	7	-	-	-
New York	(24)	12	-	12	-	-
North Carolina	(24)	12	-	12	-	-
Pennsylvania[2]	(30)	15	14	1	-	-
Rhode Island	(8)	4	4	-	-	-
South Carolina[2]	(16)	8	7	-	-	1
Vermont[1]	(8)	3	3	-	-	-
Virginia	(42)	21	-	21	-	-
Totals	**(270)**	**132**	**77**	**50**	**4**	**1**

1. Two Maryland electors and one Vermont elector did not vote.
2. For explanation of split electoral votes. See p. 6.
3. Two votes for each elector, see text p. 19.

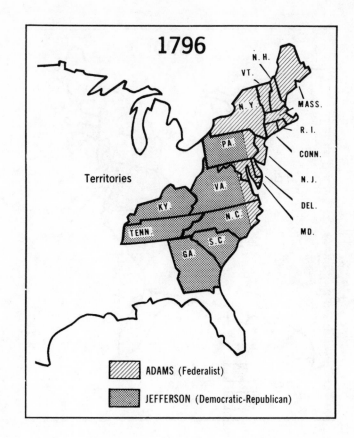

ADAMS (Federalist)

JEFFERSON (Democratic-Republican)

States	Electoral Votes [2]	J. Adams	Jefferson	T. Pinckney	Burr	S. Adams	Ellsworth	Clinton	Jay	Iredell	Henry	Johnston	Washington	C. Pinckney
Connecticut [1]	(18)	9	-	4	-	-	-	-	5	-	-	-	-	-
Delaware	(6)	3	-	3	-	-	-	-	-	-	-	-	-	-
Georgia	(8)	-	4	-	-	-	-	4	-	-	-	-	-	-
Kentucky	(8)	-	4	-	4	-	-	-	-	-	-	-	-	-
Maryland [1]	(20)	7	4	4	3	-	-	-	-	-	2	-	-	-
Massachusetts [1]	(32)	16	-	13	-	-	1	-	-	-	-	2	-	-
New Hampshire	(12)	6	-	-	-	-	6	-	-	-	-	-	-	-
New Jersey	(14)	7	-	7	-	-	-	-	-	-	-	-	-	-
New York	(24)	12	-	12	-	-	-	-	-	-	-	-	-	-
North Carolina [1]	(24)	1	11	1	6	-	-	-	-	3	-	-	1	1
Pennsylvania [1]	(30)	1	14	2	13	-	-	-	-	-	-	-	-	-
Rhode Island	(8)	4	-	-	-	-	4	-	-	-	-	-	-	-
South Carolina	(16)	-	8	8	-	-	-	-	-	-	-	-	-	-
Tennessee	(6)	-	3	-	3	-	-	-	-	-	-	-	-	-
Vermont	(8)	4	-	4	-	-	-	-	-	-	-	-	-	-
Virginia [1]	(42)	1	20	1	1	15	-	3	-	-	-	-	1	-
Totals	(276)	71	68	59	30	15	11	7	5	3	2	2	2	1

1. For explanation of split electoral votes, see p. 6.
2. Two votes for each elector, see text p. 19.

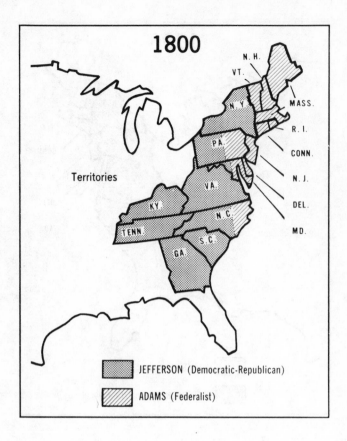

States	Electoral Votes[2]	Jefferson[3]	Burr[3]	Adams	Pinckney	Jay
Connecticut	(18)	-	-	9	9	-
Delaware	(6)	-	-	3	3	-
Georgia	(8)	4	4	-	-	-
Kentucky	(8)	4	4	-	-	-
Maryland[1]	(20)	5	5	5	5	-
Massachusetts	(32)	-	-	16	16	-
New Hampshire	(12)	-	-	6	6	-
New Jersey	(14)	-	-	7	7	-
New York	(24)	12	12	-	-	-
North Carolina[1]	(24)	8	8	4	4	-
Pennsylvania[1]	(30)	8	8	7	7	-
Rhode Island[1]	(8)	-	-	4	3	1
South Carolina	(16)	8	8	-	-	-
Tennessee	(6)	3	3	-	-	-
Vermont	(8)	-	-	4	4	-
Virginia	(42)	21	21	-	-	-
Totals	**(276)**	**73**	**73**	**65**	**64**	**1**

1. For explanation of split electoral votes, see p. 6.
2. Two votes for each elector, see text p. 19.
3. For explanation and result of tie vote, see p. 6.

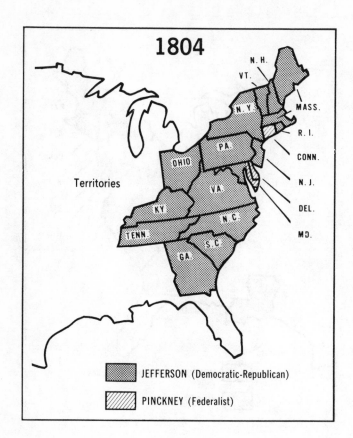

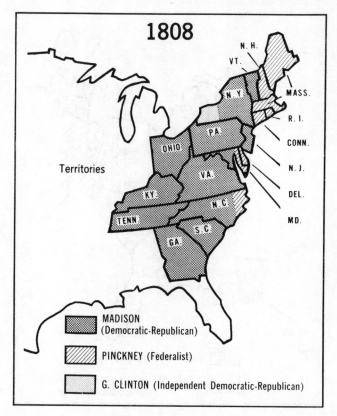

States	Electoral Votes	Jefferson	Pinckney
Connecticut	(9)	-	9
Delaware	(3)	-	3
Georgia	(6)	6	-
Kentucky	(8)	8	-
Maryland[1]	(11)	9	2
Massachusetts	(19)	19	-
New Hampshire	(7)	7	-
New Jersey	(8)	8	-
New York	(19)	19	-
North Carolina	(14)	14	-
Ohio	(3)	3	-
Pennsylvania	(20)	20	-
Rhode Island	(4)	4	-
South Carolina	(10)	10	-
Tennessee	(5)	5	-
Vermont	(6)	6	-
Virginia	(24)	24	-
Totals	**(176)**	**162**	**14**

1. For explanation of split electoral votes, see p. 6.

States	Electoral Votes	Madison	Pinckney	Clinton
Connecticut	(9)	-	9	-
Delaware	(3)	-	3	-
Georgia	(6)	6	-	-
Kentucky[1]	(8)	7	-	-
Maryland[2]	(11)	9	2	-
Massachusetts	(19)	-	19	-
New Hampshire	(7)	-	7	-
New Jersey	(8)	8	-	-
New York[2]	(19)	13	-	6
North Carolina[2]	(14)	11	3	-
Ohio	(3)	3	-	-
Pennsylvania	(20)	20	-	-
Rhode Island	(4)	-	4	-
South Carolina	(10)	10	-	-
Tennessee	(5)	5	-	-
Vermont	(6)	6	-	-
Virginia	(24)	24	-	-
Totals	**(176)**	**122**	**47**	**6**

1. One Kentucky elector did not vote.
2. For explanation of split electoral votes, see p. 6.

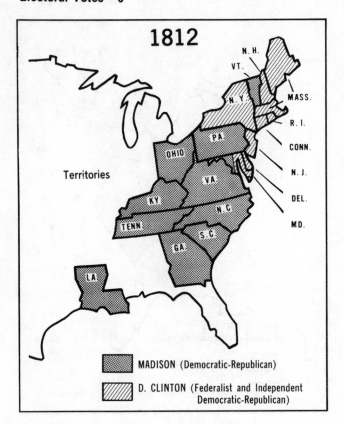

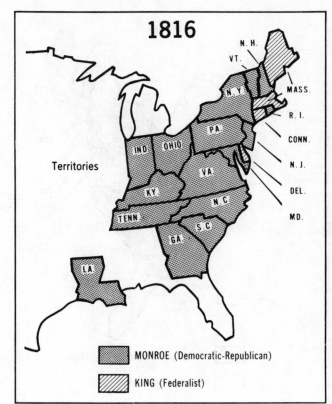

States	Electoral Votes	Madison	Clinton
Connecticut	(9)	-	9
Delaware	(4)	-	4
Georgia	(8)	8	-
Kentucky	(12)	12	-
Louisiana	(3)	3	-
Maryland[1]	(11)	6	5
Massachusetts	(22)	-	22
New Hampshire	(8)	-	8
New Jersey	(8)	-	8
New York	(29)	-	29
North Carolina	(15)	15	-
Ohio[2]	(8)	7	-
Pennsylvania	(25)	25	-
Rhode Island	(4)	-	4
South Carolina	(11)	11	-
Tennessee	(8)	8	-
Vermont	(8)	8	-
Virginia	(25)	25	-
Totals	**(218)**	**128**	**89**

1. For explanation of split electoral votes, see p. 6.
2. One Ohio elector did not vote.

States	Electoral Votes	Monroe	King
Connecticut	(9)	-	9
Delaware[1]	(4)	-	3
Georgia	(8)	8	-
Indiana	(3)	3	-
Kentucky	(12)	12	-
Louisiana	(3)	3	-
Maryland[1]	(11)	8	-
Massachusetts	(22)	-	22
New Hampshire	(8)	8	-
New Jersey	(8)	8	-
New York	(29)	29	-
North Carolina	(15)	15	-
Ohio	(8)	8	-
Pennsylvania	(25)	25	-
Rhode Island	(4)	4	-
South Carolina	(11)	11	-
Tennessee	(8)	8	-
Vermont	(8)	8	-
Virginia	(25)	25	-
Totals	**(221)**	**183**	**34**

1. One Delaware and three Maryland electors did not vote.

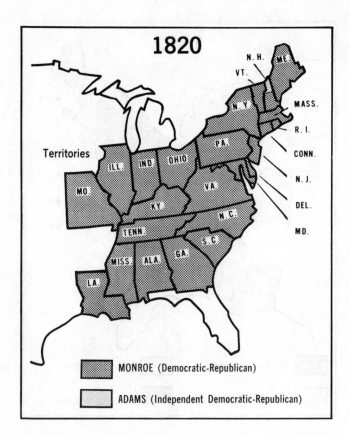

1820

MONROE (Democratic-Republican)

ADAMS (Independent Democratic-Republican)

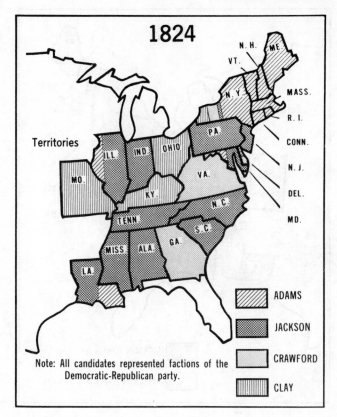

1824

Note: All candidates represented factions of the Democratic-Republican party.

ADAMS

JACKSON

CRAWFORD

CLAY

States	Electoral Votes	Monroe	Adams
Alabama	(3)	3	-
Connecticut	(9)	9	-
Delaware	(4)	4	-
Georgia	(8)	8	-
Illinois	(3)	3	-
Indiana	(3)	3	-
Kentucky	(12)	12	-
Louisiana	(3)	3	-
Maine	(9)	9	-
Maryland	(11)	11	-
Massachusetts	(15)	15	-
Mississippi [1]	(3)	2	-
Missouri	(3)	3	-
New Hampshire [2]	(8)	7	1
New Jersey	(8)	8	-
New York	(29)	29	-
North Carolina	(15)	15	-
Ohio	(8)	8	-
Pennsylvania [1]	(25)	24	-
Rhode Island	(4)	4	-
South Carolina	(11)	11	-
Tennessee [1]	(8)	7	-
Vermont	(8)	8	-
Virginia	(25)	25	-
Totals	**(235)**	**231**	**1**

1. One elector each from Mississippi, Pennsylvania and Tennessee did not vote.
2. For explanation of split electoral votes, see p. 6.

States	Electoral Votes	Jackson	Adams	Crawford	Clay
Alabama	(5)	5	-	-	-
Connecticut	(8)	-	8	-	-
Delaware [1]	(3)	-	1	2	-
Georgia	(9)	-	-	9	-
Illinois [1]	(3)	2	1	-	-
Indiana	(5)	5	-	-	-
Kentucky	(14)	-	-	-	14
Louisiana [1]	(5)	3	2	-	-
Maine	(9)	-	9	-	-
Maryland [1]	(11)	7	3	1	-
Massachusetts	(15)	-	15	-	-
Mississippi	(3)	3	-	-	-
Missouri	(3)	-	-	-	3
New Hampshire	(8)	-	8	-	-
New Jersey	(8)	8	-	-	-
New York [1]	(36)	1	26	5	4
North Carolina	(15)	15	-	-	-
Ohio	(16)	-	-	-	16
Pennsylvania	(28)	28	-	-	-
Rhode Island	(4)	-	4	-	-
South Carolina	(11)	11	-	-	-
Tennessee	(11)	11	-	-	-
Vermont	(7)	-	7	-	-
Virginia	(24)	-	-	24	-
Totals	**(261)**	**99** [2]	**84**	**41**	**37**

1. For explanation of split electoral votes, see p. 6.
2. As no candidate received a majority of the electoral votes, the election was decided by the House of Representatives. See p. 7.

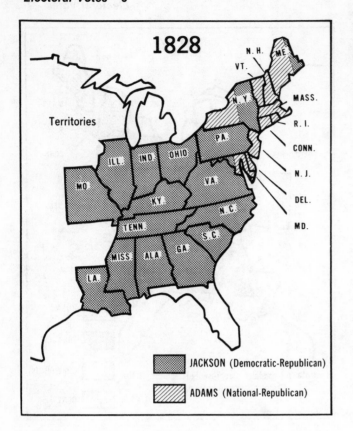

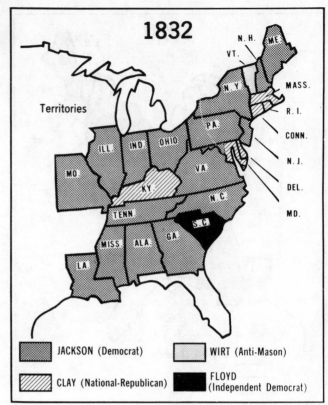

States	Electoral Votes	Jackson	Adams
Alabama	(5)	5	-
Connecticut	(8)	-	8
Delaware	(3)	-	3
Georgia	(9)	9	-
Illinois	(3)	3	-
Indiana	(5)	5	-
Kentucky	(14)	14	-
Louisiana	(5)	5	-
Maine[1]	(9)	1	8
Maryland[1]	(11)	5	6
Massachusetts	(15)	-	15
Mississippi	(3)	3	-
Missouri	(3)	3	-
New Hampshire	(8)	-	8
New Jersey	(8)	-	8
New York[1]	(36)	20	16
North Carolina	(15)	15	-
Ohio	(16)	16	-
Pennsylvania	(28)	28	-
Rhode Island	(4)	-	4
South Carolina	(11)	11	-
Tennessee	(11)	11	-
Vermont	(7)	-	7
Virginia	(24)	24	-
Totals	**(261)**	**178**	**83**

1. For explanation of split electoral votes, see p. 6.

States	Electoral Votes	Jackson	Clay	Floyd	Wirt
Alabama	(7)	7	-	-	-
Connecticut	(8)	-	8	-	-
Delaware	(3)	-	3	-	-
Georgia	(11)	11	-	-	-
Illinois	(5)	5	-	-	-
Indiana	(9)	9	-	-	-
Kentucky	(15)	-	15	-	-
Louisiana	(5)	5	-	-	-
Maine	(10)	10	-	-	-
Maryland[1]	(10)	3	5	-	-
Massachusetts	(14)	-	14	-	-
Mississippi	(4)	4	-	-	-
Missouri	(4)	4	-	-	-
New Hampshire	(7)	7	-	-	-
New Jersey	(8)	8	-	-	-
New York	(42)	42	-	-	-
North Carolina	(15)	15	-	-	-
Ohio	(21)	21	-	-	-
Pennsylvania	(30)	30	-	-	-
Rhode Island	(4)	-	4	-	-
South Carolina	(11)	-	-	11	-
Tennessee	(15)	15	-	-	-
Vermont	(7)	-	-	-	7
Virginia	(23)	23	-	-	-
Totals	**(288)**	**219**	**49**	**11**	**7**

1. Two Maryland electors did not vote. For explanation of split electoral votes, see p. 6.

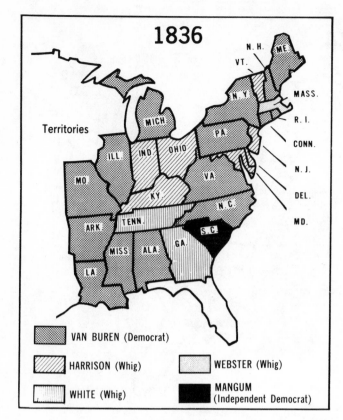

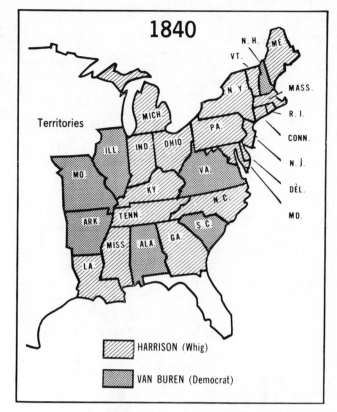

States	Electoral Votes	Van Buren	Harrison[1]	White[1]	Webster[1]	Mangum
Alabama	(7)	7	-	-	-	-
Arkansas	(3)	3	-	-	-	-
Connecticut	(8)	8	-	-	-	-
Delaware	(3)	-	3	-	-	-
Georgia	(11)	-	-	11	-	-
Illinois	(5)	5	-	-	-	-
Indiana	(9)	-	9	-	-	-
Kentucky	(15)	-	15	-	-	-
Louisiana	(5)	5	-	-	-	-
Maine	(10)	10	-	-	-	-
Maryland	(10)	-	10	-	-	-
Massachusetts	(14)	-	-	-	14	-
Michigan	(3)	3	-	-	-	-
Mississippi	(4)	4	-	-	-	-
Missouri	(4)	4	-	-	-	-
New Hampshire	(7)	7	-	-	-	-
New Jersey	(8)	-	8	-	-	-
New York	(42)	42	-	-	-	-
North Carolina	(15)	15	-	-	-	-
Ohio	(21)	-	21	-	-	-
Pennsylvania	(30)	30	-	-	-	-
Rhode Island	(4)	4	-	-	-	-
South Carolina	(11)	-	-	-	-	11
Tennessee	(15)	-	-	15	-	-
Vermont	(7)	-	7	-	-	-
Virginia	(23)	23	-	-	-	-
Totals	**(294)**	**170**	**73**	**26**	**14**	**11**

States	Electoral Votes	Harrison	Van Buren
Alabama	(7)	-	7
Arkansas	(3)	-	3
Connecticut	(8)	8	-
Delaware	(3)	3	-
Georgia	(11)	11	-
Illinois	(5)	-	5
Indiana	(9)	9	-
Kentucky	(15)	15	-
Louisiana	(5)	5	-
Maine	(10)	10	-
Maryland	(10)	10	-
Massachusetts	(14)	14	-
Michigan	(3)	3	-
Mississippi	(4)	4	-
Missouri	(4)	-	4
New Hampshire	(7)	-	7
New Jersey	(8)	8	-
New York	(42)	42	-
North Carolina	(15)	15	-
Ohio	(21)	21	-
Pennsylvania	(30)	30	-
Rhode Island	(4)	4	-
South Carolina	(11)	-	11
Tennessee	(15)	15	-
Vermont	(7)	7	-
Virginia	(23)	-	23
Totals	**(294)**	**234**	**60**

1. For explanation of three Whig presidential candidates, see p. 5.

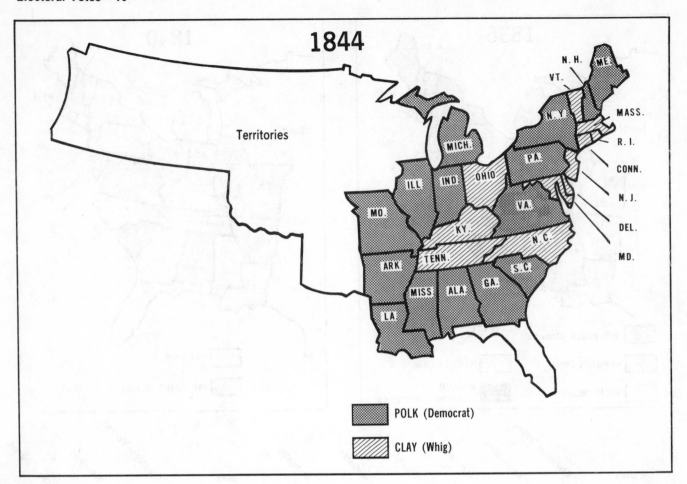

1844

Territories

POLK (Democrat)

CLAY (Whig)

States	Electoral Votes	Polk	Clay
Alabama	(9)	9	-
Arkansas	(3)	3	-
Connecticut	(6)	-	6
Delaware	(3)	-	3
Georgia	(10)	10	-
Illinois	(9)	9	-
Indiana	(12)	12	-
Kentucky	(12)	-	12
Louisiana	(6)	6	-
Maine	(9)	9	-
Maryland	(8)	-	8
Massachusetts	(12)	-	12
Michigan	(5)	5	-
Mississippi	(6)	6	-
Missouri	(7)	7	-
New Hampshire	(6)	6	-
New Jersey	(7)	-	7
New York	(36)	36	-
North Carolina	(11)	-	11
Ohio	(23)	-	23
Pennsylvania	(26)	26	-
Rhode Island	(4)	-	4
South Carolina	(9)	9	-
Tennessee	(13)	-	13
Vermont	(6)	-	6
Virginia	(17)	17	-
Totals	**(275)**	**170**	**105**

1848

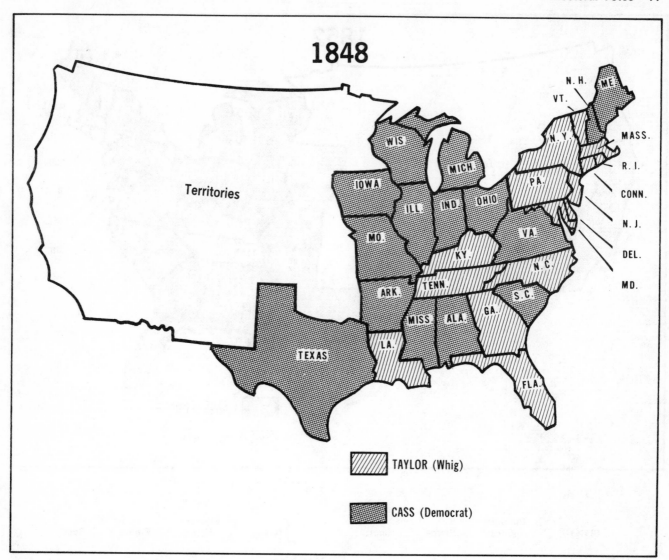

States	Electoral Votes	Taylor	Cass	States	Electoral Votes	Taylor	Cass
Alabama	(9)	-	9	**Mississippi**	(6)	-	6
Arkansas	(3)	-	3	**Missouri**	(7)	-	7
Connecticut	(6)	6	-	**New Hampshire**	(6)	-	6
Delaware	(3)	3	-	**New Jersey**	(7)	7	-
Florida	(3)	3	-	**New York**	(36)	36	-
Georgia	(10)	10	-	**North Carolina**	(11)	11	-
Illinois	(9)	-	9	**Ohio**	(23)	-	23
Indiana	(12)	-	12	**Pennsylvania**	(26)	26	-
Iowa	(4)	-	4	**Rhode Island**	(4)	4	-
Kentucky	(12)	12	-	**South Carolina**	(9)	-	9
Louisiana	(6)	6	-	**Tennessee**	(13)	13	-
Maine	(9)	-	9	**Texas**	(4)	-	4
Maryland	(8)	8	-	**Vermont**	(6)	6	-
Massachusetts	(12)	12	-	**Virginia**	(17)	-	17
Michigan	(5)	-	5	**Wisconsin**	(4)	-	4
				Totals	(290)	163	127

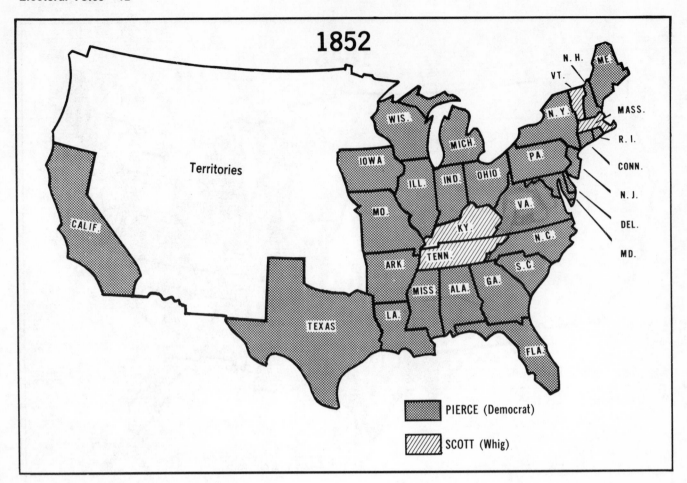

1852

PIERCE (Democrat)

SCOTT (Whig)

States	Electoral Votes	Pierce	Scott	States	Electoral Votes	Pierce	Scott
Alabama	(9)	9	-	Mississippi	(7)	7	-
Arkansas	(4)	4	-	Missouri	(9)	9	-
California	(4)	4	-	New Hampshire	(5)	5	-
Connecticut	(6)	6	-	New Jersey	(7)	7	-
Delaware	(3)	3	-	New York	(35)	35	-
Florida	(3)	3	-	North Carolina	(10)	10	-
Georgia	(10)	10	-	Ohio	(23)	23	-
Illinois	(11)	11	-	Pennsylvania	(27)	27	-
Indiana	(13)	13	-	Rhode Island	(4)	4	-
Iowa	(4)	4	-	South Carolina	(8)	8	-
Kentucky	(12)	-	12	Tennessee	(12)	-	12
Louisiana	(6)	6	-	Texas	(4)	4	-
Maine	(8)	8	-	Vermont	(5)	-	5
Maryland	(8)	8	-	Virginia	(15)	15	-
Massachusetts	(13)	-	13	Wisconsin	(5)	5	-
Michigan	(6)	6	-	**Totals**	**(296)**	**254**	**42**

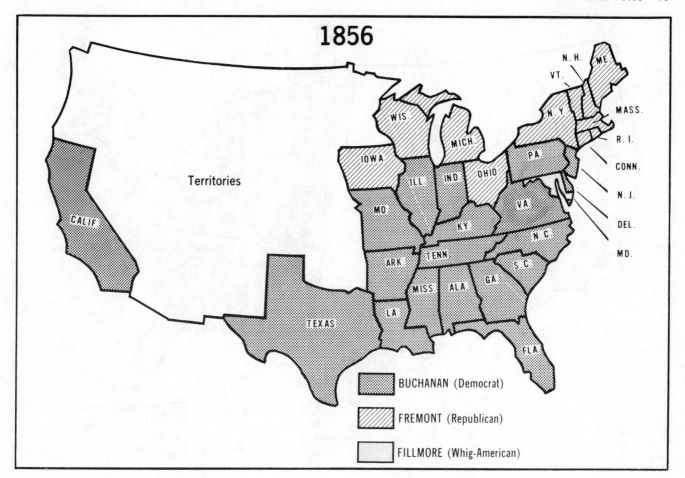

1856

Territories

BUCHANAN (Democrat)

FREMONT (Republican)

FILLMORE (Whig-American)

States	Electoral Votes	Buchanan	Fremont	Fillmore	States	Electoral Votes	Buchanan	Fremont	Fillmore
Alabama	(9)	9	-	-	Mississippi	(7)	7	-	-
Arkansas	(4)	4	-	-	Missouri	(9)	9	-	-
California	(4)	4	-	-	New Hampshire	(5)	-	5	-
Connecticut	(6)	-	6	-	New Jersey	(7)	7	-	-
Delaware	(3)	3	-	-	New York	(35)	-	35	-
Florida	(3)	3	-	-	North Carolina	(10)	10	-	-
Georgia	(10)	10	-	-	Ohio	(23)	-	23	-
Illinois	(11)	11	-	-	Pennsylvania	(27)	27	-	-
Indiana	(13)	13	-	-	Rhode Island	(4)	-	4	-
Iowa	(4)	-	4	-	South Carolina	(8)	8	-	-
Kentucky	(12)	12	-	-	Tennessee	(12)	12	-	-
Louisiana	(6)	6	-	-	Texas	(4)	4	-	-
Maine	(8)	-	8	-	Vermont	(5)	-	5	-
Maryland	(8)	-	-	8	Virginia	(15)	15	-	-
Massachusetts	(13)	-	13	-	Wisconsin	(5)	-	5	-
Michigan	(6)	-	6	-	**Totals**	**(296)**	**174**	**114**	**8**

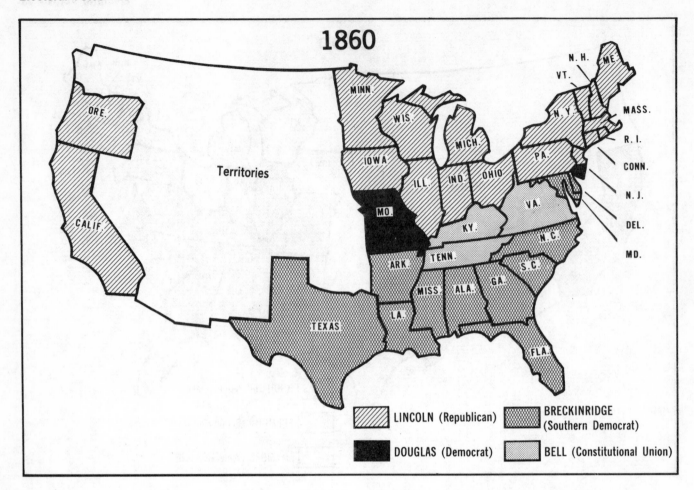

1860

Territories

LINCOLN (Republican)

DOUGLAS (Democrat)

BRECKINRIDGE
(Southern Democrat)

BELL (Constitutional Union)

States	Electoral Votes	Lincoln	Breckinridge	Bell	Douglas
Alabama	(9)	-	9	-	-
Arkansas	(4)	-	4	-	-
California	(4)	4	-	-	-
Connecticut	(6)	6	-	-	-
Delaware	(3)	-	3	-	-
Florida	(3)	-	3	-	-
Georgia	(10)	-	10	-	-
Illinois	(11)	11	-	-	-
Indiana	(13)	13	-	-	-
Iowa	(4)	4	-	-	-
Kentucky	(12)	-	-	12	-
Louisiana	(6)	-	6	-	-
Maine	(8)	8	-	-	-
Maryland	(8)	-	8	-	-
Massachusetts	(13)	13	-	-	-
Michigan	(6)	6	-	-	-
Minnesota	(4)	4	-	-	-

States	Electoral Votes	Lincoln	Breckinridge	Bell	Douglas
Mississippi	(7)	-	7	-	-
Missouri	(9)	-	-	-	9
New Hampshire	(5)	5	-	-	-
New Jersey[1]	(7)	4	-	-	3
New York	(35)	35	-	-	-
North Carolina	(10)	-	10	-	-
Ohio	(23)	23	-	-	-
Oregon	(3)	3	-	-	-
Pennsylvania	(27)	27	-	-	-
Rhode Island	(4)	4	-	-	-
South Carolina	(8)	-	8	-	-
Tennessee	(12)	-	-	12	-
Texas	(4)	-	4	-	-
Vermont	(5)	5	-	-	-
Virginia	(15)	-	-	15	-
Wisconsin	(5)	5	-	-	-
Totals	**(303)**	**180**	**72**	**39**	**12**

1. For explanation of split electoral votes, see p. 6.

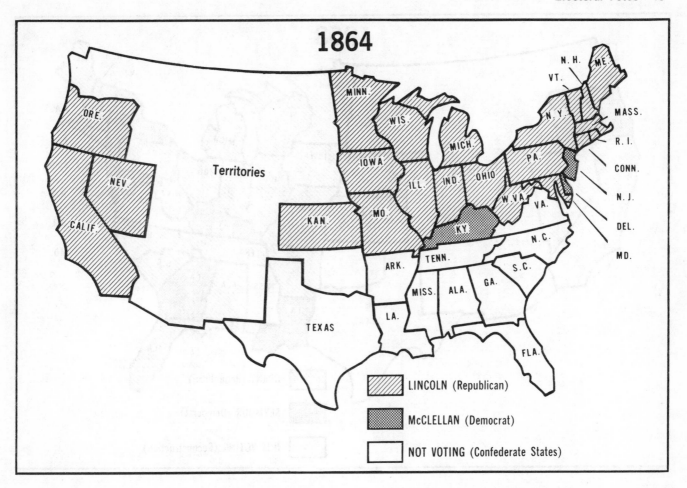

1864

LINCOLN (Republican)

McCLELLAN (Democrat)

NOT VOTING (Confederate States)

States[1]	Electoral Votes	Lincoln	McClellan	States[1]	Electoral Votes	Lincoln	McClellan
California	(5)	5	-	Missouri	(11)	11	-
Connecticut	(6)	6	-	Nevada[2]	(3)	2	-
Delaware	(3)	-	3	New Hampshire	(5)	5	-
Illinois	(16)	16	-	New Jersey	(7)	-	7
Indiana	(13)	13	-	New York	(33)	33	-
Iowa	(8)	8	-	Ohio	(21)	21	-
Kansas	(3)	3	-	Oregon	(3)	3	-
Kentucky	(11)	-	11	Pennsylvania	(26)	26	-
Maine	(7)	7	-	Rhode Island	(4)	4	-
Maryland	(7)	7	-	Vermont	(5)	5	-
Massachusetts	(12)	12	-	West Virginia	(5)	5	-
Michigan	(8)	8	-	Wisconsin	(8)	8	-
Minnesota	(4)	4	-	**Totals**	**(234)**	**212**	**21**

1. Eleven southern states—Alabama, Arkansas, Florida, Georgia, Louisiana, Mississippi, North Carolina, South Carolina, Tennessee, Texas and Virginia had seceded from the Union and did not vote.
2. One Nevada elector did not vote.

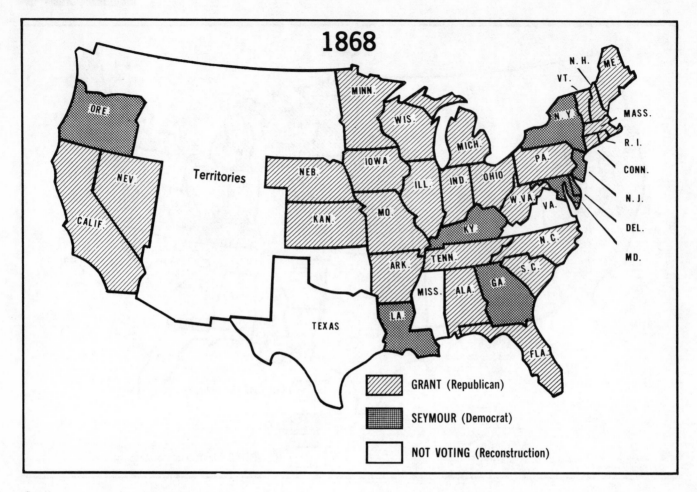

1868

GRANT (Republican)

SEYMOUR (Democrat)

NOT VOTING (Reconstruction)

States[1]	Electoral Votes	Grant	Seymour	States[1]	Electoral Votes	Grant	Seymour
Alabama	(8)	8	-	Missouri	(11)	11	-
Arkansas	(5)	5	-	Nebraska	(3)	3	-
California	(5)	5	-	Nevada	(3)	3	-
Connecticut	(6)	6	-	New Hampshire	(5)	5	-
Delaware	(3)	-	3	New Jersey	(7)	-	7
Florida	(3)	3	-	New York	(33)	-	33
Georgia	(9)	-	9	North Carolina	(9)	9	-
Illinois	(16)	16	-	Ohio	(21)	21	-
Indiana	(13)	13	-	Oregon	(3)	-	3
Iowa	(8)	8	-	Pennsylvania	(26)	26	-
Kansas	(3)	3	-	Rhode Island	(4)	4	-
Kentucky	(11)	-	11	South Carolina	(6)	6	-
Louisiana	(7)	-	7	Tennessee	(10)	10	-
Maine	(7)	7	-	Vermont	(5)	5	-
Maryland	(7)	-	7	West Virginia	(5)	5	-
Massachusetts	(12)	12	-	Wisconsin	(8)	8	-
Michigan	(8)	8	-				
Minnesota	(4)	4	-	**Totals**	**(294)**	**214**	**80**

1. Mississippi, Texas and Virginia were not yet readmitted to the Union and did not participate in the election.

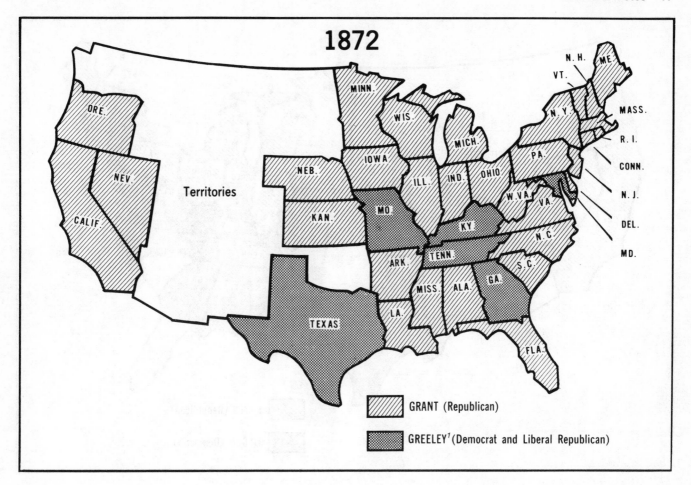

1872

GRANT (Republican)

GREELEY[1] (Democrat and Liberal Republican)

States	Electoral Votes	Grant	Hendricks[1]	Brown[1]	Jenkins[1]	Davis[1]
Alabama	(10)	10	-	-	-	-
Arkansas[2]	(6)	-	-	-	-	-
California	(6)	6	-	-	-	-
Connecticut	(6)	6	-	-	-	-
Delaware	(3)	3	-	-	-	-
Florida	(4)	4	-	-	-	-
Georgia[3]	(11)	-	-	6	2	-
Illinois	(21)	21	-	-	-	-
Indiana	(15)	15	-	-	-	-
Iowa	(11)	11	-	-	-	-
Kansas	(5)	5	-	-	-	-
Kentucky	(12)	-	8	4	-	-
Louisiana[2]	(8)	-	-	-	-	-
Maine	(7)	7	-	-	-	-
Maryland	(8)	-	8	-	-	-
Massachusetts	(13)	13	-	-	-	-
Michigan	(11)	11	-	-	-	-
Minnesota	(5)	5	-	-	-	-
Mississippi	(8)	8	-	-	-	-
Missouri	(15)	-	6	8	-	1
Nebraska	(3)	3	-	-	-	-
Nevada	(3)	3	-	-	-	-
New Hampshire	(5)	5	-	-	-	-
New Jersey	(9)	9	-	-	-	-
New York	(35)	35	-	-	-	-
North Carolina	(10)	10	-	-	-	-
Ohio	(22)	22	-	-	-	-
Oregon	(3)	3	-	-	-	-
Pennsylvania	(29)	29	-	-	-	-
Rhode Island	(4)	4	-	-	-	-
South Carolina	(7)	7	-	-	-	-
Tennessee	(12)	-	12	-	-	-
Texas	(8)	-	8	-	-	-
Vermont	(5)	5	-	-	-	-
Virginia	(11)	11	-	-	-	-
West Virginia	(5)	5	-	-	-	-
Wisconsin	(10)	10	-	-	-	-
Totals	(366)	286	42	18	2	1

1. For explanation of Democratic electoral vote, cast after Greeley's death, see p. 5.
2. Congress refused to accept electoral votes of Arkansas and Louisiana because of disruptive conditions during Reconstruction.
3. Three Georgia electoral votes cast for Greeley were not counted.

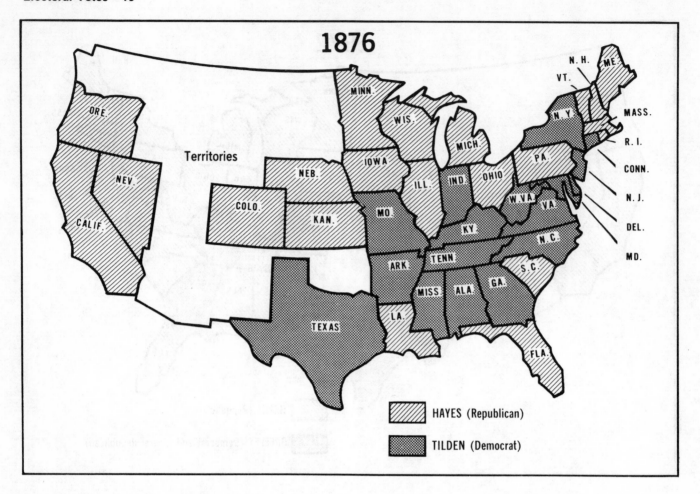

1876

HAYES (Republican)

TILDEN (Democrat)

States	Electoral Votes	Hayes	Tilden	States	Electoral Votes	Hayes	Tilden
Alabama	(10)	-	10	Missouri	(15)	-	15
Arkansas	(6)	-	6	Nebraska	(3)	3	-
California	(6)	6	-	Nevada	(3)	3	-
Colorado	(3)	3	-	New Hampshire	(5)	5	-
Connecticut	(6)	-	6	New Jersey	(9)	-	9
Delaware	(3)	-	3	New York	(35)	-	35
Florida[1]	(4)	4	-	North Carolina	(10)	-	10
Georgia	(11)	-	11	Ohio	(22)	22	-
Illinois	(21)	21	-	Oregon[1]	(3)	3	-
Indiana	(15)	-	15	Pennsylvania	(29)	29	-
Iowa	(11)	11	-	Rhode Island	(4)	4	-
Kansas	(5)	5	-	South Carolina[1]	(7)	7	-
Kentucky	(12)	-	12	Tennessee	(12)	-	12
Louisiana[1]	(8)	8	-	Texas	(8)	-	8
Maine	(7)	7	-	Vermont	(5)	5	-
Maryland	(8)	-	8	Virginia	(11)	-	11
Massachusetts	(13)	13	-	West Virginia	(5)	-	5
Michigan	(11)	11	-	Wisconsin	(10)	10	-
Minnesota	(5)	5	-	**Totals**	**(369)**	**185**	**184**
Mississippi	(8)	-	8				

1. For explanation of disputed electoral votes of Florida, Louisiana, Oregon and South Carolina, see p. 11.

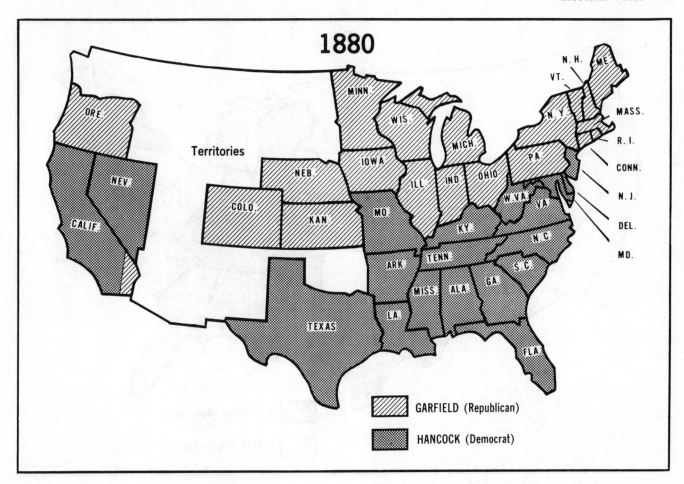

1880

GARFIELD (Republican)

HANCOCK (Democrat)

States	Electoral Votes	Garfield	Hancock	States	Electoral Votes	Garfield	Hancock
Alabama	(10)	-	10	Mississippi	(8)	-	8
Arkansas	(6)	-	6	Missouri	(15)	-	15
California[1]	(6)	1	5	Nebraska	(3)	3	-
Colorado	(3)	3	-	Nevada	(3)	-	3
Connecticut	(6)	6	-	New Hampshire	(5)	5	-
Delaware	(3)	-	3	New Jersey	(9)	-	9
Florida	(4)	-	4	New York	(35)	35	-
Georgia	(11)	-	11	North Carolina	(10)	-	10
Illinois	(21)	21	-	Ohio	(22)	22	-
Indiana	(15)	15	-	Oregon	(3)	3	-
Iowa	(11)	11	-	Pennsylvania	(29)	29	-
Kansas	(5)	5	-	Rhode Island	(4)	4	-
Kentucky	(12)	-	12	South Carolina	(7)	-	7
Louisiana	(8)	-	8	Tennessee	(12)	-	12
Maine	(7)	7	-	Texas	(8)	-	8
Maryland	(8)	-	8	Vermont	(5)	5	-
Massachusetts	(13)	13	-	Virginia	(11)	-	11
Michigan	(11)	11	-	West Virginia	(5)	-	5
Minnesota	(5)	5	-	Wisconsin	(10)	10	-
				Totals	**(369)**	**214**	**155**

1. For explanation of split electoral votes, see p. 6.

1884

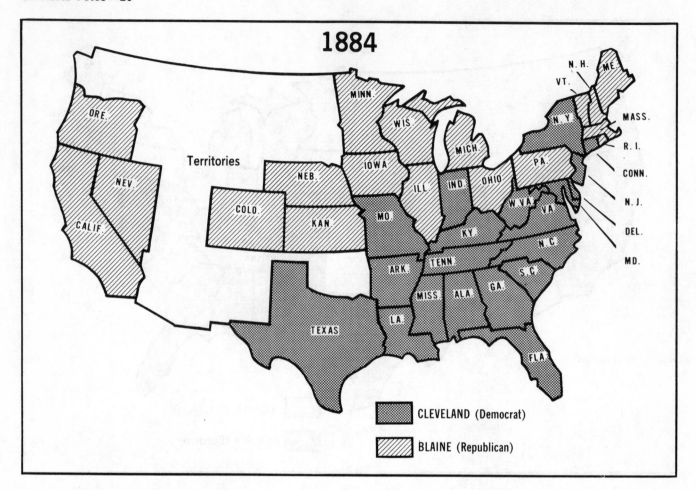

CLEVELAND (Democrat)

BLAINE (Republican)

States	Electoral Votes	Cleveland	Blaine	States	Electoral Votes	Cleveland	Blaine
Alabama	(10)	10	-	Mississippi	(9)	9	-
Arkansas	(7)	7	-	Missouri	(16)	16	-
California	(8)	-	8	Nebraska	(5)	-	5
Colorado	(3)	-	3	Nevada	(3)	-	3
Connecticut	(6)	6	-	New Hampshire	(4)	-	4
Delaware	(3)	3	-	New Jersey	(9)	9	-
Florida	(4)	4	-	New York	(36)	36	-
Georgia	(12)	12	-	North Carolina	(11)	11	-
Illinois	(22)	-	22	Ohio	(23)	-	23
Indiana	(15)	15	-	Oregon	(3)	-	3
Iowa	(13)	-	13	Pennsylvania	(30)	-	30
Kansas	(9)	-	9	Rhode Island	(4)	-	4
Kentucky	(13)	13	-	South Carolina	(9)	9	-
Louisiana	(8)	8	-	Tennessee	(12)	12	-
Maine	(6)	-	6	Texas	(13)	13	-
Maryland	(8)	8	-	Vermont	(4)	-	4
Massachusetts	(14)	-	14	Virginia	(12)	12	-
Michigan	(13)	-	13	West Virginia	(6)	6	-
Minnesota	(7)	-	7	Wisconsin	(11)	-	11
				Totals	**(401)**	**219**	**182**

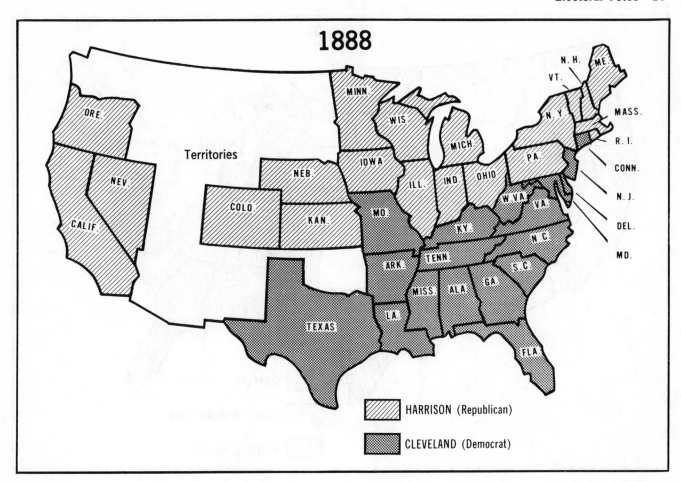

1888

| HARRISON (Republican) |
| CLEVELAND (Democrat) |

States	Electoral Votes	Harrison	Cleveland	States	Electoral Votes	Harrison	Cleveland
Alabama	(10)	-	10	Mississippi	(9)	-	9
Arkansas	(7)	-	7	Missouri	(16)	-	16
California	(8)	8	-	Nebraska	(5)	5	-
Colorado	(3)	3	-	Nevada	(3)	3	-
Connecticut	(6)	-	6	New Hampshire	(4)	4	-
Delaware	(3)	-	3	New Jersey	(9)	-	9
Florida	(4)	-	4	New York	(36)	36	-
Georgia	(12)	-	12	North Carolina	(11)	-	11
Illinois	(22)	22	-	Ohio	(23)	23	-
Indiana	(15)	15	-	Oregon	(3)	3	-
Iowa	(13)	13	-	Pennsylvania	(30)	30	-
Kansas	(9)	9	-	Rhode Island	(4)	4	-
Kentucky	(13)	-	13	South Carolina	(9)	-	9
Louisiana	(8)	-	8	Tennessee	(12)	-	12
Maine	(6)	6	-	Texas	(13)	-	13
Maryland	(8)	-	8	Vermont	(4)	4	-
Massachusetts	(14)	14	-	Virginia	(12)	-	12
Michigan	(13)	13	-	West Virginia	(6)	-	6
Minnesota	(7)	7	-	Wisconsin	(11)	11	-
				Totals	**(401)**	**233**	**168**

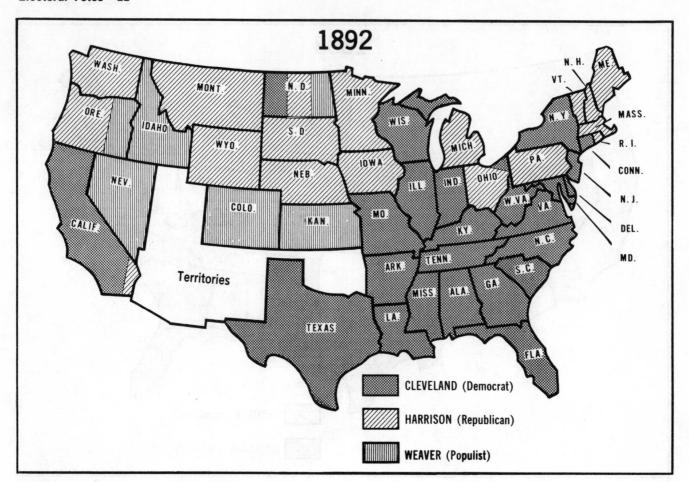

1892

CLEVELAND (Democrat)

HARRISON (Republican)

WEAVER (Populist)

States	Electoral Votes	Cleveland	Harrison	Weaver	States	Electoral Votes	Cleveland	Harrison	Weaver
Alabama	(11)	11	-	-	**Montana**	(3)	-	3	-
Arkansas	(8)	8	-	-	**Nebraska**	(8)	-	8	-
California[1]	(9)	8	1	-	**Nevada**	(3)	-	-	3
Colorado	(4)	-	-	4	**New Hampshire**	(4)	-	4	-
Connecticut	(6)	6	-	-	**New Jersey**	(10)	10	-	-
Delaware	(3)	3	-	-	**New York**	(36)	36	-	-
Florida	(4)	4	-	-	**North Carolina**	(11)	11	-	-
Georgia	(13)	13	-	-	**North Dakota**[1]	(3)	1	1	1
Idaho	(3)	-	-	3	**Ohio**[1]	(23)	1	22	-
Illinois	(24)	24	-	-	**Oregon**[1]	(4)	-	3	1
Indiana	(15)	15	-	-	**Pennsylvania**	(32)	-	32	-
Iowa	(13)	-	13	-	**Rhode Island**	(4)	-	4	-
Kansas	(10)	-	-	10	**South Carolina**	(9)	9	-	-
Kentucky	(13)	13	-	-	**South Dakota**	(4)	-	4	-
Louisiana	(8)	8	-	-	**Tennessee**	(12)	12	-	-
Maine	(6)	-	6	-	**Texas**	(15)	15	-	-
Maryland	(8)	8	-	-	**Vermont**	(4)	-	4	-
Massachusetts	(15)	-	15	-	**Virginia**	(12)	12	-	-
Michigan[1]	(14)	5	9	-	**Washington**	(4)	-	4	-
Minnesota	(9)	-	9	-	**West Virginia**	(6)	6	-	-
Mississippi	(9)	9	-	-	**Wisconsin**	(12)	12	-	-
Missouri	(17)	17	-	-	**Wyoming**	(3)	-	3	-
					Totals	**(444)**	**277**	**145**	**22**

1. For explanation of split electoral votes, see p. 6.

1896

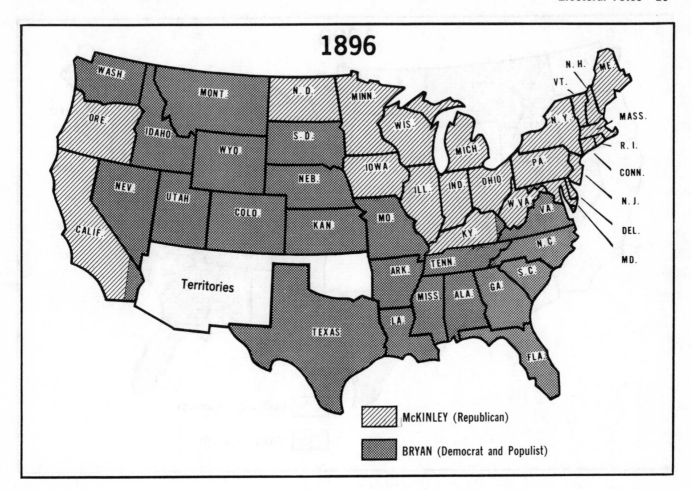

McKINLEY (Republican)

BRYAN (Democrat and Populist)

States	Electoral Votes	McKinley	Bryan	States	Electoral Votes	McKinley	Bryan
Alabama	(11)	-	11	Nebraska	(8)	-	8
Arkansas	(8)	-	8	Nevada	(3)	-	3
California[1]	(9)	8	1	New Hampshire	(4)	4	-
Colorado	(4)	-	4	New Jersey	(10)	10	-
Connecticut	(6)	6	-	New York	(36)	36	-
Delaware	(3)	3	-	North Carolina	(11)	-	11
Florida	(4)	-	4	North Dakota	(3)	3	-
Georgia	(13)	-	13	Ohio	(23)	23	-
Idaho	(3)	-	3	Oregon	(4)	4	-
Illinois	(24)	24	-	Pennsylvania	(32)	32	-
Indiana	(15)	15	-	Rhode Island	(4)	4	-
Iowa	(13)	13	-	South Carolina	(9)	-	9
Kansas	(10)	-	10	South Dakota	(4)	-	4
Kentucky[1]	(13)	12	1	Tennessee	(12)	-	12
Louisiana	(8)	-	8	Texas	(15)	-	15
Maine	(6)	6	-	Utah	(3)	-	3
Maryland	(8)	8	-	Vermont	(4)	4	-
Massachusetts	(15)	15	-	Virginia	(12)	-	12
Michigan	(14)	14	-	Washington	(4)	-	4
Minnesota	(9)	9	-	West Virginia	(6)	6	-
Mississippi	(9)	-	9	Wisconsin	(12)	12	-
Missouri	(17)	-	17	Wyoming	(3)	-	3
Montana	(3)	-	3	**Totals**	**(447)**	**271**	**176**

1. For explanation of split electoral votes, see p. 6.

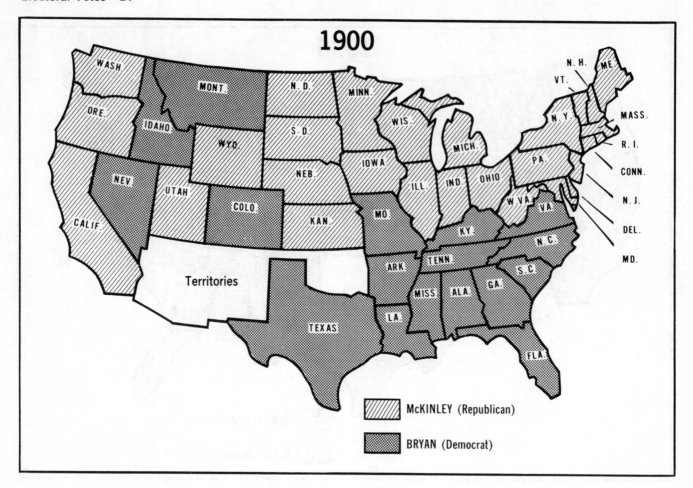

1900

McKINLEY (Republican)

BRYAN (Democrat)

States	Electoral Votes	McKinley	Bryan	States	Electoral Votes	McKinley	Bryan
Alabama	(11)	-	11	Nebraska	(8)	8	-
Arkansas	(8)	-	8	Nevada	(3)	-	3
California	(9)	9	-	New Hampshire	(4)	4	-
Colorado	(4)	-	4	New Jersey	(10)	10	-
Connecticut	(6)	6	-	New York	(36)	36	-
Delaware	(3)	3	-	North Carolina	(11)	-	11
Florida	(4)	-	4	North Dakota	(3)	3	-
Georgia	(13)	-	13	Ohio	(23)	23	-
Idaho	(3)	-	3	Oregon	(4)	4	-
Illinois	(24)	24	-	Pennsylvania	(32)	32	-
Indiana	(15)	15	-	Rhode Island	(4)	4	-
Iowa	(13)	13	-	South Carolina	(9)	-	9
Kansas	(10)	10	-	South Dakota	(4)	4	-
Kentucky	(13)	-	13	Tennessee	(12)	-	12
Louisiana	(8)	-	8	Texas	(15)	-	15
Maine	(6)	6	-	Utah	(3)	3	-
Maryland	(8)	8	-	Vermont	(4)	4	-
Massachusetts	(15)	15	-	Virginia	(12)	-	12
Michigan	(14)	14	-	Washington	(4)	4	-
Minnesota	(9)	9	-	West Virginia	(6)	6	-
Mississippi	(9)	-	9	Wisconsin	(12)	12	-
Missouri	(17)	-	17	Wyoming	(3)	3	-
Montana	(3)	-	3	**Totals**	**(447)**	**292**	**155**

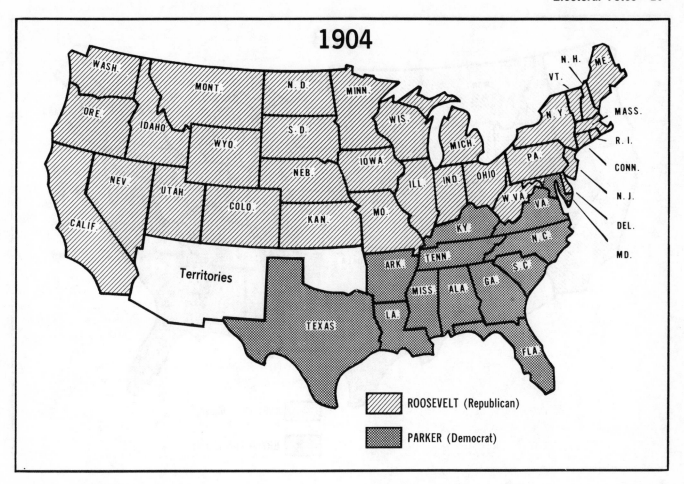

1904

ROOSEVELT (Republican)

PARKER (Democrat)

States	Electoral Votes	Roosevelt	Parker	States	Electoral Votes	Roosevelt	Parker
Alabama	(11)	-	11	Nebraska	(8)	8	-
Arkansas	(9)	-	9	Nevada	(3)	3	-
California	(10)	10	-	New Hampshire	(4)	4	-
Colorado	(5)	5	-	New Jersey	(12)	12	-
Connecticut	(7)	7	-	New York	(39)	39	-
Delaware	(3)	3	-	North Carolina	(12)	-	12
Florida	(5)	-	5	North Dakota	(4)	4	-
Georgia	(13)	-	13	Ohio	(23)	23	-
Idaho	(3)	3	-	Oregon	(4)	4	-
Illinois	(27)	27	-	Pennsylvania	(34)	34	-
Indiana	(15)	15	-	Rhode Island	(4)	4	-
Iowa	(13)	13	-	South Carolina	(9)	-	9
Kansas	(10)	10	-	South Dakota	(4)	4	-
Kentucky	(13)	-	13	Tennessee	(12)	-	12
Louisiana	(9)	-	9	Texas	(18)	-	18
Maine	(6)	6	-	Utah	(3)	3	-
Maryland[1]	(8)	1	7	Vermont	(4)	4	-
Massachusetts	(16)	16	-	Virginia	(12)	-	12
Michigan	(14)	14	-	Washington	(5)	5	-
Minnesota	(11)	11	-	West Virginia	(7)	7	-
Mississippi	(10)	-	10	Wisconsin	(13)	13	-
Missouri	(18)	18	-	Wyoming	(3)	3	-
Montana	(3)	3	-	**Totals**	**(476)**	**336**	**140**

1. For explanation of split electoral votes, see p. 6.

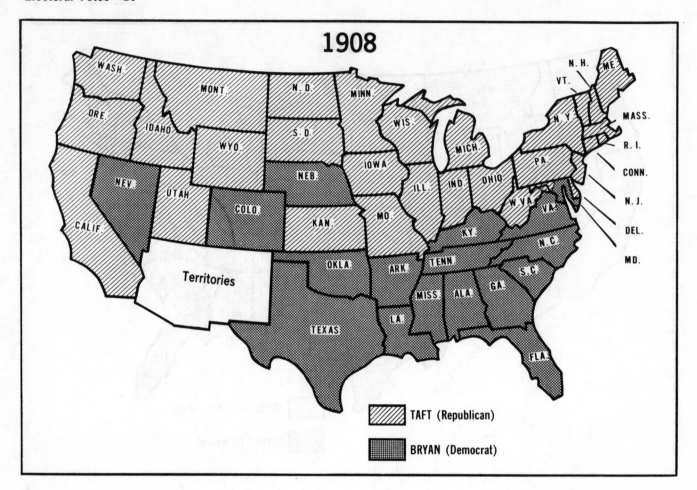

1908

TAFT (Republican)

BRYAN (Democrat)

States	Electoral Votes	Taft	Bryan	States	Electoral Votes	Taft	Bryan
Alabama	(11)	-	11	Nebraska	(8)	-	8
Arkansas	(9)	-	9	Nevada	(3)	-	3
California	(10)	10	-	New Hampshire	(4)	4	-
Colorado	(5)	-	5	New Jersey	(12)	12	-
Connecticut	(7)	7	-	New York	(39)	39	-
Delaware	(3)	3	-	North Carolina	(12)	-	12
Florida	(5)	-	5	North Dakota	(4)	4	-
Georgia	(13)	-	13	Ohio	(23)	23	-
Idaho	(3)	3	-	Oklahoma	(7)	-	7
Illinois	(27)	27	-	Oregon	(4)	4	-
Indiana	(15)	15	-	Pennsylvania	(34)	34	-
Iowa	(13)	13	-	Rhode Island	(4)	4	-
Kansas	(10)	10	-	South Carolina	(9)	-	9
Kentucky	(13)	-	13	South Dakota	(4)	4	-
Louisiana	(9)	-	9	Tennessee	(12)	-	12
Maine	(6)	6	-	Texas	(18)	-	18
Maryland[1]	(8)	2	6	Utah	(3)	3	-
Massachusetts	(16)	16	-	Vermont	(4)	4	-
Michigan	(14)	14	-	Virginia	(12)	-	12
Minnesota	(11)	11	-	Washington	(5)	5	-
Mississippi	(10)	-	10	West Virginia	(7)	7	-
Missouri	(18)	18	-	Wisconsin	(13)	13	-
Montana	(3)	3	-	Wyoming	(3)	3	-
				Totals	**(483)**	**321**	**162**

1. For explanation of split electoral votes, see p. 6.

1912

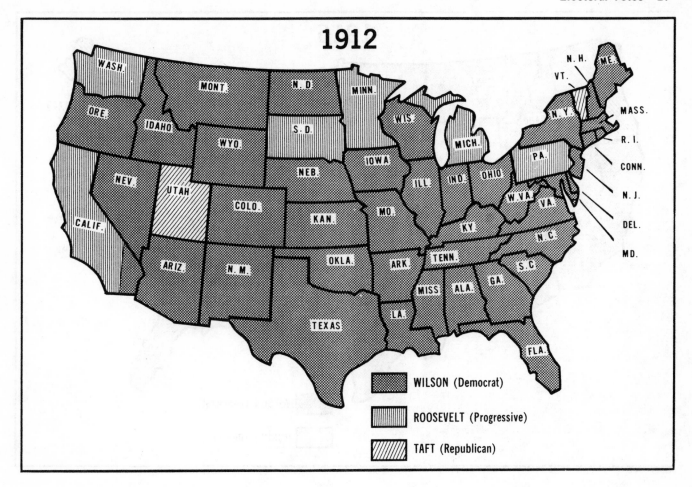

WILSON (Democrat)

ROOSEVELT (Progressive)

TAFT (Republican)

States	Electoral Votes	Wilson	Roosevelt	Taft	States	Electoral Votes	Wilson	Roosevelt	Taft
Alabama	(12)	12	-	-	Nebraska	(8)	8	-	-
Arizona	(3)	3	-	-	Nevada	(3)	3	-	-
Arkansas	(9)	9	-	-	New Hampshire	(4)	4	-	-
California[1]	(13)	2	11	-	New Jersey	(14)	14	-	-
Colorado	(6)	6	-	-	New Mexico	(3)	3	-	-
Connecticut	(7)	7	-	-	New York	(45)	45	-	-
Delaware	(3)	3	-	-	North Carolina	(12)	12	-	-
Florida	(6)	6	-	-	North Dakota	(5)	5	-	-
Georgia	(14)	14	-	-	Ohio	(24)	24	-	-
Idaho	(4)	4	-	-	Oklahoma	(10)	10	-	-
Illinois	(29)	29	-	-	Oregon	(5)	5	-	-
Indiana	(15)	15	-	-	Pennsylvania	(38)	-	38	-
Iowa	(13)	13	-	-	Rhode Island	(5)	5	-	-
Kansas	(10)	10	-	-	South Carolina	(9)	9	-	-
Kentucky	(13)	13	-	-	South Dakota	(5)	-	5	-
Louisiana	(10)	10	-	-	Tennessee	(12)	12	-	-
Maine	(6)	6	-	-	Texas	(20)	20	-	-
Maryland	(8)	8	-	-	Utah	(4)	-	-	4
Massachusetts	(18)	18	-	-	Vermont	(4)	-	-	4
Michigan	(15)	-	15	-	Virginia	(12)	12	-	-
Minnesota	(12)	-	12	-	Washington	(7)	-	7	-
Mississippi	(10)	10	-	-	West Virginia	(8)	8	-	-
Missouri	(18)	18	-	-	Wisconsin	(13)	13	-	-
Montana	(4)	4	-	-	Wyoming	(3)	3	-	-
					Totals	**(531)**	**435**	**88**	**8**

1. For explanation of split electoral votes, see p. 6.

1916

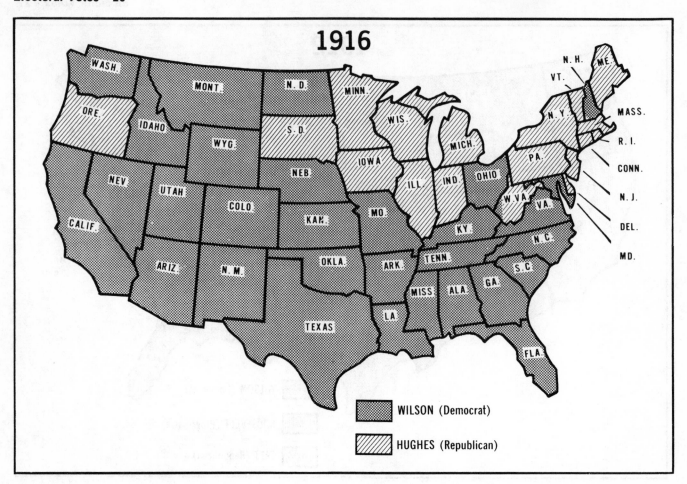

WILSON (Democrat)

HUGHES (Republican)

States	Electoral Votes	Wilson	Hughes	States	Electoral Votes	Wilson	Hughes
Alabama	(12)	12	-	Nebraska	(8)	8	-
Arizona	(3)	3	-	Nevada	(3)	3	-
Arkansas	(9)	9	-	New Hampshire	(4)	4	-
California	(13)	13	-	New Jersey	(14)	-	14
Colorado	(6)	6	-	New Mexico	(3)	3	-
Connecticut	(7)	-	7	New York	(45)	-	45
Delaware	(3)	-	3	North Carolina	(12)	12	-
Florida	(6)	6	-	North Dakota	(5)	5	-
Georgia	(14)	14	-	Ohio	(24)	24	-
Idaho	(4)	4	-	Oklahoma	(10)	10	-
Illinois	(29)	-	29	Oregon	(5)	-	5
Indiana	(15)	-	15	Pennsylvania	(38)	-	38
Iowa	(13)	-	13	Rhode Island	(5)	-	5
Kansas	(10)	10	-	South Carolina	(9)	9	-
Kentucky	(13)	13	-	South Dakota	(5)	-	5
Louisiana	(10)	10	-	Tennessee	(12)	12	-
Maine	(6)	-	6	Texas	(20)	20	-
Maryland	(8)	8	-	Utah	(4)	4	-
Massachusetts	(18)	-	18	Vermont	(4)	-	4
Michigan	(15)	-	15	Virginia	(12)	12	-
Minnesota	(12)	-	12	Washington	(7)	7	-
Mississippi	(10)	10	-	West Virginia[1]	(8)	1	7
Missouri	(18)	18	-	Wisconsin	(13)	-	13
Montana	(4)	4	-	Wyoming	(3)	3	-
				Totals	**(531)**	**277**	**254**

1. For explanation of split electoral votes, see p. 6.

1920

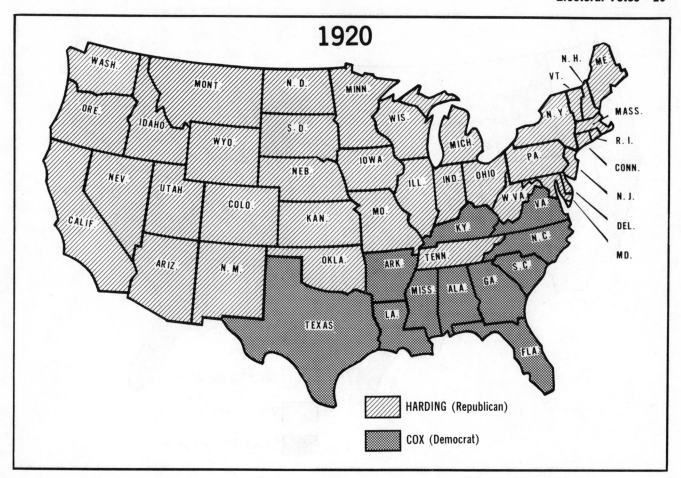

HARDING (Republican)

COX (Democrat)

States	Electoral Votes	Harding	Cox	States	Electoral Votes	Harding	Cox
Alabama	(12)	-	12	Nebraska	(8)	8	-
Arizona	(3)	3	-	Nevada	(3)	3	-
Arkansas	(9)	-	9	New Hampshire	(4)	4	-
California	(13)	13	-	New Jersey	(14)	14	-
Colorado	(6)	6	-	New Mexico	(3)	3	-
Connecticut	(7)	7	-	New York	(45)	45	-
Delaware	(3)	3	-	North Carolina	(12)	-	12
Florida	(6)	-	6	North Dakota	(5)	5	-
Georgia	(14)	-	14	Ohio	(24)	24	-
Idaho	(4)	4	-	Oklahoma	(10)	10	-
Illinois	(29)	29	-	Oregon	(5)	5	-
Indiana	(15)	15	-	Pennsylvania	(38)	38	-
Iowa	(13)	13	-	Rhode Island	(5)	5	-
Kansas	(10)	10	-	South Carolina	(9)	-	9
Kentucky	(13)	-	13	South Dakota	(5)	5	-
Louisiana	(10)	-	10	Tennessee	(12)	12	-
Maine	(6)	6	-	Texas	(20)	-	20
Maryland	(8)	8	-	Utah	(4)	4	-
Massachusetts	(18)	18	-	Vermont	(4)	4	-
Michigan	(15)	15	-	Virginia	(12)	-	12
Minnesota	(12)	12	-	Washington	(7)	7	-
Mississippi	(10)	-	10	West Virginia	(8)	8	-
Missouri	(18)	18	-	Wisconsin	(13)	13	-
Montana	(4)	4	-	Wyoming	(3)	3	-
				Totals	**(531)**	**404**	**127**

1924

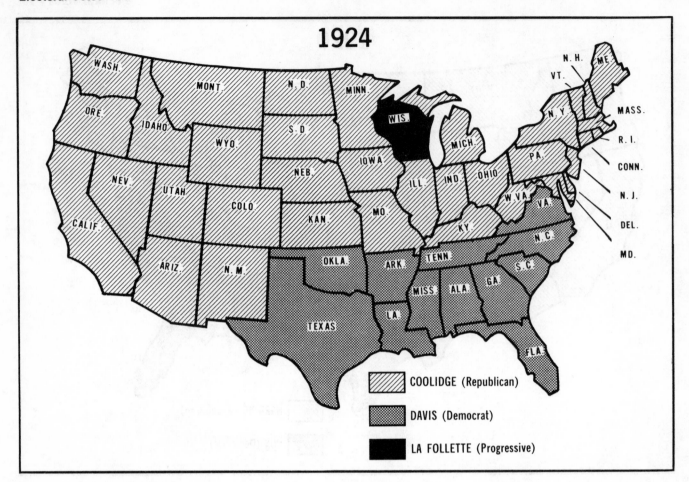

☐☐☐ COOLIDGE (Republican)

■■■ DAVIS (Democrat)

■■■ LA FOLLETTE (Progressive)

States	Electoral Votes	Coolidge	Davis	La Follette	States	Electoral Votes	Coolidge	Davis	La Follette
Alabama	(12)	-	12	-	Nebraska	(8)	8	-	-
Arizona	(3)	3	-	-	Nevada	(3)	3	-	-
Arkansas	(9)	-	9	-	New Hampshire	(4)	4	-	-
California	(13)	13	-	-	New Jersey	(14)	14	-	-
Colorado	(6)	6	-	-	New Mexico	(3)	3	-	-
Connecticut	(7)	7	-	-	New York	(45)	45	-	-
Delaware	(3)	3	-	-	North Carolina	(12)	-	12	-
Florida	(6)	-	6	-	North Dakota	(5)	5	-	-
Georgia	(14)	-	14	-	Ohio	(24)	24	-	-
Idaho	(4)	4	-	-	Oklahoma	(10)	-	10	-
Illinois	(29)	29	-	-	Oregon	(5)	5	-	-
Indiana	(15)	15	-	-	Pennsylvania	(38)	38	-	-
Iowa	(13)	13	-	-	Rhode Island	(5)	5	-	-
Kansas	(10)	10	-	-	South Carolina	(9)	-	9	-
Kentucky	(13)	13	-	-	South Dakota	(5)	5	-	-
Louisiana	(10)	-	10	-	Tennessee	(12)	-	12	-
Maine	(6)	6	-	-	Texas	(20)	-	20	-
Maryland	(8)	8	-	-	Utah	(4)	4	-	-
Massachusetts	(18)	18	-	-	Vermont	(4)	4	-	-
Michigan	(15)	15	-	-	Virginia	(12)	-	12	-
Minnesota	(12)	12	-	-	Washington	(7)	7	-	-
Mississippi	(10)	-	10	-	West Virginia	(8)	8	-	-
Missouri	(18)	18	-	-	Wisconsin	(13)	-	-	13
Montana	(4)	4	-	-	Wyoming	(3)	3	-	-
					Totals	**(531)**	**382**	**136**	**13**

1928

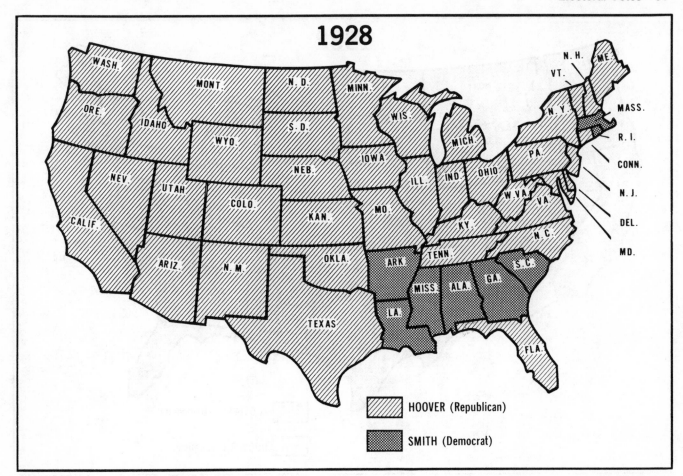

HOOVER (Republican)

SMITH (Democrat)

States	Electoral Votes	Hoover	Smith
Alabama	(12)	-	12
Arizona	(3)	3	-
Arkansas	(9)	-	9
California	(13)	13	-
Colorado	(6)	6	-
Connecticut	(7)	7	-
Delaware	(3)	3	-
Florida	(6)	6	-
Georgia	(14)	-	14
Idaho	(4)	4	-
Illinois	(29)	29	-
Indiana	(15)	15	-
Iowa	(13)	13	-
Kansas	(10)	10	-
Kentucky	(13)	13	-
Louisiana	(10)	-	10
Maine	(6)	6	-
Maryland	(8)	8	-
Massachusetts	(18)	-	18
Michigan	(15)	15	-
Minnesota	(12)	12	-
Mississippi	(10)	-	10
Missouri	(18)	18	-
Montana	(4)	4	-

States	Electoral Votes	Hoover	Smith
Nebraska	(8)	8	-
Nevada	(3)	3	-
New Hampshire	(4)	4	-
New Jersey	(14)	14	-
New Mexico	(3)	3	-
New York	(45)	45	-
North Carolina	(12)	12	-
North Dakota	(5)	5	-
Ohio	(24)	24	-
Oklahoma	(10)	10	-
Oregon	(5)	5	-
Pennsylvania	(38)	38	-
Rhode Island	(5)	-	5
South Carolina	(9)	-	9
South Dakota	(5)	5	-
Tennessee	(12)	12	-
Texas	(20)	20	-
Utah	(4)	4	-
Vermont	(4)	4	-
Virginia	(12)	12	-
Washington	(7)	7	-
West Virginia	(8)	8	-
Wisconsin	(13)	13	-
Wyoming	(3)	3	-
Totals	**(531)**	**444**	**87**

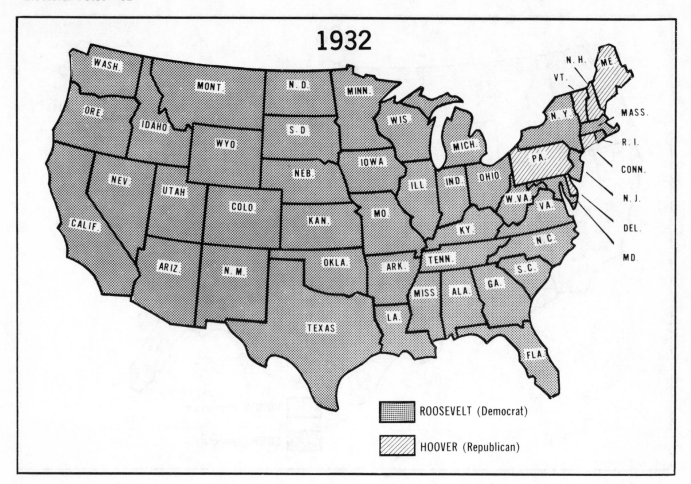

1932

ROOSEVELT (Democrat)

HOOVER (Republican)

States	Electoral Votes	Roosevelt	Hoover	States	Electoral Votes	Roosevelt	Hoover
Alabama	(11)	11	-	Nebraska	(7)	7	-
Arizona	(3)	3	-	Nevada	(3)	3	-
Arkansas	(9)	9	-	New Hampshire	(4)	-	4
California	(22)	22	-	New Jersey	(16)	16	-
Colorado	(6)	6	-	New Mexico	(3)	3	-
Connecticut	(8)	-	8	New York	(47)	47	-
Delaware	(3)	-	3	North Carolina	(13)	13	-
Florida	(7)	7	-	North Dakota	(4)	4	-
Georgia	(12)	12	-	Ohio	(26)	26	-
Idaho	(4)	4	-	Oklahoma	(11)	11	-
Illinois	(29)	29	-	Oregon	(5)	5	-
Indiana	(14)	14	-	Pennsylvania	(36)	-	36
Iowa	(11)	11	-	Rhode Island	(4)	4	-
Kansas	(9)	9	-	South Carolina	(8)	8	-
Kentucky	(11)	11	-	South Dakota	(4)	4	-
Louisiana	(10)	10	-	Tennessee	(11)	11	-
Maine	(5)	-	5	Texas	(23)	23	-
Maryland	(8)	8	-	Utah	(4)	4	-
Massachusetts	(17)	17	-	Vermont	(3)	-	3
Michigan	(19)	19	-	Virginia	(11)	11	-
Minnesota	(11)	11	-	Washington	(8)	8	-
Mississippi	(9)	9	-	West Virginia	(8)	8	-
Missouri	(15)	15	-	Wisconsin	(12)	12	-
Montana	(4)	4	-	Wyoming	(3)	3	-
				Totals	**(531)**	**472**	**59**

1936

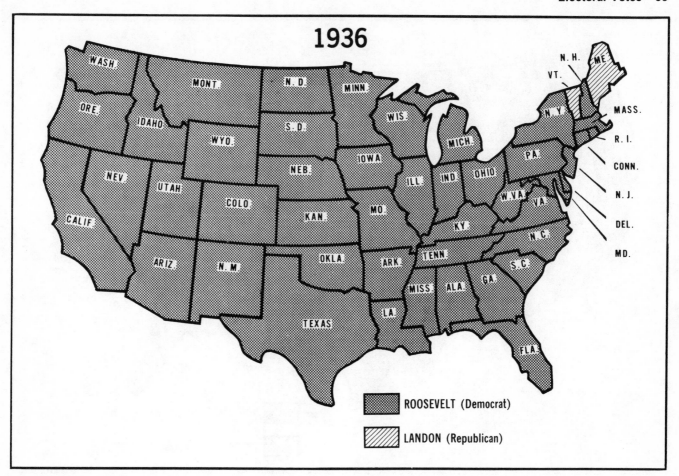

ROOSEVELT (Democrat)

LANDON (Republican)

States	Electoral Votes	Roosevelt	Landon	States	Electoral Votes	Roosevelt	Landon
Alabama	(11)	11	-	Nebraska	(7)	7	-
Arizona	(3)	3	-	Nevada	(3)	3	-
Arkansas	(9)	9	-	New Hampshire	(4)	4	-
California	(22)	22	-	New Jersey	(16)	16	-
Colorado	(6)	6	-	New Mexico	(3)	3	-
Connecticut	(8)	8	-	New York	(47)	47	-
Delaware	(3)	3	-	North Carolina	(13)	13	-
Florida	(7)	7	-	North Dakota	(4)	4	-
Georgia	(12)	12	-	Ohio	(26)	26	-
Idaho	(4)	4	-	Oklahoma	(11)	11	-
Illinois	(29)	29	-	Oregon	(5)	5	-
Indiana	(14)	14	-	Pennsylvania	(36)	36	-
Iowa	(11)	11	-	Rhode Island	(4)	4	-
Kansas	(9)	9	-	South Carolina	(8)	8	-
Kentucky	(11)	11	-	South Dakota	(4)	4	-
Louisiana	(10)	10	-	Tennessee	(11)	11	-
Maine	(5)	-	5	Texas	(23)	23	-
Maryland	(8)	8	-	Utah	(4)	4	-
Massachusetts	(17)	17	-	Vermont	(3)	-	3
Michigan	(19)	19	-	Virginia	(11)	11	-
Minnesota	(11)	11	-	Washington	(8)	8	-
Mississippi	(9)	9	-	West Virginia	(8)	8	-
Missouri	(15)	15	-	Wisconsin	(12)	12	-
Montana	(4)	4	-	Wyoming	(3)	3	-
				Totals	**(531)**	**523**	**8**

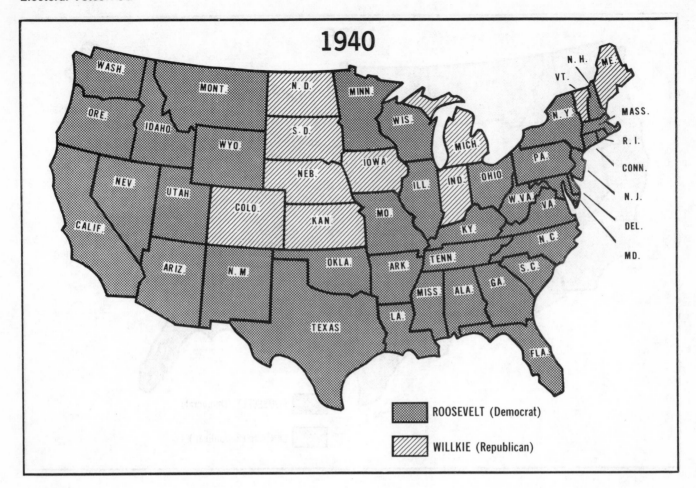

1940

ROOSEVELT (Democrat)

WILLKIE (Republican)

States	Electoral Votes	Roosevelt	Willkie	States	Electoral Votes	Roosevelt	Willkie
Alabama	(11)	11	-	Nebraska	(7)	-	7
Arizona	(3)	3	-	Nevada	(3)	3	-
Arkansas	(9)	9	-	New Hampshire	(4)	4	-
California	(22)	22	-	New Jersey	(16)	16	-
Colorado	(6)	-	6	New Mexico	(3)	3	-
Connecticut	(8)	8	-	New York	(47)	47	-
Delaware	(3)	3	-	North Carolina	(13)	13	-
Florida	(7)	7	-	North Dakota	(4)	-	4
Georgia	(12)	12	-	Ohio	(26)	26	-
Idaho	(4)	4	-	Oklahoma	(11)	11	-
Illinois	(29)	29	-	Oregon	(5)	5	-
Indiana	(14)	-	14	Pennsylvania	(36)	36	-
Iowa	(11)	-	11	Rhode Island	(4)	4	-
Kansas	(9)		9	South Carolina	(8)	8	-
Kentucky	(11)	11	-	South Dakota	(4)	-	4
Louisiana	(10)	10	-	Tennessee	(11)	11	-
Maine	(5)	-	5	Texas	(23)	23	-
Maryland	(8)	8	-	Utah	(4)	4	-
Massachusetts	(17)	17	-	Vermont	(3)	-	3
Michigan	(19)	-	19	Virginia	(11)	11	-
Minnesota	(11)	11	-	Washington	(8)	8	-
Mississippi	(9)	9	-	West Virginia	(8)	8	-
Missouri	(15)	15	-	Wisconsin	(12)	12	-
Montana	(4)	4	-	Wyoming	(3)	3	-
				Totals	**(531)**	**449**	**82**

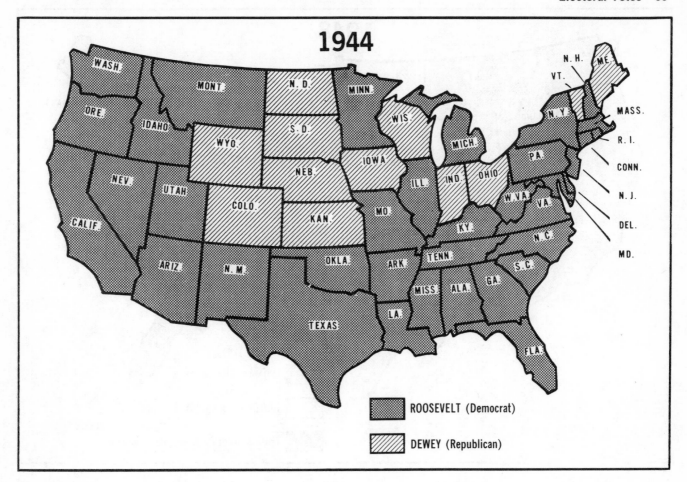

1944

ROOSEVELT (Democrat)

DEWEY (Republican)

States	Electoral Votes	Roosevelt	Dewey	States	Electoral Votes	Roosevelt	Dewey
Alabama	(11)	11	-	Nebraska	(6)	-	6
Arizona	(4)	4	-	Nevada	(3)	3	-
Arkansas	(9)	9	-	New Hampshire	(4)	4	-
California	(25)	25	-	New Jersey	(16)	16	-
Colorado	(6)	-	6	New Mexico	(4)	4	-
Connecticut	(8)	8	-	New York	(47)	47	-
Delaware	(3)	3	-	North Carolina	(14)	14	-
Florida	(8)	8	-	North Dakota	(4)	-	4
Georgia	(12)	12	-	Ohio	(25)	-	25
Idaho	(4)	4	-	Oklahoma	(10)	10	-
Illinois	(28)	28	-	Oregon	(6)	6	-
Indiana	(13)	-	13	Pennsylvania	(35)	35	-
Iowa	(10)	-	10	Rhode Island	(4)	4	-
Kansas	(8)	-	8	South Carolina	(8)	8	-
Kentucky	(11)	11	-	South Dakota	(4)	-	4
Louisiana	(10)	10	-	Tennessee	(12)	12	-
Maine	(5)	-	5	Texas	(23)	23	-
Maryland	(8)	8	-	Utah	(4)	4	-
Massachusetts	(16)	16	-	Vermont	(3)	-	3
Michigan	(19)	19	-	Virginia	(11)	11	-
Minnesota	(11)	11	-	Washington	(8)	8	-
Mississippi	(9)	9	-	West Virginia	(8)	8	-
Missouri	(15)	15	-	Wisconsin	(12)	-	12
Montana	(4)	4	-	Wyoming	(3)	-	3
				Totals	**(531)**	**432**	**99**

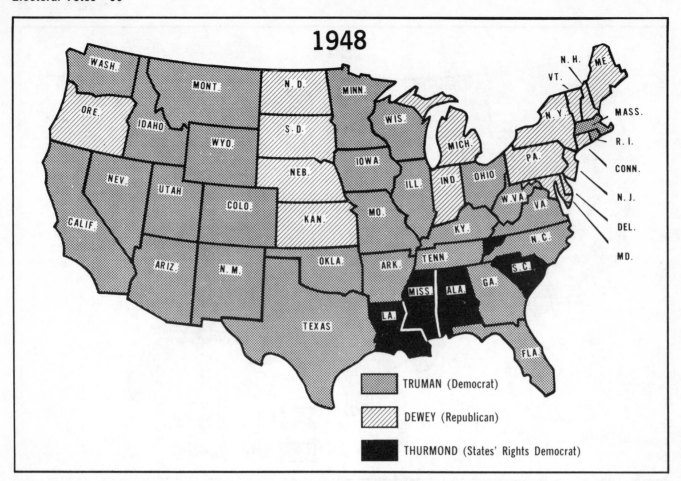

1948

TRUMAN (Democrat)

DEWEY (Republican)

THURMOND (States' Rights Democrat)

States	Electoral Votes	Truman	Dewey	Thurmond	States	Electoral Votes	Truman	Dewey	Thurmond
Alabama	(11)	-	-	11	Nebraska	(6)	-	6	-
Arizona	(4)	4	-	-	Nevada	(3)	3	-	-
Arkansas	(9)	9	-	-	New Hampshire	(4)	-	4	-
California	(25)	25	-	-	New Jersey	(16)	-	16	-
Colorado	(6)	6	-	-	New Mexico	(4)	4	-	-
Connecticut	(8)	-	8	-	New York	(47)	-	47	-
Delaware	(3)	-	3	-	North Carolina	(14)	14	-	-
Florida	(8)	8	-	-	North Dakota	(4)	-	4	-
Georgia	(12)	12	-	-	Ohio	(25)	25	-	-
Idaho	(4)	4	-	-	Oklahoma	(10)	10	-	-
Illinois	(28)	28	-	-	Oregon	(6)	-	6	-
Indiana	(13)	-	13	-	Pennsylvania	(35)	-	35	-
Iowa	(10)	10	-	-	Rhode Island	(4)	4	-	-
Kansas	(8)	-	8	-	South Carolina	(8)	-	-	8
Kentucky	(11)	11	-	-	South Dakota	(4)	-	4	-
Louisiana	(10)	-	-	10	Tennessee[1]	(12)	11	-	1
Maine	(5)	-	5	-	Texas	(23)	23	-	-
Maryland	(8)	-	8	-	Utah	(4)	4	-	-
Massachusetts	(16)	16	-	-	Vermont	(3)	-	3	-
Michigan	(19)	-	19	-	Virginia	(11)	11	-	-
Minnesota	(11)	11	-	-	Washington	(8)	8	-	-
Mississippi	(9)	-	-	9	West Virginia	(8)	8	-	-
Missouri	(15)	15	-	-	Wisconsin	(12)	12	-	-
Montana	(4)	4	-	-	Wyoming	(3)	3	-	-
					Totals	**(531)**	**303**	**189**	**39**

1. For explanation of split electoral votes, see p. 6.

1952

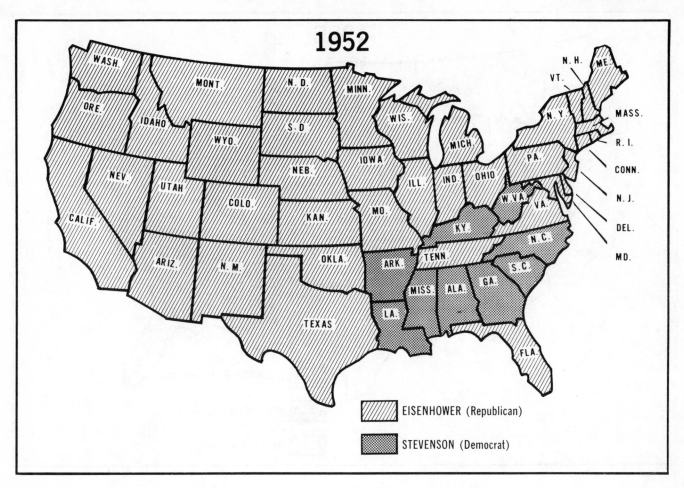

☒ EISENHOWER (Republican)

▨ STEVENSON (Democrat)

States	Electoral Votes	Eisenhower	Stevenson	States	Electoral Votes	Eisenhower	Stevenson
Alabama	(11)	-	11	Nebraska	(6)	6	-
Arizona	(4)	4	-	Nevada	(3)	3	-
Arkansas	(8)	-	8	New Hampshire	(4)	4	-
California	(32)	32	-	New Jersey	(16)	16	-
Colorado	(6)	6	-	New Mexico	(4)	4	-
Connecticut	(8)	8	-	New York	(45)	45	-
Delaware	(3)	3	-	North Carolina	(14)	-	14
Florida	(10)	10	-	North Dakota	(4)	4	-
Georgia	(12)	-	12	Ohio	(25)	25	-
Idaho	(4)	4	-	Oklahoma	(8)	8	-
Illinois	(27)	27	-	Oregon	(6)	6	-
Indiana	(13)	13	-	Pennsylvania	(32)	32	-
Iowa	(10)	10	-	Rhode Island	(4)	4	-
Kansas	(8)	8	-	South Carolina	(8)	-	8
Kentucky	(10)	-	10	South Dakota	(4)	4	-
Louisiana	(10)	-	10	Tennessee	(11)	11	-
Maine	(5)	5	-	Texas	(24)	24	-
Maryland	(9)	9	-	Utah	(4)	4	-
Massachusetts	(16)	16	-	Vermont	(3)	3	-
Michigan	(20)	20	-	Virginia	(12)	12	-
Minnesota	(11)	11	-	Washington	(9)	9	-
Mississippi	(8)	-	8	West Virginia	(8)	-	8
Missouri	(13)	13	-	Wisconsin	(12)	12	-
Montana	(4)	4	-	Wyoming	(3)	3	-
				Totals	**(531)**	**442**	**89**

1956

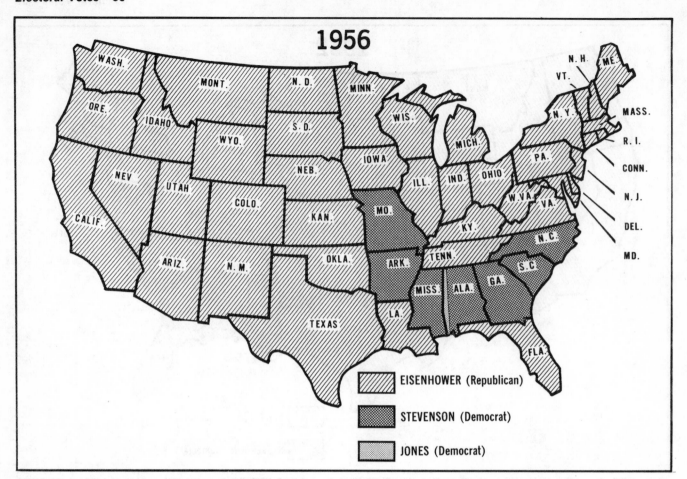

☐ EISENHOWER (Republican)

■ STEVENSON (Democrat)

▨ JONES (Democrat)

States	Electoral Votes	Eisenhower	Stevenson	Jones	States	Electoral Votes	Eisenhower	Stevenson	Jones
Alabama[1]	(11)	-	10	1	Nebraska	(6)	6	-	-
Arizona	(4)	4	-	-	Nevada	(3)	3	-	-
Arkansas	(8)	-	8	-	New Hampshire	(4)	4	-	-
California	(32)	32	-	-	New Jersey	(16)	16	-	-
Colorado	(6)	6	-	-	New Mexico	(4)	4	-	-
Connecticut	(8)	8	-	-	New York	(45)	45	-	-
Delaware	(3)	3	-	-	North Carolina	(14)	-	14	-
Florida	(10)	10	-	-	North Dakota	(4)	4	-	-
Georgia	(12)	-	12	-	Ohio	(25)	25	-	-
Idaho	(4)	4	-	-	Oklahoma	(8)	8	-	-
Illinois	(27)	27	-	-	Oregon	(6)	6	-	-
Indiana	(13)	13	-	-	Pennsylvania	(32)	32	-	-
Iowa	(10)	10	-	-	Rhode Island	(4)	4	-	-
Kansas	(8)	8	-	-	South Carolina	(8)	-	8	-
Kentucky	(10)	10	-	-	South Dakota	(4)	4	-	-
Louisiana	(10)	10	-	-	Tennessee	(11)	11	-	-
Maine	(5)	5	-	-	Texas	(24)	24	-	-
Maryland	(9)	9	-	-	Utah	(4)	4	-	-
Massachusetts	(16)	16	-	-	Vermont	(3)	3	-	-
Michigan	(20)	20	-	-	Virginia	(12)	12	-	-
Minnesota	(11)	11	-	-	Washington	(9)	9	-	-
Mississippi	(8)	-	8	-	West Virginia	(8)	8	-	-
Missouri	(13)	-	13	-	Wisconsin	(12)	12	-	-
Montana	(4)	4	-	-	Wyoming	(3)	3	-	-
					Totals	**(531)**	**457**	**73**	**1**

1. For explanation of split electoral votes, see p. 6.

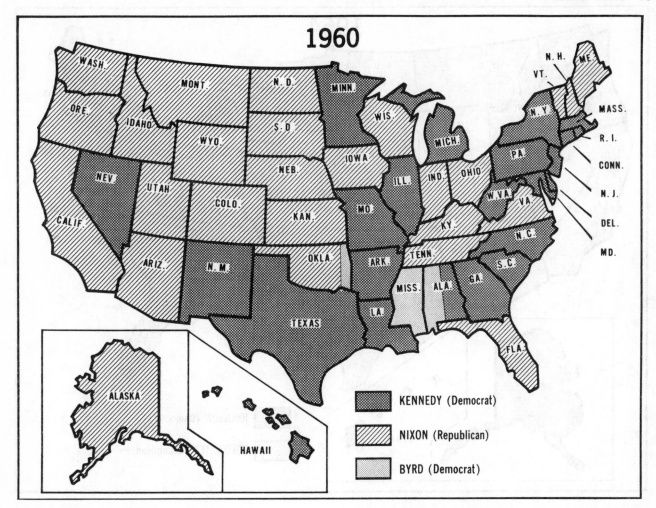

1960

KENNEDY (Democrat)

NIXON (Republican)

BYRD (Democrat)

States	Electoral Votes	Kennedy	Nixon	Byrd	States	Electoral Votes	Kennedy	Nixon	Byrd
Alabama[1]	(11)	5	-	6	Montana	(4)	-	4	-
Alaska	(3)	-	3	-	Nebraska	(6)	-	6	-
Arizona	(4)	-	4	-	Nevada	(3)	3	-	-
Arkansas	(8)	8	-	-	New Hampshire	(4)	-	4	-
California	(32)	-	32	-	New Jersey	(16)	16	-	-
Colorado	(6)	-	6	-	New Mexico	(4)	4	-	-
Connecticut	(8)	8	-	-	New York	(45)	45	-	-
Delaware	(3)	3	-	-	North Carolina	(14)	14	-	-
Florida	(10)	-	10	-	North Dakota	(4)	-	4	-
Georgia	(12)	12	-	-	Ohio	(25)	-	25	-
Hawaii	(3)	3	-	-	Oklahoma[1]	(8)	-	7	1
Idaho	(4)	-	4	-	Oregon	(6)	-	6	-
Illinois	(27)	27	-	-	Pennsylvania	(32)	32	-	-
Indiana	(13)	-	13	-	Rhode Island	(4)	4	-	-
Iowa	(10)	-	10	-	South Carolina	(8)	8	-	-
Kansas	(8)	-	8	-	South Dakota	(4)	-	4	-
Kentucky	(10)	-	10	-	Tennessee	(11)	-	11	-
Louisiana	(10)	10	-	-	Texas	(24)	24	-	-
Maine	(5)	-	5	-	Utah	(4)	-	4	-
Maryland	(9)	9	-	-	Vermont	(3)	-	3	-
Massachusetts	(16)	16	-	-	Virginia	(12)	-	12	-
Michigan	(20)	20	-	-	Washington	(9)	-	9	-
Minnesota	(11)	11	-	-	West Virginia	(8)	8	-	-
Mississippi	(8)	-	-	8	Wisconsin	(12)	-	12	-
Missouri	(13)	13	-	-	Wyoming	(3)	-	3	-
					Totals	**(537)**	**303**	**219**	**15**

1. For explanation of split electoral votes, see p. 6.

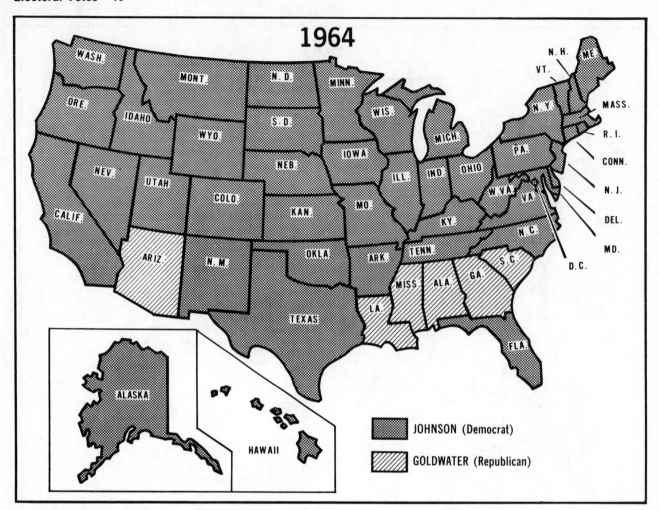

1964

JOHNSON (Democrat)

GOLDWATER (Republican)

States	Electoral Votes	Johnson	Goldwater	States	Electoral Votes	Johnson	Goldwater
Alabama	(10)	-	10	Montana	(4)	4	-
Alaska	(3)	3	-	Nebraska	(5)	5	-
Arizona	(5)	-	5	Nevada	(3)	3	-
Arkansas	(6)	6	-	New Hampshire	(4)	4	-
California	(40)	40	-	New Jersey	(17)	17	-
Colorado	(6)	6	-	New Mexico	(4)	4	-
Connecticut	(8)	8	-	New York	(43)	43	-
Delaware	(3)	3	-	North Carolina	(13)	13	-
District of Columbia	(3)	3	-	North Dakota	(4)	4	-
Florida	(14)	14	-	Ohio	(26)	26	-
Georgia	(12)	-	12	Oklahoma	(8)	8	-
Hawaii	(4)	4	-	Oregon	(6)	6	-
Idaho	(4)	4	-	Pennsylvania	(29)	29	-
Illinois	(26)	26	-	Rhode Island	(4)	4	-
Indiana	(13)	13	-	South Carolina	(8)	-	8
Iowa	(9)	9	-	South Dakota	(4)	4	-
Kansas	(7)	7	-	Tennessee	(11)	11	-
Kentucky	(9)	9	-	Texas	(25)	25	-
Louisiana	(10)	-	10	Utah	(4)	4	-
Maine	(4)	4	-	Vermont	(3)	3	-
Maryland	(10)	10	-	Virginia	(12)	12	-
Massachusetts	(14)	14	-	Washington	(9)	9	-
Michigan	(21)	21	-	West Virginia	(7)	7	-
Minnesota	(10)	10	-	Wisconsin	(12)	12	-
Mississippi	(7)	-	7	Wyoming	(3)	3	-
Missouri	(12)	12	-	**Totals**	**(538)**	**486**	**52**

1968

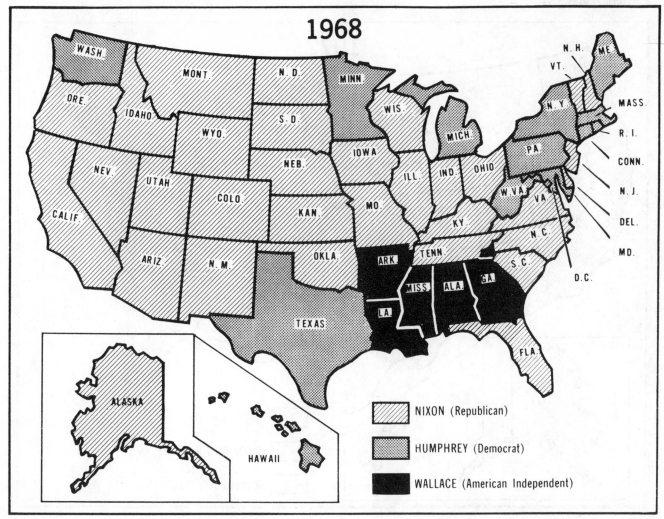

NIXON (Republican)

HUMPHREY (Democrat)

WALLACE (American Independent)

States	Electoral Votes	Nixon	Humphrey	Wallace	States	Electoral Votes	Nixon	Humphrey	Wallace
Alabama	(10)	-	-	10	Montana	(4)	4	-	-
Alaska	(3)	3	-	-	Nebraska	(5)	5	-	-
Arizona	(5)	5	-	-	Nevada	(3)	3	-	-
Arkansas	(6)	-	-	6	New Hampshire	(4)	4	-	-
California	(40)	40	-	-	New Jersey	(17)	17	-	-
Colorado	(6)	6	-	-	New Mexico	(4)	4	-	-
Connecticut	(8)	-	8	-	New York	(43)	-	43	-
Delaware	(3)	3	-	-	North Carolina[1]	(13)	12	-	1
District of Columbia	(3)	-	3	-	North Dakota	(4)	4	-	-
Florida	(14)	14	-	-	Ohio	(26)	26	-	-
Georgia	(12)	-	-	12	Oklahoma	(8)	8	-	-
Hawaii	(4)	-	4	-	Oregon	(6)	6	-	-
Idaho	(4)	4	-	-	Pennsylvania	(29)	-	29	-
Illinois	(26)	26	-	-	Rhode Island	(4)	-	4	-
Indiana	(13)	13	-	-	South Carolina	(8)	8	-	-
Iowa	(9)	9	-	-	South Dakota	(4)	4	-	-
Kansas	(7)	7	-	-	Tennessee	(11)	11	-	-
Kentucky	(9)	9	-	-	Texas	(25)	-	25	-
Louisiana	(10)	-	-	10	Utah	(4)	4	-	-
Maine	(4)	-	4	-	Vermont	(3)	3	-	-
Maryland	(10)	-	10	-	Virginia	(12)	12	-	-
Massachusetts	(14)	-	14	-	Washington	(9)	-	9	-
Michigan	(21)	-	21	-	West Virginia	(7)	-	7	-
Minnesota	(10)	-	10	-	Wisconsin	(12)	12	-	-
Mississippi	(7)	-	-	7	Wyoming	(3)	3	-	-
Missouri	(12)	12	-	-	**Totals**	**(538)**	**301**	**191**	**46**

1. For explanation of split electoral votes, see p. 6.

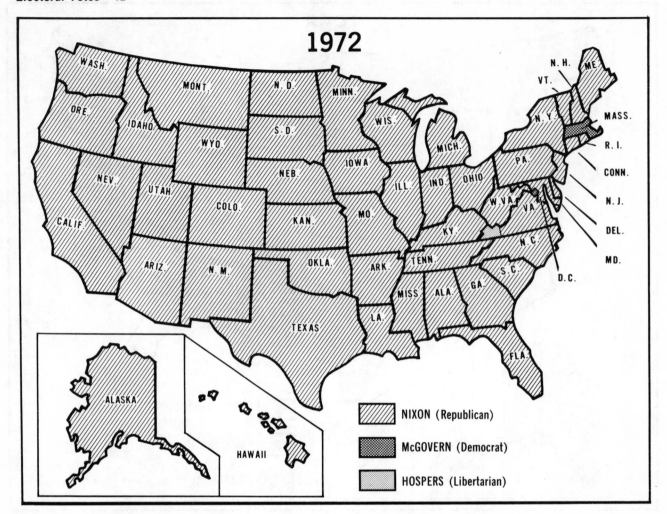

1972

NIXON (Republican)

McGOVERN (Democrat)

HOSPERS (Libertarian)

States	Electoral Votes	Nixon	McGovern	Hospers
Alabama	(9)	9	-	-
Alaska	(3)	3	-	-
Arizona	(6)	6	-	-
Arkansas	(6)	6	-	-
California	(45)	45	-	-
Colorado	(7)	7	-	-
Connecticut	(8)	8	-	-
Delaware	(3)	3	-	-
District of Columbia	(3)	-	3	-
Florida	(17)	17	-	-
Georgia	(12)	12	-	-
Hawaii	(4)	4	-	-
Idaho	(4)	4	-	-
Illinois	(26)	26	-	-
Indiana	(13)	13	-	-
Iowa	(8)	8	-	-
Kansas	(7)	7	-	-
Kentucky	(9)	9	-	-
Louisiana	(10)	10	-	-
Maine	(4)	4	-	-
Maryland	(10)	10	-	-
Massachusetts	(14)	-	14	-
Michigan	(21)	21	-	-
Minnesota	(10)	10	-	-
Mississippi	(7)	7	-	-
Missouri	(12)	12	-	-
Montana	(4)	4	-	-
Nebraska	(5)	5	-	-
Nevada	(3)	3	-	-
New Hampshire	(4)	4	-	-
New Jersey	(17)	17	-	-
New Mexico	(4)	4	-	-
New York	(4)	41	-	-
North Carolina	(13)	13	-	-
North Dakota	(3)	3	-	-
Ohio	(25)	25	-	-
Oklahoma	(8)	8	-	-
Oregon	(6)	6	-	-
Pennsylvania	(27)	27	-	-
Rhode Island	(4)	4	-	-
South Carolina	(8)	8	-	-
South Dakota	(4)	4	-	-
Tennessee	(10)	10	-	-
Texas	(26)	26	-	-
Utah	(4)	4	-	-
Vermont	(3)	3	-	-
Virginia[1]	(12)	11	-	1
Washington	(9)	9	-	-
West Virginia	(6)	6	-	-
Wisconsin	(11)	11	-	-
Wyoming	(3)	3	-	-
Totals	**(538)**	**520**	**17**	**1**

1. For explanation of split electoral votes, see p. 6.

1976

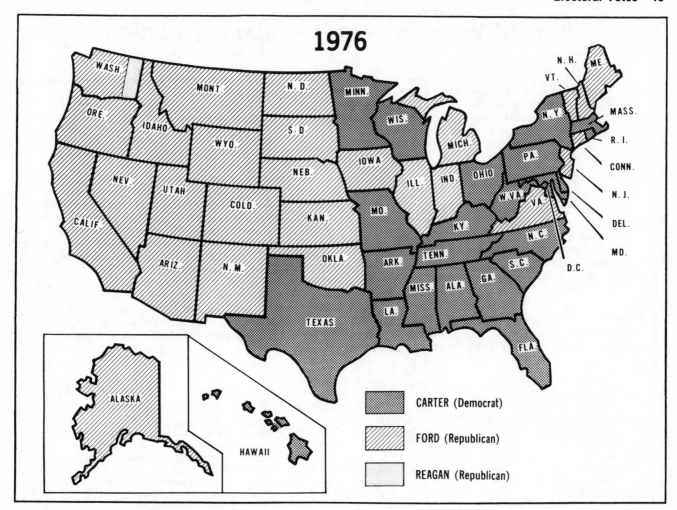

CARTER (Democrat)

FORD (Republican)

REAGAN (Republican)

States	Electoral Votes	Carter	Ford	Reagan
Alabama	(9)	9	-	-
Alaska	(3)	-	3	-
Arizona	(6)	-	6	-
Arkansas	(6)	6	-	-
California	(45)	-	45	-
Colorado	(7)	-	7	-
Connecticut	(8)	-	8	-
Delaware	(3)	3	-	-
District of Columbia	(3)	3	-	-
Florida	(17)	17	-	-
Georgia	(12)	12	-	-
Hawaii	(4)	4	-	-
Idaho	(4)	-	4	-
Illinois	(26)	-	26	-
Indiana	(13)	-	13	-
Iowa	(8)	-	8	-
Kansas	(7)	-	7	-
Kentucky	(9)	9	-	-
Louisiana	(10)	10	-	-
Maine	(4)	-	4	-
Maryland	(10)	10	-	-
Massachusetts	(14)	14	-	-
Michigan	(21)	-	21	-
Minnesota	(10)	10	-	-
Mississippi	(7)	7	-	-
Missouri	(12)	12	-	-

States	Electoral Votes	Carter	Ford	Reagan
Montana	(4)	-	4	
Nebraska	(5)	-	5	-
Nevada	(3)	-	3	-
New Hampshire	(4)	-	4	-
New Jersey	(17)	-	17	-
New Mexico	(4)	-	4	-
New York	(41)	41	-	-
North Carolina	(13)	13	-	-
North Dakota	(3)	-	3	-
Ohio	(25)	25	-	-
Oklahoma	(8)	-	8	-
Oregon	(6)	-	6	-
Pennsylvania	(27)	27	-	-
Rhode Island	(4)	4	-	-
South Carolina	(8)	8	-	-
South Dakota	(4)	-	4	-
Tennessee	(10)	10	-	-
Texas	(26)	26	-	-
Utah	(4)	-	4	-
Vermont	(3)	-	3	-
Virginia	(12)	-	12	-
Washington[1]	(9)	-	8	1
West Virginia	(6)	6	-	-
Wisconsin	(11)	11	-	-
Wyoming	(3)	-	3	-
Totals	**(538)**	**297**	**240**	**1**

1. For explanation of split electoral votes, see p. 6.

Electoral Votes for Vice President, 1804-1976

The following list gives the electoral votes for vice president from 1804 to 1976. Unless indicated by a *footnote,* the state-by-state breakdown of electoral votes for each vice presidential candidate was the same as for his party's presidential candidate. These state-by-state votes are given in the section on presidential electoral votes *(pp. 19-61).*

Electoral Votes 1789-1800

Prior to 1804, under Article II, Section 1 of the Constitution, each elector cast two votes — each vote for a different person. The electors did not distinguish between votes for president and vice president. The candidate receiving the second highest total became vice president. The 12th Amendment, ratified in 1804, required electors to vote separately for president and vice president. *(Electoral votes for 1789, 1792, 1796 and 1800, pp. 19-22)*

Candidates

In some cases persons have received electoral votes although they had never been formally nominated. The word *candidate* is used in this section to designate persons receiving electoral votes.

Sources: Votes and Parties

The *Senate Manual* (U.S. Government Printing Office, 1977) was the source used for vice presidential electoral votes.

For political party designation, the basic source was *A Statistical History of the American Presidential Elections* (Frederick Ungar, New York, 1968) by Svend Petersen; Petersen gives the party designation of *presidential candidates only.* Congressional Quarterly adopted Petersen's party designations for the running mates of presidential candidates. To supplement Petersen, Congressional Quarterly consulted the *Biographical Directory of the American Congress, 1774-1971,* U.S. Government Printing Office, 1971; the *Dictionary of American Biography,* Charles Scribner's, New York, 1928-1936; the *Encyclopedia of American Biography,* Harper and Row, New York, 1974 and *Who Was Who in America, 1607-1968,* Marquis Co., Chicago, 1943-1968.

Year	Candidate	Electoral Votes
1804	George Clinton (Democratic-Republican)	162
	Rufus King (Federalist)	14
1808	George Clinton (Democratic-Republican)[1]	113
	John Langdon (Democratic-Republican)	9
	James Madison (Democratic-Republican)	3
	James Monroe (Democratic-Republican)	3
	Rufus King (Federalist)	47
1812	Elbridge Gerry (Democratic-Republican)[2]	131
	Jared Ingersoll (Federalist)	86
1816	Daniel D. Tompkins (Democratic-Republican)	183
	John E. Howard (Federalist)[3]	22
	James Ross (Federalist)	5
	John Marshall (Federalist)	4
	Robert G. Harper (Federalist)	3
1820	Daniel D. Tompkins (Democratic-Republican)[4]	218
	Richard Rush (Democratic-Republican)	1
	Richard Stockton (Federalist)	8
	Daniel Rodney (Federalist)	4
	Robert G. Harper (Federalist)	1
1824	John C. Calhoun (Democratic-Republican)[5]	182
	Nathan Sanford (Democratic-Republican)	30
	Nathaniel Macon (Democratic-Republican)	24
	Andrew Jackson (Democratic-Republican)	13
	Martin Van Buren (Democratic-Republican)	9
	Henry Clay (Democratic-Republican)	2
1828	John C. Calhoun (Democratic-Republican)[6]	171

Year	Candidate	Electoral Votes
	William Smith (Independent Democratic-Republican)	7
	Richard Rush (National Republican)	83
1832	Martin Van Buren (Democratic)[7]	189
	William Wilkins (Democratic)	30
	Henry Lee (Independent Democratic)	11
	John Sergeant (National Republican)	49
	Amos Ellmaker (Anti-Masonic)	7
1836	Richard M. Johnson (Democratic)[8]	147
	William Smith (Independent Democratic)	23
	Francis Granger (Whig)	77
	John Tyler (Whig)	47
1840	John Tyler (Whig)	234
	Richard M. Johnson (Democratic)[9]	48
	L. W. Tazewell (Democratic)	11
	James K. Polk (Democratic)	1
1844	George M. Dallas (Democratic)	170
	Theodore Frelinghuysen (Whig)	105
1848	Millard Fillmore (Whig)	163
	William O. Butler (Democratic)	127
1852	William R. King (Democratic)	254
	William A. Graham (Whig)	42
1856	John C. Breckinridge (Democratic)	174
	William L. Dayton (Republican)	114
	Andrew J. Donelson (American)	8
1860	Hannibal Hamlin (Republican)	180
	Joseph Lane (Southern Democratic)	72
	Edward Everett (Constitutional Union)	39
	Herschel V. Johnson (Democratic)	12
1864	Andrew Johnson (Republican)	212
	George H. Pendleton (Democratic)	21
1868	Schuyler Colfax (Republican)	214
	Francis P. Blair (Democratic)	80
1872	Henry Wilson (Republican)	286
	Benjamin G. Brown (Democratic)[10]	47
	Alfred H. Colquitt (Democratic)	5
	John M. Palmer (Democratic)	3
	Thomas E. Bramlette (Democratic)	3
	William S. Groesbeck (Democratic)	1
	Willis B. Machen (Democratic)	1

	George W. Julian (Liberal Republican)	5
	Nathaniel P. Banks (Liberal Republican)	1
1876	William A. Wheeler (Republican)	185
	Thomas A. Hendricks (Democratic)	184
1880	Chester A. Arthur (Republican)	214
	William H. English (Democratic)	155
1884	Thomas A. Hendricks (Democratic)	219
	John A. Logan (Republican)	182
1888	Levi P. Morton (Republican)	233
	Allen G. Thurman (Democratic)	168
1892	Adlai E. Stevenson (Democratic)	277
	Whitelaw Reid (Republican)	145
	James G. Field (Populist)	22
1896	Garret A. Hobart (Republican)	271
	Arthur Sewall (Democratic)[11]	149
	Thomas E. Watson (Populist)	27
1900	Theodore Roosevelt (Republican)	292
	Adlai E. Stevenson (Democratic)	155
1904	Charles W. Fairbanks (Republican)	336
	Henry G. Davis (Democratic)	140
1908	James S. Sherman (Republican)	321
	John W. Kern (Democratic)	162
1912	Thomas R. Marshall (Democratic)	435
	Hiram W. Johnson (Progressive)	88
	Nicholas M. Butler (Republican)	8
1916	Thomas R. Marshall (Democratic)	277
	Charles W. Fairbanks (Republican)	254
1920	Calvin Coolidge (Republican)	404
	Franklin D. Roosevelt (Democratic)	127
1924	Charles G. Dawes (Republican)	382
	Charles W. Bryan (Democratic)	136
	Burton K. Wheeler (Progressive)	13

1928	Charles Curtis (Republican)	444
	Joseph T. Robinson (Democratic)	87
1932	John N. Garner (Democratic)	472
	Charles Curtis (Republican)	59
1936	John N. Garner (Democratic)	523
	Frank Knox (Republican)	8
1940	Henry A. Wallace (Democratic)	449
	Charles L. McNary (Republican)	82
1944	Harry S Truman (Democratic)	432
	John W. Bricker (Republican)	99
1948	Alben W. Barkley (Democratic)	303
	Earl Warren (Republican)	189
	Fielding L. Wright (States' Rights Democratic)	39
1952	Richard M. Nixon (Republican)	442
	John J. Sparkman (Democratic)	89
1956	Richard M. Nixon (Republican)	457
	Estes Kefauver (Democratic)	73
	Herman Talmadge (Democratic)	1
1960	Lyndon B. Johnson (Democratic)	303
	J. Strom Thurmond (Democratic)[12]	14
	Henry Cabot Lodge (Republican)	219
	Barry Goldwater (Republican)	1
1964	Hubert H. Humphrey (Democratic)	486
	William E. Miller (Republican)	52
1968	Spiro T. Agnew (Republican)	301
	Edmund S. Muskie (Democratic)	191
	Curtis E. LeMay (American Independent)	46
1972	Spiro T. Agnew (Republican)	520
	R. Sargent Shriver (Democratic)	17
	Theodora Nathan (Libertarian)	1
1976	Walter F. Mondale (Democratic)	297
	Robert J. Dole (Republican)[13]	241

Footnotes

1. New York cast 13 presidential electoral votes for Democratic-Republican James Madison and 6 votes for Clinton; for vice president, New York cast 13 votes for Clinton, 3 votes for Madison and 3 votes for Monroe.

Langdon received Ohio's three votes and Vermont's 6 votes.

2. The state-by-state vote for Gerry was the same as for Democratic-Republican presidential candidate Madison except for Massachusetts and New Hampshire. Massachusetts cast 2 votes for Gerry and 20 votes for Ingersoll; New Hampshire cast 1 vote for Gerry and 7 votes for Ingersoll.

3. Four Federalists received vice presidential electoral votes: Howard—Massachusetts, 22 votes; Ross—Connecticut, 5 votes; Marshall—Connecticut, 4 votes; Harper—Delaware, 3 votes.

4. The state-by-state vote for Tompkins was the same as for Democratic-Republican presidential candidate James Monroe except for Delaware, Maryland and Massachusetts. Delaware cast 4 votes for Rodney; Maryland cast 10 votes for Tompkins and one for Harper; Massachusetts cast 7 votes for Tompkins and 8 for Stockton.

New Hamsphire, which cast 7 presidential electoral votes for Monroe and 1 vote for John Quincy Adams, cast 7 vice presidential electoral votes for Tompkins and 1 vote for Rush.

5. The state-by-state vice presidential electoral vote was as follows:

Calhoun—Alabama, 5 votes; Delaware, 1 vote; Illinois, 3 votes; Indiana, 5 votes; Kentucky, 7 votes; Louisiana, 5 votes; Maine, 9 votes; Maryland, 10 votes; Massachusetts, 15 votes; Mississippi, 3 votes; New Hampshire, 7 votes; New Jersey, 8 votes; New York, 29 votes; North Carolina, 15 votes; Pennsylvania, 28 votes; Rhode Island, 3 votes; South Carolina, 11 votes; Tennessee, 11 votes; Vermont, 7 votes.

Sanford—Kentucky, 7 votes; New York, 7 votes; Ohio, 16 votes.

Macon—Virginia, 24 votes.

Jackson—Connecticut, 8 votes; Maryland, 1 vote; Missouri, 3 votes; New Hamphire, 1 vote.

Van Buren—Georgia, 9 votes.

Clay—Delaware, 2 votes.

6. The state-by-state vote for Calhoun was the same as for Democratic-Republican presidential candidate Jackson except for Georgia, which cast 2 votes for Calhoun and 7 votes for Smith.

7. The state-by-state vote for Van Buren was the same as for Democratic presidential candidate Jackson except for Pennsylvania which cast 30 votes for Wilkins.

South Carolina cast 11 presidential electoral votes for Independent Democratic presidential candidate Floyd and 11 votes for Independent Democratic vice presidential candidate Lee.

Vermont cast 7 presidential electoral votes for Anti-Masonic candidate Wirt and 7 vice presidential electoral votes for Wirt's running mate, Ellmaker.

8. The state-by-state vote for Johnson was the same as for Democratic presidential candidate Van Buren except for Virginia which cast 23 votes for Smith.

Granger's state-by-state vote was the same as for Whig presidential candidate Harrison except for Maryland and Massachusetts. Maryland cast 10 presidential electoral votes for Harrison and 10 vice presidential votes for Tyler; Massachusetts cast 14 presidential electoral votes for Whig candidate Webster and 14 vice presidential votes for Granger.

Tyler received 11 votes from Georgia, 10 from Maryland, 11 from South Carolina and 15 from Tennessee.

No vice presidential candidate received a majority of the electoral vote. As a result, the Senate, for the only time in history, selected the vice president under the provisions of the 12th Amendment. Johnson was elected vice president by a vote of 33 to 16 for Granger.

9. The Democratic Party did not nominate a vice presidential candidate in 1840. Johnson's state-by-state vote was the same as for presidential candidate Van Buren except for South Carolina and Virginia.

South Carolina cast 11 votes for Tazewell.

Virginia cast 23 presidential electoral votes for Van Buren, 22 vice presidential votes for Johnson and 1 vice presidential vote for Polk.

10. Liberal Republican and Democratic presidential candidate Horace Greeley died Nov. 29, 1872. As a result, 18 electors pledged to Greeley cast their presidential electoral votes for Brown, Greeley's running mate.

The vice presidential electoral vote was as follows:

Brown—Georgia, 5 votes; Kentucky, 8 votes; Maryland, 8 votes; Missouri, 6 votes; Tennessee, 12 votes, Texas, 8 votes.

Colquitt—Georgia, 5 votes.

Palmer—Missouri, 3 votes.

Bramlette—Kentucky, 3 votes.

Groesbeck—Missouri, 1 vote.

Machen—Kentucky, 1 vote.

Julian—Missouri, 5 votes.

Banks—Georgia, 1 vote.

11. The state-by-state vote for Sewell was the same as for Democratic-Populist candidate William Jennings Bryan except for the following states which cast electoral votes for Thomas E. Watson: Arkansas—3 votes; Louisiana—4 votes; Missouri—4 votes; Montana—1 vote; Nebraska—4 votes; North Carolina—5 votes; South Dakota—2 votes; Utah—1 vote; Washington—2 votes; Wyoming—1 vote.

12. Democratic electors carried Alabama's 11 electoral votes. Five of the electors were pledged to the national Democratic ticket of John F. Kennedy and Lyndon B. Johnson. Six electors ran unpledged and voted for Harry F. Byrd for president and Thurmond for vice president.

Mississippi's 8 electors voted for Byrd and Thurmond.

In Oklahoma, the Republican ticket of Richard M. Nixon and Henry Cabot Lodge carried the state, but one of the state's 8 electors voted for Byrd for president and Goldwater for vice president.

13. One Republican elector from the state of Washington cast his presidential electoral vote for Ronald Reagan instead of the Republican nominee, Gerald R. Ford. But he voted for Robert J. Dole, Ford's running mate, for vice president. Thus Dole received one more electoral vote than Ford.

Popular Votes for President

CQ

Sources for Popular Returns

The popular election returns presented in this section (pages 67-111) were obtained, except for 1976 or where indicated by a footnote, from the Historical Archive of the Inter-University Consortium for Political Research (ICPR) at the University of Michigan. The 1976 returns and party designations were taken from Richard M. Scammon's *America Votes 12* (Washington: Congressional Quarterly, 1977). The returns cover the period from 1824 through the 1976 presidential election. The starting date for the ICPR collection was based on consideration of such factors as the pronounced trend by 1824 for the election of presidential electors by popular vote, as well as the availability, accessibility and quality of the returns. The bulk of the ICPR election data collection consists of returns at the county level in computer readable form.

The collection of ICPR presidential returns — part of a larger project involving gubernatorial, House and Senate returns — began in 1962 under grants from the Social Science Research Council and the National Science Foundation. Scholars searched state and local archives, newspaper files and other sources for the data. In as many cases as possible, multiple sources were consulted. Although general preference was given to official sources, these scholars were charged with evaluating all available sources in terms of their quality and completeness.

While the complete source annotations for the collection are too extensive to publish here, information on the sources for returns from specific elections can be obtained through the ICPR.

For each presidential election from 1824 to 1976, the following information is provided in the tables (pages 67-102) for the popular returns:

● The total nationwide popular vote and the plurality of the candidate who received the greatest number of votes.

● Names and party affiliations of major candidates.

● State-by-state breakdown of the popular vote and the percentage of the vote received by each candidate.

● The plurality received by the candidate who carried each state.

● The total national popular vote and percentage of the vote received by each candidate.

● The aggregate vote and percentage of the total vote received in each state by minor party candidates, minor parties running unpledged electors or unidentified votes. These figures appear in the column designated "Other." A complete breakdown of the votes included in the "Other" column appears on pages 103-111. An index of all candidates is on page 185.

Party Designation

In the ICPR data, the distinct — and in many cases, *multiple* — party designations appearing in the original sources are preserved. Thus, in the ICPR returns for 1968, George C. Wallace ran for President under a variety of party designations in different states — "Democratic," "American," "American Independent," "Independent," "George Wallace Party," "Conservative," "American Party of Missouri," "Independent American," "Courage" and "George Wallace and Independent."

In order to provide a single party designation for presidential candidates, Congressional Quarterly has aggregated under a *single party designation* the votes of candidates who are listed in the ICPR data as receiving votes under more than one party designation. Two sources were used for assigning party designation. For the elections 1824 through 1964, the source for party designation is Svend Petersen's *A Statistical History of the American Presidential Elections* (Frederick Ungar, New York, 1968).

For the 1968, 1972 and 1976 elections, the source for party designation is Scammon's *America Votes 8* (Washington: Congressional Quarterly, 1970), *America Votes 10* (1973) and *America Votes 12* (1977). For 1968, Scammon lists Wallace as an "American Independent," and Congressional Quarterly follows this usage.

Vote Totals and Percentages

The total popular vote for each candidate in a given election was determined by adding the votes received by that candidate in each state (including write-in votes where available), even though the vote totals for some states may have come from sources other than ICPR.

The percentage of the vote received in each state by any candidate or party has been calculated to two decimal places and rounded to one place; thus, 0.05 percent is listed as 0.1 percent. The percentage of the nationwide vote was calculated to three decimal places and rounded to two; thus, 0.005 percent is listed as 0.01 percent. Due to rounding, state percentages and national percentages do not always equal 100 percent.

Pluralities

The plurality column represents the difference between the vote received by the first and second place finishers in each state. In a few cases, votes included in the "Other" column were needed to calculate the plurality. In these cases, a footnote provides an explanation. *(See, for example, Georgia in the 1916 election, p. 87)*

1824 Presidential Election

Total Popular Votes: 365,833
Jackson's Plurality: 38,149

STATE	JOHN Q. ADAMS (Democratic-Republican) Votes	%	ANDREW JACKSON (Democratic-Republican) Votes	%	HENRY CLAY (Democratic-Republican) Votes	%	WILLIAM H. CRAWFORD (Democratic-Republican) Votes	%	OTHER[1] Votes	%	PLURALITY
Alabama	2,422	17.8	9,429	69.3	96	.2	1,656	12.2			7,007
Connecticut	7,494	70.4					1,965	18.5	1,188	11.2	5,529
Illinois	1,516	32.5	1,272	27.2	1,036	22.2	847	18.1			244
Indiana	3,071	19.4	7,444	47.0	5,316	33.6			7		2,128
Kentucky			6,356	27.2	16,982	72.8					10,626
Maine[2]	10,289	81.5					2,336	18.5			7,953
Maryland[2]	14,632	44.1	14,523	43.7	695	2.1	3,364	10.1			109
Massachusetts	30,687	73.0							11,369	27.0	24,071[3]
Mississippi	1,654	33.8	3,121	63.8			119	2.4			1,467
Missouri	159	4.6	1,166	34.0	2,042	59.5	32	.9	33	1.0	876
New Hampshire[2]	9,389	93.6					643	6.4			8,746
New Jersey	8,309	41.9	10,332	52.1			1,196	6.0			2,023
North Carolina			20,231	56.0			15,622	43.3	256	.7	4,609
Ohio[2]	12,280	24.5	18,489	37.0	19,255	38.5					766
Pennsylvania	5,441	11.6	35,736	75.9	1,690	3.6	4,206	8.9			30,295
Rhode Island	2,144	91.5							200	8.5	1,944
Tennessee[2]	216	1.0	20,197	97.5			312	1.5			19,885
Virginia	3,419	22.2	2,975	19.4	419	2.7	8,558	55.7			5,139
Totals	**113,122**	**30.92**	**151,271**	**41.34**	**47,531**	**12.99**	**40,856**	**11.17**	**13,053**	**3.57**	

1828 Presidential Election

Total Popular Votes: 1,148,018
Jackson's Plurality: 141,656

STATE	ANDREW JACKSON (Democratic-Republican) Votes	%	JOHN Q. ADAMS (National-Republican) Votes	%	OTHER[1] Votes	%	PLURALITY
Alabama	16,736	89.9	1,878	10.1	4		14,858
Connecticut	4,448	23.0	13,829	71.4	1,101	5.7	9,381
Georgia[2]	19,362	96.8	642	3.2			18,720
Illinois	9,560	67.2	4,662	32.8			4,898
Indiana	22,201	56.6	17,009	43.4			5,192
Kentucky	39,308	55.5	31,468	44.5			7,840
Louisiana	4,605	53.0	4,082	47.0			523
Maine	13,927	40.0	20,773	59.7	89	.3	6,846
Maryland	22,782	49.8	23,014	50.3			232
Massachusetts	6,012	15.4	29,836	76.4	3,226	8.3	23,824
Mississippi	6,763	81.1	1,581	19.0			5,182
Missouri	8,232	70.6	3,422	29.4			4,810
New Hampshire	20,212	45.9	23,823	54.1			3,611
New Jersey	21,809	47.9	23,753	52.1	8		1,944
New York	139,412	51.5	131,563	48.6			7,849
North Carolina	37,814	73.1	13,918	26.9	15		23,896
Ohio	67,596	51.6	63,453	48.4			4,143
Pennsylvania	101,457	66.7	50,763	33.4			50,694
Rhode Island	820	22.9	2,755	77.0	5	.1	1,935
Tennessee[4]	44,293	95.2	2,240	4.8			42,053
Vermont	8,350	25.4	24,363	74.2	120	.4	16,013
Virginia	26,854	69.0	12,070	31.0			14,784
Totals	**642,553**	**55.97**	**500,897**	**43.63**	**4,568**	**.40**	

1. For breakdown of "Other" vote, see minor candidate vote totals, p. 103.
2. Figures from Svend Petersen, A Statistical History of the American Presidential Elections, (New York, 1968), p. 18.

3. Plurality of 24,071 votes is calculated on the basis of 6,616 for unpledged electors.
4. Figures from Petersen, op cit., p. 20.

1832 Presidential Election

Total Popular Votes: 1,293,973
Jackson's Plurality: 217,575

STATE	ANDREW JACKSON (Democrat)		HENRY CLAY (National-Republican)		WILLIAM WIRT (Anti-Masonic)		OTHER[1]		PLURALITY
	Votes	%	Votes	%	Votes	%	Votes	%	
Alabama	14,286	99.9	5	.1					14,281
Connecticut	11,269	34.3	18,155	55.3	3,409	10.4			6,886
Delaware	4,110	49.0	4,276	51.0					166
Georgia [2]	20,750	100.0							20,750
Illinois	14,609	68.0	6,745	31.4	97	.5	30	.1	7,864
Indiana	31,652	55.4	25,473	44.6	27	.1			6,179
Kentucky	36,292	45.5	43,449	54.5					7,157
Louisiana	3,908	61.7	2,429	38.3					1,479
Maine	33,978	54.7	27,331	44.0	844	1.4			6,647
Maryland	19,156	50.0	19,160	50.0					4
Massachusetts	13,933	20.6	31,963	47.3	14,692	21.7	7,031	10.4	17,271
Mississippi	5,750	100.0							5,750
Missouri [2]	5,192	100.0							5,192
New Hampshire	24,855	56.8	18,938	43.2					5,917
New Jersey	23,826	49.9	23,466	49.1	468	1.0			360
New York	168,497	52.1	154,896	47.9					13,601
North Carolina	25,261	84.8	4,538	15.2					20,723
Ohio	81,246	51.3	76,566	48.4	538	.3			4,680
Pennsylvania	90,973	57.7			66,706	42.3			24,267
Rhode Island	2,051	35.7	2,871	50.0	819	14.3	6	.1	820
Tennessee	28,078	95.4	1,347	4.6					26,731
Vermont	7,865	24.3	11,161	34.5	13,112	40.5	206	.6	1,951
Virginia	34,243	75.0	11,436	25.0	3				22,807
Totals	**701,780**	**54.23**	**484,205**	**37.42**	**100,715**	**7.78**	**7,273**	**.56**	

1836 Presidential Election

Total Popular Votes: 1,503,534
Van Buren's Plurality: 213,360

STATE	MARTIN VAN BUREN (Democrat)		WILLIAM H. HARRISON (Whig)		HUGH L. WHITE (Whig)		DANIEL WEBSTER (Whig)		OTHER[1]		PLURALITY
	Votes	%	Votes	%	Votes	%	Votes	%	Votes	%	
Alabama	20,638	55.3			16,658	44.7					3,980
Arkansas	2,380	64.1			1,334	35.9					1,046
Connecticut	19,294	50.7	18,799	49.4							495
Delaware	4,154	46.7	4,736	53.2					5	.1	582
Georgia	22,778	48.2			24,481	51.8					1,703
Illinois	18,369	54.7	15,220	45.3							3,149
Indiana	33,084	44.5	41,339	55.6							8,255
Kentucky	33,229	47.4	36,861	52.6							3,632
Louisiana	3,842	51.7			3,583	48.3					259
Maine	22,825	58.9	14,803	38.2					1,112	2.9	8,022
Maryland	22,267	46.3	25,852	53.7							3,585
Massachusetts	33,486	44.8					41,201	55.1	45	.1	7,715
Michigan	6,507	54.0	5,545	46.0							962
Mississippi	10,297	51.3			9,782	48.7					515
Missouri [3]	10,995	60.0			7,337	40.0					3,658
New Hampshire	18,697	75.0	6,228	25.0							12,469
New Jersey	25,592	49.5	26,137	50.5							545
New York	166,795	54.6	138,548	45.4							28,247
North Carolina	26,631	53.1			23,521	46.9			1		3,110
Ohio	97,122	47.9	105,809	52.1							8,687
Pennsylvania	91,466	51.2	87,235	48.8							4,231
Rhode Island	2,962	52.2	2,710	47.8					1		252
Tennessee	26,170	42.1			36,027	57.9					9,857
Vermont	14,040	40.0	20,994	59.8					65	.2	6,954
Virginia	30,556	56.6			23,384	43.4			5		7,172
Totals	**764,176**	**50.83**	**550,816**	**36.63**	**146,107**	**9.72**	**41,201**	**2.74**	**1,234**	**.08**	

1. For breakdown of "Other" vote, see minor candidate vote totals, p. 103.
2. Figures from Petersen, op. cit., p. 21.
3. Figures from Petersen, op. cit., p. 22.

1840 Presidential Election

Total Popular Votes: 2,411,808
Harrison's Plurality: 146,536

STATE	WILLIAM H. HARRISON (Whig)		MARTIN VAN BUREN (Democrat)		JAMES G. BIRNEY (Liberty)		OTHER[1]		PLURALITY
	Votes	%	Votes	%	Votes	%	Votes	%	
Alabama	28,515	45.6	33,996	54.4					5,481
Arkansas	5,160	43.6	6,679	56.4					1,519
Connecticut	31,598	55.6	25,281	44.5					6,317
Delaware	5,967	55.0	4,872	44.9			13	.1	1,095
Georgia	40,339	55.8	31,983	44.2					8,356
Illinois	45,574	48.9	47,441	50.9	160	.2			1,867
Indiana	65,280	55.5	51,696	44.0	30		599	.5	13,584
Kentucky	58,488	64.2	32,616	35.8					25,872
Louisiana	11,296	59.7	7,616	40.3					3,680
Maine	46,612	50.2	46,190	49.8					422
Maryland	33,528	53.8	28,752	46.2					4,776
Massachusetts	72,852	57.4	52,355	41.3	1,618	1.3			20,497
Michigan	22,933	52.1	21,096	47.9					1,837
Mississippi	19,515	53.4	17,010	46.6					2,505
Missouri	22,954	43.4	29,969	56.6					7,015
New Hampshire	26,310	43.9	32,774	54.7	872	1.5			6,464
New Jersey	33,351	51.7	31,034	48.2	69	.1			2,317
New York	226,001	51.2	212,733	48.2	2,809	.6			13,268
North Carolina	46,567	57.7	34,168	42.3					12,399
Ohio	148,043	54.3	123,944	45.4	903	.3			24,099
Pennsylvania	144,023	50.1	143,672	49.9					351
Rhode Island	5,213	60.4	3,263	37.8	19	.2	136	1.6	1,950
Tennessee	60,194	55.7	47,951	44.3					12,243
Vermont	32,440	63.9	18,006	35.5	317	.6	19		14,434
Virginia	42,637	49.4	43,757	50.7					1,120
Totals	**1,275,390**	**52.88**	**1,128,854**	**46.81**	**6,797**	**.28**	**767**	**.03**	

1844 Presidential Election

Total Popular Votes: 2,703,659
Polk's Plurality: 39,490

STATE	JAMES K. POLK (Democrat)		HENRY CLAY (Whig)		JAMES G. BIRNEY (Liberty)		OTHER[1]		PLURALITY
	Votes	%	Votes	%	Votes	%	Votes	%	
Alabama	37,401	59.0	26,002	41.0					11,399
Arkansas	9,546	63.0	5,604	37.0					3,942
Connecticut	29,841	46.2	32,832	50.8	1,943	3.0			2,991
Delaware	5,970	48.8	6,271	51.2			6	.1	301
Georgia	44,147	51.2	42,100	48.8					2,047
Illinois	58,795	53.9	45,854	42.1	3,469	3.2	939	.9	12,941
Indiana	70,183	50.1	67,866	48.4	2,108	1.5			2,317
Kentucky	51,988	45.9	61,249	54.1					9,261
Louisiana	13,782	51.3	13,083	48.7					699
Maine	45,719	53.8	34,378	40.5	4,836	5.7			11,341
Maryland	32,706	47.6	35,984	52.4					3,278
Massachusetts	53,039	40.2	67,062	50.8	10,830	8.2	1,106	.8	14,023
Michigan	27,737	49.9	24,185	43.5	3,638	6.6			3,552
Mississippi	25,846	57.4	19,158	42.6					6,688
Missouri	41,322	57.0	31,200	43.0					10,122
New Hampshire	27,160	55.2	17,866	36.3	4,161	8.5			9,294
New Jersey	37,495	49.4	38,318	50.5	131	.2			823
New York	237,588	48.9	232,482	47.9	15,812	3.3			5,106
North Carolina	39,287	47.6	43,232	52.4			2		3,945
Ohio	149,127	47.8	155,091	49.7	8,082	2.6			5,964
Pennsylvania	167,311	50.5	161,195	48.6	3,139	1.0			6,116
Rhode Island	4,867	39.9	7,322	60.1			5		2,455
Tennessee	59,917	50.0	60,040	50.1					123
Vermont	18,041	37.0	26,770	54.9	3,954	8.1			8,729
Virginia	50,679	53.1	44,860	47.0					5,819
Totals	**1,339,494**	**49.54**	**1,300,004**	**48.08**	**62,103**	**2.30**	**2,058**	**.08**	

1. For breakdown of "Other" vote, see minor candidate vote totals, p. 103.

1848 Presidential Election

Total Popular Votes: 2,879,184
Taylor's Plurality: 137,933

STATE	ZACHARY TAYLOR (Whig)		LEWIS CASS (Democrat)		MARTIN VAN BUREN (Free Soil)		OTHER [1]		PLURALITY
	Votes	%	Votes	%	Votes	%	Votes	%	
Alabama	30,482	49.4	31,173	50.6			4		691
Arkansas	7,587	44.9	9,301	55.1					1,714
Connecticut	30,318	48.6	27,051	43.4	5,005	8.0	24		3,267
Delaware	6,440	51.8	5,910	47.5	82	.7			530
Florida	4,120	57.2	3,083	42.8					1,037
Georgia	47,532	51.5	44,785	48.5					2,747
Illinois	52,853	42.4	55,952	44.9	15,702	12.6	89	.1	3,099
Indiana	69,668	45.7	74,695	49.0	8,031	5.3			5,027
Iowa	9,930	44.6	11,238	50.5	1,103	5.0			1,308
Kentucky	67,145	57.5	49,720	42.5					17,425
Louisiana	18,487	54.6	15,379	45.4					3,108
Maine	35,273	40.3	40,195	45.9	12,157	13.9			4,922
Maryland	37,702	52.1	34,528	47.7	129	.2			3,174
Massachusetts	61,072	45.3	35,281	26.2	38,333	28.5	62	.1	22,739
Michigan	23,947	36.8	30,742	47.2	10,393	16.0			6,795
Mississippi	25,911	49.4	26,545	50.6					634
Missouri	32,671	44.9	40,077	55.1					7,406
New Hampshire	14,781	29.5	27,763	55.4	7,560	15.1			12,982
New Jersey	40,015	51.5	36,901	47.5	829	1.1			3,114
New York	218,583	47.9	114,319	25.1	120,497	26.4	2,545	.6	98,086
North Carolina	44,054	55.2	35,772	44.8					8,282
Ohio	138,656	42.2	154,782	47.1	35,523	10.8	26		16,126
Pennsylvania	185,730	50.3	172,186	46.7	11,176	3.0			13,544
Rhode Island	6,705	60.7	3,613	32.7	726	6.6	5	.1	3,092
Tennessee	64,321	52.5	58,142	47.5					6,179
Texas	5,281	31.1	11,644	68.5			75	.4	6,363
Vermont	23,117	48.3	10,943	22.9	13,837	28.9			9,280
Virginia	45,265	49.2	46,739	50.8					1,474
Wisconsin	13,747	35.1	15,001	38.3	10,418	26.6			1,254
Totals	1,361,393	47.28	1,223,460	42.49	291,501	10.12	2,830	.10	

1. For breakdown of "Other" vote, see minor candidate vote totals, p. 103.

1852 Presidential Election

Total Popular Votes: 3,161,830
Pierce's Plurality: 220,568

STATE	FRANKLIN PIERCE (Democrat)		WINFIELD SCOTT (Whig)		JOHN P. HALE (Free Soil)		OTHER[1]		PLURALITY
	Votes	%	Votes	%	Votes	%	Votes	%	
Alabama	26,881	60.9	15,061	34.1			2,205	5.0	11,820
Arkansas	12,173	62.2	7,404	37.8					4,769
California	40,721	53.0	35,972	46.8	61	.1	56	.1	4,749
Connecticut	33,249	49.8	30,359	45.5	3,161	4.7	12		2,890
Delaware	6,318	49.9	6,293	49.7	62	.5			25
Florida	4,318	60.0	2,875	40.0					1,443
Georgia [2]	40,516	64.7	16,660	26.6			5,450	8.7	23,856
Illinois	80,378	51.9	64,733	41.8	9,863	6.4			15,645
Indiana	95,340	52.1	80,907	44.2	6,929	3.8			14,433
Iowa	17,763	50.2	15,856	44.8	1,606	4.5	139	.4	1,907
Kentucky	53,949	48.3	57,428	51.4	266	.2			3,479
Louisiana	18,647	51.9	17,255	48.1					1,392
Maine	41,609	50.6	32,543	39.6	8,030	9.8			9,066
Maryland	40,022	53.3	35,077	46.7	21				4,945
Massachusetts	44,569	35.1	52,683	41.5	28,023	22.1	1,828	1.4	8,114
Michigan	41,842	50.5	33,860	40.8	7,237	8.7			7,982
Mississippi	26,896	60.5	17,558	39.5					9,338
Missouri	38,817	56.4	29,984	43.6					8,833
New Hampshire	28,503	56.4	15,486	30.6	6,546	13.0			13,017
New Jersey	44,301	52.8	38,551	45.9	336	.4	738	.9	5,750
New York	262,083	50.2	234,882	45.0	25,329	4.9			27,201
North Carolina	39,788	50.4	39,043	49.5			60	.1	745
Ohio	169,193	47.9	152,577	43.2	31,133	8.8			16,616
Pennsylvania	198,568	51.2	179,182	46.2	8,500	2.2	1,670	.4	19,386
Rhode Island	8,735	51.4	7,626	44.9	644	3.8			1,109
Tennessee	56,900	49.3	58,586	50.7					1,686
Texas	14,857	73.5	5,356	26.5			10	.1	9,501
Vermont	13,044	29.8	22,173	50.6	8,621	19.7			9,129
Virginia	73,872	55.7	58,732	44.3					15,140
Wisconsin	33,658	52.0	22,240	34.4	8,842	13.7			11,418
Totals	**1,607,510**	**50.84**	**1,386,942**	**43.87**	**155,210**	**4.91**	**12,168**	**.38**	

1. For breakdown of "Other" vote, see minor candidate vote totals, p. 103.
2. Figures from Petersen, op. cit., p. 31.

1856 Presidential Election

Total Popular Votes: 4,054,647
Buchanan's Plurality: 493,727

STATE	JAMES BUCHANAN (Democrat)		JOHN C. FREMONT (Republican)		MILLARD FILLMORE (Whig-American)		OTHER [1]		PLURALITY
	Votes	%	Votes	%	Votes	%	Votes	%	
Alabama	46,739	62.1			28,552	37.9			18,187
Arkansas	21,910	67.1			10,732	32.9			11,178
California	53,342	48.4	20,704	18.8	36,195	32.8	14		17,147
Connecticut	35,028	43.6	42,717	53.2	2,615	3.3			7,689
Delaware	8,004	54.8	310	2.1	6,275	43.0	9	.1	1,729
Florida	6,358	56.8			4,833	43.2			1,525
Georgia	56,581	57.1			42,439	42.9			14,142
Illinois	105,528	44.1	96,275	40.2	37,531	15.7			9,253
Indiana	118,670	50.4	94,375	40.1	22,356	9.5			24,295
Iowa	37,568	40.7	45,073	48.8	9,669	10.5			7,505
Kentucky	74,642	52.5			67,416	47.5			7,226
Louisiana	22,164	51.7			20,709	48.3			1,455
Maine	39,140	35.7	67,279	61.3	3,270	3.0			28,139
Maryland	39,123	45.0	285	.3	47,452	54.6			8,329
Massachusetts	39,244	23.1	108,172	63.6	19,626	11.5	3,006	1.8	68,928
Michigan	52,136	41.5	71,762	57.2	1,660	1.3			19,626
Mississippi	35,456	59.4			24,191	40.6			11,265
Missouri	57,964	54.4			48,522	45.6			9,442
New Hampshire	31,891	45.7	37,473	53.7	410	.6			5,582
New Jersey	46,943	47.2	28,338	28.5	24,115	24.3			18,605
New York	195,878	32.8	276,004	46.3	124,604	20.9			80,126
North Carolina	48,243	56.8			36,720	43.2			11,523
Ohio	170,874	44.2	187,497	48.5	28,121	7.3	148		16,623
Pennsylvania	230,772	50.1	147,963	32.1	82,202	17.8			82,809
Rhode Island	6,680	33.7	11,467	57.9	1,675	8.5			4,787
Tennessee	69,704	52.2			63,878	47.8			5,826
Texas	31,995	66.7			16,010	33.4			15,985
Vermont	10,569	20.9	39,561	78.1	545	1.1			28,992
Virginia	90,083	60.0			60,150	40.0			29,933
Wisconsin	52,843	43.9	67,090	55.7	580	.5			14,247
Totals	1,836,072	45.28	1,342,345	33.11	873,053	21.53	3,177	.08	

1. For breakdown of "Other" vote, see minor candidate vote totals, p. 103.

1860 Presidential Election

Total Popular Vote: 4,685,561
Lincoln's Plurality: 485,706

STATE	ABRAHAM LINCOLN (Republican)		STEPHEN A. DOUGLAS (Democrat)		JOHN C. BRECKINRIDGE (Southern Democrat)		JOHN BELL (Constitutional Union)		OTHER[1]		PLURALITY
	Votes	%	Votes	%	Votes	%	Votes	%	Votes	%	
Alabama			13,618	15.1	48,669	54.0	27,835	30.9			20,834
Arkansas			5,357	9.9	28,732	53.1	20,063	37.1			8,669
California	38,733	32.3	37,999	31.7	33,969	28.4	9,111	7.6	15		734
Connecticut	43,488	58.1	15,431	20.6	14,372	19.2	1,528	2.0			28,057
Delaware	3,822	23.7	1,066	6.6	7,339	45.5	3,888	24.1			3,451
Florida			223	1.7	8,277	62.2	4,801	36.1			3,476
Georgia			11,581	10.9	52,176	48.9	42,960	40.3			9,216
Illinois	172,171	50.7	160,215	47.2	2,331	.7	4,914	1.5	35		11,956
Indiana	139,033	51.1	115,509	42.4	12,295	4.5	5,306	2.0			23,524
Iowa	70,302	54.6	55,639	43.2	1,035	.8	1,763	1.4			14,663
Kentucky[2]	1,364	.9	25,651	17.5	53,143	36.3	66,058	45.2			12,915
Louisiana			7,625	15.1	22,681	44.9	20,204	40.0			2,477
Maine	62,811	62.2	29,693	29.4	6,368	6.3	2,046	2.0			33,118
Maryland	2,294	2.5	5,966	6.5	42,482	45.9	41,760	45.1			722
Massachusetts	106,684	62.8	34,370	20.2	6,163	3.6	22,331	13.2	328	.2	72,314
Michigan	88,481	57.2	65,057	42.0	805	.5	415	.3			23,424
Minnesota	22,069	63.4	11,920	34.3	748	2.2	50	.1	17	.1	10,149
Mississippi			3,282	4.8	40,768	59.0	25,045	36.4			15,723
Missouri	17,028	10.3	58,801	35.5	31,362	18.9	58,372	35.3			429
New Hampshire	37,519	56.9	25,887	39.3	2,125	3.2	412	.6			11,632
New Jersey[2]	58,346	48.1	62,869	51.9							4,523
New York	362,646	53.7	312,510	46.3							50,136
North Carolina			2,737	2.8	48,846	50.5	45,129	46.7			3,717
Ohio	231,709	52.3	187,421	42.3	11,406	2.6	12,194	2.8	136		44,288
Oregon	5,329	36.1	4,136	28.0	5,075	34.4	218	1.5			254
Pennsylvania	268,030	56.3	16,765	3.5	178,871	37.5	12,776	2.7			89,159
Rhode Island	12,244	61.4	7,707	38.6							4,537
Tennessee			11,281	7.7	65,097	44.6	69,728	47.7			4,631
Texas			18		47,454	75.5	15,383	24.5			32,071
Vermont	33,808	75.7	8,649	19.4	218	.5	1,969	4.4			25,159
Virginia	1,887	1.1	16,198	9.7	74,325	44.5	74,481	44.6			156
Wisconsin	86,110	56.6	65,021	42.7	887	.6	161	.1			21,089
Totals	**1,865,908**	**39.82**	**1,380,202**	**29.46**	**848,019**	**18.09**	**590,901**	**12.61**	**531**	**.01**	

1. For breakdown of "Other" vote, see minor candidate vote totals, p. 103.
2. Figures from Petersen, op. cit., p. 37.

1864 Presidential Election

Total Popular Votes: 4,031,887
Lincoln's Plurality: 405,581

STATE[2]	ABRAHAM LINCOLN (Republican)		GEORGE B. MCCLELLAN (Democrat)		OTHER[1]		PLURALITY
	Votes	%	Votes	%	Votes	%	
California	62,053	58.6	43,837	41.4			18,216
Connecticut	44,673	51.4	42,285	48.6			2,388
Delaware	8,155	48.2	8,767	51.8			612
Illinois	189,512	54.4	158,724	45.6			30,788
Indiana	149,887	53.5	130,230	46.5			19,657
Iowa	83,858	63.1	49,089	36.9			34,769
Kansas	17,089	79.2	3,836	17.8	655	3.0	13,253
Kentucky	27,787	30.2	64,301	69.8			36,514
Maine	67,805	59.1	46,992	40.9			20,813
Maryland	40,153	55.1	32,739	44.9			7,414
Massachusetts	126,742	72.2	48,745	27.8	6		77,997
Michigan	91,133	55.1	74,146	44.9			16,987
Minnesota	25,031	59.0	17,376	41.0	26	.1	7,655
Missouri	72,750	69.7	31,596	30.3			41,154
Nevada	9,826	59.8	6,594	40.2			3,232
New Hampshire	36,596	52.6	33,034	47.4			3,562
New Jersey	60,724	47.2	68,020	52.8			7,296
New York	368,735	50.5	361,986	49.5			6,749
Ohio	265,674	56.4	205,609	43.6			60,065
Oregon	9,888	53.9	8,457	46.1	5		1,431
Pennsylvania	296,292	51.6	277,443	48.4			18,849
Rhode Island	14,349	62.2	8,718	37.8			5,631
Vermont	42,419	76.1	13,321	23.9			29,098
West Virginia	23,799	68.2	11,078	31.8			12,721
Wisconsin	83,458	55.9	65,884	44.1			17,574
Totals	**2,218,388**	**55.02**	**1,812,807**	**44.96**	**692**	**.02**	

1. For breakdown of "Other" vote, see minor candidate vote totals, p. 103.
2. Eleven Confederate states did not participate in election because of the Civil War.

1868 Presidential Election

Total Popular Votes: 5,722,440
Grant's Plurality: 304,906

STATE[2]	ULYSSES S. GRANT (Republican)		HORATIO SEYMOUR (Democrat)		OTHER[1]		PLURALITY
	Votes	%	Votes	%	Votes	%	
Alabama	76,667	*51.3*	72,921	*48.8*	6		**3,746**
Arkansas	22,112	*53.7*	19,078	*46.3*			**3,034**
California	54,588	*50.2*	54,068	*49.8*			**520**
Connecticut	50,789	*51.5*	47,781	*48.5*			**3,008**
Delaware	7,614	*41.0*	10,957	*59.0*			**3,343**
Georgia	57,109	*35.7*	102,707	*64.3*			**45,598**
Illinois	250,304	*55.7*	199,116	*44.3*			**51,188**
Indiana	176,548	*51.4*	166,980	*48.6*			**9,568**
Iowa	120,399	*61.9*	74,040	*38.1*			**46,359**
Kansas	30,027	*68.8*	13,600	*31.2*	3		**16,427**
Kentucky	39,566	*25.5*	115,889	*74.6*			**76,323**
Louisiana	33,263	*29.3*	80,225	*70.7*			**46,962**
Maine	70,502	*62.4*	42,460	*37.6*			**28,042**
Maryland	30,438	*32.8*	62,357	*67.2*			**31,919**
Massachusetts	136,379	*69.8*	59,103	*30.2*	26		**77,276**
Michigan	128,563	*57.0*	97,069	*43.0*			**31,494**
Minnesota	43,545	*60.8*	28,075	*39.2*			**15,470**
Missouri	86,860	*57.0*	65,628	*43.0*			**21,232**
Nebraska	9,772	*63.9*	5,519	*36.1*			**4,253**
Nevada	6,474	*55.4*	5,215	*44.6*			**1,259**
New Hampshire	37,718	*55.2*	30,575	*44.8*	11		**7,143**
New Jersey	80,132	*49.1*	83,001	*50.9*			**2,869**
New York	419,888	*49.4*	429,883	*50.6*			**9,995**
North Carolina	96,939	*53.4*	84,559	*46.6*			**12,380**
Ohio	280,159	*54.0*	238,506	*46.0*			**41,653**
Oregon	10,961	*49.6*	11,125	*50.4*			**164**
Pennsylvania	342,280	*52.2*	313,382	*47.8*			**28,898**
Rhode Island	13,017	*66.7*	6,494	*33.3*			**6,523**
South Carolina	62,301	*57.9*	45,237	*42.1*			**17,064**
Tennessee	56,628	*68.4*	26,129	*31.6*			**30,499**
Vermont	44,173	*78.6*	12,051	*21.4*			**32,122**
West Virginia	29,015	*58.8*	20,306	*41.2*			**8,709**
Wisconsin	108,920	*56.3*	84,708	*43.8*			**24,212**
Totals	**3,013,650**	**52.66**	**2,708,744**	**47.34**	**46**		

1. For breakdown of "Other" vote, see minor candidate vote totals, p. 103.
2. Mississippi, Texas and Virginia did not participate in the election due to Reconstruction. In Florida the state legislature cast the electoral vote.

1872 Presidential Election

Total Popular Votes: 6,467,679
Grant's Plurality: 763,474

STATE	ULYSSES S. GRANT (Republican)		HORACE GREELEY (Democrat, Liberal Republican)		CHARLES O'CONOR (Straight Out Democrat)		OTHER[1]		PLURALITY
	Votes	%	Votes	%	Votes	%	Votes	%	
Alabama	90,272	53.2	79,444	46.8					10,828
Arkansas	41,373	52.2	37,927	47.8					3,446
California	54,007	56.4	40,717	42.5	1,061	1.1			13,290
Connecticut	50,307	52.4	45,685	47.6					4,622
Delaware	11,129	51.0	10,205	46.8	488	2.2			924
Florida	17,763	53.5	15,427	46.5					2,336
Georgia	62,550	45.0	76,356	55.0					13,806
Illinois	241,936	56.3	184,884	43.0	3,151	.7			57,052
Indiana	186,147	53.2	163,632	46.8					22,515
Iowa	131,566	60.8	71,189	32.9	2,221	1.0	11,389	5.2	60,377
Kansas	66,805	66.5	32,970	32.8	156	.2	581	.5	33,835
Kentucky	88,766	46.4	99,995	52.3	2,374	1.2			11,229
Louisiana	71,663	55.7	57,029	44.3					14,634
Maine	61,426	67.9	29,097	32.1					32,329
Maryland	66,760	49.7	67,687	50.3					927
Massachusetts	133,455	69.3	59,195	30.7					74,260
Michigan	138,768	62.6	78,651	35.5	2,879	1.3	1,271	.6	60,117
Minnesota	56,040	61.4	35,131	38.5			168	.2	20,909
Mississippi	82,175	63.5	47,282	36.5					34,893
Missouri	119,196	43.7	151,434	55.5	2,429	.9			32,238
Nebraska	18,329	70.7	7,603	29.3					10,726
Nevada	8,413	57.4	6,236	42.6					2,177
New Hampshire	37,168	53.9	31,425	45.6			313	.5	5,743
New Jersey	91,656	54.5	76,456	45.5					15,200
New York	440,738	53.2	387,282	46.8					53,456
North Carolina	94,772	57.4	70,130	42.5	261	.2			24,642
Ohio	281,852	53.2	244,320	46.2	1,163	.2	2,100	.4	37,532
Oregon	11,818	58.8	7,742	38.5	547	2.7			4,076
Pennsylvania	349,589	62.3	212,040	37.8					137,549
Rhode Island	13,665	71.9	5,329	28.1					8,336
South Carolina	72,290	75.7	22,699	23.8	204	.2	259	.3	49,591
Tennessee	85,655	47.8	93,391	52.2					7,736
Texas	47,910	41.4	67,675	58.5	115	.1			19,765
Vermont	41,481	79.2	10,927	20.9					30,554
Virginia	93,463	50.5	91,647	49.5	85	.1			1,816
West Virginia	32,320	51.7	29,532	47.3	615	1.0			2,788
Wisconsin	105,012	54.6	86,390	44.9	853	.4			18,622
Totals	**3,598,235**	**55.63**	**2,834,761**	**43.83**	**18,602**	**.29**	**16,081**	**.25**	

1. For breakdown of "Other" vote, see minor candidate vote totals, p. 103.

1876 Presidential Election [2]

Total Popular Votes: 8,413,101
Tilden's Plurality: 254,235

STATE	RUTHERFORD B. HAYES [2] (Republican) Votes	%	SAMUEL J. TILDEN [2] (Democrat) Votes	%	PETER COOPER (Greenback) Votes	%	OTHER [1] Votes	%	PLURALITY
Alabama	68,708	40.0	102,989	60.0			2		34,281
Arkansas	38,649	39.9	58,086	59.9	211	.2			19,437
California	79,258	50.9	76,460	49.1	47		19		2,798
Connecticut	59,033	48.3	61,927	50.7	774	.6	400	.3	2,894
Delaware	10,752	44.6	13,381	55.5					2,629
Florida	23,849	51.0	22,927	49.0					922
Georgia	50,533	28.0	130,157	72.0					79,624
Illinois	278,232	50.2	258,611	46.7	17,207	3.1	318	.1	19,621
Indiana	208,011	48.3	213,529	49.5	9,533	2.2			5,518
Iowa	171,326	58.4	112,121	38.2	9,431	3.2	520	.2	59,205
Kansas	78,324	63.1	37,902	30.5	7,770	6.3	138	.1	40,422
Kentucky	97,568	37.4	160,060	61.4			2,998	1.2	62,492
Louisiana	75,315	51.7	70,508	48.4					4,807
Maine	66,300	56.6	49,917	42.7			828	.7	16,383
Maryland	71,980	44.0	91,779	56.1					19,799
Massachusetts	150,063	57.8	108,777	41.9			779	.3	41,286
Michigan	166,901	52.4	141,665	44.5	9,023	2.8	837	.3	25,236
Minnesota	72,962	58.8	48,799	39.3	2,399	1.9			24,163
Mississippi	52,603	31.9	112,173	68.1					59,570
Missouri	145,027	41.4	202,086	57.6	3,497	1.0			57,059
Nebraska	31,915	64.8	17,343	35.2					14,572
Nevada	10,383	52.7	9,308	47.3					1,075
New Hampshire	41,540	51.8	38,510	48.1			93	.1	3,030
New Jersey	103,517	47.0	115,962	52.7	714	.3			12,445
New York	489,207	48.2	521,949	51.4	1,978	.2	2,369	.2	32,742
North Carolina	108,484	46.4	125,427	53.6					16,943
Ohio	330,698	50.2	323,182	49.1	3,058	.5	1,712	.3	7,516
Oregon	15,207	50.9	14,157	47.4	509	1.7			1,050
Pennsylvania	384,157	50.6	366,204	48.3	7,209	1.0	1,403	.2	17,953
Rhode Island	15,787	59.6	10,712	40.4					5,075
South Carolina	91,786	50.2	90,897	49.8					889
Tennessee	89,566	40.2	133,177	59.8					43,611
Texas	45,013	29.7	106,372	70.2			46		61,359
Vermont	44,092	68.4	20,254	31.4			114	.2	23,838
Virginia	95,518	40.4	140,770	59.6					45,252
West Virginia	41,997	42.2	56,546	56.8	1,104	1.1			14,549
Wisconsin	130,050	50.6	123,922	48.2	1,509	.6	1,695	.7	6,128
Totals	**4,034,311**	**47.95**	**4,288,546**	**50.97**	**75,973**	**.90**	**14,271**	**.17**	

1. *For breakdown of "Other" vote, see minor candidate vote totals, p. 103.*
2. *For resolution of disputed 1876 election, see introduction, p. 11.*

1880 Presidential Election

Total Popular Votes: 9,210,420
Garfield's Plurality: 1,898

STATE	JAMES A. GARFIELD (Republican)		WINFIELD S. HANCOCK (Democrat)		JAMES B. WEAVER (Greenback)		OTHER[1]		PLURALITY
	Votes	%	Votes	%	Votes	%	Votes	%	
Alabama	56,350	37.1	91,130	60.0	4,422	2.9			34,780
Arkansas	41,661	38.7	60,489	56.1	4,079	3.8	1,543	1.4	18,828
California	80,282	48.9	80,426	49.0	3,381	2.1	129	.1	144
Colorado	27,450	51.3	24,647	46.0	1,435	2.7	14		2,803
Connecticut	67,071	50.5	64,411	48.5	868	.7	448	.3	2,660
Delaware	14,148	48.0	15,181	51.5	129	.4			1,033
Florida	23,654	45.8	27,964	54.2					4,310
Georgia	54,470	34.6	102,981	65.4					48,511
Illinois	318,036	51.1	277,321	44.6	26,358	4.2	590	.1	40,715
Indiana	232,169	49.3	225,523	47.9	13,066	2.8			6,646
Iowa	183,904	56.9	105,845	32.8	32,327	10.0	1,064	.3	78,059
Kansas	121,520	60.4	59,789	29.7	19,710	9.8	35		61,731
Kentucky	106,490	39.9	148,875	55.7	11,506	4.3	233	.1	42,385
Louisiana	38,978	37.3	65,047	62.3	437	.4			26,069
Maine	74,052	51.5	65,211	45.3	4,409	3.1	231	.2	8,841
Maryland	78,515	45.6	93,706	54.4					15,191
Massachusetts	165,198	58.5	111,960	39.6	4,548	1.6	799	.3	53,238
Michigan	185,335	52.5	131,596	37.3	34,895	9.9	1,250	.4	53,739
Minnesota	93,939	62.3	53,314	35.4	3,267	2.2	286	.2	40,625
Mississippi	34,844	29.8	75,750	64.7	5,797	5.0	677	.6	40,906
Missouri	153,647	38.7	208,600	52.5	35,042	8.8			54,953
Nebraska	54,979	62.9	28,523	32.7	3,853	4.4			26,456
Nevada	8,732	47.6	9,611	52.4					879
New Hampshire	44,856	51.9	40,797	47.2	528	.6	180	.2	4,059
New Jersey	120,555	49.0	122,565	49.8	2,617	1.1	191	.1	2,010
New York	555,544	50.3	534,511	48.4	12,373	1.1	1,517	.1	21,033
North Carolina	115,616	48.0	124,204	51.6	1,126	.5			8,588
Ohio	375,048	51.7	340,867	47.0	6,456	.9	2,613	.4	34,181
Oregon	20,619	50.5	19,955	48.9	267	.7			664
Pennsylvania	444,704	50.8	407,428	46.6	20,667	2.4	1,984	.2	37,276
Rhode Island	18,195	62.2	10,779	36.9	236	.8	25	.1	7,416
South Carolina	57,954	34.1	111,236	65.5	567	.3	36		53,282
Tennessee	107,677	44.3	129,569	53.3	6,017	2.5			21,892
Texas	50,217	21.5	156,010	66.8	27,405	11.7			105,793
Vermont	45,567	70.0	18,316	28.1	1,215	1.9			27,251
Virginia	83,533	39.5	128,083	60.5					44,550
West Virginia	46,243	41.1	57,390	51.0	9,008	8.0			11,147
Wisconsin	144,406	54.0	114,650	42.9	7,986	3.0	160	.1	29,756
Totals	4,446,158	48.27	4,444,260	48.25	305,997	3.32	14,005	.15	

1. For breakdown of "Other" vote, see minor candidate vote totals, p. 103.

1884 Presidential Election

Total Popular Votes: 10,049,754
Cleveland's Plurality: 25,685

STATE	GROVER CLEVELAND (Democrat)		JAMES G. BLAINE (Republican)		BENJAMIN F. BUTLER (Greenback)		JOHN P. ST. JOHN (Prohibition)		OTHER[1]		PLURALITY
	Votes	%	Votes	%	Votes	%	Votes	%	Votes	%	
Alabama	92,736	60.4	59,444	38.7	762	.5	610	.4	72	.1	33,292
Arkansas	72,734	57.8	51,198	40.7	1,847	1.5					21,536
California	89,288	45.3	102,369	52.0	2,037	1.0	2,965	1.5	329	.2	13,081
Colorado	27,723	41.7	36,084	54.3	1,956	2.9	756	1.1			8,361
Connecticut	67,167	49.0	65,879	48.0	1,682	1.2	2,493	1.8			1,288
Delaware	16,957	56.6	12,953	43.2	10		64	.2			4,004
Florida	31,769	53.0	28,031	46.7			72	.1	118	.2	3,738
Georgia	94,667	65.9	48,603	33.8	145	.1	195	.1			46,064
Illinois	312,351	46.4	337,469	50.2	10,776	1.6	12,074	1.8			25,118
Indiana	244,989	49.8	238,466	48.5	8,194	1.7					6,523
Iowa	177,316	47.0	197,089	52.3			1,499	.4	1,297	.3	19,773
Kansas	90,111	33.9	154,410	58.1	16,341	6.2	4,311	1.6	468	.2	64,299
Kentucky	152,961	55.3	118,690	42.9	1,691	.6	3,139	1.1			34,271
Louisiana	62,594	57.2	46,347	42.4	120	.1	338	.3			16,247
Maine	52,153	40.0	72,217	55.3	3,955	3.0	2,160	1.7	6		20,064
Maryland	96,866	52.1	85,748	46.1	578	.3	2,827	1.5			11,118
Massachusetts	122,352	40.3	146,724	48.4	24,382	8.0	9,923	3.3	2		24,372
Michigan	149,835	37.2	192,669	47.8	42,252	10.5	18,403	4.6			42,834
Minnesota	70,065	36.9	111,685	58.8	3,583	1.9	4,684	2.5			41,620
Mississippi	77,653	64.3	43,035	35.7							34,618
Missouri	236,023	53.5	203,081	46.0			2,164	.5			32,942
Nebraska	54,391	40.5	76,912	57.3			2,899	2.2			22,521
Nevada	5,577	43.6	7,176	56.2	26	.2					1,599
New Hampshire	39,198	46.3	43,254	51.1	554	.7	1,580	1.9			4,056
New Jersey	127,747	49.0	123,436	47.3	3,486	1.3	6,156	2.4	28		4,311
New York	563,048	48.3	562,001	48.2	16,955	1.5	24,999	2.1			1,047
North Carolina	142,905	53.3	125,021	46.6			430	.2			17,884
Ohio	368,280	46.9	400,092	51.0	5,179	.7	11,069	1.4			31,812
Oregon	24,598	46.7	26,845	51.0	726	1.4	479	.9	35	.1	2,247
Pennsylvania	394,772	43.9	472,792	52.6	16,992	1.9	15,154	1.7			78,020
Rhode Island	12,391	37.8	19,030	58.1	422	1.3	928	2.8			6,639
South Carolina	69,845	75.3	21,730	23.4					1,237	1.3	48,115
Tennessee	133,770	51.5	124,101	47.7	957	.4	1,150	.4			9,669
Texas	223,209	69.5	91,234	28.4	3,310	1.0	3,489	1.1			131,975
Vermont	17,331	29.2	39,514	66.5	785	1.3	1,752	3.0	27	.1	22,183
Virginia	145,491	51.1	139,356	48.9			130	.1			6,135
West Virginia	67,311	50.9	63,096	47.8	799	.6	939	.7			4,215
Wisconsin	146,447	45.8	161,155	50.4	4,594	1.4	7,651	2.4			14,708
Totals	4,874,621	48.50	4,848,936	48.25	175,096	1.74	147,482	1.47	3,619	.04	

1. For breakdown of "Other" vote, see minor candidate vote totals, p. 103.

1888 Presidential Election

Total Popular Votes: 11,383,320
Cleveland's Plurality: 90,596[2]

STATE	BENJAMIN HARRISON (Republican)		GROVER CLEVELAND (Democrat)		CLINTON B. FISK (Prohibition)		ALSON J. STREETER (Union Labor)		OTHER[1]		PLURALITY
	Votes	%	Votes	%	Votes	%	Votes	%	Votes	%	
Alabama	57,177	32.7	117,314	67.0	594	.3					60,137
Arkansas	59,752	38.0	86,062	54.8	614	.4	10,630	6.8			26,310
California	124,816	49.7	117,729	46.8	5,761	2.3			3,033	1.2	7,087
Colorado	50,772	55.2	37,549	40.8	2,182	2.4	1,266	1.4	177	.2	13,223
Connecticut	74,584	48.4	74,920	48.7	4,234	2.8	240	.2			336
Delaware	12,950	43.5	16,414	55.2	399	1.3			1		3,464
Florida	26,529	39.9	39,557	59.5	414	.6					13,028
Georgia	40,499	28.3	100,493	70.3	1,808	1.3	136	.1			59,994
Illinois	370,475	49.5	348,351	46.6	21,703	2.9	7,134	1.0	150		22,124
Indiana	263,366	49.1	260,990	48.6	9,939	1.9	2,693	.5			2,376
Iowa	211,607	52.3	179,876	44.5	3,550	.9	9,105	2.3	556	.1	31,731
Kansas	182,845	55.2	102,739	31.0	6,774	2.1	37,838	11.4	937	.3	80,106
Kentucky	155,138	45.0	183,830	53.3	5,223	1.5	677	.2			28,692
Louisiana	30,660	26.5	85,032	73.4	160	.1	39				54,372
Maine	73,730	57.5	50,472	39.4	2,691	2.1	1,344	1.1	16		23,258
Maryland	99,986	47.4	106,188	50.3	4,767	2.3					6,202
Massachusetts	183,892	53.4	151,590	44.0	8,701	2.5			60		32,302
Michigan	236,387	49.7	213,469	44.9	20,945	4.4	4,555	1.0			22,918
Minnesota	142,492	54.2	104,372	39.7	15,201	5.8	1,097	.4			38,120
Mississippi	30,095	26.0	85,451	73.8	240	.2					55,356
Missouri	236,252	45.3	261,943	50.2	4,539	.9	18,625	3.6			25,691
Nebraska	108,417	53.5	80,552	39.8	9,435	4.7	4,226	2.1			27,865
Nevada	7,229	57.5	5,303	42.2	41	.3					1,926
New Hampshire	45,734	50.4	43,382	47.8	1,596	1.8			58	.1	2,352
New Jersey	144,347	47.5	151,493	49.9	7,794	2.6					7,146
New York	650,338	49.3	635,965	48.2	30,231	2.3	627	.1	2,587	.2	14,373
North Carolina	134,784	47.2	147,902	51.8	2,840	1.0			37		13,118
Ohio	416,054	49.6	395,456	47.1	24,356	2.9	3,491	.4			20,598
Oregon	33,291	53.8	26,518	42.9	1,676	2.7			404	.7	6,773
Pennsylvania	526,091	52.7	446,633	44.8	20,947	2.1	3,873	.4	24		79,458
Rhode Island	21,969	53.9	17,530	43.0	1,251	3.1	18		7		4,439
South Carolina	13,736	17.2	65,824	82.3					437	.6	52,088
Tennessee	138,978	45.8	158,699	52.3	5,969	2.0	48				19,721
Texas	88,604	25.0	232,189	65.5	4,739	1.3	28,880	8.2			143,585
Vermont	45,193	71.2	16,788	26.5	1,460	2.3			35	.1	28,405
Virginia	150,399	49.5	152,004	50.0	1,684	.6					1,605
West Virginia	78,171	49.0	78,677	49.4	1,084	.7	1,508	1.0			506
Wisconsin	176,553	49.8	155,232	43.8	14,277	4.0	8,552	2.4			21,321
Totals	5,443,892	47.82	5,534,488	48.62	249,813	2.19	146,602	1.29	8,519	.07	

1. For breakdown of "Other" vote, see minor candidate vote totals, p. 103.
2. Harrison won the election. See p. 5.

1892 Presidential Election

Total Popular Votes: 12,056,097
Cleveland's Plurality: 372,639

STATE	GROVER CLEVELAND (Democrat)		BENJAMIN HARRISON (Republican)		JAMES B. WEAVER (Populist)		JOHN BIDWELL (Prohibition)		OTHER[1]		PLURALITY
	Votes	%	Votes	%	Votes	%	Votes	%	Votes	%	
Alabama	138,135	59.4	9,184	4.0	84,984	36.6	240	.1			53,151
Arkansas	87,834	59.3	47,072	31.8	11,831	8.0	113	.1	1,267	.9	40,762
California	118,151	43.8	118,027	43.8	25,311	9.4	8,096	3.0			124
Colorado			38,620	41.1	53,584	57.1	1,677	1.8			14,964
Connecticut	82,395	50.1	77,030	46.8	809	.5	4,026	2.5	333	.2	5,365
Delaware	18,581	49.9	18,077	48.6			564	1.5	13		504
Florida	30,153	85.0			4,843	13.7	475	1.3			25,310
Georgia	129,446	58.0	48,408	21.7	41,939	18.8	988	.4	2,345	1.1	81,038
Idaho			8,599	44.3	10,520	54.2	288	1.5			1,921
Illinois	426,281	48.8	399,308	45.7	22,207	2.5	25,871	3.0			26,973
Indiana	262,740	47.5	255,615	46.2	22,208	4.0	13,050	2.4			7,125
Iowa	196,367	44.3	219,795	49.6	20,595	4.7	6,402	1.4			23,428
Kansas			156,134	48.3	162,888	50.3	4,569	1.4			6,754
Kentucky	175,461	51.5	135,462	39.7	23,500	6.9	6,441	1.9			39,999
Louisiana	87,926	76.5	26,963	23.5							60,963
Maine	48,049	41.3	62,936	54.1	2,396	2.1	3,066	2.6	4		14,887
Maryland	113,866	53.4	92,736	43.5	796	.4	5,877	2.8			21,130
Massachusetts	176,813	45.2	202,814	51.9	3,210	.8	7,539	1.9	652	.2	26,001
Michigan	202,396	43.4	222,708	47.7	20,031	4.3	20,857	4.5	925	.2	20,312
Minnesota	100,589	37.6	122,736	45.8	30,399	11.3	14,117	5.3			22,147
Mississippi	40,030	76.2	1,398	2.7	10,118	19.3	973	1.9			29,912
Missouri	268,400	49.6	227,646	42.0	41,204	7.6	4,333	.8			40,754
Montana	17,690	39.8	18,871	42.4	7,338	16.5	562	1.3			1,181
Nebraska	24,956	12.5	87,213	43.6	83,134	41.5	4,902	2.5			4,079
Nevada	703	6.5	2,811	26.0	7,226	66.8	86	.8			4,415
New Hampshire	42,081	47.1	45,658	51.1	292	.3	1,297	1.5			3,577
New Jersey	170,987	50.7	156,059	46.2	969	.3	8,133	2.4	1,337	.4	14,928
New York	654,868	49.0	609,350	45.6	16,429	1.2	38,190	2.9	17,956	1.3	45,518
North Carolina	132,951	47.4	100,346	35.8	44,336	15.8	2,637	.9			32,605
North Dakota[2]			17,519	48.5	17,700	49.0	899	2.5			181
Ohio	404,115	47.5	405,187	47.7	14,850	1.8	26,012	3.1			1,072
Oregon	14,243	18.2	35,002	44.7	26,875	34.3	2,258	2.9			8,127
Pennsylvania	452,264	45.1	516,011	51.5	8,714	.9	25,123	2.5	888	.1	63,747
Rhode Island	24,336	45.8	26,975	50.7	228	.4	1,654	3.1	3		2,639
South Carolina	54,680	77.6	13,345	18.9	2,407	3.4			72	.1	41,335
South Dakota	8,894	12.7	34,714	49.5	26,552	37.8					8,162
Tennessee	136,468	51.4	100,537	37.8	23,918	9.0	4,809	1.8			35,931
Texas	236,979	57.7	70,982	17.3	96,649	23.5	2,164	.5	4,086	1.0	140,330
Vermont	16,325	29.3	37,992	68.1	42	.1	1,424	2.6	10		21,667
Virginia	164,136	56.2	113,098	38.7	12,275	4.2	2,729	.9			51,038
Washington	29,802	33.9	36,459	41.5	19,165	21.8	2,542	2.9			6,657
West Virginia	84,467	49.4	80,292	46.9	4,167	2.4	2,153	1.3			4,175
Wisconsin	177,325	47.7	171,101	46.1	9,919	2.7	13,136	3.5			6,224
Wyoming			8,454	50.6	7,722	46.2	498	3.0	29	.2	732
Totals	**5,551,883**	**46.05**	**5,179,244**	**42.96**	**1,024,280**	**8.50**	**270,770**	**2.25**	**29,920**	**.25**	

1. For breakdown of "Other" vote, see minor candidate vote totals, p. 103.
2. Figures from Petersen, op. cit., p. 60.

1896 Presidential Election

Total Popular Votes: 13,935,738
McKinley's Plurality: 596,985

STATE	WILLIAM McKINLEY (Republican)		WILLIAM J. BRYAN (Democrat, Populist)		JOHN M. PALMER (National Democrat)		JOSHUA LEVERING (Prohibition)		OTHER[1]		PLURALITY
	Votes	%	Votes	%	Votes	%	Votes	%	Votes	%	
Alabama	55,673	28.6	130,298	67.0	6,375	3.3	2,234	1.2			74,625
Arkansas	37,512	25.1	110,103	73.7			889	.6	892	.6	72,591
California	146,756	49.2	144,877	48.5	1,730	.6	2,573	.9	2,662	.9	1,879
Colorado	26,271	13.9	161,005	84.9	1		1,717	.9	545	.3	134,734
Connecticut	110,285	63.2	56,740	32.5	4,336	2.5	1,806	1.0	1,227	.7	53,545
Delaware	20,450	53.2	16,574	43.1	966	2.5	466	1.2			3,876
Florida	11,298	24.3	32,756	70.4	1,778	3.8	656	1.4			21,458
Georgia	59,395	36.6	93,885	57.8	3,670	2.3	5,483	3.4	47		34,490
Idaho	6,324	21.3	23,135	78.1			172	.6			16,811
Illinois	607,130	55.7	465,593	42.7	6,307	.6	9,796	.9	1,940	.2	141,537
Indiana	323,754	50.8	305,538	48.0	2,145	.3	3,061	.5	2,591	.4	18,216
Iowa	289,293	55.5	223,744	42.9	4,516	.9	3,192	.6	805	.2	65,549
Kansas	159,484	47.5	173,049	51.5	1,209	.4	1,723	.5	620	.2	13,565
Kentucky	218,171	48.9	217,894	48.9	5,084	1.1	4,779	1.1			277
Louisiana	22,037	21.8	77,175	76.4	1,834	1.8					55,138
Maine	80,403	67.9	34,587	29.2	1,867	1.6	1,562	1.3			45,816
Maryland	136,959	54.7	104,150	41.6	2,499	1.0	5,918	2.4	723	.3	32,809
Massachusetts	278,976	69.5	105,414	26.3	11,749	2.9	2,998	.8	2,132	.5	173,562
Michigan	293,336	53.8	237,164	43.5	6,923	1.3	4,978	.9	3,182	.6	56,172
Minnesota	193,503	56.6	139,735	40.9	3,222	.9	4,348	1.3	954	.3	53,768
Mississippi	4,819	6.9	63,355	91.0	1,021	1.5	396	.6			58,536
Missouri	304,940	45.2	363,667	54.0	2,365	.4	2,169	.3	891	.1	58,727
Montana	10,509	19.7	42,628	79.9			193	.4			32,119
Nebraska	103,064	46.2	115,007	51.5	2,885	1.3	1,242	.6	983	.4	11,943
Nevada	1,938	18.8	8,348	81.2							6,410
New Hampshire	57,444	68.7	21,650	25.9	3,520	4.2	779	.9	277	.3	35,794
New Jersey	221,367	59.7	133,675	36.0	6,373	1.7			9,599	2.6	87,692
New York	819,838	57.6	551,369	38.7	18,950	1.3	16,052	1.1	17,667	1.2	268,469
North Carolina	155,122	46.8	174,408	52.6	578	.2	635	.2	594	.2	19,286
North Dakota	26,335	55.6	20,686	43.7			358	.8	12		5,649
Ohio	525,991	51.9	477,497	47.1	1,858	.2	5,068	.5	3,881	.4	48,494
Oregon	48,700	50.0	46,739	48.0	977	1.0	919	.9			1,961
Pennsylvania	728,300	61.0	433,228	36.3	11,000	.9	19,274	1.6	2,553	.2	295,072
Rhode Island	37,437	68.3	14,459	26.4	1,166	2.1	1,160	2.1	563	1.0	22,978
South Carolina	9,313	13.5	58,801	85.3	824	1.2					49,488
South Dakota	41,040	49.5	41,225	49.7			672	.8			185
Tennessee	148,683	46.3	167,168	52.1	1,953	.6	3,099	1.0			18,485
Texas	163,894	30.3	370,308	68.4	5,022	.9	1,794	.3			206,414
Utah	13,491	17.3	64,607	82.7							51,116
Vermont	51,127	80.1	10,367	16.7	1,341	2.1	733	1.2			40,490
Virginia	135,379	45.9	154,708	52.5	2,129	.7	2,350	.8	108		19,329
Washington	39,153	41.8	53,314	57.0			968	1.0	148	.2	14,361
West Virginia	105,379	52.2	94,480	46.8	678	.3	1,220	.6			10,899
Wisconsin	268,135	59.9	165,523	37.0	4,584	1.0	7,507	1.7	1.660	.4	102,612
Wyoming	10,072	47.8	10,862	51.6			133	.6			790
Totals	**7,108,480**	**51.01**	**6,511,495**	**46.73**	**133,435**	**.96**	**125,072**	**.90**	**57,256**	**.41**	

1. For breakdown of "Other" vote, see minor candidate vote totals, p. 103.

1900 Presidential Election

Total Popular Votes: 13,970,470
McKinley's Plurality: 859,694

STATE	WILLIAM McKINLEY (Republican) Votes	%	WILLIAM J. BRYAN (Democrat) Votes	%	JOHN C. WOOLLEY (Prohibition) Votes	%	EUGENE V. DEBS (Socialist) Votes	%	OTHER[1] Votes	%	PLURALITY
Alabama	55,612	34.8	97,129	60.8	2,763	1.7			4,188	2.6	41,517
Arkansas	44,800	35.0	81,242	63.5	584	.5			1,340	1.1	36,442
California	164,755	54.5	124,985	41.3	5,024	1.7			7,554	2.5	39,770
Colorado	92,701	42.0	122,705	55.6	3,790	1.7	686	.3	1,013	.5	30,004
Connecticut	102,572	56.9	74,014	41.1	1,617	.9	1,029	.6	963	.5	28,558
Delaware	22,535	53.7	18,852	44.9	546	1.3	56	.1			3,683
Florida	7,355	18.6	28,273	71.3	2,244	5.7	634	1.6	1,143	2.9	20,918
Georgia	34,260	28.2	81,180	66.9	1,402	1.2			4,568	3.8	46,920
Idaho	27,198	46.9	29,484	50.9	857	1.5			445	.8	2,286
Illinois	597,985	52.8	503,061	44.4	17,626	1.6	9,687	.9	3,539	.3	94,924
Indiana	336,063	50.6	309,584	46.6	13,718	2.1	2,374	.4	2,355	.4	26,479
Iowa	307,799	58.0	209,261	39.5	9,502	1.8	2,743	.5	1,040	.2	98,538
Kansas[2]	185,955	52.6	162,601	46.0	3,605	1.0	1,605	.5			23,534
Kentucky	227,132	48.5	235,126	50.2	2,890	.6	766	.2	2,351	.5	7,994
Louisiana	14,234	21.0	53,668	79.0					4		39,434
Maine	65,412	61.9	36,822	34.8	2,581	2.4	878	.8			28,590
Maryland	136,151	51.5	122,237	46.2	4,574	1.7	900	.3	524	.2	13,914
Massachusetts	238,866	57.6	156,997	37.9	6,202	1.5	9,607	2.3	3,132	.8	81,869
Michigan	316,014	58.1	211,432	38.9	11,804	2.2	2,820	.5	1,719	.3	104,582
Minnesota	190,461	60.2	112,901	35.7	8,555	2.7	3,065	1.0	1,329	.4	77,560
Mississippi	5,707	9.7	51,706	87.6					1,642	2.8	45,999
Missouri	314,092	45.9	351,922	51.5	5,965	.9	6,139	.9	5,540	.8	37,830
Montana	25,409	39.8	37,311	58.4	306	.5	711	1.1	119	.2	11,902
Nebraska	121,835	50.5	114,013	47.2	3,655	1.5	823	.3	1,104	.5	7,822
Nevada	3,849	37.8	6,347	62.3							2,498
New Hampshire	54,799	59.3	35,489	38.4	1,270	1.4	790	.9	16		19,310
New Jersey	221,707	55.3	164,808	41.1	7,183	1.8	4,609	1.2	2,743	.7	56,899
New York	822,013	53.1	678,462	43.8	22,077	1.4	12,869	.8	12,622	.8	143,551
North Carolina	132,997	45.5	157,733	53.9	990	.3			798	.3	24,736
North Dakota	35,898	62.1	20,524	35.5	735	1.3	517	.9	109	.2	15,374
Ohio	543,918	52.3	474,882	45.7	10,203	1.0	4,847	.5	6,223	.6	69,036
Oregon	46,172	55.5	32,810	39.4	2,536	3.1	1,464	1.8	269	.3	13,362
Pennsylvania	712,665	60.7	424,232	36.2	27,908	2.4	4,831	.4	3,574	.3	288,433
Rhode Island	33,784	59.7	19,812	35.0	1,529	2.7			1,423	2.5	13,972
South Carolina	3,525	7.0	47,173	93.1							43,648
South Dakota	54,574	56.8	39,538	41.1	1,541	1.6	176	.2	340	.4	15,036
Tennessee	123,108	45.0	145,240	53.0	3,844	1.4	346	.1	1,322	.5	22,132
Texas	131,174	30.9	267,945	63.1	2,642	.6	1,846	.4	20,727	4.9	136,771
Utah	47,089	50.6	44,949	48.3	205	.2	717	.8	111	.1	2,140
Vermont	42,569	75.7	12,849	22.9	383	.7	39	.1	372	.7	29,720
Virginia	115,769	43.8	146,079	55.3	2,130	.8			230	.1	30,310
Washington	57,455	53.4	44,833	41.7	2,363	2.2	2,006	1.9	866	.8	12,622
West Virginia	119,829	54.3	98,807	44.8	1,628	.7	286	.1	246	.1	21,022
Wisconsin	265,760	60.1	159,163	36.0	10,027	2.3	7,048	1.6	503	.1	106,597
Wyoming	14,482	58.6	10,164	41.1			21	.1	41	.2	4,318
Totals	**7,218,039**	**51.67**	**6,358,345**	**45.51**	**209,004**	**1.50**	**86,935**	**.62**	**98,147**	**.70**	

1. For breakdown of "Other" vote, see minor candidate vote totals, p. 103.
2. Figures from Petersen, op. cit., p. 67.

1904 Presidential Election

Total Popular Votes: 13,518,964
Roosevelt's Plurality: 2,543,695

STATE	THEODORE ROOSEVELT (Republican)		ALTON PARKER (Democrat)		EUGENE V. DEBS (Socialist)		SILAS C. SWALLOW (Prohibition)		OTHER[1]		PLURALITY
	Votes	%	Votes	%	Votes	%	Votes	%	Votes	%	
Alabama	22,472	20.7	79,797	73.4	853	.8	612	.6	5,051	4.6	57,325
Arkansas	46,760	40.2	64,434	55.4	1,816	1.6	992	.9	2,326	2.0	17,674
California	205,226	61.9	89,294	26.9	29,535	8.9	7,380	2.2	333	.1	115,932
Colorado	134,661	55.3	100,105	41.1	4,304	1.8	3,438	1.4	1,159	.5	34,556
Connecticut	111,089	58.1	72,909	38.2	4,543	2.4	1,506	.8	1,089	.6	38,180
Delaware	23,705	54.1	19,347	44.1	146	.3	607	1.4	51	.1	4,358
Florida	8,314	21.5	26,449	68.3	2,337	6.0			1,605	4.2	18,135
Georgia	24,004	18.3	83,466	63.7	196	.2	685	.5	22,635	17.3	59,462
Idaho	47,783	65.8	18,480	25.5	4,949	6.8	1,013	1.4	352	.5	29,303
Illinois	632,645	58.8	327,606	30.4	69,225	6.4	34,770	3.2	12,249	1.1	305,039
Indiana	368,289	54.0	274,356	40.2	12,023	1.8	23,496	3.4	4,042	.6	93,933
Iowa	307,907	63.4	149,141	30.7	14,847	3.1	11,601	2.4	2,207	.5	158,766
Kansas	213,455	64.9	86,164	26.2	15,869	4.8	7,306	2.2	6,253	1.9	127,291
Kentucky	205,457	47.1	217,170	49.8	3,599	.8	6,603	1.5	3,117	.7	11,713
Louisiana	5,205	9.7	47,708	88.5	995	1.9					42,503
Maine	65,432	67.4	27,642	28.5	2,102	2.2	1,510	1.6	337	.4	37,790
Maryland	109,497	48.8	109,446	48.8	2,247	1.0	3,034	1.4	5		51
Massachusetts	257,813	57.9	165,746	37.2	13,604	3.1	4,279	1.0	3,658	.8	92,067
Michigan	361,863	69.5	134,163	25.8	8,942	1.7	13,312	2.6	2,163	.4	227,700
Minnesota	216,651	74.0	55,187	18.8	11,692	4.0	6,253	2.1	3,077	1.1	161,464
Mississippi	3,280	5.6	53,480	91.1	462	.8			1,499	2.6	50,200
Missouri	321,449	49.9	296,312	46.0	13,009	2.0	7,191	1.1	5,900	.9	25,137
Montana	33,994	53.5	21,816	34.3	5,675	8.9	339	.5	1,744	2.8	12,178
Nebraska	138,558	61.4	52,921	23.4	7,412	3.3	6,323	2.8	20,518	9.1	85,637
Nevada	6,864	56.7	3,982	32.9	925	7.6			344	2.8	2,882
New Hampshire	54,157	60.1	34,071	37.8	1,090	1.2	750	.8	83	.1	20,086
New Jersey	245,164	56.7	164,566	38.1	9,587	2.2	6,845	1.6	6,085	1.4	80,598
New York	859,533	53.1	683,981	42.3	36,883	2.3	20,787	1.3	16,581	1.0	175,552
North Carolina	82,442	39.7	124,091	59.7	124	.1	342	.2	819	.4	41,649
North Dakota	52,595	75.1	14,273	20.4	2,009	2.9	1,137	1.6			38,322
Ohio	600,095	59.8	344,674	34.3	36,260	3.6	19,339	1.9	4,027	.4	255,421
Oregon	60,309	67.3	17,327	19.3	7,479	8.3	3,795	4.2	746	.8	42,982
Pennsylvania	840,949	68.0	337,998	27.3	21,863	1.8	33,717	2.7	2,211	.2	502,951
Rhode Island	41,605	60.6	24,839	36.2	956	1.4	768	1.1	488	.7	16,766
South Carolina	2,570	4.6	53,320	95.4							50,750
South Dakota	72,083	71.1	21,969	21.7	3,138	3.1	2,965	2.9	1,240	1.2	50,114
Tennessee	105,363	43.4	131,653	54.2	1,354	.6	1,889	.8	2,491	1.0	26,290
Texas	51,307	22.0	167,088	71.5	2,788	1.2	3,933	1.7	8,493	3.6	115,781
Utah	62,446	61.5	33,413	32.9	5,767	5.7					29,033
Vermont	40,459	78.0	9,777	18.8	859	1.7	792	1.5	1		30,682
Virginia	48,180	37.0	80,649	61.8	202	.2	1,379	1.1			32,469
Washington	101,540	70.0	28,098	19.4	10,023	6.9	3,229	2.2	2,261	1.6	73,442
West Virginia	132,620	55.3	100,855	42.0	1,573	.7	4,599	1.9	339	.1	31,765
Wisconsin	280,314	63.2	124,205	28.0	28,240	6.4	9,872	2.2	809	.2	156,109
Wyoming	20,489	66.9	8,930	29.2	987	3.2	208	.7			11,559
Totals	7,626,593	56.41	5,082,898	37.60	402,489	2.98	258,596	1.91	148,388	1.10	

1. For breakdown of "Other" vote, see minor candidate vote totals, p. 103.

1908 Presidential Election

Total Popular Votes: 14,882,734
Taft's Plurality: 1,269,457

STATE	WILLIAM H. TAFT (Republican)		WILLIAM J. BRYAN (Democrat)		EUGENE V. DEBS (Socialist)		EUGENE W. CHAFIN (Prohibition)		OTHER[1]		PLURALITY
	Votes	%	Votes	%	Votes	%	Votes	%	Votes	%	
Alabama	25,561	24.3	74,391	70.8	1,450	1.4	690	.7	3,060	2.9	48,830
Arkansas	56,684	37.3	87,020	57.3	5,842	3.9	1,026	.7	1,273	.8	30,336
California	214,398	55.5	127,492	33.0	28,659	7.4	11,770	3.0	4,306	1.1	86,906
Colorado	123,693	46.9	126,644	48.0	7,960	3.0	5,559	2.1	2		2,951
Connecticut	112,815	59.4	68,255	35.9	5,113	2.7	2,380	1.3	1,340	.7	44,560
Delaware	25,014	52.1	22,055	45.9	239	.5	670	1.4	29		2,959
Florida	10,654	21.6	31,104	63.0	3,747	7.6	1,356	2.8	2,499	5.1	20,450
Georgia	41,355	31.2	72,350	54.6	584	.4	1,452	1.1	16,763	12.7	30,995
Idaho	52,621	54.1	36,162	37.2	6,400	6.6	1,986	2.0	124	.1	16,459
Illinois	629,932	54.5	450,810	39.0	34,711	3.0	29,364	2.5	10,437	.9	179,122
Indiana	348,993	48.4	338,262	46.9	13,476	1.9	18,036	2.5	2,350	.3	10,731
Iowa	275,210	55.6	200,771	40.6	8,287	1.7	9,837	2.0	665	.1	74,439
Kansas	197,316	52.5	161,209	42.9	12,420	3.3	5,030	1.3	68	.2	36,107
Kentucky	235,711	48.0	244,092	49.7	4,093	.8	5,885	1.2	938	.2	8,381
Louisiana	8,958	11.9	63,568	84.6	2,514	3.4			77	.1	54,610
Maine	66,987	63.0	35,403	33.3	1,758	1.7	1,487	1.4	700	.7	31,584
Maryland	116,513	48.9	115,908	48.6	2,323	1.0	3,302	1.4	485	.2	605
Massachusetts	265,966	58.2	155,533	34.0	10,778	2.4	4,373	1.0	20,255	4.4	110,433
Michigan	333,313	61.9	174,619	32.5	11,527	2.1	16,785	3.1	1,880	.4	158,694
Minnesota	195,843	59.3	109,401	33.1	14,472	4.4	10,114	3.1	424	.1	86,442
Mississippi	4,363	6.5	60,287	90.1	978	1.5			1,276	1.9	55,924
Missouri	347,203	48.5	346,574	48.4	15,431	2.2	4,209	.6	2,424	.3	629
Montana	32,471	46.9	29,511	42.6	5,920	8.6	838	1.2	493	.7	2,960
Nebraska	126,997	47.6	131,099	49.1	3,524	1.3	5,179	1.9			4,102
Nevada	10,775	43.9	11,212	45.7	2,103	8.6			436	1.8	437
New Hampshire	53,144	59.3	33,655	37.6	1,299	1.5	905	1.0	592	.7	19,489
New Jersey	265,298	56.8	182,522	39.1	10,249	2.2	4,930	1.1	4,112	.9	82,776
New York	870,070	53.1	667,468	40.7	38,451	2.4	22,667	1.4	39,694	2.4	202,602
North Carolina	114,887	45.5	136,928	54.2	372	.2	354	.1	13		22,041
North Dakota	57,680	61.0	32,884	34.8	2,421	2.6	1,496	1.6	43	.1	24,796
Ohio	572,312	51.0	502,721	44.8	33,795	3.0	11,402	1.0	1,322	.1	69,591
Oklahoma	110,473	43.5	122,362	48.1	21,425	8.4					11,889
Oregon	62,454	56.5	37,792	34.2	7,322	6.6	2,682	2.4	289	.3	24,662
Pennsylvania	745,779	58.8	448,782	35.4	33,914	2.7	36,694	2.9	2,281	.2	296,997
Rhode Island	43,942	60.8	24,706	34.2	1,365	1.9	1,016	1.4	1,288	1.8	19,236
South Carolina	3,945	5.9	62,288	93.8	100	.2			46	.1	58,343
South Dakota	67,536	58.8	40,266	35.1	2,846	2.5	4,039	3.5	88	.1	27,270
Tennessee	117,977	45.9	135,608	52.7	1,870	.7	301	.1	1,424	.6	17,631
Texas	65,605	22.4	216,662	74.0	7,779	2.7	1,626	.6	1,241	.4	151,057
Utah	61,165	56.2	42,610	39.2	4,890	4.5			92	.1	18,555
Vermont	39,552	75.1	11,496	21.8			799	1.5	833	1.6	28,056
Virginia	52,572	38.4	82,946	60.5	255	.2	1,111	.8	181	.1	30,374
Washington	106,062	57.8	58,383	31.8	14,177	7.7	4,700	2.6	248	.1	47,679
West Virginia	137,869	53.4	111,410	43.2	3,679	1.4	5,140	2.0		.1	26,459
Wisconsin	247,744	54.5	166,662	36.7	28,147	6.2	11,565	2.5	320	.1	81,082
Wyoming	20,846	55.4	14,918	39.7	1,715	4.6	66	.2	63	.2	5,928
Totals	7,676,258	51.58	6,406,801	43.05	420,380	2.82	252,821	1.70	126,474	.85	

1. For breakdown of "Other" vote, see minor candidate vote totals, p. 103.

1912 Presidential Election

Total Popular Votes: 15,040,963
Wilson's Plurality: 2,173,945

STATE	WOODROW WILSON (Democrat)		THEODORE ROOSEVELT (Progressive)		WILLIAM H. TAFT (Republican)		EUGENE V. DEBS (Socialist)		OTHER[1]		PLURALITY
	Votes	%	Votes	%	Votes	%	Votes	%	Votes	%	
Alabama	82,438	69.9	22,680	19.2	9,807	8.3	3,029	2.6	5		59,758
Arizona	10,324	43.6	6,949	29.3	2,986	12.6	3,163	13.4	265	1.1	3,375
Arkansas	68,814	55.0	21,644	17.3	25,585	20.5	8,153	6.5	908	.7	43,229
California	283,436	41.8	283,610	41.8	3,847	.6	79,201	11.7	27,783	4.1	174
Colorado	113,912	42.8	71,752	27.0	58,386	22.0	16,366	6.2	5,538	2.1	42,160
Connecticut	74,561	39.2	34,129	17.9	68,324	35.9	10,056	5.3	3,334	1.8	6,237
Delaware	22,631	46.5	8,886	18.3	15,997	32.9	556	1.1	620	1.3	6,634
Florida	35,343	69.5	4,555	9.0	4,279	8.4	4,806	9.5	1,854	3.7	30,537
Georgia	93,087	76.6	21,985	18.1	5,191	4.3	1,058	.9	149	.1	71,102
Idaho	33,921	32.1	25,527	24.1	32,810	31.0	11,960	11.3	1,536	1.5	1,111
Illinois	405,048	35.3	386,478	33.7	253,593	22.1	81,278	7.1	19,776	1.7	18,570
Indiana	281,890	43.1	162,007	24.8	151,267	23.1	36,931	5.6	22,379	3.4	119,883
Iowa	185,322	37.6	161,819	32.9	119,805	24.3	16,967	3.5	8,440	1.7	23,503
Kansas	143,663	39.3	120,210	32.9	74,845	20.5	26,779	7.3	63		23,453
Kentucky	219,484	48.5	101,766	22.5	115,510	25.5	11,646	2.6	4,308	1.0	103,974
Louisiana	60,871	76.8	9,283	11.7	3,833	4.8	5,261	6.6			51,588
Maine	51,113	39.4	48,495	37.4	26,545	20.5	2,541	2.0	947	.7	2,618
Maryland	112,674	48.6	57,789	24.9	54,956	23.7	3,996	1.7	2,566	1.1	54,885
Massachusetts	173,408	35.5	142,228	29.1	155,948	32.0	12,616	2.6	3,856	.8	17,460
Michigan	150,201	27.4	213,243	38.9	151,434	27.6	23,060	4.2	10,033	1.8	61,809
Minnesota	106,426	31.8	125,856	37.7	64,334	19.3	27,505	8.2	10,098	3.0	19,430
Mississippi	57,324	88.9	3,549	5.5	1,560	2.4	2,050	3.2			53,775
Missouri	330,746	47.4	124,375	17.8	207,821	29.8	28,466	4.1	7,158	1.0	122,925
Montana	28,129	35.1	22,709	28.3	18,575	23.1	10,811	13.5	32		5,420
Nebraska	109,008	43.7	72,681	29.1	54,226	21.7	10,185	4.1	3,383	1.4	36,327
Nevada	7,986	39.7	5,620	27.9	3,196	15.9	3,313	16.5			2,366
New Hampshire	34,724	39.5	17,794	20.2	32,927	37.4	1,981	2.3	535	.6	1,797
New Jersey	178,638	41.2	145,679	33.6	89,066	20.5	15,948	3.7	4,332	1.0	32,959
New Mexico	20,437	41.9	8,347	17.1	17,164	35.2	2,859	5.9			3,273
New York	655,573	41.3	390,093	24.6	455,487	28.7	63,434	4.0	23,728	1.5	200,086
North Carolina	144,407	59.2	69,135	28.4	29,129	12.0	987	.4	118	.1	75,272
North Dakota	29,549	34.2	25,726	29.8	22,990	26.6	6,966	8.1	1,243	1.4	3,823
Ohio	424,834	41.0	229,807	22.2	278,168	26.8	90,164	8.7	14,141	1.4	146,666
Oklahoma	119,143	47.0			90,726	35.8	41,630	16.4	2,195	.9	28,417
Oregon	47,064	34.3	37,600	27.4	34,673	25.3	13,343	9.7	4,360	3.2	9,464
Pennsylvania	395,637	32.5	444,894	36.5	273,360	22.5	83,614	6.9	20,231	1.7	49,257
Rhode Island	30,412	39.0	16,878	21.7	27,703	35.6	2,049	2.6	852	1.1	2,709
South Carolina	48,355	95.9	1,293	2.6	536	1.1	164	.3	55	.1	47,062
South Dakota	48,942	42.1	58,811	50.6			4,664	4.0	3,910	3.4	9,869
Tennessee	133,021	52.8	54,041	21.5	60,475	24.0	3,564	1.4	832	.3	72,546
Texas	218,921	72.7	26,715	8.9	28,310	9.4	24,884	8.3	2,131	.7	190,611
Utah	36,576	32.6	24,174	21.5	42,013	37.4	8,999	8.0	510	.5	5,437
Vermont	15,350	24.4	22,129	35.2	23,303	37.1	928	1.5	1,094	1.7	1,174
Virginia	90,332	66.0	21,776	15.9	23,288	17.0	820	.6	759	.6	67,044
Washington	86,840	26.9	113,698	35.2	70,445	21.8	40,134	12.4	11,682	3.6	26,858
West Virginia	113,097	42.1	79,112	29.4	56,754	21.1	15,248	5.7	4,517	1.7	33,985
Wisconsin	164,230	41.1	62,448	15.6	130,596	32.7	33,476	8.4	9,225	2.3	33,634
Wyoming	15,310	36.2	9,232	21.8	14,560	34.4	2,760	6.5	421	1.0	750
Totals	6,293,152	41.84	4,119,207	27.39	3,486,333	23.18	900,369	5.99	241,902	1.61	

1. For breakdown of "Other" vote, see minor candidate vote totals, p. 103.

1916 Presidential Election

Total Popular Votes: 18,535,022
Wilson's Plurality: 579,511

STATE	WOODROW WILSON (Democrat) Votes	%	CHARLES E. HUGHES (Republican) Votes	%	ALLAN L. BENSON (Socialist) Votes	%	J. FRANK HANLY (Prohibition) Votes	%	OTHER[1] Votes	%	PLURALITY
Alabama	99,116	76.0	28,662	22.0	1,916	1.5	741	.6			70,454
Arizona	33,170	57.2	20,522	35.4	3,174	5.5	1,153	2.0			12,648
Arkansas	112,211	66.0	48,879	28.7	6,999	4.1	2,015	1.2			63,332
California	465,936	46.6	462,516	46.3	42,898	4.3	27,713	2.8	187		3,420
Colorado	177,496	60.8	101,388	34.7	9,951	3.4	2,793	1.0	409	.1	76,108
Connecticut	99,786	46.7	106,514	49.8	5,179	2.4	1,789	.8	606	.3	6,728
Delaware	24,753	47.8	26,011	50.2	480	.9	566	1.1			1,258
Florida	55,984	69.3	14,611	18.1	5,353	6.6	4,786	5.9			41,373
Georgia	127,754	79.5	11,294	7.0	941	.6			20,692	12.9	107,062[2]
Idaho	70,054	52.0	55,368	41.1	8,066	6.0	1,127	.8			14,686
Illinois	950,229	43.3	1,152,549	52.6	61,394	2.8	26,047	1.2	2,488	.1	202,320
Indiana	334,063	46.5	341,005	47.4	21,860	3.0	16,368	2.3	5,557	.8	6,942
Iowa	221,699	42.9	280,439	54.3	10,976	2.1	3,371	.7	2,253	.1	58,740
Kansas	314,588	50.0	277,658	44.1	24,685	3.9	12,882	2.1			36,930
Kentucky	269,990	51.9	241,854	46.5	4,734	.9	3,039	.6	461	.1	28,136
Louisiana	79,875	85.9	6,466	7.0	284	.3			6,349	6.8	73,409
Maine	64,033	47.0	69,508	51.0	2,177	1.6	596	.4			5,475
Maryland	138,359	52.8	117,347	44.8	2,674	1.0	2,903	1.1	756	.3	21,012
Massachusetts	247,885	46.6	268,784	50.5	11,058	2.1	2,993	.6	1,102	.2	20,899
Michigan	283,993	43.9	337,952	52.2	16,012	2.5	8,085	1.3	831	.1	53,959
Minnesota	179,155	46.3	179,544	46.4	20,117	5.2	7,793	2.0	758	.2	389
Mississippi	80,422	93.3	4,253	4.9	1,484	1.7			520		76,169
Missouri	398,032	50.6	369,339	46.9	14,612	1.9	3,887	.5	903	.1	28,693
Montana	101,104	56.8	66,933	37.6	9,634	5.4			338	.2	34,171
Nebraska	158,827	55.3	117,771	41.0	7,141	2.5	2,952	1.0	624	.2	41,056
Nevada	17,776	53.4	12,127	36.4	3,065	9.2	346	1.0			5,649
New Hampshire	43,781	49.1	43,725	49.1	1,318	1.5	303	.3			56
New Jersey	211,018	42.7	268,982	54.4	10,405	2.1	3,182	.6	855	.2	57,964
New Mexico	33,693	50.4	31,097	46.5	1,977	3.0	112	.2			2,596
New York	759,426	44.5	879,238	57.5	45,944	2.7	19,031	1.1	2,666	.2	119,812
North Carolina	168,383	58.1	120,890	41.7	509	.2	55				47,493
North Dakota	55,206	47.8	53,471	46.3	5,716	5.0	997	.9			1,735
Ohio	604,161	51.9	514,753	44.2	38,092	3.3	8,085	.7			89,408
Oklahoma	148,123	50.7	97,233	33.3	45,091	15.4	1,646	.6	234	.1	50,890
Oregon	120,087	45.9	126,813	48.5	9,711	3.7	4,729	1.8	310	.1	6,726
Pennsylvania	521,784	40.2	703,823	54.3	42,638	3.3	28,525	2.2	419		182,039
Rhode Island	40,394	46.0	44,858	51.1	1,914	2.2	470	.5	180	.2	4,464
South Carolina	61,845	96.7	1,550	2.4	135	.2			420	.7	60,295
South Dakota	59,191	45.9	64,217	49.8	3,760	2.9	1,774	1.4			5,026
Tennessee	153,280	56.3	116,223	42.7	2,542	.9	145	.1			37,057
Texas	287,415	77.0	64,999	17.4	18,960	5.1	1,936	.5			222,416
Utah	84,145	58.8	54,137	37.8	4,460	3.1	149	.1	254	.2	30,008
Vermont	22,708	35.2	40,250	62.4	798	1.2	709	1.1	10		17,542
Virginia	101,840	67.0	48,384	31.8	1,056	.7	678	.5	67		53,456
Washington	183,388	48.1	167,208	43.9	22,800	6.0	6,868	1.8	730	.2	16,180
West Virginia	140,403	48.5	143,124	49.4	6,144	2.1					2,721
Wisconsin	191,363	42.8	220,822	49.4	27,631	6.2	7,318	1.6			29,459
Wyoming	28,376	54.7	21,698	41.8	1,459	2.8	373	.7			6,678
Totals	**9,126,300**	**49.24**	**8,546,789**	**46.11**	**589,924**	**3.18**	**221,030**	**1.19**	**50,979**	**.28**	

1. For breakdown of "Other" vote, see minor candidate vote totals, p. 103.
2. Plurality of 107,062 votes is calculated on the basis of 20,692 votes cast for the Progressive Party.

1920 Presidential Election

Total Popular Votes: 26,753,786
Harding's Plurality: 6,992,430

STATE	WARREN G. HARDING (Republican)		JAMES M. COX (Democrat)		EUGENE V. DEBS (Socialist)		PARLEY P. CHRISTENSEN (Farmer-Labor)		OTHER[1]		PLURALITY
	Votes	%	Votes	%	Votes	%	Votes	%	Votes	%	
Alabama	74,719	31.9	156,064	66.7	2,402	1.0			766	.3	81,345
Arizona	37,016	55.6	29,546	44.4							7,470
Arkansas	71,107	38.7	107,406	58.5	5,108	2.8					36,299
California	624,992	66.2	229,191	24.3	64,076	6.8			25,672	2.7	395,801
Colorado	171,709	59.4	103,721	35.9	7,860	2.7	2,898	1.0	2,807	1.0	67,988
Connecticut	229,238	62.7	120,721	33.0	10,350	2.8	1,947	.5	3,262	.9	108,517
Delaware	52,858	55.7	39,911	42.1	988	1.0	82	.1	1,025	1.1	12,947
Florida[2]	44,853	30.8	90,515	62.0	5,189	3.6			5,124	3.5	45,662
Georgia	42,981	28.7	106,112	70.9	558	.4					63,131
Idaho	88,975	65.6	46,579	34.3	38				32		42,396
Illinois	1,420,480	67.8	534,395	25.5	74,747	3.6	49,632	2.4	15,461	.8	886,085
Indiana	696,370	55.1	511,364	40.5	24,713	2.0	16,499	1.3	14,028	1.1	185,006
Iowa	634,674	70.9	227,924	25.5	16,981	1.9	10,321	1.2	5,185	.6	406,750
Kansas	369,268	64.8	185,464	32.5	15,511	2.7			75		183,804
Kentucky	451,480	49.2	457,203	49.8	6,409	.7			3,250	.4	5,723
Louisiana	38,539	30.5	87,355	69.2					342	.3	48,816
Maine	136,355	65.5	69,306	33.3	2,210	1.1			310	.2	67,049
Maryland	236,117	55.1	180,626	42.2	8,876	2.1	1,645	.4	1,186	.3	55,491
Massachusetts	681,153	68.6	276,691	27.8	32,265	3.3			3,607	.4	404,462
Michigan	755,941	72.8	231,046	22.3	28,446	2.7	10,163	1.0	12,385	1.2	524,895
Minnesota	519,421	70.6	142,994	19.4	56,106	7.6			17,317	2.4	376,427
Mississippi	11,527	14.0	69,252	84.0	1,639	2.0					57,725
Missouri	727,252	54.6	574,799	43.2	20,342	1.5	3,108	.2	6,739	.5	152,453
Montana	109,680	61.0	57,746	32.1			12,283	6.8			51,934
Nebraska	247,498	64.7	119,608	31.3	9,600	2.5			6,037	1.6	127,890
Nevada	15,479	56.9	9,851	36.2	1,864	6.9					5,628
New Hampshire	95,196	59.8	62,662	39.4	1,234	.8					32,534
New Jersey	611,541	67.7	256,887	28.4	27,141	3.0	2,200	.2	6,114	.7	354,654
New Mexico	57,634	54.7	46,668	44.3			1,097	1.0			10,966
New York	1,871,167	64.6	781,238	27.0	203,201	7.0	18,413	.6	24,494	.9	1,089,929
North Carolina	232,819	43.2	305,367	56.7	446	.1			17		72,548
North Dakota	158,997	77.7	37,409	18.3	8,273	4.0					121,588
Ohio	1,182,022	58.5	780,037	38.6	57,147	2.8			2,447	.1	401,985
Oklahoma	243,465	50.2	215,798	44.5	25,698	5.3					27,667
Oregon	143,592	60.2	80,019	33.6	9,801	4.1			5,110	2.2	63,573
Pennsylvania	1,218,216	65.8	503,843	27.2	70,571	3.8	15,705	.9	44,282	2.4	714,373
Rhode Island	107,463	64.0	55,062	32.8	4,351	2.6			1,105	.7	52,401
South Carolina	2,244	3.4	64,170	96.1	28				366	.6	61,926
South Dakota	109,874	60.7	35,938	19.8			34,406	19.0	900	.5	73,936
Tennessee	219,229	51.2	206,558	48.3	2,249	.5					12,671
Texas	114,384	23.5	288,933	59.4	8,122	1.7			75,010	15.4	174,549
Utah	81,555	55.9	56,639	38.8	3,159	2.2	4,475	3.1			24,916
Vermont	67,964	75.8	20,884	23.3					818	.9	47,080
Virginia	87,456	37.9	141,670	61.3	808	.4	240	.1	826	.4	54,214
Washington	223,137	56.0	84,298	21.1	8,913	2.2	77,246	19.4	5,111	1.3	138,839
West Virginia	282,010	55.3	220,789	43.3	5,609	1.1			1,526	.3	61,221
Wisconsin	498,576	71.1	113,196	16.2	80,635	11.5			8,648	1.2	385,380
Wyoming	35,091	64.2	17,429	31.9			2,180	4.0			17,662
Totals	**16,133,314**	**60.30**	**9,140,884**	**34.17**	**913,664**	**3.42**	**264,540**	**.99**	**301,384**	**1.13**	

1. For breakdown of "Other" vote, see minor candidate vote totals, p. 103.
2. Figures from Petersen, op. cit., p. 83.

1924 Presidential Election

Total Popular Votes: 29,075,959
Coolidge's Plurality: 7,331,384

STATE	CALVIN COOLIDGE (Republican) Votes	%	JOHN W. DAVIS (Democrat) Votes	%	ROBERT M. LAFOLLETTE (Progressive) Votes	%	HERMAN P. FARIS (Prohibition) Votes	%	OTHER[1] Votes	%	PLURALITY
Alabama	40,615	25.0	113,138	69.7	8,040	5.0	562	.4			72,523
Arizona	30,516	41.3	26,235	35.5	17,210	23.3					4,281
Arkansas	40,518	29.3	84,759	61.2	13,146	9.5			10		44,241
California	733,196	57.2	105,514	8.2	424,649	33.1	18,436	1.4	122		308,547
Colorado	193,956	59.4	75,238	23.0	57,368	17.6					118,718
Connecticut	246,322	61.5	110,184	27.5	42,416	10.6			1,373	.3	136,138
Delaware	52,441	57.7	33,445	36.8	4,979	5.5			16		18,996
Florida	30,633	28.1	62,083	56.9	8,625	7.9	5,498	5.0	2,315	2.1	31,450
Georgia	30,300	18.2	123,260	74.1	12,687	7.6					92,960
Idaho	72,084	48.1	24,217	16.2	53,664	35.8					18,420
Illinois	1,453,321	58.8	576,975	23.4	432,027	17.5	2,367	.1	5,377	.2	876,346
Indiana	703,042	55.3	492,245	38.7	71,700	5.6	4,416	.4	987	.1	210,797
Iowa	537,458	55.0	160,382	16.4	274,448	28.1			4,482	.5	263,010
Kansas	407,671	61.5	156,320	23.6	98,462	14.9			3		251,351
Kentucky	396,758	48.8	375,543	46.1	38,465	4.7			3,093	.4	21,215
Louisiana	24,670	20.2	93,218	76.4					4,063	3.3	68,548
Maine	138,440	72.0	41,964	21.8	11,382	5.9			406	.2	96,476
Maryland	162,414	45.3	148,072	41.3	47,157	13.2			987	.3	14,342
Massachusetts	703,476	62.3	280,817	24.9	141,225	12.5			4,304	.4	422,659
Michigan	874,631	75.4	152,359	13.1	122,014	10.5	6,085	.5	5,330	.5	722,272
Minnesota	420,759	51.2	55,913	6.8	339,192	41.3			6,282	.8	81,567
Mississippi	8,384	7.5	100,057	89.4	3,448	3.1					91,673
Missouri	648,486	49.6	572,962	43.8	83,996	6.4	1,418	.1	1,231	.1	75,524
Montana	74,246	42.5	33,867	19.4	65,985	37.8			370	.2	8,261
Nebraska	218,985	47.2	137,299	29.6	105,681	22.8	1,594	.3			81,686
Nevada	11,243	41.8	5,909	22.0	9,769	36.3					1,474
New Hampshire	98,575	59.8	57,201	34.7	8,993	5.5					41,374
New Jersey	675,162	62.2	297,743	27.4	108,901	10.0	1,337	.1	2,936	.3	377,419
New Mexico	54,745	48.5	48,542	43.0	9,543	8.5					6,203
New York	1,820,058	55.8	950,796	29.1	474,913	14.6			18,172	.6	869,262
North Carolina	190,754	39.6	284,190	59.0	6,651	1.4	13				93,436
North Dakota	94,931	47.7	13,858	7.0	89,922	45.2			370	.2	5,009
Ohio	1,176,130	58.3	477,888	23.7	358,008	17.8			4,271	.2	698,242
Oklahoma	225,756	42.8	255,798	48.5	41,142	7.8			5,134	1.0	30,042
Oregon	142,579	51.0	67,589	24.2	68,403	24.5			908	.3	74,176
Pennsylvania	1,401,481	65.4	409,192	19.1	307,567	14.3	9,779	.5	16,700	.8	992,289
Rhode Island	125,286	59.6	76,606	36.5	7,628	3.6			595	.3	48,680
South Carolina	1,123	2.2	49,008	96.6	623	1.2			1		47,885
South Dakota	101,299	49.7	27,214	13.4	75,200	36.9					26,099
Tennessee	130,831	43.5	159,339	52.9	10,666	3.5	94		100		28,508
Texas	130,794	19.8	485,443	73.7	42,879	6.5					354,649
Utah	77,327	49.3	46,908	29.9	32,662	20.8					30,419
Vermont	80,498	78.2	16,124	15.7	5,943	5.8	316	.3	5		64,374
Virginia	73,328	32.8	139,717	62.5	10,369	4.6			189	.1	66,389
Washington	220,224	52.3	42,842	10.2	150,727	35.8			7,709	1.8	69,497
West Virginia	288,635	49.5	257,232	44.1	36,723	6.3			1,072	.2	31,403
Wisconsin	311,614	37.1	68,096	8.1	453,678	54.0	2,918	.4	4,441	.5	142,064
Wyoming	41,858	52.4	12,868	16.1	25,174	31.5					16,684
Totals	**15,717,553**	**54.06**	**8,386,169**	**28.84**	**4,814,050**	**16.56**	**54,833**	**.19**	**103,354**	**.36**	

1. For breakdown of "Other" vote, see minor candidate vote totals, p. 103.

1928 Presidential Election

Total Popular Votes: 36,790,364
Hoover's Plurality: 6,411,806

STATE	HERBERT C. HOOVER (Republican)		ALFRED E. SMITH (Democrat)		NORMAN M. THOMAS (Socialist)		WILLIAM Z. FOSTER (Communist)		OTHER[1]		PLURALITY
	Votes	%	Votes	%	Votes	%	Votes	%	Votes	%	
Alabama	120,725	48.5	127,796	51.3	460	.2					7,071
Arizona	52,533	57.6	38,537	42.2			184	.2			13,996
Arkansas	77,785	39.3	119,195	60.3	434	.2	317	.2			41,410
California	1,147,929	63.9	614,365	34.2	19,595	1.1	112		14,655	.8	533,564
Colorado	252,924	64.8	132,747	34.0	2,630	.7	675	.2	1,092	.3	120,177
Connecticut	296,614	53.6	252,040	45.6	3,019	.6	730	.1	622	.1	44,574
Delaware	68,860	65.8	35,354	33.8	329	.3	58	.1			33,506
Florida	144,168	57.1	100,721	39.9	4,036	1.6	3,704	1.5			43,447
Georgia	99,368	43.4	129,602	56.6	124	.1	64				30,234
Idaho	97,322	64.2	52,926	34.9	1,293	.9					44,396
Illinois	1,770,723	57.0	1,312,235	42.2	19,138	.6	3,581	.1	1,812	.1	458,488
Indiana	848,290	59.7	562,691	39.6	3,871	.3	321		6,141	.4	285,599
Iowa	623,570	61.8	379,011	37.6	2,960	.3	328		3,320	.3	244,559
Kansas	513,672	72.0	193,003	27.1	6,205	.9	319				320,669
Kentucky	558,064	59.3	381,060	40.5	846	.1	307		354		177,004
Louisiana	51,160	23.7	164,655	76.3							113,495
Maine	179,923	68.6	81,179	31.0	1,065	.4					98,744
Maryland	301,479	57.1	223,626	42.3	1,701	.3	636	.1	906	.2	77,853
Massachusetts	775,566	49.2	792,758	50.2	6,262	.4	2,461	.2	776	.1	17,192
Michigan	965,396	70.4	396,762	28.9	3,516	.3	2,881	.2	3,527	.3	568,634
Minnesota	560,977	57.8	396,451	40.8	6,774	.7	4,853	.5	1,921	.2	164,526
Mississippi	26,202	17.3	124,445	82.2					788	.5	98,243
Missouri	834,080	55.6	662,684	44.2	3,739	.3			342		171,396
Montana	113,472	58.4	78,638	40.5	1,690	.9	577	.3			34,834
Nebraska	345,745	63.2	197,950	36.2	3,433	.6					147,795
Nevada	18,327	56.5	14,090	43.5							4,237
New Hampshire	115,404	58.7	80,715	41.0	465	.2	173	.1			34,689
New Jersey	925,285	59.8	616,162	39.8	4,866	.3	1,240	.1	642		309,123
New Mexico	69,708	59.0	48,211	40.8			158	.1			21,497
New York	2,193,344	49.8	2,089,863	47.4	107,332	2.4	10,876	.3	4,211	.1	103,481
North Carolina	348,923	54.9	286,227	45.1							62,696
North Dakota	131,419	54.8	106,648	44.5	842	.4	936	.4			24,771
Ohio	1,627,546	64.9	864,210	34.5	8,683	.4	2,836	.1	5,071	.2	763,336
Oklahoma	394,046	63.7	219,174	35.4	3,924	.6			1,283	.2	174,872
Oregon	205,341	64.2	109,223	34.1	2,720	.9	1,094	.3	1,564	.5	96,118
Pennsylvania	2,055,382	65.2	1,067,586	33.9	18,647	.6	4,726	.2	4,271	.1	987,796
Rhode Island	117,522	49.6	118,973	50.2			283	.1	416	.2	1,451
South Carolina	5,858	8.5	62,700	91.4	47	.1					56,842
South Dakota	157,603	60.2	102,660	39.2	443	.2	224	.1	927	.4	54,943
Tennessee	195,195	55.5	156,169	44.4	590	.2	70				39,026
Texas	367,036	51.7	341,458	48.1	641	.1	209				25,578
Utah	94,485	53.5	80,985	45.9	954	.5	46				13,500
Vermont	90,404	66.9	44,440	32.9					347	.3	45,964
Virginia	164,609	53.9	140,146	45.9	250	.1	179	.1	180	.1	24,463
Washington	335,503	67.1	156,772	31.4	2,615	.5	1,083	.2	4,068	.8	178,731
West Virginia	375,551	58.4	263,784	41.0	1,313	.2	401	.1	1,703	.3	111,767
Wisconsin	544,205	53.5	450,259	44.3	18,213	1.8	1,528	.2	2,626	.3	93,946
Wyoming	52,748	63.7	29,299	35.4	788	1.0					23,449
Totals	21,411,991	58.20	15,000,185	40.77	266,453	.72	48,170	.13	63,565	.17	

1. For breakdown of "Other" vote, see minor candidate vote totals, p. 103.

1932 Presidential Election

Total Popular Votes: 39,749,382
Roosevelt's Plurality: 7,066,619

STATE	FRANKLIN D. ROOSEVELT (Democrat)		HERBERT C. HOOVER (Republican)		NORMAN M. THOMAS (Socialist)		WILLIAM Z. FOSTER (Communist)		OTHER[1]		PLURALITY
	Votes	%	Votes	%	Votes	%	Votes	%	Votes	%	
Alabama	207,732	84.7	34,647	14.1	2,060	.8	676	.3	13		173,085
Arizona	79,264	67.0	36,104	30.5	2,618	2.2	256	.2	9		43,160
Arkansas	186,829	86.3	27,465	12.7	1,166	.5	157	.1	952	.4	159,364
California	1,324,157	58.4	847,902	37.4	63,299	2.8			30,464	1.3	476,255
Colorado	250,151	54.9	188,364	41.3	13,591	3.0	758	.2	2,824	.6	61,787
Connecticut	281,632	47.4	288,420	48.5	20,480	3.5	1,364	.2	2,287	.4	6,788
Delaware	54,319	48.1	57,073	50.6	1,376	1.2	133	.1			2,754
Florida	206,307	74.9	69,170	25.1							137,137
Georgia	234,118	91.6	19,863	7.8	461	.2	23		1,125	.4	214,255
Idaho	109,479	58.7	71,312	38.2	526	.3	491	.3	4,660	2.5	38,167
Illinois	1,882,304	55.2	1,432,756	42.0	67,258	2.0	15,582	.5	10,026	.3	449,548
Indiana	862,054	54.7	677,184	42.9	21,388	1.4	2,187	.1	14,084	.9	184,870
Iowa	598,019	57.7	414,433	40.0	20,467	2.0	559	.1	3,209	.3	183,586
Kansas	424,204	53.6	349,498	44.1	18,276	2.3					74,706
Kentucky	580,574	59.1	394,716	40.2	3,858	.4	275		3,663	.4	185,858
Louisiana	249,418	92.8	18,853	7.0					533	.2	230,565
Maine	128,907	43.2	166,631	55.8	2,489	.8	162	.1	255	.1	37,724
Maryland	314,314	61.5	184,184	36.0	10,489	2.1	1,031	.2	1,036	.2	130,130
Massachusetts	800,148	50.6	736,959	46.6	34,305	2.2	4,821	.3	3,881	.2	63,189
Michigan	871,700	52.4	739,894	44.4	39,205	2.4	9,318	.6	4,648	.3	131,806
Minnesota	600,806	59.9	363,959	36.3	25,476	2.5	6,101	.6	6,501	.7	236,847
Mississippi	140,168	96.0	5,170	3.5	675	.5					134,998
Missouri	1,025,406	63.7	564,713	35.1	16,374	1.0	568		2,833	.2	460,693
Montana	127,476	58.8	78,134	36.0	7,902	3.7	1,801	.8	1,461	.7	49,342
Nebraska	359,082	63.0	201,177	35.3	9,876	1.7					157,905
Nevada	28,756	69.5	12,622	30.5							16,134
New Hampshire	100,680	49.0	103,629	50.4	947	.5	264	.1			2,949
New Jersey	806,394	49.5	775,406	47.6	42,981	2.6	2,908	.2	1,811	.1	30,988
New Mexico	95,089	62.8	54,146	35.7	1,771	1.2	133	.1	389	.3	40,943
New York	2,534,959	54.1	1,937,963	41.3	177,397	3.8	27,956	.6	10,339	.2	596,996
North Carolina	497,566	69.9	208,344	29.3	5,585	.8					289,222
North Dakota	178,350	69.6	71,772	28.0	3,521	1.4	830	.3	1,817	.7	106,578
Ohio	1,301,695	49.9	1,227,319	47.0	64,094	2.5	7,231	.3	9,389	.4	74,376
Oklahoma	516,468	73.3	188,165	26.7							328,303
Oregon	213,871	58.0	136,019	36.9	15,450	4.2	1,681	.5	1,730	.5	77,852
Pennsylvania	1,295,948	45.3	1,453,540	50.8	91,223	3.2	5,659	.2	12,807	.5	157,592
Rhode Island	146,604	55.1	115,266	43.3	3,138	1.2	546	.2	616	.2	31,338
South Carolina	102,347	98.0	1,978	1.9	82	.1			4		100,369
South Dakota	183,515	63.6	99,212	34.4	1,551	.5	364	.1	3,796	1.3	84,303
Tennessee	259,463	66.5	126,752	32.5	1,796	.5	254	.1	1,998	.5	132,711
Texas	767,585	88.2	97,852	11.2	4,416	.5	204		387	.1	669,733
Utah	116,749	56.6	84,513	41.0	4,087	2.0	946	.5			32,236
Vermont	56,266	41.1	78,984	57.7	1,533	1.1	195	.1	2		22,718
Virginia	203,979	68.5	89,634	30.1	2,382	.8	86		1,858	.6	114,345
Washington	353,260	57.5	208,645	33.9	17,080	2.8	2,972	.5	32,844	5.3	144,615
West Virginia	405,124	54.5	330,731	44.5	5,133	.7	444	.1	2,342	.3	74,393
Wisconsin	707,410	63.5	347,741	31.2	53,379	4.8	3,105	.3	3,165	.3	359,669
Wyoming	54,370	56.1	39,583	40.8	2,829	2.9	180	.2			14,787
Totals	22,825,016	57.42	15,758,397	39.64	883,990	2.22	102,221	.26	179,758	.45	

1. For breakdown of "Other" vote, see minor candidate vote totals, p. 103.

1936 Presidential Election

Total Popular Votes: 45,642,303
Roosevelt's Plurality: 11,068,093

STATE	FRANKLIN D. ROOSEVELT (Democrat)		ALFRED M. LANDON (Republican)		WILLIAM LEMKE (Union)		NORMAN M. THOMAS (Socialist)		OTHER[1]		PLURALITY
	Votes	%	Votes	%	Votes	%	Votes	%	Votes	%	
Alabama	238,131	86.4	35,358	12.8	543	.2	242	.1	1,397	.5	202,773
Arizona	86,722	69.9	33,433	26.9	3,307	2.7	317	.3	384	.3	53,289
Arkansas	146,756	81.8	32,049	17.9			446	.3	167	.1	114,707
California	1,766,836	67.0	836,431	31.7			11,325	.4	23,794	.9	930,405
Colorado	294,599	60.3	181,267	37.1	9,962	2.0	1,594	.3	824	.2	113,332
Connecticut	382,129	55.3	278,685	40.4	21,805	3.2	5,683	.8	2,421	.4	103,444
Delaware	69,702	54.6	54,014	42.3	442	.4	172	.1	3,273	2.5	15,688
Florida	249,117	76.1	78,248	23.9							170,869
Georgia	255,364	87.1	36,943	12.6	136	.1	68		660	.2	218,421
Idaho	125,683	63.0	66,232	33.2	7,677	3.9					59,451
Illinois	2,282,999	57.7	1,570,393	39.7	89,430	2.3	7,530	.2	5,362	.1	712,606
Indiana	934,974	56.6	691,570	41.9	19,407	1.2	3,856	.2	1,090	.1	243,404
Iowa	621,756	54.4	487,977	42.7	29,887	2.6	1,373	.1	1,944	.2	133,779
Kansas	464,520	53.7	397,727	46.0	497	.1	2,770	.3			66,793
Kentucky	541,944	58.5	369,702	39.9	12,532	1.4	649	.1	1,472	.2	172,242
Louisiana	292,802	88.8	36,697	11.1					93		256,105
Maine[2]	126,333	41.6	168,823	55.6	7,581	2.5	783	.3	720	.2	42,490
Maryland	389,612	62.4	231,435	37.0			1,629	.3	2,220	.4	158,177
Massachusetts	942,716	51.2	768,613	41.8	118,639	6.5	5,111	.3	5,278	.3	174,103
Michigan	1,016,794	56.3	699,733	38.8	75,795	4.2	8,208	.5	4,568	.3	317,061
Minnesota	698,811	61.8	350,461	31.0	74,296	6.6	2,872	.3	3,535	.3	348,350
Mississippi	157,333	97.0	4,467	2.8			342	.2			152,866
Missouri	1,111,043	60.8	697,891	38.2	14,630	.8	3,454	.2	1,617	.1	413,152
Montana	159,690	69.3	63,598	27.6	5,539	2.4	1,066	.5	609	.3	96,092
Nebraska	347,445	57.1	247,731	40.7	12,847	2.1					99,714
Nevada	31,925	72.8	11,923	27.2							20,002
New Hampshire	108,460	49.7	104,642	48.0	4,819	2.2			193	.1	3,818
New Jersey	1,083,549	59.6	719,421	39.6	9,405	.5	3,892	.2	2,860	.2	364,128
New Mexico	105,848	62.7	61,727	36.5	924	.6	343	.2	104	.1	44,121
New York	3,293,222	58.8	2,180,670	39.0			86,897	1.6	35,609	.6	1,112,552
North Carolina	616,141	73.4	223,294	26.6							392,847
North Dakota	163,148	59.6	72,751	26.6	36,708	13.4	552	.2	557	.2	90,397
Ohio	1,747,140	58.0	1,127,855	37.4	132,212	4.4			5,251	.2	619,285
Oklahoma	501,069	66.8	245,122	32.7			2,211	.3	1,328	.2	255,947
Oregon	266,733	64.4	122,706	29.6	21,831	5.3	2,143	.5	608	.2	144,027
Pennsylvania	2,353,987	56.9	1,690,200	40.8	67,478	1.6	14,599	.4	12,172	.3	663,787
Rhode Island	164,338	53.0	125,031	40.3	19,569	6.3			1,340	.4	39,307
South Carolina	113,791	98.6	1,646	1.4							112,145
South Dakota	160,137	54.0	125,977	42.5	10,338	3.5					34,160
Tennessee	328,083	68.9	146,520	30.8	296	.1	692	.2	960	.2	181,563
Texas	730,843	86.9	104,728	12.5	3,193	.4	1,067	.1	772	.1	626,115
Utah	150,248	69.3	64,555	29.8	1,121	.5	432	.2	323	.2	85,693
Vermont	62,124	43.2	81,023	56.4					542	.4	18,899
Virginia	234,980	70.2	98,336	29.4	233	.1	313	.1	728	.2	136,644
Washington	459,579	66.4	206,885	29.9	17,463	2.5	3,496	.5	4,908	.7	252,694
West Virginia	502,872	60.6	325,486	39.2			832	.1	1,173	.1	177,386
Wisconsin	802,984	63.8	380,828	30.3	60,297	4.8	10,626	.8	3,825	.3	422,156
Wyoming	62,624	60.6	38,739	37.5	1,653	1.6	200	.2	166	.2	23,885
Totals	27,747,636	60.79	16,679,543	36.54	892,492	1.96	187,785	.41	134,847	.30	

1. For breakdown of "Other" vote, see minor candidate vote totals, p. 103.
2. Figures from Petersen, op. cit., p. 94.

1940 Presidential Election

Total Popular Votes: 49,840,443
Roosevelt's Plurality: 4,927,188

STATE	FRANKLIN D. ROOSEVELT (Democrat)		WENDELL WILLKIE (Republican)		NORMAN M. THOMAS (Socialist)		ROGER W. BABSON (Prohibition)		OTHER[1]		PLURALITY
	Votes	%	Votes	%	Votes	%	Votes	%	Votes	%	
Alabama	250,723	85.2	42,167	14.3	100		698	.2	509	.2	208,556
Arizona	95,267	63.5	54,030	36.0			742	.5			41,237
Arkansas	157,258	78.4	42,122	21.0	301	.2	793	.4			115,136
California	1,877,618	57.4	1,351,419	41.3	16,506	.5	9,400	.3	13,848	.4	526,199
Colorado	265,364	48.4	279,022	50.9	1,899	.4	1,597	.3	378	.1	13,658
Connecticut	417,621	53.4	361,819	46.3					2,062	.3	55,802
Delaware	74,599	54.7	61,440	45.1	110	.1	187	.1			13,159
Florida	359,334	74.0	126,158	26.0							233,176
Georgia	265,194	84.8	46,495	14.9			983	.3	14		218,699
Idaho	127,842	54.4	106,509	45.3	484	.2			276	.1	21,333
Illinois	2,149,934	51.0	2,047,240	48.5	10,914	.3	9,190	.2			102,694
Indiana	874,063	49.0	899,466	50.5	2,075	.1	6,437	.4	706		25,403
Iowa	578,802	47.6	632,370	52.0			2,284	.2	1,976	.2	53,568
Kansas	364,725	42.4	489,169	56.9	2,347	.3	4,056	.5			124,444
Kentucky	557,312	57.4	410,384	42.3	1,062	.1	1,465	.2			146,928
Louisiana	319,751	85.9	52,446	14.1					108		267,305
Maine	156,478	48.8	163,951	51.1					411	.1	7,473
Maryland	384,552	58.3	269,534	40.8	4,093	.6	11		1,940	.3	115,018
Massachusetts	1,076,522	53.1	939,700	46.4	4,091	.2	1,370	.1	5,310	.3	136,822
Michigan	1,032,991	49.5	1,039,917	49.9	7,593	.4	1,795	.1	3,633	.2	6,926
Minnesota	644,196	51.5	596,274	47.7	5,454	.4			5,264	.4	47,922
Mississippi	168,267	95.7	7,363	4.2	193	.1					160,904
Missouri	958,476	52.3	871,009	47.5	2,226	.1	1,809	.1	209		87,467
Montana	145,698	58.8	99,579	40.2	1,443	.6	664	.3	489	.2	46,119
Nebraska	263,677	42.8	352,201	57.2							88,524
Nevada	31,945	60.1	21,229	39.9							10,716
New Hampshire	125,292	53.2	110,127	46.8							15,165
New Jersey	1,016,404	51.5	944,876	47.9	2,823	.1	852		9,260	.5	71,528
New Mexico	103,699	56.6	79,315	43.3	143	.1	100	.1			24,384
New York	3,251,918	51.6	3,027,478	48.0	18,950	.3	3,250	.1			224,440
North Carolina	609,015	74.0	213,633	26.0							395,382
North Dakota	124,036	44.2	154,590	55.1	1,279	.5	325	.1	545	.2	30,554
Ohio	1,733,139	52.2	1,586,773	47.8							146,366
Oklahoma	474,313	57.4	348,872	42.2			3,027	.4			125,441
Oregon	258,415	53.7	219,555	45.6	398	.1	154		2,678	.6	38,860
Pennsylvania	2,171,035	53.2	1,889,848	46.3	10,967	.3			6,864	.2	281,187
Rhode Island	182,182	56.7	138,653	43.2			74		239	.1	43,529
South Carolina	95,470	95.6	4,360	4.4							91,110
South Dakota	131,362	42.6	177,065	57.4							45,703
Tennessee	351,601	67.3	169,153	32.4	463	.1	1,606	.3			182,448
Texas	861,390	80.9	201,866	19.0	628	.1	928	.1	215		659,524
Utah	153,833	62.2	92,973	37.6	198	.1			191	.1	60,860
Vermont	64,269	44.9	78,371	54.8					422	.3	14,102
Virginia	235,961	68.1	109,363	31.6	282	.1	882	.3	120		126,598
Washington	462,145	58.2	322,123	40.6	4,586	.6	1,686	.2	3,293	.4	140,022
West Virginia	495,662	57.1	372,414	42.9							123,248
Wisconsin	704,811	50.2	679,206	48.3	15,071	1.1	2,148	.2	4,263	.3	25,605
Wyoming	59,287	52.8	52,633	46.9	148	.1	172	.2			6,654
Totals	27,263,448	54.70	22,336,260	44.82	116,827	.23	58,685	.12	65,223	.13	

1. For breakdown of "Other" vote, see minor candidate vote totals, p. 103.

1944 Presidential Election

Total Popular Votes: 47,974,819
Roosevelt's Plurality: 3,598,564

STATE	FRANKLIN D. ROOSEVELT (Democrat)		THOMAS E. DEWEY (Republican)		NORMAN M. THOMAS (Socialist)		CLAUDE A. WATSON (Prohibition)		OTHER[1]		PLURALITY
	Votes	%	Votes	%	Votes	%	Votes	%	Votes	%	
Alabama	198,904	81.3	44,478	18.2	189	.1	1,054	.4			154,426
Arizona	80,926	58.8	56,287	40.9			421	.3			24,639
Arkansas	148,965	70.0	63,556	29.8	438	.2					85,409
California	1,988,564	56.5	1,512,965	43.0	2,515	.1	14,770	.4	2,061	.1	475,599
Colorado[2]	234,331	46.4	268,731	53.2	1,977	.4					34,400
Connecticut	435,146	52.3	390,527	46.9	5,097	.6			1,220	.2	44,619
Delaware	68,166	54.4	56,747	45.3	154	.1	294	.2			11,419
Florida	339,377	70.3	143,215	29.7							196,162
Georgia	268,187	81.7	56,507	17.2	6		36		3,373	1.0	211,680
Idaho	107,399	51.6	100,137	48.1	282	.1	503	.2			7,262
Illinois	2,079,479	51.5	1,939,314	48.1	180		7,411	.2	9,677	.2	140,165
Indiana	781,403	46.7	875,891	52.4	2,223	.1	12,574	.8			94,488
Iowa	499,876	47.5	547,267	52.0	1,511	.1	3,752	.4	193		47,391
Kansas	287,458	39.2	442,096	60.3	1,613	.2	2,609	.4			154,638
Kentucky	472,589	54.5	392,448	45.2	535	.1	2,023	.2	317		80,141
Louisiana	281,564	80.6	67,750	19.4					69		213,814
Maine	140,631	47.5	155,434	52.4					335	.1	14,803
Maryland	315,983	52.0	292,150	48.0							23,833
Massachusetts	1,035,296	52.8	921,350	47.0			973	.1	3,046	.1	113,946
Michigan	1,106,899	50.2	1,084,423	49.2	4,598	.2	6,503	.3	2,800	.1	22,476
Minnesota	589,864	52.4	527,416	46.9	5,048	.5			3,176	.3	62,448
Mississippi[3]	168,621	93.6	11,613	6.4							157,008
Missouri	807,804	51.4	761,524	48.4	1,751	.1	1,195	.1	220		46,280
Montana	112,566	54.3	93,163	44.9	1,296	.6	340	.2			19,403
Nebraska	233,246	41.4	329,880	58.6							96,634
Nevada	29,623	54.6	24,611	45.4							5,012
New Hampshire	119,663	52.1	109,916	47.9	46						9,747
New Jersey	987,874	50.3	961,335	49.0	3,358	.2	4,255	.2	6,939	.4	26,539
New Mexico	81,338	53.5	70,559	46.4			147	.1			10,779
New York	3,304,238	52.3	2,987,647	47.3	10,553	.2			14,352	.2	316,591
North Carolina	527,408	66.7	263,155	33.3							264,253
North Dakota	100,144	45.5	118,535	53.8	954	.4	549	.3			18,391
Ohio	1,570,763	49.8	1,582,293	50.2							11,530
Oklahoma	401,549	55.6	319,424	44.2			1,663	.2			82,125
Oregon	248,635	51.8	225,365	46.9	3,785	.8	2,362	.5			23,270
Pennsylvania	1,940,481	51.1	1,835,054	48.4	11,721	.3	5,751	.2	1,789	.1	105,427
Rhode Island	175,356	58.6	123,487	41.3			433	.1			51,869
South Carolina	90,601	87.6	4,617	4.5			365	.4	7,799	7.5	82,802[4]
South Dakota	96,711	41.7	135,365	58.3							38,654
Tennessee	308,707	60.5	200,311	39.2	792	.2	882	.2			108,396
Texas	820,048	71.4	191,372	16.7	592	.1	1,013	.1	135,661	11.8	628,676
Utah	150,088	60.5	97,833	39.4	340	.1					52,255
Vermont	53,806	43.0	71,420	57.0					14		17,614
Virginia	242,276	62.4	145,243	37.4	417	.1	459	.1	90		97,033
Washington	486,774	56.8	361,689	42.2	3,824	.5	2,396	.3	1,645	.2	125,085
West Virginia	392,777	54.9	322,819	45.1							69,958
Wisconsin	650,413	48.6	674,532	50.4	13,205	1.0			1,002	.1	24,119
Wyoming	49,419	48.8	51,921	51.2							2,502
Totals	25,611,936	53.39	22,013,372	45.89	79,000	.16	74,733	.16	195,778	.41	

1. For breakdown of "Other" vote, see minor candidate vote totals, p. 103.
2. Figures from Richard M. Scammon, America at the Polls, (Pittsburgh, 1965), p. 71.
3. Ibid., p. 250.
4. Plurality of 82,802 votes is calculated on the basis of 7,799 votes cast for Southern Democratic electors.

1948 Presidential Election

Total Popular Votes: 48,692,442
Truman's Plurality: 2,135,570

STATE	HARRY S TRUMAN (Democrat)		THOMAS E. DEWEY (Republican)		J. STROM THURMOND (States' Rights Democrat)		HENRY A. WALLACE (Progressive)		OTHER[1]		PLURALITY
	Votes	%	Votes	%	Votes	%	Votes	%	Votes	%	
Alabama			40,930	19.0	171,443	79.7	1,522	.7	1,026	.5	130,513
Arizona	95,251	53.8	77,597	43.8			3,310	1.9	907	.5	17,654
Arkansas	149,659	61.7	50,959	21.0	40,068	16.5	751	.3	1,038	.4	98,700
California	1,913,134	47.6	1,895,269	47.1	1,228		190,381	4.7	21,526	.5	17,865
Colorado	267,288	51.9	239,714	46.5			6,115	1.2	2,120	.4	27,574
Connecticut	423,297	47.9	437,754	49.6			13,713	1.6	8,754	1.0	14,457
Delaware	67,813	48.8	69,588	50.0			1,050	.8	622	.5	1,775
Florida	281,988	48.8	194,280	33.6	89,755	15.5	11,620	2.0			87,708
Georgia	254,646	60.8	76,691	18.3	85,135	20.3	1,636	.4	736	.2	169,511
Idaho	107,370	50.0	101,514	47.3			4,972	2.3	960	.4	5,856
Illinois	1,994,715	50.1	1,961,103	49.2					28,228	.7	33,612
Indiana	807,833	48.8	821,079	49.6			9,649	.6	17,653	1.1	13,246
Iowa	522,380	50.3	494,018	47.6			12,125	1.2	9,749	.9	28,362
Kansas	351,902	44.6	423,039	53.6			4,603	.6	9,275	1.2	71,137
Kentucky	466,756	56.7	341,210	41.5	10,411	1.3	1,567	.2	2,714	.3	125,546
Louisiana	136,344	32.8	72,657	17.5	204,290	49.1	3,035	.7	10		67,946
Maine	111,916	42.4	150,234	56.9			1,884	.7			38,318
Maryland	286,521	47.8	294,814	49.2	2,467	.4	9,983	1.7	5,235	.9	8,293
Massachusetts	1,151,788	54.7	909,370	43.2			38,157	1.8	7,832	.4	242,418
Michigan	1,003,448	47.6	1,038,595	49.2			46,515	2.2	21,051	1.0	35,147
Minnesota	692,966	57.2	483,617	39.9			27,866	2.3	7,777	.6	209,349
Mississippi	19,384	10.1	4,995	2.5	167,538	87.2	225	.1			148,154
Missouri	917,315	58.1	655,039	41.5	42		3,998	.3	2,234	.1	262,276
Montana	119,071	53.1	96,770	43.2			7,307	3.3	1,124	.5	22,301
Nebraska	224,165	45.9	264,774	54.2							40,609
Nevada	31,290	50.4	29,357	47.3			1,469	2.4			1,933
New Hampshire	107,995	46.7	121,299	52.4	7		1,970	.9	169	.1	13,304
New Jersey	895,455	45.9	981,124	50.3			42,683	2.2	30,293	1.6	85,669
New Mexico	105,240	56.3	80,303	43.0			1,037	.6	253	.1	24,937
New York	2,780,204	45.0	2,841,163	46.0			509,559	8.3	46,283	.7	60,959
North Carolina	459,070	58.0	258,572	32.7	69,652	8.8	3,915	.5			200,498
North Dakota	95,812	43.4	115,139	52.2	374	.2	8,391	3.8	1,000	.5	19,327
Ohio	1,452,791	49.5	1,445,684	49.2			37,487	1.3			7,107
Oklahoma	452,782	62.8	268,817	37.3							183,965
Oregon	243,147	46.4	260,904	49.8			14,978	2.9	5,051	1.0	17,757
Pennsylvania	1,752,426	46.9	1,902,197	50.9			55,161	1.5	25,564	.7	149,771
Rhode Island	188,736	57.6	135,787	41.4			2,619	.8	560	.2	52,949
South Carolina	34,423	24.1	5,386	3.8	102,607	72.0	154	.1	1		68,184
South Dakota	117,653	47.0	129,651	51.8			2,801	1.1			11,998
Tennessee	270,402	49.1	202,914	36.9	73,815	13.4	1,864	.3	1,288	.2	67,488
Texas	750,700	65.4	282,240	24.6	106,909	9.3	3,764	.3	3,632	.3	468,460
Utah	149,151	54.0	124,402	45.0			2,679	1.0	74		24,749
Vermont	45,557	36.9	75,926	61.5			1,279	1.0	619	.5	30,369
Virginia	200,786	47.9	172,070	41.0	43,393	10.4	2,047	.5	960	.2	28,716
Washington	476,165	52.6	386,315	42.7			31,692	3.5	10,887	1.2	89,850
West Virginia	429,188	57.3	316,251	42.2			3,311	.4			112,937
Wisconsin	647,310	50.7	590,959	46.3			25,282	2.0	13,249	1.0	56,351
Wyoming	52,354	51.6	47,947	47.3			931	.9	193	.2	4,407
Totals	**24,105,587**	**49.51**	**21,970,017**	**45.12**	**1,169,134**	**2.40**	**1,157,057**	**2.38**	**290,647**	**.60**	

1. For breakdown of "Other" vote, see minor candidate vote totals, p. 103.

1952 Presidential Election

Total Popular Votes: 61,551,118
Eisenhower's Plurality: 6,621,485

STATE	DWIGHT D. EISENHOWER (Republican) Votes	%	ADLAI E. STEVENSON (Democrat) Votes	%	VINCENT HALLINAN (Progressive) Votes	%	STUART HAMBLEN (Prohibition) Votes	%	OTHER[1] Votes	%	PLURALITY
Alabama	149,231	35.0	275,075	64.6			1,814	.4			125,844
Arizona	152,042	58.4	108,528	41.7							43,514
Arkansas	177,155	43.8	226,300	55.9			886	.2	459	.1	49,145
California	2,897,310	56.3	2,197,548	42.7	24,692	.5	16,117	.3	7,561	.2	699,762
Colorado	379,782	60.3	245,504	39.0	1,919	.3			2,898	.5	134,278
Connecticut	611,012	55.7	481,649	43.9	1,466	.1			2,779	.3	129,363
Delaware	90,059	51.8	83,315	47.9	155	.1	234	.1	262	.1	6,744
Florida	544,036	55.0	444,950	45.0							99,086
Georgia	198,961	30.3	456,823	69.7					1		257,862
Idaho	180,707	65.4	95,081	34.4	443	.2					85,626
Illinois	2,457,327	54.8	2,013,920	44.9					9,811	.2	443,407
Indiana	1,136,259	58.1	801,530	41.0	1,222	.1	15,335	.8	979	.1	334,729
Iowa	808,906	63.8	451,513	35.6	5,085	.4	2,882	.2	358		357,393
Kansas	616,302	68.8	273,296	30.5			6,038	.7	530	.1	343,006
Kentucky	495,029	49.8	495,729	49.9	336		1,161	.1	893	.1	700
Louisiana	306,925	47.1	345,027	52.9							38,102
Maine	232,353	66.2	118,806	33.8							113,547
Maryland	499,424	55.4	395,337	43.8	7,313	.8					104,087
Massachusetts	1,292,325	54.2	1,083,525	45.5	4,636	.2	886		2,026	.1	208,800
Michigan	1,551,529	55.4	1,230,657	44.0	3,922	.1	10,331	.4	2,153	.1	320,872
Minnesota	763,211	55.3	608,458	44.1	2,666	.2	2,147	.2	3,001	.2	154,753
Mississippi	112,966	39.6	172,553	60.4							59,587
Missouri	959,429	50.7	929,830	49.1	987	.1	885	.1	931	.1	29,599
Montana	157,394	59.4	106,213	40.1	723	.3	548	.2	159	.1	51,181
Nebraska	421,603	69.2	188,057	30.9							233,546
Nevada	50,502	61.5	31,688	38.6							18,814
New Hampshire	166,287	60.9	106,663	39.1							59,624
New Jersey	1,373,613	56.8	1,015,902	42.0	5,589	.2	989		22,461	.9	357,711
New Mexico	132,170	55.5	105,435	44.2	225	.1	297	.1	250	.1	26,735
New York	3,952,815	55.5	3,104,601	43.6	64,211	.9			6,614	.1	848,214
North Carolina	558,107	46.1	652,803	53.9							94,696
North Dakota	191,712	71.0	76,694	28.4	344	.1	302	.1	1,075	.4	115,018
Ohio	2,100,391	56.8	1,600,367	43.2							500,024
Oklahoma	518,045	54.6	430,939	45.4							87,106
Oregon	420,815	60.5	270,579	38.9	3,665	.5					150,236
Pennsylvania	2,415,789	52.7	2,146,269	46.9	4,222	.1	8,951	.2	5,738	.1	269,520
Rhode Island	210,935	50.9	203,293	49.1	187	.1			83		7,642
South Carolina	168,043	49.3	172,957	50.7			1				4,914
South Dakota	203,857	69.3	90,426	30.7							113,431
Tennessee	446,147	50.0	443,710	49.7	887	.1	1,432	.2	379		2,437
Texas	1,102,818	53.1	969,227	46.7	294		1,983	.1	1,563	.1	133,591
Utah	194,190	58.9	135,364	41.1							58,826
Vermont	109,717	71.5	43,299	28.2	282	.2			203	.1	66,418
Virginia	349,037	56.3	268,677	43.4	311	.1			1,664	.3	80,360
Washington	599,107	54.3	492,845	44.7	2,460	.2			8,296	.8	106,262
West Virginia	419,970	48.1	453,578	51.9							33,608
Wisconsin	979,744	61.0	622,175	38.7	2,174	.1			3,277	.2	357,569
Wyoming	81,049	62.7	47,934	37.1			194	.2	76	.1	33,115
Totals	33,936,137	55.13	27,314,649	44.38	140,416	.23	73,413	.12	86,503	.14	

1. For breakdown of "Other" vote, see minor candidate vote totals, p. 103.

1956 Presidential Election

Total Popular Votes: 62,025,372
Eisenhower's Plurality: 9,555,073

STATE	DWIGHT D. EISENHOWER (Republican)		ADLAI E. STEVENSON (Democrat)		T. COLEMAN ANDREWS (Constitution)		ERIC HASS (Socialist-Labor)		OTHER[1]		PLURALITY
	Votes	%	Votes	%	Votes	%	Votes	%	Votes	%	
Alabama	195,694	39.5	279,542	56.4					20,333	4.1	83,848
Arizona	176,990	61.0	112,880	38.9	303	.1					64,110
Arkansas	186,287	45.8	213,277	52.5	7,008	1.7					26,990
California	3,027,668	55.4	2,420,135	44.3	6,087	.1	300		12,168	.2	607,533
Colorado	394,479	59.5	263,997	39.8	759	.1	3,308	.5	531	.1	130,482
Connecticut	711,837	63.7	405,079	36.3							306,758
Delaware	98,057	55.1	79,421	44.6			110	.1	400	.2	18,636
Florida	643,849	57.2	480,371	42.7					1,542	.1	163,478
Georgia	222,778	33.3	444,688	66.4					2,189	.3	221,910
Idaho	166,979	61.2	105,868	38.8	126	.1			16		61,111
Illinois	2,623,327	59.5	1,775,682	40.3			8,342	.2	56		847,645
Indiana	1,182,811	59.9	783,908	39.7			1,334	.1	6,554	.3	398,903
Iowa	729,187	59.1	501,858	40.7	3,202	.3	125		192		227,329
Kansas	566,878	65.4	296,317	34.2					3,048	.4	270,561
Kentucky[2]	572,192	54.3	476,453	45.2			358		4,802	.5	95,739
Louisiana	329,047	53.3	243,977	39.5					44,520	7.2	85,070
Maine	249,238	70.9	102,468	29.1							146,770
Maryland	559,738	60.0	372,613	40.0							187,125
Massachusetts	1,393,197	59.3	948,190	40.4			5,573	.2	1,546	.1	445,007
Michigan	1,713,647	55.6	1,359,898	44.2					6,923	.2	353,749
Minnesota	719,302	53.7	617,525	46.1			2,080	.2	1,098	.1	101,777
Mississippi	60,683	24.5	144,453	58.2					42,961	17.3	83,770
Missouri	914,289	49.9	918,273	50.1							3,984
Montana	154,933	57.1	116,238	42.9							38,695
Nebraska	378,108	65.5	199,029	34.5							179,079
Nevada	56,049	58.0	40,640	42.0							15,409
New Hampshire	176,519	66.1	90,364	33.8	111						86,155
New Jersey	1,606,942	64.7	850,337	34.2	5,317	.2	6,736	.3	14,980	.6	756,605
New Mexico	146,788	57.8	106,098	41.8	364	.1	69		607	.2	40,690
New York	4,340,340	61.2	2,750,769	38.8							1,589,571
North Carolina	575,069	49.3	590,530	50.7							15,461
North Dakota	156,766	61.7	96,742	38.1	483	.2					60,024
Ohio	2,262,610	61.1	1,439,655	38.9							822,955
Oklahoma	473,769	55.1	385,581	44.9							88,188
Oregon	406,393	55.3	329,204	44.8							77,189
Pennsylvania	2,585,252	56.5	1,981,769	43.3			7,447	.2	2,035		603,483
Rhode Island	225,819	58.3	161,790	41.7							64,029
South Carolina	75,634	25.2	136,278	45.4	2				88,509	29.5	47,769[3]
South Dakota	171,569	58.4	122,288	41.6							49,281
Tennessee	462,288	49.2	456,507	48.6	19,820	2.1			789	.1	5,781
Texas	1,080,619	55.3	859,958	44.0	14,591	.8					220,661
Utah	215,631	64.6	118,364	35.4							97,267
Vermont	110,390	72.2	42,540	27.8					39		67,850
Virginia	386,459	55.4	267,760	38.4	42,964	6.2	351	.1	444	.1	118,699
Washington	620,430	53.9	523,002	45.4			7,457	.7			97,428
West Virginia	449,297	54.1	381,534	45.9							67,763
Wisconsin	954,844	61.6	586,768	37.8	6,918	.5	710	.1	1,318	.1	368,076
Wyoming	74,573	60.1	49,554	39.9							25,019
Totals	35,585,245	57.37	26,030,172	41.97	108,055	.17	44,300	.07	257,600	.42	

1. For breakdown of "Other" vote, see minor candidate vote totals, p. 103.
2. Figures from Petersen, op. cit., p. 109.
3. Plurality of 47,769 votes is calculated on the basis of Stevenson's vote and the 88,-509 votes cast for unpledged electors.

1960 Presidential Election

Total Popular Votes: 68,828,960
Kennedy's Plurality: 114,673

STATE	JOHN F. KENNEDY (Democrat) Votes	%	RICHARD M. NIXON (Republican) Votes	%	ERIC HASS (Socialist-Labor) Votes	%	UNPLEDGED Votes	%	OTHER[1] Votes	%	PLURALITY
Alabama	318,303	56.8	236,110	42.1					6,083	1.1	82,193
Alaska	29,809	49.1	30,953	50.9							1,144
Arizona	176,781	44.4	221,241	55.5	469	.1					44,460
Arkansas[2]	215,049	50.2	184,508	43.1					28,952	6.8	30,541
California	3,224,099	49.6	3,259,722	50.1	1,051				21,706	.3	35,623
Colorado	330,629	44.9	402,242	54.6	2,803	.4			563	.1	71,613
Connecticut	657,055	53.7	565,813	46.3							91,242
Delaware	99,590	50.6	96,373	49.0	82				638	.3	3,217
Florida	748,700	48.5	795,476	51.5							46,776
Georgia	458,638	62.5	274,472	37.4					245		184,166
Hawaii	92,410	50.0	92,295	50.0							115
Idaho	138,853	46.2	161,597	53.8							22,744
Illinois	2,377,846	50.0	2,368,988	49.8	10,560	.2			15		8,858
Indiana	952,358	44.6	1,175,120	55.0	1,136	.1			6,746	.3	222,762
Iowa	550,565	43.2	722,381	56.7	230				634	.1	171,816
Kansas	363,213	39.1	561,474	60.5					4,138	.5	198,261
Kentucky	521,855	46.4	602,607	53.6							80,752
Louisiana	407,339	50.4	230,980	28.6					169,572	21.0	176,359
Maine	181,159	43.0	240,608	57.1							59,449
Maryland	565,808	53.6	489,538	46.4					3		76,270
Massachusetts	1,487,174	60.2	976,750	39.6	3,892	.2			1,664	.1	510,424
Michigan	1,687,269	50.9	1,620,428	48.8	1,718	.1			8,682	.3	66,841
Minnesota	779,933	50.6	757,915	49.2	962	.1			3,077	.2	22,018
Mississippi	108,362	36.3	73,561	24.7			116,248[3]	39.0			7,886
Missouri	972,201	50.3	962,218	49.7							9,983
Montana	134,891	48.6	141,841	51.1					847	.3	6,950
Nebraska	232,542	37.9	380,553	62.1							148,011
Nevada	54,880	51.2	52,387	48.8							2,493
New Hampshire	137,772	46.6	157,989	53.4							20,217
New Jersey	1,385,415	50.0	1,363,324	49.2	4,262	.2			20,110	.7	22,091
New Mexico	156,027	50.2	153,733	49.4	570	.2			777	.3	2,294
New York	3,830,085	52.5	3,446,419	47.3					14,319	.2	383,666
North Carolina	713,136	52.1	655,420	47.9							57,716
North Dakota	123,963	44.5	154,310	55.4					158	.1	30,347
Ohio	1,944,248	46.7	2,217,611	53.3							273,363
Oklahoma	370,111	41.0	533,039	59.0							162,928
Oregon	367,402	47.3	408,065	52.6					959	.1	40,663
Pennsylvania	2,556,282	51.1	2,439,956	48.7	7,185	.1			3,118	.1	116,326
Rhode Island	258,032	63.6	147,502	36.4							110,530
South Carolina	198,121	51.2	188,558	48.8					1		9,563
South Dakota	128,070	41.8	178,417	58.2							50,347
Tennessee	481,453	45.8	556,577	52.9					13,746	1.3	75,124
Texas	1,167,935	50.5	1,121,693	48.5					22,213	1.0	46,242
Utah	169,248	45.2	205,361	54.8					100		36,113
Vermont	69,186	41.4	98,131	58.7					7		28,945
Virginia	362,327	47.0	404,521	52.4	397	.1			4,204	.5	42,194
Washington	599,298	48.3	629,273	50.7	10,895	.9			2,106	.2	29,975
West Virginia	441,786	52.7	395,995	47.3							45,791
Wisconsin	830,805	48.1	895,175	51.8	1,310	.1			1,792	.1	64,370
Wyoming	63,331	45.0	77,451	55.0							14,120
Totals	34,221,344	49.72	34,106,671	49.55	47,522	.07	116,248	.17	337,175	.48	

1. For breakdown of "Other" vote, see minor candidate vote totals, p. 103.
2. Figures from Petersen, op. cit., p. 113.
3. Votes for unpledged electors who cast electoral votes for Harry F. Byrd (D Va.), which carried the state.

1964 Presidential Election

Total Popular Votes: 70,641,104
Johnson's Plurality: 15,948,746

STATE	LYNDON B. JOHNSON (Democrat)		BARRY M. GOLDWATER (Republican)		ERIC HASS (Socialist-Labor)		CLIFTON DEBERRY (Socialist Workers)		OTHER[1]		PLURALITY
	Votes	%	Votes	%	Votes	%	Votes	%	Votes	%	
Alabama			479,085	69.5					210,732	30.6	268,353[3]
Alaska	44,329	65.9	22,930	34.1							21,399
Arizona	237,753	49.5	242,535	50.5	482	.1					4,782
Arkansas	314,197	56.1	243,264	43.4					2,965	.5	70,933
California	4,171,877	59.1	2,879,108	40.8	489		378		5,725	.1	1,292,769
Colorado	476,024	61.3	296,767	38.2	302		2,537	.3	1,355	.2	179,257
Connecticut	826,269	67.8	390,996	32.1					1,313	.1	435,273
Delaware	122,704	61.0	78,078	38.8	113	.1			425	.2	44,626
D.C.[2]	169,796	85.5	28,801	14.5							140,995
Florida	948,540	51.2	905,941	48.9							42,599
Georgia	522,163	45.9	616,584	54.1					195		94,421
Hawaii	163,249	78.8	44,022	21.2							119,227
Idaho	148,920	50.9	143,557	49.1							5,363
Illinois	2,796,833	59.5	1,905,946	40.5					62		890,887
Indiana	1,170,848	56.0	911,118	43.6	1,374	.1			8,266	.4	259,730
Iowa	733,030	61.9	449,148	37.9	182		159		2,020	.2	283,882
Kansas	464,028	54.1	386,579	45.1	1,901	.2			5,393	.6	77,449
Kentucky	669,659	64.0	372,977	35.7					3,469	.3	296,682
Louisiana	387,068	43.2	509,225	56.8							122,157
Maine	262,264	68.8	118,701	31.2							143,563
Maryland	730,912	65.5	385,495	34.5							345,417
Massachusetts	1,786,422	76.2	549,727	23.4	4,755	.2			3,894	.2	1,236,695
Michigan	2,136,615	66.7	1,060,152	33.1	1,704	.1	3,817	.1	814		1,076,463
Minnesota	991,117	63.8	559,624	36.0	2,544	.2	1,177	.1			431,493
Mississippi	52,616	12.9	356,512	87.1							303,896
Missouri	1,164,344	64.1	653,535	36.0							510,809
Montana	164,246	59.0	113,032	40.6			332	.1	1,018	.4	51,214
Nebraska	307,307	52.6	276,847	47.4							30,460
Nevada	79,339	58.6	56,094	41.4							23,245
New Hampshire	182,065	63.6	104,029	36.4							78,036
New Jersey	1,867,671	65.6	963,843	33.9	7,075	.3	8,181	.3			903,828
New Mexico	194,015	59.0	132,838	40.4	1,217	.4			543	.2	61,177
New York	4,913,156	68.6	2,243,559	31.3	6,086	.1	3,211		268		2,669,597
North Carolina	800,139	56.2	624,841	43.9							175,298
North Dakota	149,784	58.0	108,207	41.9			224	.1	174	.1	41,577
Ohio	2,498,331	62.9	1,470,865	37.1							1,027,466
Oklahoma	519,834	55.8	412,665	44.3							107,169
Oregon	501,017	63.7	282,779	36.0					2,509	.3	218,238
Pennsylvania	3,130,954	64.9	1,673,657	34.7	5,092	.1	10,456	.2	2,531	.1	1,457,297
Rhode Island	315,463	80.9	74,615	19.1							240,848
South Carolina	215,723	41.1	309,048	58.9					8		93,325
South Dakota	163,010	55.6	130,108	44.4							32,902
Tennessee	635,047	55.5	508,965	44.5					34		126,082
Texas	1,663,185	63.3	958,566	36.5					5,060	.2	704,619
Utah	219,628	54.7	181,785	45.3							37,843
Vermont	108,127	66.3	54,942	33.7					20		53,185
Virginia	558,038	53.5	481,334	46.2	2,895	.3					76,704
Washington	779,699	62.0	470,366	37.4	7,772	.6	537				309,333
West Virginia	538,087	67.9	253,953	32.1							284,134
Wisconsin	1,050,424	62.1	638,495	37.7	1,204	.1	1,692	.1			411,929
Wyoming	80,718	56.6	61,998	43.4							18,720
Totals	**43,126,584**	**61.05**	**27,177,838**	**38.47**	**45,187**	**.06**	**32,701**	**.05**	**258,794**	**.37**	

1. For breakdown of "Other" vote, see minor candidate vote totals, p. 103.
2. Figures from Richard M. Scammon, America at the Polls, (Pittsburgh, 1965), p. 521.
3. Plurality of 268,353 votes is calculated on the basis of Goldwater's vote and the 210,732 votes cast for unpledged Democrats.

1968 Presidential Election

Total Popular Votes: 73,203,370
Nixon's Plurality: 510,645

STATE	RICHARD M. NIXON (Republican)		HUBERT H. HUMPHREY (Democrat)		GEORGE C. WALLACE (American Independent)		HENNING A. BLOMEN (Socialist Labor)		OTHER[1]		PLURALITY
	Votes	%	Votes	%	Votes	%	Votes	%	Votes	%	
Alabama	146,591	14.0	195,918	18.8	687,664	65.8			14,332	1.4	491,746
Alaska	37,600	45.3	35,411	42.7	10,024	12.1					2,189
Arizona	266,721	54.8	170,514	35.0	46,573	9.6	75		3,053	.6	96,207
Arkansas[2]	190,759	30.8	188,228	30.4	240,982	38.9					50,223
California	3,467,664	47.8	3,244,318	44.7	487,270	6.7	341		51,994	.7	223,346
Colorado	409,345	50.5	335,174	41.3	60,813	7.5	3,016	.4	2,851	.3	74,171
Connecticut	556,721	44.3	621,561	49.5	76,650	6.1			1,300	.1	64,840
Delaware	96,714	45.1	89,194	41.6	28,459	13.3					7,520
D.C.[3]	31,012	18.2	139,566	81.8							108,554
Florida	886,804	40.5	676,794	30.9	624,207	28.5					210,010
Georgia	380,111	30.4	334,440	26.8	535,550	42.8			173		155,439
Hawaii	91,425	38.7	141,324	59.8	3,469	1.5					49,899
Idaho	165,369	56.8	89,273	30.7	36,541	12.6					76,096
Illinois	2,174,774	47.1	2,039,814	44.2	390,958	8.5	13,878	.3	325		134,960
Indiana	1,067,885	50.3	806,659	38.0	243,108	11.5			5,909	.3	261,226
Iowa	619,106	53.0	476,699	40.8	66,422	5.7	241		5,463	.5	142,407
Kansas	478,674	54.8	302,996	34.7	88,921	10.2			2,192	.3	175,678
Kentucky	462,411	43.8	397,541	37.7	193,098	18.3			2,843	.3	64,870
Louisiana	257,535	23.5	309,615	28.2	530,300	48.3					220,685
Maine	169,254	43.1	217,312	55.3	6,370	1.6					48,058
Maryland	517,995	41.9	538,310	43.6	178,734	14.5					20,315
Massachusetts	766,844	32.9	1,469,218	63.0	87,088	3.7	6,180	.3	2,422	.1	702,374
Michigan	1,370,665	41.5	1,593,082	48.2	331,968	10.0	1,762	.1	8,773	.3	222,417
Minnesota	658,643	41.5	857,738	54.0	68,931	4.3	285		2,909	.2	199,095
Mississippi	88,516	13.5	150,644	23.0	415,349	63.5					264,705
Missouri	811,932	44.9	791,444	43.7	206,126	11.4					20,488
Montana	138,835	50.6	114,117	41.6	20,015	7.3			1,437	.5	24,718
Nebraska	321,163	59.8	170,784	31.8	44,904	8.4					150,379
Nevada	73,188	47.5	60,598	39.3	20,432	13.3					12,590
New Hampshire	154,903	52.1	130,589	43.9	11,173	3.8			633	.2	24,314
New Jersey	1,325,467	46.1	1,264,206	44.0	262,187	9.1	6,784	.2	16,751	.6	61,261
New Mexico	169,692	51.9	130,081	39.8	25,737	7.9			1,771	.5	39,611
New York	3,007,932	44.3	3,378,470	49.8	358,864	5.3	8,432	.1	36,368	.5	370,538
North Carolina	627,192	39.5	464,113	29.2	496,188	31.3					131,004
North Dakota	138,669	55.9	94,769	38.2	14,244	5.8			200	.1	43,900
Ohio	1,791,014	45.2	1,700,586	43.0	467,495	11.8	120		483		90,428
Oklahoma	449,697	47.7	301,658	32.0	191,731	20.3					148,039
Oregon	408,433	49.8	358,866	43.8	49,683	6.1			2,640	.3	49,567
Pennsylvania	2,090,017	44.0	2,259,403	47.6	378,582	8.0	4,977	.1	14,947	.3	169,386
Rhode Island	122,359	31.8	246,518	64.0	15,678	4.1			383		124,159
South Carolina	254,062	38.1	197,486	29.6	215,430	32.3					38,632
South Dakota	149,841	53.3	118,023	42.0	13,400	4.8					31,818
Tennessee	472,592	37.9	351,233	28.1	424,792	34.0					47,800
Texas	1,227,844	39.9	1,266,804	41.1	584,269	19.0			489		38,960
Utah	238,728	56.5	156,665	37.1	26,906	6.4			269	.1	82,063
Vermont	85,142	52.8	70,255	43.5	5,104	3.2			903	.6	14,887
Virginia	590,319	43.4	442,387	32.5	320,272	23.6	4,671	.3	2,281	.2	147,932
Washington	588,510	45.2	616,037	47.3	96,990	7.4	491		2,319	.2	27,527
West Virginia	307,555	40.8	374,091	49.6	72,560	9.6					66,536
Wisconsin	809,997	47.9	748,804	44.3	127,835	7.6	1,338	.1	3,564	.2	61,193
Wyoming	70,927	55.8	45,173	35.5	11,105	8.7					25,754
Totals	31,785,148	43.42	31,274,503	42.72	9,901,151	13.53	52,591	.07	189,977	.26	

1. *For breakdown of "Other" vote, see minor candidate vote totals, p. 103.*
2. *Figures from Richard M. Scammon,* America Votes *8, (Washington, 1970), p. 26.*
3. *Ibid., p. 433.*

1972 Presidential Election

Total Popular Votes: 77,727,590
Nixon's Plurality: 17,998,388

STATE	RICHARD M. NIXON (Republican) Votes	%	GEORGE S. MCGOVERN (Democrat) Votes	%	JOHN G. SCHMITZ (American) Votes	%	BENJAMIN SPOCK (People's) Votes	%	OTHER[1] Votes	%	PLURALITY
Alabama[2]	728,701	72.4	256,923	25.5	11,928	1.1			8,559	.9	471,778
Alaska	55,349	58.1	32,967	34.6	6,903	7.3					22,382
Arizona	402,812	61.6	198,540	30.4	21,208	3.3			30,945	4.7	204,272
Arkansas	448,541	68.9	199,892	30.7	2,887	.4					248,649
California	4,602,096	55.0	3,475,847	41.5	232,554	2.8	55,167	.7	2,198		1,126,249
Colorado	597,189	62.6	329,980	34.6	17,269	1.8	2,403	.3	7,043	.8	267,209
Connecticut	810,763	58.6	555,498	40.1	17,239	1.3			777	.1	255,265
Delaware	140,357	59.6	92,283	39.2	2,638	1.1			238	.1	48,074
D.C.[3]	35,226	21.6	127,627	78.1					568	.3	92,401
Florida	1,857,759	71.9	718,117	27.8					7,407	.3	1,139,642
Georgia	881,490	75.3	289,529	24.7							591,961
Hawaii	168,933	62.5	101,433	37.5							67,500
Idaho	199,384	64.2	80,826	26.0	28,869	9.3	903	.3	397	.1	118,558
Illinois	2,788,179	59.0	1,913,472	40.5	2,471	.1			19,114	.4	874,707
Indiana	1,405,154	66.1	708,568	33.3			4,544	.2	7,263	.3	696,586
Iowa	706,207	57.6	496,206	40.5	22,056	1.8			1,475	.1	210,001
Kansas	619,812	67.7	270,287	29.5	21,808	2.4			4,188	.5	349,525
Kentucky	676,446	63.4	371,159	34.8	17,627	1.7	1,118	.1	1,149	.1	305,287
Louisiana[4]	686,852	66.0	298,142	28.6	44,127	4.2			12,169	1.2	388,710
Maine	256,458	61.5	160,584	38.5							95,874
Maryland	829,305	61.3	505,781	37.4	18,726	1.4					323,524
Massachusetts	1,112,078	45.2	1,332,540	54.2	2,877	.1	101		11,160	.5	220,462
Michigan	1,961,721	56.2	1,459,435	41.8	63,321	1.8			5,848	.2	502,286
Minnesota	898,269	51.6	802,346	46.1	31,407	1.8	2,805	.2	6,825	.4	95,923
Mississippi	505,125	78.2	126,782	19.6	11,598	1.8			2,458	.4	378,343
Missouri	1,154,058	62.3	698,531	37.7							455,527
Montana	183,976	57.9	120,197	37.9	13,430	4.2					63,779
Nebraska	406,298	70.5	169,991	29.5							236,307
Nevada	115,750	63.7	66,016	36.3							49,734
New Hampshire	213,724	64.0	116,435	34.9	3,386	1.0			510	.2	97,289
New Jersey	1,845,502	61.6	1,102,211	36.8	34,378	1.2	5,355	.2	9,783	.3	743,291
New Mexico	235,606	61.1	141,084	36.6	8,767	2.3			474	.1	94,522
New York	4,192,778	57.3	2,951,084	40.3					17,968	.3	1,241,694
North Carolina	1,054,889	69.5	438,705	28.9	25,018	1.7					616,184
North Dakota	174,109	62.1	100,384	35.8	5,646	2.0			375	.1	73,725
Ohio	2,441,827	59.6	1,558,889	38.1	80,067	2.0			14,004	.3	882,938
Oklahoma	759,025	73.7	247,147	24.0	23,728	2.3					511,878
Oregon	486,686	52.5	392,760	42.3	46,211	5.0			2,289	.3	93,926
Pennsylvania	2,714,521	59.1	1,796,951	39.1	70,593	1.5			10,040	.2	917,570
Rhode Island	220,383	53.0	194,645	46.8					729	.2	25,738
South Carolina	477,044	70.8	186,824	27.7	10,075	1.5			17		290,220
South Dakota	166,476	54.2	139,945	45.5					994	.3	26,531
Tennessee	813,147	67.7	357,293	29.8	30,373	2.5			369		455,854
Texas	2,298,896	66.2	1,154,289	33.3	6,039	.2			12,057	.4	1,144,607
Utah	323,643	67.6	126,284	26.4	28,549	6.0					197,359
Vermont	117,149	62.9	68,174	36.6			1,010	.5			48,975
Virginia	988,493	67.8	438,887	30.1	19,721	1.4			9,918	.7	549,606
Washington	837,135	56.9	568,334	38.6	58,906	4.0	2,644	.2	3,828	.3	68,801
West Virginia	484,964	63.6	277,435	36.4							207,529
Wisconsin	989,430	53.4	810,174	43.7	47,525	2.6	2,701	.2	3,060	.1	179,256
Wyoming	100,464	69.0	44,358	30.5	748	.5					56,106
Totals	47,170,179	60.69	29,171,791	37.53	1,090,673	1.40	78,751	.10	216,196	.28	

1. For breakdown of "other" vote, see minor candidate vote totals, p. 103.
2. Figures from Richard Scammon *America Votes*, 10, (Washington, 1973), p. 25.
3. *Ibid.*, p. 415.
4. *Ibid.*, p. 156.

1976 Presidential Election

Total Popular Votes: 81,555,889
Carter's Plurality: 1,682,970

STATE	JIMMY CARTER (Democrat) Votes	%	GERALD R. FORD (Republican) Votes	%	EUGENE J. McCARTHY (Independent) Votes	%	ROGER MacBRIDE (Libertarian) Votes	%	OTHER[1] Votes	%	PLURALITY
Alabama	659,170	55.7	504,070	42.6	99	—	1,481	0.1	18,030	1.5	155,100
Alaska	44,058	35.7	71,555	57.9			6,785	5.5	1,176	1.0	27,497
Arizona	295,602	39.8	418,642	56.4	19,229	2.6	7,647	1.0	1,599	0.2	123,040
Arkansas	498,604	65.0	267,903	34.9	639	0.1			389	0.1	230,701
California	3,742,284	47.6	3,882,244	49.3	58,412	0.7	56,388	0.7	127,789	1.6	139,960
Colorado	460,353	42.6	584,367	54.0	26,107	2.4	5,330	0.5	5,397	0.5	124,014
Connecticut	647,895	46.9	719,261	52.1	3,759	0.3	209	—	10,402	0.8	71,366
Delaware	122,596	52.0	109,831	46.6	2,437	1.0			970	0.4	12,765
D.C.	137,818	81.6	27,873	16.5			274	0.2	2,865	1.7	109,945
Florida	1,636,000	51.9	1,469,531	46.6	23,643	0.8	103	—	21,354	0.7	166,469
Georgia	979,409	66.7	483,743	33.0	991	0.1	175	—	3,140	0.2	495,666
Hawaii	147,375	50.6	140,003	48.1			3,923	1.3			7,372
Idaho	126,549	36.8	204,151	59.3	1,194	0.3	3,558	1.0	8,619	2.5	77,602
Illinois	2,271,295	48.1	2,364,269	50.1	55,939	1.2	8,057	0.2	19,354	0.4	92,974
Indiana	1,014,714	45.7	1,183,958	53.3					21,690	1.0	169,244
Iowa	619,931	48.5	632,863	49.5	20,051	1.6	1,452	0.1	5,009	0.4	12,932
Kansas	430,421	44.9	502,752	52.5	13,185	1.4	3,242	0.3	8,245	0.9	72,331
Kentucky	615,717	52.8	531,852	45.6	6,837	0.6	814	0.1	11,922	1.0	83,865
Louisiana	661,365	51.7	587,446	46.0	6,588	0.5	3,325	0.3	19,715	1.5	73,919
Maine	232,279	48.1	236,320	48.9	10,874	2.3	11	—	3,732	0.8	4,041
Maryland	759,612	52.8	672,661	46.7	4,541	0.3	255	—	2,828	0.2	86,951
Massachusetts	1,429,475	56.1	1,030,276	40.4	65,637	2.6	135	—	22,035	0.9	399,199
Michigan	1,696,714	46.4	1,893,742	51.8	47,905	1.3	5,406	0.1	9,982	0.3	197,028
Minnesota	1,070,440	54.9	819,395	42.0	35,490	1.8	3,529	0.2	21,077	1.1	251,045
Mississippi	381,309	49.6	366,846	47.7	4,074	0.5	2,788	0.4	14,344	1.9	14,463
Missouri	998,387	51.1	927,443	47.5	24,029	1.2			3,741	0.2	70,944
Montana	149,259	45.4	173,703	52.8					5,772	1.8	24,444
Nebraska	233,692	38.5	359,705	59.2	9,409	1.5	1,482	0.2	3,380	0.6	126,013
Nevada	92,479	45.8	101,273	50.2			1,519	0.8	6,605	3.3	8,794
New Hampshire	147,635	43.5	185,935	54.7	4,095	1.2	936	0.3	1,017	0.3	38,300
New Jersey	1,444,653	47.9	1,509,688	50.1	32,717	1.1	9,449	0.3	17,965	0.6	65,035
New Mexico	201,148	48.1	211,419	50.5	1,161	0.3	1,110	0.3	3,571	0.9	10,271
New York	3,389,558	51.9	3,100,791	47.5	4,303	0.1	12,197	0.2	27,321	0.4	288,767
North Carolina	927,365	55.2	741,960	44.2	780	—	2,219	0.1	6,590	0.4	185,405
North Dakota	136,078	45.8	153,470	51.6	2,952	1.0	253	0.1	4,435	1.5	17,392
Ohio	2,011,621	48.9	2,000,505	48.7	58,258	1.4	8,961	0.2	32,528	0.8	11,116
Oklahoma	532,442	48.7	545,708	50.0	14,101	1.3					13,266
Oregon	490,407	47.6	492,120	47.8	40,207	3.9			7,142	0.7	1,713
Pennsylvania	2,328,677	50.4	2,205,604	47.7	50,584	1.1			35,922	0.8	123,073
Rhode Island	227,636	55.4	181,249	44.1	479	0.1	715	0.2	1,091	0.3	46,387
South Carolina	450,807	56.2	346,149	43.1	289	—	53	—	5,285	0.7	104,658
South Dakota	147,068	48.9	151,505	50.4			1,619	0.5	486	0.2	4,437
Tennessee	825,879	55.9	633,969	42.9	5,004	0.3	1,375	0.1	10,118	0.7	191,910
Texas	2,082,319	51.1	1,953,300	48.0	20,118	0.5	189	—	15,958	0.4	129,019
Utah	182,110	33.6	337,908	62.4	3,907	0.7	2,438	0.5	14,835	2.7	155,798
Vermont	80,954	43.1	102,085	54.4	4,001	2.1			725	0.4	21,131
Virginia	813,896	48.0	836,554	49.3			4,648	0.3	41,996	2.5	22,658
Washington	717,323	46.1	777,732	50.0	36,986	2.4	5,042	0.3	18,451	1.2	60,409
West Virginia	435,914	58.0	314,760	41.9	113	—	16	—	161	—	121,154
Wisconsin	1,040,232	49.4	1,004,987	47.8	34,943	1.7	3,814	0.2	20,199	1.0	35,245
Wyoming	62,239	39.8	92,717	59.3	624	0.4	89	0.1	674	0.4	30,478
Totals	**40,830,763**	**50.1**	**39,147,793**	**48.0**	**756,691**	**0.9**	**173,011**	**0.2**	**647,631**	**0.8**	

1. For breakdown of "Other" vote, see minor candidate vote totals, p. 103.

Popular Returns: Minor Candidates and Parties

This section (pages 103 to 111) contains popular vote returns for all minor candidates and parties which were aggregated in the columns labeled "Other" in the tables of presidential election returns (pages 67 to 102).

The source for these data, except for 1976 and where indicated by a footnote, is the Historical Archive of the Inter-University Consortium for Political Research (ICPR). For 1976, the source was Scammon's *America Votes 12.* Footnotes are on page 111. *(Details on ICPR data, p. 66)*

The material is presented in the following order:

● Year of presidential election.

● Name of candidate and party, if available from the ICPR data. "Unknown" is used where ICPR sources indicated votes but neither candidate nor a party.

● State name, votes and percent. Statewide percentages were calculated to two decimal places and rounded to one place. Thus, 0.05 percent is listed as 0.1 percent.

● Nationwide vote totals and percent. Totals and percentages were calculated only where a candidate or party received votes in more than one state. Percentages were calculated to three decimal places and rounded to two. Thus, 0.005 percent is listed as 0.01 percent.

1824

Unpledged Republican

Massachusetts: 6,616 votes, 15.7 per cent of Mass. vote.

Unknown:

Connecticut: 1,188 votes, 11.2 per cent; Indiana: 7; Massachusetts: 4,753, 11.3; Missouri: 33, 1.0; North Carolina: 256, 0.7; Rhode Island: 200, 8.5.

1828

Unknown:

Alabama: 4 votes; Connecticut: 1,101, 5.7 per cent; Maine: 89, 0.3; Massachusetts: 3,226, 8.3; New Jersey: 8; North Carolina: 15; Rhode Island: 5, 0.1; Vermont: 120, 0.4.

1832

Unknown:

Illinois: 30 votes, 0.1 per cent; Massachusetts: 7,031, 10.4; Rhode Island: 6, 0.1; Vermont: 206, 0.6.

1836

Unknown:

Delaware: 5 votes, 0.1 per cent; Maine: 1,112, 2.9; Massachusetts: 45, 0.1; North Carolina; 1; Rhode Island; 1; Vermont: 65, 0.2; Virginia: 5.

1840

Unknown:

Delaware: 13 votes, 0.1 per cent; Indiana: 599, 0.5; Rhode Island: 136, 1.6; Vermont: 19.

1844

Unknown:

Delaware: 6 votes, 0.1 per cent; Illinois, 939, 0.9; Massachusetts: 1,106, 0.8; North Carolina: 2; Rhode Island: 5.

1848

Gerrit Smith (Liberty)

New York: 2,545 votes, 0.6 per cent of N.Y. vote.

Party Designation

In the ICPR data, the distinct party designations appearing in the original sources are preserved. Thus, in the ICPR returns for 1880, John W. Phelps received votes under the following 4 party designations: "Anti-Masonic" — California 5 votes, Illinois 150 votes and Pennsylvania 44 votes; "Anti-Secret" — Kansas 25 votes; "National American" — Michigan 312 votes and "American" — Rhode Island 4 votes and Wisconsin 91 votes.

In order to provide a single party designation for each minor candidate, Congressional Quarterly has aggregated under a single party designation the votes of minor candidates who are listed in the ICPR data as receiving votes under more than one party designation. The source for the designation is Svend Petersen's *A Statistical History of the American Presidential Elections* (Frederick Ungar, New York 1968) where Petersen gives a party designation. In the 1880 election cited above, Petersen lists John W. Phelps as an "American" party candidate. Where Petersen lists no party designation, Congressional Quarterly selected the party designation for a candidate which appeared most frequently in the ICPR returns.

Henry Clay (Clay Whig)

Illinois: 89 votes, 0.1 per cent of Ill. vote.

Unknown:

Alabama: 4 votes; Connecticut: 24; Massachusetts: 62, 0.1 per cent; North Carolina: 26; Rhode Island: 5, 0.1; Texas: 75, 0.4.

1852

Daniel Webster (Whig)[1]

Georgia: 5,324 votes, 8.5 per cent; Massachusetts: 1,670 votes, 1.3 per cent.

Totals: 6,994, .22%.

—Broome (Native American)

Massachusetts: 158 votes, 0.1 per cent; New Jersey: 738, 0.9; Pennsylvania: 1,670, 0.4.

Totals: 2,566, 0.08%.

George Michael Troup (Southern Rights)[2]

Alabama: 2,205 votes, 5.0 per cent; Georgia: 126, 0.2.

Totals: 2,331 votes, 0.07%.

Unknown:

California: 56 votes, 0.1 per cent; Connecticut: 12; Iowa: 139, 0.4; North Carolina: 60, 0.1; Texas: 10, 0.1.

1856

Unknown:

California: 14 votes; Delaware: 9, 0.1 per cent; Massachusetts: 3,006, 1.8; Ohio, 148.

1860

Gerrit Smith (Union)

Illinois: 35 votes; Ohio: 136.

Unknown:

California: 15 votes; Massachusetts: 328, 0.2 per cent; Minnesota: 17, 0.1.

1864

E. Cheeseborough

Kansas: 543 votes, 2.5 per cent of Kan. vote.

Unknown:

Kansas: 112 votes, 0.5 per cent; Massachusetts: 6; Minnesota: 26, 0.1; Oregon: 5.

1868

S. J. Crawford
Kansas: 1 vote.

C. B. Lines
Kansas: 1 vote.

Walter Ross
Kansas: 1 vote.

Unknown:
Alabama: 6 votes; Massachusetts: 26; New Hampshire: 11.

1872

James Black (Prohibition)
Michigan: 1,271 votes, 0.6 per cent; Ohio: 2,100, 0.4.
Totals: 3,371, 0.05%

George W. Slocum
Iowa: 424 votes, 0.2 per cent of Iowa vote.

James Baird Weaver
Iowa: 309 votes, 0.1 per cent of Iowa vote.

William Palmer
Kansas: 440 votes, 0.4 per cent of Kan. vote.

Liberal Republican Elector
Iowa: 10,447 votes, 4.8 per cent of Iowa vote.

Unknown:
Iowa: 209 votes, 0.1 per cent; Kansas: 141, 0.1; Minnesota: 168, 0.2; New Hampshire: 313, 0.5; South Carolina: 259, 0.3.

1876

Green Clay Smith (Prohibition)
Connecticut: 374 votes, 0.3 per cent; Illinois: 141; Kansas: 110, 0.1; Michigan: 766, 0.2; New York: 2,369, 0.2; Ohio: 1,636, 0.3; Pennsylvania: 1,320, 0.2; Wisconsin: 27.
Totals: 6,743; 0.08%

James B. Walker (American)
Illinois: 177 votes; Kansas: 23; Michigan: 71; Ohio: 76; Pennsylvania: 83; Wisconsin: 29.
Totals: 459; 0.01%

Louis Brookwater
Iowa: 97 votes.

Communist
Wisconsin: 32 votes.

Unknown:
Alabama: 2 votes; California: 19; Connecticut: 26; Iowa: 423, 0.1 per cent; Kansas: 5; Kentucky: 2,998, 1.2; Maine: 828, 0.7; Massachusetts: 779, 0.3; New Hampshire: 93, 0.1; Texas: 46; Vermont: 114, 0.2; Wisconsin: 1,607, 0.6.

1880

Neal Dow (Prohibition)
California: 54 votes; Connecticut: 409, 0.3 per cent; Illinois: 440, 0.1; Kansas: 10; Kentucky: 233, 0.1; Maine: 92, 0.1; Massachusetts: 682, 0.2; Michigan: 938, 0.3; Minnesota: 286, 0.2; New Hampshire: 180, 0.2; New Jersey: 191, 0.1; New York: 1,517, 0.1; Ohio: 2,613, 0.4; Pennsylvania: 1,940, 0.2; Rhode Island: 20, 0.1; Wisconsin: 69.
Totals 9,674, 0.11%

John W. Phelps (American)
California: 5 votes; Illinois: 150; Kansas: 25; Michigan: 312, 0.1 per cent; Pennsylvania: 44; Rhode Island: 4; Wisconsin: 91.
Totals 631, 0.01%

A. C. Brewer (Independent Democrat)
Arkansas: 322 votes, 0.3 per cent of Ark. vote.

W. Pitt Norris
Iowa: 433 votes, 0.1 per cent of Iowa vote.

H. Scott Howells
Iowa: 159 votes, 0.1 per cent of Iowa vote.

Unknown:
Arkansas: 1,221 votes, 1.1 per cent; California: 70; Colorado: 14; Connecticut: 39; Iowa: 472, 0.2; Maine: 139, 0.1; Massachusetts: 117; Mississippi: 677, 0.6; Rhode Island: 1; South Carolina: 36.

1884

Unknown:
Alabama: 72 votes, 0.1 per cent; California: 329, 0.2; Florida: 118, 0.2; Iowa: 1,297, 0.3; Kansas: 468, 0.2; Maine: 6; Massachusetts: 2; New Jersey: 28; Oregon: 35, 0.1; South Carolina: 1,237, 1.3; Vermont: 27, 0.1.

1888

Robert H. Cowdrey (United Labor)
Illinois: 150 votes; New York: 519; Oregon: 351; 0.6 per cent.
Totals 1,020, 0.01%

Socialist Labor
New York: 2,068 votes, 0.2 per cent.
Totals 2,068, 0.02%

James Langdon Curtis (American)
California: 1,591 votes, 0.6 per cent; Pennsylvania: 24.
Totals: 1,615, 0.01%

E.W. Perry
Iowa: 399 votes, 0.1 per cent of Iowa vote.

Unknown:
California: 1,442 votes, 0.6 per cent; Colorado: 177, 0.2; Delaware: 1; Iowa: 157; Kansas: 937, 0.3; Maine: 16; Massachusetts: 60; New Hampshire: 58, 0.1; North Carolina: 37; Oregon: 53, 0.1; Rhode Island: 7; South Carolina: 437, 0.6; Vermont: 35, 0.1.

1892

Simon Wing (Socialist Labor)
Connecticut: 333 votes, 0.2 per cent; Massachusetts: 649, 0.2; New Jersey: 1,337, 0.4; New York: 17,956, 1.3; Pennsylvania: 888, 0.1.
Totals: 21,163; 0.18%

Unknown:
Arkansas: 1,267 votes, 0.9 per cent; Delaware: 13; Georgia: 2,345, 1.1 Maine: 4; Massachusetts: 3; Michigan: 925, 0.2; Rhode Island: 3; South Carolina: 72, 0.1; Texas: 4,086, 1.0; Vermont: 10; Wyoming: 29, 0.2.

1896

Charles Horatio Matchett (Socialist Labor)
California: 1,611 votes, 0.5 per cent; Colorado: 159, 0.1; Connecticut: 1,223, 0.7; Illinois: 1,147, 0.1; Indiana: 324, 0.1; Iowa: 453, 0.1; Maryland: 587, 0.2; Massachusetts: 2,112, 0.5; Michigan: 293, 0.1; Minnesota: 954, 0.3; Missouri: 599, 0.1; Nebraska: 186, 0.1; New Hampshire: 228, 0.3; New Jersey: 3,985, 1.1: New York: 17,667, 1.2; Ohio: 1,165, 0.1; Pennsylvania: 1,683, 0.1; Rhode Island: 558, 1.0; Virginia: 108; Wisconsin: 1,314, 0.3.
Totals: 36,356; 0.26%

Charles Eugene Bentley (National Prohibition)
Arkansas: 892 votes, 0.6 per cent; California: 1,047, 0.4; Colorado: 386, 0.2; Illinois: 793, 0.1; Indiana: 2,267, 0.4; Iowa: 352, 0.1; Kansas: 620, 0.2; Maryland: 136, 0.1; Michigan: 1,816, 0.3; Missouri: 292; Nebraska: 797, 0.4; New Hampshire: 49, 0.1; New Jersey: 5,614, 1.5; North Carolina: 222, 0.1; Ohio: 2,716, 0.3; Pennsylvania: 870, 0.1; Washington: 148, 0.2; Wisconsin: 346, 0.1.
Totals: 19,363; 0.14%

W. C. Douglass

North Carolina: 51 votes.

Unknown:

California: 4 votes; Connecticut: 4; Georgia: 47; Massachusetts: 20; Michigan: 1,073, 0.2 per cent; North Carolina: 321, 0.1; North Dakota: 12; Rhode Island: 5.

1900

Wharton Barker (Populist)

Alabama: 4,188 votes, 2.6 per cent; Arkansas: 972, 0.8; Colorado: 333, 0.2; Florida: 1,143, 2.9; Georgia: 4,568, 3.8; Idaho: 445, 0.8; Illinois: 1,141, 0.1; Indiana: 1,438, 0.2; Iowa: 615, 0.1; Kentucky: 1,961, 0.4; Michigan: 889, 0.2; Mississippi: 1,642, 2.8; Missouri: 4,244; 0.6; Nebraska: 1,104, 0.5; New Jersey: 669, 0.2; North Carolina: 798, 0.3; North Dakota: 109, 0.2; Ohio: 251; Oregon: 269, 0.3; Pennsylvania: 638, 0.1; South Dakota: 340, 0.4; Tennessee: 1,322, 0.5; Texas: 20,565, 4.9; Vermont: 367, 0.7; Virginia: 63; West Virginia: 246, 0.1; Wyoming: 20, 0.1.

Totals: 50,340; 0.36%

Joseph F. Malloney (Socialist Labor)

California: 7,554 votes, 2.5 per cent; Colorado: 654, 0.3; Connecticut: 908, 0.5; Illinois: 1,374, 0.1; Indiana: 663, 0.1; Iowa: 259, 0.1; Kentucky: 390, 0.1; Maryland: 382, 0.1; Massachusetts: 2,599, 0.6; Michigan: 830, 0.2; Minnesota: 1,329, 0.4: Missouri: 1,296, 0.2; Montana: 119, 0.2; New Jersey: 2,074, 0.5; New York: 12,622, 0.8; Ohio: 1,688, 0.2; Pennsylvania: 2,936, 0.3; Rhode Island: 1,423, 2.5; Texas: 162; Utah: 102, 0.1; Virginia: 167, 0.1; Washington: 866, 0.8; Wisconsin: 503, 0.1.

Totals: 40,900; 0.29%

Seth Hockett Ellis (Union Reform)

Arkansas: 341 votes, 0.3 per cent; Illinois: 672, 0.1; Indiana: 254; Maryland: 142, 0.1; Ohio: 4,284, 0.4.

Totals: 5,693; 0.04%

Jonah Fitz Randolph Leonard (United Christian)

Illinois: 352 votes; Iowa: 166.
Totals: 518.

E. W. Perrin

Arkansas: 27 votes.

W. J. Palmer

Colorado: 26 votes.

Edward Waldo Emerson

Massachusetts: 342 votes, 0.1 per cent of Mass. vote.

G. W. Pape

Vermont: 1 vote.

S. W. Cook

Wyoming: 21 votes, 0.1 per cent of Wyo. vote.

Anti-Imperialist

Connecticut: 45 votes.

Unknown:

Connecticut: 10 votes; Louisiana: 4; Massachusetts: 191, 0.1; New Hampshire: 16; Utah: 9; Vermont: 4.

1904

Thomas Edward Watson (Populist)

Alabama: 5,051 votes, 4.6 per cent; Arkansas: 2,326, 2.0; Colorado: 824, 0.3; Connecticut: 495, 0.3; Delaware: 51, 0.1; Florida: 1,605, 4.2; Georgia: 22,635, 17.3; Idaho: 352, 0.5; Illinois: 6,725, 0.6; Indiana: 2,444, 0.4; Iowa: 2,207, 0.5; Kansas: 6,253, 1.9; Kentucky: 2,521, 0.6; Maine: 337, 0.4; Maryland: 1; Massachusetts: 1,294, 0.3; Michigan: 1,145, 0.2; Minnesota: 2,103, 0.7; Mississippi: 1,499, 2.6; Missouri: 4,226, 0.7; Montana: 1,531, 2.4; Nebraska: 20,518, 9.1; Nevada: 344, 2.8; New Hampshire: 82, 0.1; New Jersey: 3,705, 0.9; New York: 7,459, 0.5; North Carolina: 819, 0.4; Ohio: 1,392, 0.1; Oregon: 746, 0.8; South

Dakota: 1,240, 1.2; Tennessee: 2,491, 1.0; Texas: 8,062, 3.5; Washington: 669, 0.5; West Virginia: 339, 0.1; Wisconsin: 560, 0.1.

Totals: 114,051; 0.84%

Charles Hunter Corregan (Socialist Labor)

Colorado: 335 votes, 0.1 per cent; Connecticut: 583, 0.3; Illinois: 4,698, 0.4; Indiana: 1,598, 0.2; Kentucky: 596, 0.1; Massachusetts: 2,359, 0.5; Michigan: 1,018, 0.2; Minnesota: 974, 0.3; Missouri: 1,674, 0.3; Montana: 213, 0.3; New Jersey: 2,380, 0.6; New York: 9,122, 0.6; Ohio: 2,635, 0.3; Pennsylvania: 2,211, 0.2; Rhode Island: 488, 0.7; Texas: 431, 0.2; Washington: 1,592, 1.1; Wisconsin: 249, 0.1.

Totals: 33,156; 0.25%

Austin Holcomb (Continental)

Illinois: 826 votes, 0.1 per cent of Ill. vote.

Thomas O. Clark

Maryland: 4 votes.

Unknown:

California: 333 votes, 0.1 per cent; Connecticut: 11; Massachusetts: 5; New Hampshire: 1; Vermont: 1.

1908

Thomas L. Hisgen (Independence)

Alabama: 497 votes, 0.5 per cent; Arkansas: 286, 0.2; California: 4,278, 1.1; Connecticut: 728, 0.4; Delaware: 29, 0.1; Florida: 553, 1.1; Georgia: 76, 0.1; Idaho: 124, 0.1; Illinois: 7,724, 0.7; Indiana: 514, 0.1; Iowa: 404, 0.1; Kansas: 68; Kentucky: 200; Louisiana: 77, 0.1; Maine: 700, 0.7; Maryland; 485; 0.2; Massachusetts: 19,235, 4.2; Michigan: 734, 0.1; Minnesota: 424, 0.1; Missouri: 392, 0.1; Montana: 493, 0.7; Nevada: 436, 1.8; New Hampshire: 584, 0.7; New Jersey: 2,916, 0.6; New York: 35,817, 2.2; North Dakota: 43, 0.1; Ohio: 439; Oregon: 289, 0.3; Pennsylvania: 1,057, 0.1; Rhode Island: 1,105, 1.5; South Carolina: 46, 0.1; South Dakota: 88, 0.1; Tennessee: 332, 0.1; Texas: 106; Utah: 92, 0.1; Vermont: 804, 1.5; Virginia: 51; Washington: 248, 0.1; Wyoming: 63, 0.2.

Totals: 82,537; 0.55%

Thomas Edward Watson (Populist)

Alabama: 1,576 votes, 1.5 per cent; Arkansas: 987, 0.7; Florida: 1,946, 3.9; Georgia: 16,687, 12.6; Illinois: 633, 0.1; Indiana: 1,193, 0.2; Iowa: 261, 0.1; Kentucky: 333, 0.1; Mississippi: 1,276, 1.9; Missouri: 1,165, 0.2; Ohio: 162; Tennessee: 1,092, 0.4; Texas: 960, 0.3; Virginia: 105, 0.1.

Totals: 28,376; 0.19%

August Gillhaus (Socialist Labor)

Connecticut: 608 votes, 0.3 per cent; Illinois: 1,680, 0.2; Indiana: 643, 0.1; Kentucky: 405, 0.1; Massachusetts: 1,011, 0.2; Michigan: 1,085, 0.2; Missouri: 867, 0.1; New Jersey: 1,196, 0.3; New York: 3,877, 0.2; Ohio: 721, 0.1; Pennsylvania: 1,224, 0.1; Rhode Island: 183, 0.3; Texas: 175, 0.1; Virginia: 25; Wisconsin: 318; 0.1.

Totals: 14,018; 0.09%

Daniel Braxton Turney (United Christian)

Illinois: 400 votes; Michigan: 61.

S. H. Lasiter

Colorado: 1 vote.

B. J. McGrue

Colorado: 1 vote.

Edwin H. Lentz

New Hampshire: 8 votes.

Edward Clark

North Carolina: 13 votes.

Republican (Davidson Faction)

Alabama: 987 votes; 0.9 per cent of Ala. vote.

Unknown:

California: 28 votes; Connecticut: 4, Massachusetts: 9; Vermont: 29, 0.1 per cent; Wisconsin: 2.

1912

Eugene W. Chafin (Prohibition)

Arizona: 265 votes, 1.1 per cent; Arkansas: 908, 0.7; California: 23,366, 3.5; Colorado: 5,063, 1.9; Connecticut: 2,068, 1.1; Delaware: 620, 1.3; Florida: 1,854, 3.7; Georgia: 149, 0.1; Idaho: 1,536, 1.5; Illinois: 15,710, 1.4; Indiana: 19,249, 2.9; Iowa: 8,440, 1.7; Kentucky: 3,253, 0.7; Maine: 947, 0.7; Maryland: 2,244, 1.0; Massachusetts: 2,753, 0.6; Michigan: 8,794, 1.6; Minnesota: 7,886, 2.4; Missouri: 5,380, 0.8; Montana: 32; Nebraska: 3,383, 1.4; New Hampshire: 535, 0.6; New Jersey: 2,936, 0.7; New York: 19,455, 1.2; North Carolina: 118, 0.1; North Dakota: 1,243, 1.4; Ohio: 11,511, 1.1; Oklahoma: 2,195, 0.9; Oregon: 4,360, 3.2; Pennsylvania: 19,525, 1.6; Rhode Island: 616, 0.8; South Dakota: 3,910, 3.4; Tennessee: 832, 0.3; Texas: 1,701, 0.6; Vermont: 1,094, 1.7; Virginia: 709, 0.5; Washington: 9,810, 3.0; West Virginia: 4,517, 1.7; Wisconsin: 8,584, 2.2; Wyoming: 421, 1.0.

Totals: 207,972; 1.38%

Arthur E. Reimer (Socialist Labor)

Colorado: 475 votes, 0.2 per cent; Connecticut: 1,260, 0.7; Illinois: 4,066, 0.4; Indiana: 3,130, 0.5; Kentucky: 1,055, 0.2; Maryland: 322, 0.1; Massachusetts: 1,102, 0.2; Michigan: 1,239, 0.2; Minnesota: 2,212; 0.7; Missouri: 1,778, 0.3; New Jersey: 1,396, 0.3; New York: 4,273, 0.3; Ohio: 2,630, 0.3; Pennsylvania: 706, 0.1; Rhode Island: 236, 0.3; Texas: 430, 0.1; Utah: 510, 0.5; Virginia: 50; Washington: 1,872, 0.6; Wisconsin: 632, 0.2.

Totals: 29,374; 0.2%

Independent

Alabama: 5 votes.

Unknown

California: 4,417, 0.7 per cent; Connecticut: 6; Kansas: 63; Massachusetts: 1; South Carolina: 55, 0.1; Wisconsin: 9.

1916

Arthur E. Reimer (Socialist Labor)

Connecticut: 606 votes, 0.3 per cent; Illinois: 2,488, 0.1; Indiana: 1,659, 0.2; Iowa: 460, 0.1; Kentucky: 332, 0.1; Maryland: 756, 0.3; Massachusetts: 1,096, 0.2; Michigan: 831, 0.1; Minnesota: 468, 0.1; Missouri: 903, 0.1; Nebraska: 624, 0.2; New Jersey: 855, 0.2; New York: 2,666, 0.2; Pennsylvania: 419; Rhode Island: 180, 0.2; Utah: 144, 0.1; Virginia: 67; Washington: 730, 0.2.

Totals: 15,284; 0.08%

Progressive [3]

Colorado: 409 votes, 0.1 per cent; Georgia: 20,692, 12.9; Indiana: 3,898, 0.5; Iowa: 1,793, 0.4; Kentucky: 129; Louisiana: 6,349, 6.8; Minnesota: 290, 0.1; Mississippi: 520, 0.6; Montana: 338, 0.2; Oklahoma: 234, 0.1; Oregon: 310, 0.1; South Carolina: 162, 0.3; Utah: 110, 0.1

Totals 35,234; 0.19%

Unknown:

California: 187 votes; Massachusetts: 6; South Carolina: 258, 0.4 per cent; Vermont: 10.

1920

Aaron Sherman Watkins (Prohibition) [4]

Alabama: 766 votes, 0.3 per cent; California: 25,085, 2.7; Colorado: 2,807; 1.0; Connecticut: 1,771; 0.5; Delaware: 986, 1.0; Florida: 5,124, 3.5; Idaho: 11,216, 0.5; Illinois: 11,216, 1.1; Indiana: 13,462, 1.1; Iowa: 4,197, 0.5; Kentucky: 3,250, 0.4; Michigan: 9,510, 0.9; Minnesota: 11,489, 1.6; Missouri: 5,152, 0.4; Nebraska: 5,947, 1.6; New Jersey: 4,674, 0.5; New York: 19,653, 0.7; North Carolina: 17; Oregon: 3,595, 1.5; Pennsylvania: 42,696, 2.3; Rhode Island: 510,

0.3; South Dakota: 900, 0.5; Vermont: 762, 0.9; Virginia: 826, 0.4; Washington: 3,790, 1.0; West Virginia: 1,526, 0.3; Wisconsin: 8,648, 1.2.

Totals: 188,391, 0.7%

James Edward Ferguson (American)

Texas: 47,812 votes, 9.8 per cent.

William W. Cox (Socialist Labor)

Connecticut: 1,491 votes, 0.4 per cent; Illinois: 3,471, 0.2; Iowa: 982, 0.1; Maryland: 1,178, 0.3; Massachusetts: 3,583, 0.4; Michigan: 2,450, 0.2; Minnesota: 5,828, 0.8; Missouri: 1,587, 0.1; New Jersey: 923, 0.1; New York: 4,841, 0.2; Oregon: 1,515, 0.6; Pennsylvania: 753; Rhode Island: 495, 0.3; Washington: 1,321, 0.3.

Totals: 30,418; 0.11%

Robert Colvin Macauley (Single Tax)

Delaware: 39 votes; Illinois: 774; Indiana: 566; Maine: 310, 0.2 per cent; Michigan: 425; New Jersey: 517, 0.1; Ohio: 2,153, 0.1; Pennsylvania: 806; Rhode Island: 100, 0.1.

Totals: 5,690; 0.02%

Black and Tan Republican

Texas: 27,198, 5.6 per cent.

Independent Republican

Louisiana: 342 votes, 0.3 percent.

Insurgent Referendum

South Carolina: 366 votes, 0.6 per cent.

Unknown:

California: 587 votes, 0.1 per cent; Iowa: 6; Kansas: 75; Maryland: 8; Massachusetts: 24; Nebraska: 90; Ohio: 294; Pennsylvania: 27; Vermont: 56, 0.1.

1924

Frank T. Johns (Socialist Labor)

Connecticut: 1,373 votes, 0.3 per cent; Illinois: 2,334, 0.1; Kentucky: 1,512, 0.2; Maine: 406, 0.2; Maryland: 987, 0.3; Massachusetts: 1,668, 0.2; Minnesota: 1,855, 0.2; Missouri: 1,066, 0.1; New Jersey: 819, 0.1; New York: 9,928, 0.3; Ohio: 3,025, 0.2; Oregon: 908, 0.3; Pennsylvania: 634; Rhode Island: 268, 0.1; Vermont: 3; Virginia: 189, 0.1; Washington: 982, 0.2; Wisconsin: 411, 0.1.

Totals: 28,368, 0.1%

William Zebulon Foster (Communist)

Illinois: 2,622 votes, 0.1 per cent; Indiana: 987, 0.1; Iowa: 4,037, 0.4; Massachusetts: 2,634, 0.2; Michigan: 5,330, 0.5; Minnesota: 4,427, 0.5; Montana: 370, 0.2; New Jersey: 1,540, 0.1; New York: 8,244, 0.3; North Dakota: 370, 0.2; Pennsylvania: 2,735, 0.1; Rhode Island: 289, 0.1; Washington: 736, 0.2; Wisconsin: 3,759, 0.5.

Totals: 38,080; 0.13%

Gilbert Owen Nations (American)

Arkansas: 10 votes; Florida: 2,315, 2.1 per cent; Kentucky: 1,334, 0.2; New Jersey: 358; Pennsylvania: 13,035, 0.6; Tennessee: 100; Washington: 5,991, 1.4; West Virginia: 1,072, 0.2.

Totals: 24,215; 0.08%

William J. Wallace (Commonwealth Land)

Delaware: 16 votes; Illinois: 421; Kentucky: 247; Missouri: 165; New Jersey: 219; Ohio: 1,246, 0.1 per cent; Pennsylvania: 296; Rhode Island: 38; Wisconsin: 271.

Totals: 2,919; 0.01%

Andrew Gump

South Carolina: 1 vote.

Socialist

Oklahoma: 5,134 votes, 1.0 percent.

Unknown:

California: 122 votes; Iowa: 445, 0.1 per cent; Kansas: 3; Louisiana: 4,063, 3.3; Massachusetts: 2; Vermont: 2.

1928

Verne L. Reynolds (Socialist Labor)

Connecticut: 622 votes, 0.1 per cent; Illinois: 1,812, 0.1; Indiana: 645, 0.1; Iowa: 230; Kentucky: 354; Maryland: 906, 0.2; Massachusetts: 772, 0.1; Michigan: 799, 0.1; Minnesota: 1,921, 0.2; Missouri: 342; New Jersey: 488; New York: 4,211, 0.1; Ohio: 1,515, 0.1; Oregon: 1,564, 0.5; Pennsylvania: 382; Rhode Island: 416, 0.2; Virginia: 180, 0.1; Washington: 4,068, 0.8; Wisconsin: 381.

Totals: 21,608; 0.6%

William Frederick Varney (Prohibition)

California: 14,394 votes, 0.8 per cent; Indiana: 5,496, 0.4; Michigan: 2,728, 0.2; New Jersey: 154; Ohio: 3,556, 0.1; Pennsylvania: 3,875, 0.1; Vermont: 338, 0.3; West Virginia: 1,703, 0.3; Wisconsin: 2,245, 0.2.

Totals: 34,489; 0.09%.

Frank Elbridge Webb (Farmer Labor)

Colorado: 1,092 votes, 0.3 per cent; Iowa: 3,088, 0.3; Oklahoma: 1,283, 0.2; South Dakota: 927, 0.4.

Totals: 6,390; 0.02%.

Benjamin Gitlow

California: 104 votes.

H. Morgan

California: 6 votes.

W. O. Ligon

Mississippi: 524 votes, 0.4 per cent of Miss. vote.

Z. A. Rogers

Mississippi: 264 votes, 0.2 per cent of Miss. vote.

Unknown:

California: 151 votes; Iowa: 2; Massachusetts: 4; Pennsylvania: 14; Vermont: 9.

1932

William David Upshaw (Prohibition)

Alabama: 13 votes; California: 20,637, 0.9 per cent; Colorado: 1,928, 0.4; Georgia: 1,125, 0.4; Illinois: 6,388, 0.2; Indiana: 10,399, 0.7; Iowa: 2,111, 0.2; Kentucky: 2,263, 0.2; Massachusetts: 1,142, 0.1; Michigan: 2,893, 0.2; Missouri: 2,429, 0.2; New Jersey: 757, 0.1; Ohio: 7,421, 0.3; Pennsylvania: 11,369, 0.4; Rhode Island: 183, 0.1; South Dakota: 463, 0.2; Tennessee: 1,998, 0.5; Virginia: 1,843, 0.6; Washington: 1,540, 0.3; West Virginia: 2,342, 0.3; Wisconsin: 2,672, 0.2.

Totals: 81,916; 0.21%

William Hope Harvey (Liberty)

Arkansas: 952 votes, 0.4 per cent; California: 9,827, 0.4; Idaho: 4,660, 2.5; Michigan: 217; Montana: 1,461, 0.7; New Mexico: 389, 0.3; North Dakota: 1,817, 0.7; South Dakota: 3,333, 1.2; Texas: 235; Washington: 30,308, 4.9.

Totals: 53,199, 0.13%

Verne L. Reynolds (Socialist Labor)

Colorado: 427 votes, 0.1 per cent; Connecticut: 2,287, 0.4; Illinois: 3,638, 0.1; Indiana: 2,070, 0.1; Kentucky: 1,400, 0.1; Maine: 255, 0.1; Maryland: 1,036, 0.2; Massachusetts: 2,668, 0.2; Michigan: 1,401, 0.1; Minnesota: 770, 0.1; Missouri: 404; New Jersey: 1,054, 0.1; New York: 10,339, 0.2; Ohio: 1,968, 0.1; Oregon: 1,730, 0.5; Pennsylvania: 659; Rhode Island: 433, 0.2; Washington: 996, 0.2; Wisconsin: 493.

Totals: 34,028; 0.09%

Jacob Sechler Coxey (Farmer Labor)

Colorado: 469 votes, 0.1 per cent; Iowa: 1,094, 0.1; Michigan: 137; Minnesota: 5,731, 0.6.

Totals: 7,431; 0.02%

John Zahnd (National)

Indiana: 1,615 votes, 0.1 per cent of Ind. vote.

James R. Cox (Jobless)

Pennsylvania: 726 votes; Virginia: 15.
Totals: 741.

Arizona Progressive Democrat

Arizona: 9 votes.

Independent

Louisiana: 533 votes, 0.2 per cent of La. vote.

Jacksonian

Texas: 152 votes.

Populist

South Carolina: 4 votes.

Unknown:

Iowa: 4 votes; Massachusetts: 71; Pennsylvania: 53; Vermont: 2.

1936

Earl Russell Browder (Communist)[5]

Alabama: 678 votes, 0.3 per cent; Arkansas: 167, 0.1; California: 10,877, 0.4; Colorado: 497, 0.1; Connecticut: 1,193, 0.2; Delaware: 51; Indiana: 1,090, 0.1; Iowa: 506; Kentucky: 210; Maine: 257, 0.1; Maryland: 915, 0.2; Massachusetts: 2,930, 0.2; Michigan: 3,384, 0.2; Minnesota: 2,574, 0.2; Missouri: 417; Montana: 385, 0.2; New Hampshire: 193, 0.1; New Jersey: 1,595, 0.1; New Mexico: 43; New York: 35,609, 0.6; North Dakota: 360, 0.1; Ohio: 5,251, 0.2; Pennsylvania: 4,061, 0.1; Rhode Island: 411, 0.1; Tennessee: 326, 0.1; Texas: 253; Utah: 280, 0.1; Vermont: 405, 0.3; Virginia: 98; Washington: 1,907, 0.3; Wisconsin: 2,197, 0.2; Wyoming: 91, 0.1.

Totals: 79,211; 0.17%

David Leigh Colvin (Prohibition)[5]

Alabama: 719 votes, 0.3 per cent; Arizona: 384, 0.3; California: 12,917, 0.5; Georgia: 660, 0.2; Illinois: 3,438, 0.1; Iowa: 1,182, 0.1; Kentucky: 952, 0.1; Maine: 334, 0.1 ; Massachusetts: 1,032, 0.1; Michigan: 579; Missouri: 908, 0.1; Montana: 224, 0.1; New Jersey: 916, 0.1; New Mexico: 61; North Dakota: 197, 0.1; Oklahoma: 1,328, 0.2; Pennsylvania: 6,687, 0.2; Tennessee: 634, 0.1; Texas: 519, 0.1; Utah: 43; Virginia: 594, 0.2; Washington: 1,041, 0.2; West Virginia: 1,173, 0.1; Wisconsin: 1,071, 0.1; Wyoming: 75, 0.1.

Totals: 37,668; 0.08%

John W. Aiken (Socialist Labor)[5]

Colorado: 327 votes, 0.1 per cent; Connecticut: 1,228, 0.2; Illinois: 1,924, 0.1; Iowa: 252; Kentucky: 310; Maine: 129; Maryland: 1,305, 0.2; Massachusetts: 1,305, 0.1; Michigan: 600; Minnesota: 961, 0.1; Missouri: 292; New Jersey: 349; Oregon: 500, 0.1; Pennsylvania: 1,424; Rhode Island: 929, 0.3; Virginia: 36; Washington: 362, 0.1; Wisconsin: 557.

Totals: 12,790; 0.03%

William Dudley Pelley (Christian)

Washington: 1,598 votes, 0.2 per cent of Wash. vote.

Independent Republican

Delaware: 3,222, 2.5 per cent of Del. vote.

Unknown:

Iowa: 4 votes; Louisiana: 93; Massachusetts: 11; Michigan: 5; Oregon: 108; Vermont: 137, 0.1 per cent.

1940

Earl Russell Browder (Communist)

Alabama: 509 votes, 0.2 per cent; California: 13,586, 0.4; Colorado: 378, 0.1; Connecticut: 1,091, 0.1; Idaho: 276, 0.1; Iowa: 1,524, 0.1; Maine: 411, 0.1; Maryland: 1,274, 0.2; Massachusetts: 3,806, 0.2; Michigan: 2,834, 0.1; Minnesota: 2,711, 0.2; Montana: 489, 0.2; New Jersey: 8,814, 0.5; Oregon: 191; Pennsylvania: 4,519, 0.1; Rhode Island: 239, 0.1; Texas: 215; Utah: 191, 0.1; Vermont: 411, 0.3; Virginia: 72; Washington: 2,626, 0.3; Wisconsin: 2,381, 0.2.

Totals: 48,548; 0.1%

John W. Aiken (Socialist Labor)

Connecticut: 971 votes, 0.1 per cent; Indiana: 706; Iowa: 452; Maryland: 657, 0.1; Massachusetts: 1,492, 0.1; Michigan: 795; Minnesota: 2,553, 0.2; Missouri: 209; New Jersey: 446; Oregon: 2,487, 0.5; Pennsylvania: 1,518; Virginia: 48; Washington: 667, 0.1; Wisconsin: 1,882, 0.1.

Totals: 14,883, 0.03%

Alfred Knutson (Independent)

North Dakota: 545 votes, 0.2 per cent of N.D. vote.

Independent

Louisiana: 108 votes.

Unknown:

California: 262 votes; Georgia: 14; Maryland: 9; Massachusetts: 12; Michigan: 4; Pennsylvania: 827; Vermont: 11.

1944

Edward A. Teichert (Socialist Labor)

California: 180 votes; Connecticut: 1,220, 0.2 per cent; Illinois: 9,677, 0.2; Iowa: 193; Kentucky: 317; Maine: 335, 0.1; Massachusetts: 2,780, 0.1; Michigan: 1,264, 0.1; Minnesota: 3,176, 0.3; Missouri: 220; New Jersey: 6,939, 0.4; New York: 14,352, 0.2; Pennsylvania: 1,789, 0.1; Virginia: 90; Washington: 1,645, 0.2; Wisconsin: 1,002, 0.1.

Totals: 45,179; 0.09%

Gerald L. K. Smith (America First)

Michigan: 1,530 votes, 0.1 per cent; Texas: 250.
Totals: 1,780

Darlington Hoopes (Socialist)

California: 1,408 votes.

Anla A. Albaugh

California: 147 votes.

Independent

Louisiana: 69 votes.

Independent Democrat

Georgia: 3,373 votes, 1.0 per cent of Ga. vote.

Southern Democrat

South Carolina: 7,799, 7.5 per cent of S.C. vote.

Texas Regulars

Texas: 135,411, 11.8 per cent of Texas vote.

Unknown:

California: 326 votes; Massachusetts: 266; Michigan: 6; Vermont: 14.

1948

Norman M. Thomas (Socialist)

Arkansas: 1,037 votes, 0.4 per cent; California: 3,459, 0.1; Colorado: 1,678, 0.3; Connecticut: 6,964, 0.8; Delaware: 250, 0.2; Georgia: 3; Idaho: 332, 0.2; Illinois: 11,522, 0.3; Indiana: 2,179, 0.1; Iowa: 1,829, 0.2; Kansas: 2,807, 0.4; Kentucky: 1,284, 0.2; Maryland: 2,941, 0.5; Michigan: 6,063, 0.3; Minnesota: 4,646, 0.4; Missouri: 2,222, 0.1; Montana: 695, 0.3; New Hampshire: 86; New Jersey: 10,521, 0.5; New Mexico: 80; New York: 40,879, 0.7; North Dakota: 1,000, 0.5; Oregon: 5,051, 1.0; Pennsylvania: 11,325, 0.3; Rhode Island: 429, 0.1; South Carolina: 1; Tennessee: 1,288, 0.2; Texas: 874, 0.1; Vermont: 584, 0.5; Virginia: 726, 0.2; Washington: 3,534, 1.0; Wisconsin: 12,547, 1.0; Wyoming: 137, 0.1.

Totals: 138,973; 0.29%

Claude A. Watson (Prohibition)

Alabama: 1,026 votes, 0.5 per cent, Arizona: 786, 0.4; Arkansas: 1; California: 16,926, 0.4; Delaware: 343, 0.3; Georgia: 732, 0.2; Idaho: 628, 0.3; Illinois: 11,959, 0.3; Indiana: 14,711, 0.9; Iowa: 3,382, 0.3; Kansas: 6,468, 0.8; Kentucky: 1,245, 0.2; Massachusetts: 1,663, 0.1; Michigan: 13,052, 0.6; Missouri: 8;

Montana: 429, 0.2; New Jersey: 10,593, 0.5; New Mexico: 124, 0.1; Pennsylvania: 10,538, 0.3; Texas: 2,758, 0.2; Washington: 6,117, 0.7.

Totals: 103,489; 0.21%

Edward A. Teichert (Socialist Labor)

Arizona: 121 votes, 0.1 per cent; California: 195; Colorado: 214; Connecticut: 1,184, 0.1; Delaware: 29; Illinois: 3,118, 0.1; Indiana: 763, 0.1; Iowa: 4,274, 0.4; Kentucky: 185; Massachusetts: 5,535, 0.3; Michigan: 1,263, 0.1; Minnesota: 2,525, 0.2; Missouri: 3; New Hampshire: 83; New Jersey: 3,354, 0.2; New Mexico: 49; New York: 2,729; Pennsylvania: 1,461; Rhode Island: 131; Virginia: 234, 0.1; Washington: 1,133, 0.1; Wisconsin: 399; Wyoming: 56, 0.1.

Totals: 29,038; 0.06%

Farrell Dobbs (Socialist Workers)

California: 133 votes; Colorado: 228; Connecticut: 606, 0.1 per cent; Iowa: 256; Michigan: 672; Minnesota: 606, 0.1; New Jersey: 5,825, 0.3; New York: 2,675; Pennsylvania: 2,133, 0.1; Utah: 74; Washington: 103; Wisconsin: 303.

Totals: 13,614, 0.03%

Gerald L. K. Smith

California: 42 votes.

John G. Scott

California: 6 votes.

John Maxwell

California: 4 votes.

Morgan Blake

Georgia: 1 vote.

Fielding H. Wright

Maryland: 2,294 votes, 0.4 per cent of Md. vote.

Dwight David Eisenhower

Missouri: 1 vote.

Unknown:

California: 761 votes; Illinois: 1,629; Iowa: 8; Louisiana: 10; Massachusetts: 634; Michigan: 1; Pennsylvania: 107; Vermont: 35.

1952

Eric Hass (Socialist Labor)

Arkansas: 1 vote; California: 273; Colorado: 352, 0.1 per cent; Connecticut: 535, 0.1; Delaware: 242, 0.1; Illinois: 9,363, 0.2; Indiana: 979, 0.1; Iowa: 139; Kentucky: 893, 0.1; Massachusetts: 1,957, 0.1; Michigan: 1,495, 0.1; Minnesota: 2,383, 0.2; Missouri: 169; New Jersey: 5,815, 0.2; New Mexico: 35; New York: 1,560; Pennsylvania: 1,377; Rhode Island: 83; Virginia: 1,160, 0.2; Washington: 633, 0.1; Wisconsin: 770, 0.1; Wyoming: 36.

Totals: 30,250; 0.05%

Darlington Hoopes (Socialist)

California: 206 votes; Colorado: 365, 0.1 per cent; Connecticut: 2,244, 0.2; Delaware: 20; Iowa: 219; Kansas: 530, 0.1; Missouri: 227; Montana: 159, 0.1; New Jersey: 8,593, 0.4; New York: 2,664; Pennsylvania: 2,698, 0.1; Vermont: 185, 0.1; Virginia: 504, 0.1; Washington: 254; Wisconsin: 1,157, 0.1; Wyoming: 40.

Totals: 20,065; 0.03%

Douglas MacArthur (Constitution)

Arkansas: 458 votes, 0.1 per cent; California: 3,504, 0.1; Colorado: 2,181, 0.4; Missouri: 535; New Mexico: 215, 0.1; North Dakota: 1,075, 0.4; Tennessee: 379; Texas: 1,563, 0.1; Washington: 7,290, 0.7.

Totals: 17,200; 0.03%

Farrell Dobbs (Socialist Worker)

Michigan: 655 votes; Minnesota: 618; New Jersey: 3,850, 0.2 per cent; New York: 2,212; Pennsylvania: 1,508; Washington: 119; Wisconsin: 1,350, 0.1.

Totals: 10,312; 0.02%

Henry Krajewski (Poor Man's)

New Jersey: 4,203 votes, 0.2 per cent of N.J. vote.

Unknown:

California: 3,578 votes, 0.1 per cent; Georgia: 1; Idaho: 23; Illinois: 448; Massachusetts: 69; Michigan: 3; New York: 178; Pennsylvania: 155; Vermont: 18.

1956

Harry Flood Byrd (States' Rights)[6]

Kentucky: 2,657 votes, 0.3 per cent of Ky. vote.

Enoch A. Holtwick (Prohibition)[6]

California: 11,119 votes, 0.2 per cent; Delaware: 400, 0.2; Indiana: 6,554, 0.3; Kansas: 3,048, 0.4; Kentucky: 2,145, 0.2; Massachusetts: 1,205, 0.1; Michigan: 6,923, 0.2; New Jersey: 9,147, 0.4; New Mexico: 607, 0.2; Tennessee: 789, 0.1.

Totals: 41,937; 0.07%

Farrell Dobbs (Socialist Workers)

California: 96 votes; Minnesota: 1,098, 0.1 per cent; New Jersey: 4,004, 0.2; Pennsylvania: 2,035; Wisconsin: 564.

Totals: 7,797; 0.01%

Darlington Hoopes (Socialist)

California: 123 votes; Colorado: 531, 0.1 per cent; Iowa: 192; Virginia: 444, 0.1; Wisconsin: 754, 0.1.

Totals: 2,044

Henry Krajewski (American Third Party)

New Jersey: 1,829 votes, 0.1 per cent of N.J. vote.

Gerald L. K. Smith

California: 11 votes.

Independent

Mississippi: 42,961, 17.3 per cent of Miss. vote.

Unpledged

Alabama: 20,323 votes, 4.1 per cent; Louisiana: 44,520, 7.2; South Carolina: 88,509, 29.5.

Unknown:

Alabama: 10 votes; California: 819; Florida: 1,542, 0.1 per cent; Georgia: 2,189, 0.3; Idaho: 16; Illinois: 56; Massachusetts: 341; Vermont: 39.

1960

Rutherford L. Decker (Prohibition)

California: 21,706 votes, 0.3 per cent; Delaware: 284, 0.1; Indiana: 6,746, 0.3; Kansas: 4,138, 0.5; Massachusetts: 1,633, 0.1; Michigan: 2,029, 0.1; Montana: 456, 0.2; New Mexico: 777, 0.3; Tennessee: 2,450, 0.2; Texas: 3,868, 0.2.

Totals: 44,087; 0.06%

Orval E. Faubus (National States Rights)[7]

Alabama: 4,367 votes, 0.8 per cent; Arkansas: 28,952, 6.8; Delaware: 354, 0.2; Louisiana: 169,572, 21.0; Tennessee: 11,296, 1.1.

Totals: 209,314; 0.3%

Farrell Dobbs (Socialist Workers)

Colorado: 563 votes, 0.1 per cent; Iowa: 634, 0.1; Michigan: 4,347, 0.1; Minnesota: 3,077, 0.2; Montana: 391, 0.1; New Jersey: 11,402, 0.4; New York: 14,319, 0.2; North Dakota: 158, 0.1; Pennsylvania: 2,678, 0.1; Utah: 100; Washington: 705, 0.1; Wisconsin: 1,792, 0.1.

Totals: 40,166; 0.06%

Charles Loten Sullivan (Constitutional)

Texas: 18,170 votes, 0.8 per cent.
Total: 0.03%

J. Bracken Lee (Conservative)

New Jersey: 8,708 votes, 0.3 per cent.
Total: 0.01%

C. Benton Coiner (Virginia Conservative)

Virginia: 4,204 votes, 0.5 per cent of Va. vote.

Lar Daly (Tax Cut)

Michigan: 1,767 votes, 0.1 per cent of Mich. vote.

Clennon King (Independent Afro-American Unity)

Alabama: 1,485 votes, 0.3 per cent of Ala. vote.

Merritt B. Curtis (Constitution)

Washington: 1,401 votes, 0.1 per cent of Wash. vote.

T. Coleman Andrews

Maryland: 2 votes.

Barry Goldwater

Maryland: 1 vote.

Stuart Symington

South Carolina: 1 vote.

Independent American

Michigan: 539 votes.

Unknown:

Alabama: 231 votes; Georgia: 245; Illinois: 15; Massachusetts: 31; Oregon: 959, 0.1 per cent; Pennsylvania: 440; Texas: 175; Vermont: 7.

1964

E. Harold Munn (Prohibition)

California: 305 votes; Colorado: 1,355, 0.2 per cent; Delaware: 425, 0.2; Indiana: 8,266, 0.4; Iowa: 1,902, 0.2; Kansas: 5,393, 0.6; Massachusetts: 3,735, 0.2; Michigan: 669; Montana: 499, 0.2; New Mexico: 543, 0.2; North Dakota: 174, 0.1.

Totals: 23,266; 0.03%

John Kasper (National States Rights)

Arkansas: 2,965 votes, 0.5 per cent; Kentucky: 3,469, 0.3; Montana: 519, 0.2.

Totals: 6,953; 0.01%

Joseph B. Lightburn (Constitution)

Texas: 5,060 votes, 0.2 per cent.
Total: 0.01%

James Hensley (Universal Party)

California: 19 votes.

George C. Wallace

Georgia: 60 votes.

Richard B. Russell

Georgia: 50 votes.

Unpledged Democrat

Alabama: 210,732 votes, 30.6 per cent of Ala. vote.

Unknown:

Alabama: 1 vote; California: 5,401, 0.1 per cent; Connecticut: 1,313, 0.1; Georgia: 85; Illinois: 62; Iowa: 118; Massachusetts: 159; Michigan: 145; New York: 268; Oregon: 2,509, 0.3; Pennsylvania: 2,531, 0.1; South Carolina: 8; Tennessee: 34; Vermont: 20.

1968

Dick Gregory (Peace and Freedom)

California: 3,230 votes; Colorado: 1,393, 0.2 per cent; New Jersey: 8,084, 0.3; New York: 24,517, 0.4; Ohio: 372; Pennsylvania: 7,821, 0.2; Virginia: 1,680, 0.1.

Totals: 47,097, 0.06%

Fred Halstead (Socialist Workers)

Arizona: 85 votes; Colorado: 235; Indiana: 1,293, 0.1 per cent; Iowa: 3,377, 0.3; Kentucky: 2,843, 0.3; Michigan: 4,099, 0.1; Minnesota: 807, 0.1; Montana: 457, 0.2; New Hampshire: 104; New Jersey: 8,667, 0.3; New Mexico: 252, 0.1; New York: 11,851, 0.2;

North Dakota: 128, 0.1; Ohio: 69; Pennsylvania: 4,862, 0.1; Rhode Island: 383, 0.1; Utah: 89; Vermont: 295, 0.2; Washington: 272; Wisconsin: 1,222, 0.1.
Totals: 41,390; 0.06%

Eldridge Cleaver (Peace and Freedom)

Arizona: 217 votes; Iowa: 1,332, 0.1 per cent; Michigan: 4,585, 0.1; Minnesota: 933, 0.1; Washington: 1,669, 0.1.
Totals: 8,736; 0.01%

Eugene McCarthy

Arizona: 2,751 votes, 0.6 per cent; California: 20,721, 0.3; Minnesota: 584; Oregon: 1,496, 0.2.
Totals: 25,552; 0.03%

E. Harold Munn (Prohibition)

Alabama: 3,814 votes, 0.4 per cent; California: 59; Colorado: 275; Indiana: 4,616, 0.2; Iowa: 362; Kansas: 2,192, 0.3; Massachusetts: 2,369, 0.1; Michigan: 60: Montana: 510, 0.2; North Dakota: 38; Ohio: 19; Virginia: 601.
Totals: 14,915; 0.02%

Ventura Chavez (People's Constitution)

New Mexico: 1,519 votes, 0.5 per cent of N.M. vote.

Charlene Mitchell (Communist)

California: 260 votes; Minnesota: 415; Ohio: 23; Washington: 378.

James Hensley (Universal)

Iowa: 142 votes.

Richard K. Troxell (Constitution)

North Dakota: 34 votes.

Kent M. Soeters (Berkeley Defense Group)

California: 17 votes.

Nelson A. Rockefeller

Oregon: 69 votes.

American Independent Democrat

Alabama: 10,518 votes; 1.0 per cent of Ala. vote.

New Party

New Hampshire: 421 votes, 0.1 per cent; Vermont: 579, 0.4.

New Reform

Montana: 470 votes, 0.2 per cent of Mont. vote.

Peace and Freedom

California: 27,707 votes, 0.4 per cent; Utah: 180.
Totals: 27,887 votes; 0.04%

Unknown:

Colorado: 948 votes, 0.1 per cent; Connecticut: 1,300, 0.1; Georgia: 173; Illinois: 325; Iowa: 250; Massachusetts: 53; Michigan: 29; Minnesota: 170; New Hampshire: 108; Oregon: 1,075, 0.1; Pennsylvania: 2,264, 0.1; Texas: 489; Vermont: 29; Wisconsin: 2,342, 0.1.

1972

Linda Jenness (Socialist Workers)

California: 574 votes; Colorado: 666, 0.1 per cent; Idaho: 397, 0.1; Iowa: 488; Kentucky: 685, 0.1; Massachusetts: 10,600, 0.4; Michigan: 1,603, 0.1; Minnesota: 940, 0.1; Mississippi: 2,458, 0.4; New Hampshire: 368, 0.1; New Jersey: 2,233, 0.1; New Mexico: 474, 0.1; North Dakota: 288, 0.1; Pennsylvania: 4,639, 0.1; Rhode Island: 729, 0.2; South Dakota: 994, 0.3; Texas: 8,664, 0.3; Washington: 623.
Totals: 37,423; 0.05%

Louis Fisher (Socialist Labor)

California: 197 votes; Colorado: 4,361, 0.5 per cent; Illinois: 12,344, 0.3; Indiana: 1,688, 0.1; Iowa: 195; Massachusetts: 129; Michigan: 2,437, 0.1; Minnesota: 4,261, 0.2; New Jersey: 4,544, 0.2; New York: 4,530, 0.1; Ohio: 7,107, 0.2; Virginia: 9,918, 0.7; Washington: 1,102, 0.1; Wisconsin: 998, 0.1.
Totals: 53,811, 0.07%

Gus Hall (Communist)

California: 373 votes; Colorado: 432, 0.1 per cent; Illinois: 4,541, 0.1; Iowa: 272; Kentucky: 464; Massachusetts: 46; Michigan: 1,210; Minnesota: 662; New Jersey: 1,263; New York: 5,641, 0.1; North Dakota: 87; Ohio: 6,437, 0.2; Pennsylvania: 2,686, 0.1; Washington: 566; Wisconsin: 663.
Totals: 25,343; 0.03%

E. Harold Munn (Prohibition)[8]

Alabama: 8,559 votes, 0.9 per cent; California: 53; Colorado: 467, 0.1; Delaware: 238, 0.1; Kansas: 4,188, 0.5.
Totals: 12,818; 0.02%

John Hospers (Libertarian)

California: 980 votes; Colorado: 1,111, 0.1 per cent; Massachusetts: 43; Washington: 1,537, 0.1.
Totals: 3,671

John V. Mahalchik (America First)

New Jersey: 1,743 votes, 0.1 per cent of N.J. vote.

Gabriel Green (Universal)

California: 21 votes; Iowa: 199.

John Beno

Colorado: 6 votes.

Evelyn Reed (Socialist Workers)

Indiana: 5,575 votes, 0.3 per cent; New York: 7,797, 0.1; Wisconsin: 506.
Totals: 13,878; 0.02%

Edward A. Wallace

Ohio: 460 votes.

Socialist Worker

Arizona: 30,945, 4.7 per cent; Louisiana: 12,169, 1.2.

Unknown:

Connecticut: 777 votes, 0.1 per cent; Florida: 7,407, 0.3; Illinois: 2,229, 0.1; Iowa: 321; Massachusetts: 342; Michigan: 598; Minnesota: 962, 0.1; New Hampshire: 142; Oregon: 2,289, 0.3; Pennsylvania: 2,715, 0.1; South Carolina: 17; Tennessee: 369; Texas: 3,393, 0.1; Wisconsin: 893, 0.1; District of Columbia: 568, 0.3.

1976

Lester Maddox (American Independent)

Alabama: 9,198 votes, 0.8 per cent; Arizona: 85; California: 51,098, 0.6; Connecticut: 7,101, 0.5; Georgia: 1,071, 0.1; Idaho: 5,935, 1.7; Kansas: 2,118, 0.2; Kentucky: 2,328, 0.2; Louisiana: 10,058, 0.8; Maine: 8; Maryland: 171; Mississippi: 4,861, 0.6; Nebraska: 3,380, 0.6; Nevada: 1,497, 0.7; New Jersey: 7,716, 0.3; New Mexico: 31; New York: 97; North Dakota: 269, 0.1; Ohio: 15,529, 0.4; Pennsylvania: 25,344, 0.5; Rhode Island: 1; South Carolina: 1,950, 0.2; Tennessee: 2,303, 0.2; Texas: 41; Utah: 1,162, 0.2; Washington: 8,585, 0.6; West Virginia: 12; Wisconsin: 8,552, 0.4; Wyoming: 30.
Totals: 170,531; 0.2%

Thomas J. Anderson (American)

Alabama: 70 votes; Arizona: 564, 0.1 per cent; Arkansas: 389, 0.1; California: 4,565, 0.1; Colorado: 397; Connecticut: 155; Delaware: 645, 0.3; Florida: 21,325, 0.7; Georgia: 1,168, 0.1; Idaho: 493, 0.1; Illinois: 387; Indiana: 14,048, 0.6; Iowa: 3,040, 0.2; Kansas: 4,724, 0.5; Kentucky: 8,308, 0.7; Maine: 28; Maryland:

321; Massachusetts: 7,555, 0.3; Minnesota: 13,592, 0.7; Mississippi: 6,678, 0.9; Montana: 5,772, 1.8; New Mexico: 106; New York: 451; North Carolina: 5,607, 0.3; North Dakota: 3,796, 1.3; Oregon: 1,035, 0.1; Rhode Island: 24; South Carolina: 2,996, 0.4; Tennessee: 5,769, 0.4; Texas: 11,442, 0.3; Utah: 13,284, 2.5; Virginia: 16,686, 1.0; Washington: 5,046, 0.3; West Virginia: 17; Wyoming: 290, 0.2.

Totals: 160,773; 0.2%.

Peter Camejo (Socialist Workers)

Alabama: 1 vote; Arizona: 928, 0.1 per cent; California: 17,259, 0.2; Colorado: 1,126, 0.1; Connecticut: 42; District of Columbia: 545, 0.3; Georgia: 43; Idaho: 14; Illinois: 3,615, 0.1; Indiana: 5,695, 0.3; Iowa: 267; Kentucky: 350; Louisiana: 2,240, 0.2; Maine: 1; Maryland: 261; Massachusetts: 8,138, 0.3; Michigan: 1,804; Minnesota: 4,149, 0.2; Mississippi: 2,805, 0.4; New Hampshire: 161; New Jersey: 1,184; New Mexico: 2,462, 0.6; New York: 6,996, 0.1; North Dakota: 43; Ohio: 4,717, 0.1; Pennsylvania: 3,009, 0.1; Rhode Island: 462, 0.1; South Carolina: 8; South Dakota: 168, 0.1; Texas: 1,723; Utah: 268; Vermont: 430, 0.2; Virginia: 17,802, 1.0; Washington: 905, 0.1; West Virginia: 2; Wisconsin: 1,691, 0.1.

Totals: 91,314, 0.1%

Gus Hall (Communist)

Alabama: 1,954 votes, 0.2 per cent; California: 12,766, 0.2; Colorado: 403; Connecticut: 186; District of Columbia: 219, 0.1; Georgia: 3; Idaho: 5; Illinois: 9,250, 0.2; Iowa: 554; Kentucky: 426; Louisiana: 7,417, 0.6; Maine: 14; Maryland: 68; Minnesota: 1,092, 0.1; New Jersey: 1,662, 0.1; New Mexico: 19; New York: 10,270, 0.2; North Dakota: 84; Ohio: 7,817, 0.2; Pennsylvania: 1,891; Rhode Island: 334, 0.1; South Carolina: 1; South Dakota: 318, 0.1; Tennessee: 547; Utah: 121; Washington: 817, 0.1; West Virginia: 5; Wisconsin: 749.

Totals: 58,992; 0.07%.

Margaret Wright (People's Party)

California: 41,731 votes, 0.5 per cent; Connecticut: 1; Idaho: 1; Maryland: 8; Massachusetts: 33; Michigan: 3,504, 0.1; Minnesota: 635; New Jersey: 1,044; Washington: 1,124, 0.1; Wisconsin: 943.

Totals: 49,024; 0.06%.

Lyndon H. LaRouche (U.S. Labor)

Alabama: 1 vote; Colorado: 567, 0.1 per cent; Connecticut: 1,789, 0.1; Delaware: 136, 0.1; District of Columbia: 157, 0.1; Georgia: 1; Idaho: 739, 0.2; Illinois: 2,018; Indiana: 1,947, 0.1; Iowa: 241; Kentucky: 510; Maryland: 21; Massachusetts: 4,922, 0.2; Michigan: 1,366; Minnesota: 543; New Hampshire: 186, 0.1; New Jersey: 1,650, 0.1; New Mexico: 1; New York: 5,413, 0.1;

North Carolina: 755; North Dakota: 142; Ohio: 4,335, 0.1; Pennsylvania: 2,744, 0.1; South Carolina: 2; Tennessee: 512; Vermont: 196, 0.1; Virginia: 7,508, 0.4; Washington: 903, 0.1; Wisconsin: 738.

Totals: 40,043; 0.05%.

Benjamin C. Bubar (Prohibition)

Alabama: 6,669 votes, 0.6 per cent; California: 34; Colorado: 2,882, 0.3; Delaware: 103; Kansas: 1,403, 0.1; Maine: 3,495, 0.7; Maryland: 2; Massachusetts: 14; New Jersey: 554; New Mexico: 211, 0.1; North Dakota: 63; Ohio: 62; Tennessee: 442.

Totals: 15,934; 0.02%.

Jules Levin (Socialist Labor)

California: 222 votes; Colorado: 14; Connecticut: 1; Delaware: 86; Florida: 19; Georgia: 2; Illinois: 2,422, 0.1 per cent; Iowa: 167; Maine: 1; Maryland: 7; Massachusetts: 19; Michigan: 1,148; Minnesota: 370; New Hampshire: 66; New Jersey: 3,686, 0.1; New York: 28; Ohio: 68; Rhode Island: 188; Washington: 713; Wisconsin: 389.

Totals: 9,616; 0.01%.

Frank P. Zeidler (Socialist)

Connecticut: 5 votes; Florida: 8; Georgia: 2; Idaho: 2; Iowa: 234; Maryland: 16; Minnesota: 354; New Jersey: 469; New Mexico: 240, 0.1 per cent; New York: 14; North Dakota: 38; Washington: 358; Wisconsin: 4,298, 0.2.

Totals: 6,038; 0.01%.

Ernest L. Miller (Restoration)

California: 26 votes; Colorado: 6; Florida: 2; Georgia: 3; Maryland: 8; Tennessee: 316.

Totals: 361.

Frank Taylor (United American)

Arizona: 22 votes; California: 14.

Totals: 36.

Unknown

Alabama: 137 votes; Alaska: 1,176, 1.0 per cent; California: 74; Colorado: 2; Connecticut: 1,122, 0.1; District of Columbia: 1,944, 1.2; Georgia: 847, 0.1; Idaho: 1,430, 0.4; Illinois: 1,662; Iowa: 506; Maine: 185; Maryland: 1,945, 0.1; Massachusetts: 1,354, 0.1; Michigan: 2,160, 0.1; Minnesota: 342; Missouri: 3,741, 0.2; Nevada: 5,108, 2.5; New Hampshire: 604, 0.2; New Mexico: 501, 0.1; New York: 4,052, 0.1; North Carolina: 228; Oregon: 6,107, 0.6; Pennsylvania: 2,934, 0.1; Rhode Island: 82; South Carolina: 328; Tennessee: 229; Texas: 2,752, 0.1; Vermont: 99, 0.1; West Virginia: 125; Wisconsin: 2,839, 0.1; Wyoming: 354, 0.2.

Totals: 44,969; 0.06%.

1. *Georgia figures for Webster obtained from Petersen, Svend, A Statistical History of the American Presidential Elections, Frederick Ungar, New York, 1963, 1968, p. 31.*
2. *Troup figures obtained from Petersen, ibid.*
3. *Iowa and Mississippi figures from Petersen, op. cit., p. 81. Petersen lists these votes, as well as Progressive votes in all other states, for Theodore Roosevelt. In the ICPR data for 1916, votes are listed for Progressive electors; Roosevelt's name does not appear. Since Roosevelt declined to be a candidate, Congressional Quarterly followed ICPR listing these votes as Progressive.*

4. *Florida figures for Watkins obtained from Petersen, op. cit., p. 83.*
5. *Maine figures for Browder, Colvin and Aiken obtained from Petersen, op. cit., p. 94.*
6. *Kentucky figures for Byrd and Holtwick obtained from Petersen, op. cit., p. 109.*
7. *Arkansas figures for Faubus obtained from Petersen, op. cit., p. 113.*
8. *Alabama figures for Munn obtained from Scammon, Richard M., America Votes (10), Congressional Quarterly, 1973, p. 28.*

Political Party Nominees

CQ

Political Party Nominees, 1831-1976

The following pages contain a comprehensive list of major and minor party nominees for president and vice president since 1831 when the first nominating convention was held by the Anti-Masonic Party.

In many cases, minor parties made only token efforts at a presidential campaign. Often, third party candidates declined to run after being nominated by the convention, or their names appeared on the ballots of only a few states. In some cases the names of minor candidates did not appear on any state ballots and they received only a scattering of write-in votes, if any. As a result, some of these candidates do not appear in the presidential elections returns. *(pp. 67-111)*

The basic source used to compile the list was Joseph Nathan Kane's *Facts About the Presidents,* 3rd edition, The H. W. Wilson Co., New York, 1974. To verify the names appearing in Kane, Congressional Quarterly consulted the following additional sources: Richard M. Scammon's *America at the Polls,* University of Pittsburgh Press, 1965; *America Votes 8* (1968), Congressional Quarterly, 1969; *America Votes 10* (1972), Congressional Quarterly, 1973; *Encyclopedia of American History,* edited by Richard B. Morris, Harper and Row, New York, 1965; *Dictionary of American Biography,* Charles Scribner's Sons, 1928-1936; *Facts on File,* Facts on File Inc., New York 1945-75; *History of U.S. Political Parties,* Vols. I-IV, edited by Arthur M. Schlesinger, Bowker, New York, 1973; *History of American Presidential Elections, 1789-1968,* edited by Arthur M. Schlesinger, McGraw Hill, New York, 1971; and *Who Was Who in America,* Vol. I-V (1607-1968), Marquis Who's Who, Chicago. The source for the 1976 candidates was Richard M. Scammon's *America Votes 12* (1976), Congressional Quarterly, 1977.

When these sources contained information in conflict with Kane, the conflicting information is included in a footnote. Where a candidate appears in Kane, *but could not be verified in another source,* an asterisk appears beside the candidate's name on the list. *(Footnotes, p. 121)*

Election of 1832

Democratic Party
President: Andrew Jackson, Tennessee
Vice President: Martin Van Buren, New York
National Republican Party
President: Henry Clay, Kentucky
Vice President: John Sergeant, Pennsylvania
Independent Party
President: John Floyd, Virginia
Vice President: Henry Lee, Massachusetts
Anti-Masonic Party
President: William Wirt, Maryland
Vice President: Amos Ellmaker, Pennsylvania

Election of 1836

Democratic Party
President: Martin Van Buren, New York
Vice President: Richard Mentor Johnson, Kentucky
Whig Party
President: William Henry Harrison, Hugh Lawson White, Daniel Webster
Vice President: Francis Granger, John Tyler.

The Whigs nominated regional candidates in 1836 hoping that each candidate would carry his region and deny Democrat Van Buren an electoral vote majority. Webster was the Whig candidate in Massachusetts; Harrison in the rest of New England, the middle Atlantic states and the West; and White in the South.

Granger was the running mate of Harrison and Webster. Tyler was White's running mate.

Election of 1840

Whig Party
President: William Henry Harrison, Ohio
Vice President: John Tyler, Virginia
Democratic Party
President: Martin Van Buren, New York

The Democratic convention adopted a resolution which left the choice of vice presidential candidates to the states. Democratic electors divided their vice presidential votes among incumbent Richard M. Johnson (48 votes), Littleton W. Tazewell (11 votes) and James K. Polk (1 vote).
Liberty Party
President: James Gillespie Birney, New York
Vice President: Thomas Earle, Pennsylvania

Election of 1844

Democratic Party
President: James Knox Polk, Tennessee
Vice President: George Mifflin Dallas, Pennsylvania
Whig Party
President: Henry Clay, Kentucky
Vice President: Theodore Frelinghuysen, New Jersey
Liberty Party
President: James Gillespie Birney, New York
Vice President: Thomas Morris, Ohio
National Democratic
President: John Tyler, Virginia
Vice President: None
Tyler withdrew from the race in favor of the Democrat, Polk.

Election of 1848

Whig Party
President: Zachary Taylor, Louisiana
Vice President: Millard Fillmore, New York
Democratic Party
President: Lewis Cass, Michigan
Vice President: William Orlando Butler, Kentucky
Free Soil Party
President: Martin Van Buren, New York
Vice President: Charles Francis Adams, Massachusetts
Free Soil (Barnburners—Liberty Party)
President: John Parker Hale, New Hampshire
Vice President: Leicester King, Ohio
Later John Parker Hale relinquished the nomination.

National Liberty Party
President: Gerrit Smith, New York
Vice President: Charles C. Foote, Michigan

Election of 1852

Democratic Party
President: Franklin Pierce, New Hampshire
Vice President: William Rufus De Vane King, Alabama

Whig Party
President: Winfield Scott, New Jersey
Vice President: William Alexander Graham, North Carolina

Free Soil
President: John Parker Hale, New Hampshire
Vice President: George Washington Julian, Indiana

Election of 1856

Democratic Party
President: James Buchanan, Pennsylvania
Vice President: John Cabell Breckinridge, Kentucky

Republican Party
President: John Charles Fremont, California
Vice President: William Lewis Dayton, New Jersey

American (Know-Nothing) Party
President: Millard Fillmore, New York
Vice President: Andrew Jackson Donelson, Tennessee

Whig Party (the "Silver Grays")
President: Millard Fillmore, New York
Vice President: Andrew Jackson Donelson, Tennessee

North American Party
President: Nathaniel Prentice Banks, Massachusetts
Vice President: William Freame Johnson, Pennsylvania
Banks and Johnson declined the nominations and gave their support to the Republicans.

Election of 1860

Republican Party
President: Abraham Lincoln, Illinois
Vice President: Hannibal Hamlin, Maine

Democratic Party
President: Stephen Arnold Douglas, Illinois
Vice President: Herschel Vespasian Johnson, Georgia

Southern Democratic Party
President: John Cabell Breckinridge, Kentucky
Vice President: Joseph Lane, Oregon

Constitutional Union Party
President: John Bell, Tennessee
Vice President: Edward Everett, Massacusetts

Election of 1864

Republican Party
President: Abraham Lincoln, Illinois
Vice President: Andrew Johnson, Tennessee

Democratic Party
President: George Brinton McClellan, New York
Vice President: George Hunt Pendleton, Ohio

Independent Republican Party
President: John Charles Fremont, California
Vice President: John Cochrane, New York
Fremont and Cochrane declined and gave their support to the Republican Party nominees

Election of 1868

Republican Party
President: Ulysses Simpson Grant, Illinois
Vice President: Schuyler Colfax, Indiana

Democratic Party
President: Horatio Seymour, New York
Vice President: Francis Preston Blair, Jr., Missouri

Election of 1872

Republican Party
President: Ulysses Simpson Grant, Illinois
Vice President: Henry Wilson, Massachusetts

Liberal Republican Party
President: Horace Greeley, New York
Vice President: Benjamin Gratz Brown, Missouri

Independent Liberal Republican Party (Opposition Party)
President: William Slocum Groesbeck, Ohio
Vice President: Frederick Law Olmsted, New York

Democratic Party
President: Horace Greeley, New York
Vice President: Benjamin Gratz Brown, Missouri

Straight-out Democratic Party
President: Charles O'Conor, New York
Vice President: John Quincy Adams, Massachusetts

Prohibition Party
President: James Black, Pennsylvania
Vice President: John Russell, Michigan

People's Party (Equal Rights Party)
President: Victoria Claflin Woodhull, New York
Vice President: Frederick Douglass

Labor Reform Party
President: David Davis, Illinois
Vice President: Joel Parker, New Jersey

Liberal Republican Party of Colored Men
President: Horace Greeley, New York
Vice President: Benjamin Gratz Brown, Missouri

National Working Men's Party
President: Ulysses Simpson Grant, Illinois
Vice President: Henry Wilson, Massachusetts

Election of 1876

Republican Party
President: Rutherford Birchard Hayes, Ohio
Vice President: William Almon Wheeler, New York

Democratic Party
President: Samuel Jones Tilden, New York
Vice President: Thomas Andrews Hendricks, Indiana

Greenback Party
President: Peter Cooper, New York
Vice President: Samuel Fenton Cary, Ohio

Prohibition Party
President: Green Clay Smith, Kentucky
Vice President: Gideon Tabor Stewart, Ohio

American National Party
President: James B. Walker, Illinois
Vice President: Donald Kirkpatrick, New York*

Election of 1880

Republican Party
President: James Abram Garfield, Ohio
Vice President: Chester Alan Arthur, New York

Democratic Party
President: Winfield Scott Hancock, Pennsylvania
Vice President: William Hayden English, Indiana

Greenback Labor Party
President: James Baird Weaver, Iowa
Vice President: Benjamin J. Chambers, Texas

Prohibition Party
President: Neal Dow, Maine
Vice President: Henry Adams Thompson, Ohio

American Party
President: John Wolcott Phelps, Vermont
Vice President: Samuel Clarke Pomeroy, Kansas*

Election of 1884

Democratic Party
President: Grover Cleveland, New York
Vice President: Thomas Andrews Hendricks, Indiana

Republican Party
President: James Gillespie Blaine, Maine
Vice President: John Alexander Logan, Illinois

Anti-Monopoly Party
President: Benjamin Franklin Butler, Massachusetts
Vice President: Absolom Madden West, Mississippi

Greenback Party
President: Benjamin Franklin Butler, Massachusetts
Vice President: Absolom Madden West, Mississippi

Prohibition Party
President: John Pierce St. John, Kansas
Vice President: William Daniel, Maryland
American Prohibition Party
President: Samuel Clarke Pomeroy, Kansas
Vice President: John A. Conant, Connecticut
Equal Rights Party
President: Belva Ann Bennett Lockwood, District of Columbia
Vice President: Marietta Lizzie Bell Stow, California

Election of 1888

Republican Party
President: Benjamin Harrison, Indiana
Vice President: Levi Parsons Morton, New York
Democratic Party
President: Grover Cleveland, New York
Vice President: Allen Granberry Thurman, Ohio
Prohibition Party
President: Clinton Bowen Fisk, New Jersey
Vice President: John Anderson Brooks, Missouri*
Union Labor Party
President: Alson Jenness Streeter, Illinois
Vice President: Charles E. Cunningham, Arkansas*
United Labor Party
President: Robert Hall Cowdrey, Illinois
Vice President: William H. T. Wakefield, Kansas*
American Party
President: James Langdon Curtis, New York
Vice President: Peter Dinwiddie Wigginton, California*
Equal Rights Party
President: Belva Ann Bennett Lockwood, District of Columbia
Vice President: Alfred Henry Love, Pennsylvania*
Industrial Reform Party
President: Albert E. Redstone, California*
Vice President: John Colvin, Kansas*

Election of 1892

Democratic Party
President; Grover Cleveland, New York
Vice President: Adlai Ewing Stevenson, Illinois
Republican Party
President: Benjamin Harrison, Indiana
Vice President: Whitelaw Reid, New York
People's Party of America
President: James Baird Weaver, Iowa
Vice President: James Gaven Field, Virginia
Prohibition Party
President: John Bidwell, California
Vice President: James Britton Cranfill, Texas
Socialist Labor Party
President: Simon Wing, Massachusetts
Vice President: Charles Horatio Matchett, New York*

Election of 1896

Republican Party
President: William McKinley, Ohio
Vice President: Garret Augustus Hobart, New Jersey
Democratic Party
President: William Jennings Bryan, Nebraska
Vice President: Arthur Sewall, Maine
People's Party (Populist)
President: William Jennings Bryan, Nebraska
Vice President: Thomas Edward Watson, Georgia
National Democratic Party
President: John McAuley Palmer, Illinois
Vice President: Simon Bolivar Buckner, Kentucky
Prohibition Party
President: Joshua Levering, Maryland
Vice President: Hale Johnson, Illinois*
Socialist Labor Party
President: Charles Horatio Matchett, New York
Vice President: Matthew Maguire, New Jersey
National Party
President: Charles Eugene Bentley, Nebraska
Vice President: James Haywood Southgate, North Carolina*

National Silver Party (Bi-Metallic League)
President: William Jennings Bryan, Nebraska
Vice President: Arthur Sewall, Maine

Election of 1900

Republican Party
President: William McKinley, Ohio
Vice President: Theodore Roosevelt, New York
Democratic Party
President: William Jennings Bryan, Nebraska
Vice President: Adai Ewing Stevenson, Illinois
Prohibition Party
President: John Granville Woolley, Illinois
Vice President: Henry Brewer Metcalf, Rhode Island
Social-Democratic Party
President: Eugene Victor Debs, Indiana
Vice President: Job Harriman, California
People's Party (Populist—Anti-Fusionist faction)
President: Wharton Barker, Pennsylvania
Vice President: Ignatius Donnelly, Minnesota
Socialist Labor Party
President: Joseph Francis Malloney, Massachusetts
Vice President: Valentine Remmel, Pennsylvania
Union Reform Party
President: Seth Hockett Ellis, Ohio
Vice President: Samuel T. Nicholson, Pennsylvania
United Christian Party
President: Jonah Fitz Randolph Leonard, Iowa
Vice President: David H. Martin, Pennsylvania
People's Party (Populist—Fusionist faction)
President: William Jennings Bryan, Nebraska
Vice President: Adlai Ewing Stevenson, Illinois
Silver Republican Party
President: William Jennings Bryan, Nebraska
Vice President: Adlai Ewing Stevenson, Illinois
National Party
President: Donelson Caffery, Louisiana
Vice President: Archibald Murray Howe, Massachusetts*

Election of 1904

Republican Party
President: Theodore Roosevelt, New York
Vice President: Charles Warren Fairbanks, Indiana
Democratic Party
President: Alton Brooks Parker, New York
Vice President: Henry Gassaway Davis, West Virginia
Socialist Party
President: Eugene Victor Debs, Indiana
Vice President: Benjamin Hanford, New York
Prohibition Party
President: Silas Comfort Swallow, Pennsylvania
Vice President: George W. Carroll, Texas
People's Party (Populists)
President: Thomas Edward Watson, Georgia
Vice President: Thomas Henry Tibbles, Nebraska
Socialist Labor Party
President: Charles Hunter Corregan, New York
Vice President: William Wesley Cox, Illinois
Continental Party
President: Austin Holcomb
Vice President: A. King, Missouri

Election of 1908

Republican Party
President: William Howard Taft, Ohio
Vice President: James Schoolcraft Sherman, New York
Democratic Party
President: William Jennings Bryan, Nebraska
Vice President: John Worth Kern, Indiana
Socialist Party
President: Eugene Victor Debs
Vice President: Benjamin Hanford
Prohibition Party
President: Eugene Wilder Chafin, Illinois
Vice President: Aaron Sherman Watkins, Ohio

Independence Party
President: Thomas Louis Hisgen, Massachusetts
Vice President: John Temple Graves, Georgia
People's Party (Populist)
President: Thomas Edward Watson, Georgia
Vice President: Samuel Williams, Indiana
Socialist Labor Party
President: August Gillhaus, New York
Vice President: Donald L. Munro, Virginia
United Christian Party
President: Daniel Braxton Turney, Illinois
Vice President: Lorenzo S. Coffin, Iowa

Election of 1912

Democratic Party
President: Woodrow Wilson, New Jersey
Vice President: Thomas Riley Marshall, Indiana
Progressive Party ("Bull Moose" Party)
President: Theodore Roosevelt, New York
Vice President: Hiram Warren Johnson, California
Republican Party
President: William Howard Taft, Ohio
Vice President: James Schoolcraft Sherman, New York
Sherman died Oct. 30; replaced by Nicholas Murray Butler, New York
Socialist Party
President: Eugene Victor Debs, Indiana
Vice President: Emil Seidel, Wisconsin
Prohibition Party
President: Eugene Wilder Chafin, Illinois
Vice President: Aaron Sherman Watkins, Ohio
Socialist Labor Party
President: Arthur Elmer Reimer, Massachusetts
Vice President: August Gillhaus, New York[1]

Election of 1916

Democratic Party
President: Woodrow Wilson, New Jersey
Vice President: Thomas Riley Marshall, Indiana
Republican Party
President: Charles Evans Hughes, New York
Vice President: Charles Warren Fairbanks, Indiana
Socialist Party
President: Allan Louis Benson, New York
Vice President: George Ross Kirkpatrick, New Jersey
Prohibition Party
President: James Franklin Hanly, Indiana
Vice President: Ira Landrith, Tennessee
Socialist Labor Party
President: Arthur Elmer Reimer, Massachusetts*
Vice President: Caleb Harrison, Illinois*
Progressive Party
President: Theodore Roosevelt, New York
Vice President: John Milliken Parker, Louisiana

Election of 1920

Republican Party
President: Warren Gamaliel Harding, Ohio
Vice President: Calvin Coolidge, Massachusetts
Democratic Party
President: James Middleton Cox, Ohio
Vice President: Franklin Delano Roosevelt, New York
Socialist Party
President: Eugene Victor Debs, Indiana
Vice President: Seymour Stedman, Illinois
Farmer Labor Party
President: Parley Parker Christensen, Utah
Vice President: Maximilian Sebastian Hayes, Ohio
Prohibition Party
President: Aaron Sherman Watkins, Ohio
Vice President: David Leigh Colvin, New York
Socialist Labor Party
President: William Wesley Cox, Missouri
Vice President: August Gillhaus, New York
Single Tax Party
President: Robert Colvin Macauley, Pennsylvania
Vice President: R. G. Barnum, Ohio

American Party
President: James Edward Ferguson, Texas
Vice President: William J. Hough

Election of 1924

Republican Party
President: Calvin Coolidge, Massachusetts
Vice President: Charles Gates Dawes, Illinois
Democratic Party
President: John William Davis, West Virginia
Vice President: Charles Wayland Bryan, Nebraska
Progressive Party
President: Robert La Follette, Wisconsin
Vice President: Burton Kendall Wheeler, Montana
Prohibition Party
President: Herman Preston Faris, Missouri
Vice President: Marie Caroline Brehm, California
Socialist Labor Party
President: Frank T. Johns, Oregon
Vice President: Verne L. Reynolds, New York
Socialist Party
President: Robert La Follette, New York
Vice President: Burton Kendall Wheeler, Montana
Workers Party (Communist Party)
President: William Zebulon Foster, Illinois
Vice President: Benjamin Gitlow, New York
American Party
President: Gilbert Owen Nations, District of Columbia
Vice President: Charles Hiram Randall, California[2]
Commonwealth Land Party
President: William J. Wallace, New Jersey
Vice President: John Cromwell Lincoln, Ohio
Farmer Labor Party
President: Duncan McDonald, Illinois*
Vice President: William Bouck, Washington*
Greenback Party
President: John Zahnd, Indiana*
Vice President: Roy M. Harrop, Nebraska*

Election of 1928

Republican Party
President: Herbert Clark Hoover, California
Vice President: Charles Curtis, Kansas
Democratic Party
President: Alfred Emanuel Smith, New York
Vice President: Joseph Taylor Robinson, Arkansas
Socialist Party
President: Norman Mattoon Thomas, New York
Vice President: James Hudson Maurer, Pennsylvania
Workers Party (Communist Party)
President: William Zebulon Foster, Illinois
Vice President: Benjamin Gitlow, New York
Socialist Labor Party
President: Verne L. Reynolds, Michigan
Vice President: Jeremiah D. Crowley, New York
Prohibition Party
President: William Frederick Varney, New York
Vice President: James Arthur Edgerton, Virginia
Farmer Labor Party
President: Frank Elbridge Webb, California
Vice President: Will Vereen, Georgia[3]
Greenback Party
President: John Zahnd, Indiana*
Vice President: Wesley Henry Bennington, Ohio*

Election of 1932

Democratic Party
President: Franklin Delano Roosevelt, New York
Vice President: John Nance Garner, Texas
Republican Party
President: Herbert Clark Hoover, California
Vice President: Charles Curtis, Kansas
Socialist Party
President: Norman Mattoon Thomas, New York
Vice President: James Hudson Maurer, Pennsylvania

Communist Party
President: William Zebulon Foster, Illinois
Vice President: James William Ford, New York
Prohibition Party
President: William David Upshaw, Georgia
Vice President: Frank Stewart Regan, Illinois
Liberty Party
President: William Hope Harvey, Arkansas
Vice President: Frank B. Hemenway, Washington
Socialist Labor Party
President: Verne L. Reynolds, New York
Vice President: John W. Aiken, Massachusetts
Farmer Labor Party
President: Jacob Sechler Coxey, Ohio
Vice President: Julius J. Reiter, Minnesota
Jobless Party
President: James Renshaw Cox, Pennsylvania
Vice President: V. C. Tisdal, Oklahoma
National Party
President: Seymour E. Allen, Massachusetts

Election of 1936

Democratic Party
President: Franklin Delano Roosevelt, New York
Vice President: John Nance Garner, Texas
Republican Party
President: Alfred Mossman Landon, Kansas
Vice President: Frank Knox, Illinois
Union Party
President: William Lemke, North Dakota
Vice President: Thomas Charles O'Brien, Massachusetts
Socialist Party
President: Norman Mattoon Thomas, New York
Vice President: George A. Nelson, Wisconsin
Communist Party
President: Earl Russell Browder, Kansas
Vice President: James William Ford, New York
Prohibition Party
President: David Leigh Colvin, New York
Vice President: Alvin York, Tennessee
Socialist Labor Party
President: John W. Aikin, Massachusetts
Vice President: Emil F. Teichert, New York
National Greenback Party
President: John Zahnd, Indiana*
Vice President: Florence Garvin, Rhode Island*

Election of 1940

Democratic Party
President: Franklin Delano Roosevelt, New York
Vice President: Henry Agard Wallace, Iowa
Republican Party
President: Wendell Lewis Willkie, New York
Vice President: Charles Linza McNary, Oregon
Socialist Party
President: Norman Mattoon Thomas, New York
Vice President: Maynard C. Krueger, Illinois
Prohibition Party
President: Roger Ward Babson, Massachusetts
Vice President: Edgar V. Moorman, Illinois
Communist Party (Workers Party)
President: Earl Russell Browder, Kansas
Vice President: James William Ford, New York
Socialist Labor Party
President: John W. Aiken, Massachusetts
Vice President: Aaron M. Orange, New York
Greenback Party
President: John Zahnd, Indiana*
Vice President: James Elmer Yates, Arizona*

Election of 1944

Democratic Party
President: Franklin Delano Roosevelt, New York
Vice President: Harry S Truman, Missouri
Republican Party
President: Thomas Edmund Dewey, New York

Vice President: John William Bricker, Ohio
Socialist Party
President: Norman Mattoon Thomas, New York
Vice President: Darlington Hoopes, Pennsylvania
Prohibition Party
President: Claude A. Watson, California
Vice President: Andrew Johnson, Kentucky
Socialist Labor Party
President: Edward A. Teichert, Pennsylvania
Vice President: Arla A. Albaugh, Ohio
America First Party
President: Gerald Lyman Kenneth Smith, Michigan
Vice President: Henry A. Romer, Ohio

Election of 1948

Democratic Party
President: Harry S Truman, Missouri
Vice President: Alben William Barkley, Kentucky
Republican Party
President: Thomas Edmund Dewey, New York
Vice President: Earl Warren, California
States' Rights Democratic Party
President: James Strom Thurmond, South Carolina
Vice President: Fielding Lewis Wright, Mississippi
Progressive Party
President: Henry Agard Wallace, Iowa
Vice President: Glen Hearst Taylor, Idaho
Socialist Party
President: Norman Mattoon Thomas, New York
Vice President: Tucker Powell Smith, Michigan
Prohibition Party
President: Claude A. Watson, California
Vice President: Dale Learn, Pennsylvania
Socialist Labor Party
President: Edward A. Teichert, Pennsylvania
Vice President: Stephen Emery, New York
Socialist Workers Party
President: Farrell Dobbs, New York
Vice President: Grace Carlson, Minnesota
Christian Nationalist Party
President: Gerald Lyman Kenneth Smith, Missouri
Vice President: Henry A. Romer, Ohio
Greenback Party
President: John G. Scott, New York
Vice President: Granville B. Leeke, Indiana*
Vegetarian Party
President: John Maxwell, Illinois
Vice President: Symon Gould, New York*

Election of 1952

Republican Party
President: Dwight David Eisenhower, New York
Vice President: Richard Milhous Nixon, California
Democratic Party
President: Adlai Ewing Stevenson, Illinois
Vice President: John Jackson Sparkman, Alabama
Progressive Party
President: Vincent William Hallinan, California
Vice President: Charlotta A. Bass, New York
Prohibition Party
President: Stuart Hamblen, California
Vice President: Enoch Arden Holtwick, Illinois
Socialist Labor Party
President: Eric Hass, New York
Vice President: Stephen Emery, New York
Socialist Party
President: Darlington Hoopes, Pennsylvania
Vice President: Samuel Herman Friedman, New York
Socialist Workers Party
President: Farrell Dobbs, New York
Vice President: Myra Tanner Weiss, New York
America First Party
President: Douglas MacArthur, Wisconsin
Vice President: Harry Flood Byrd, Virginia

American Labor Party
President: Vincent William Hallinan, California
Vice President: Charlotta A. Bass, New York

American Vegetarian Party
President: Daniel J. Murphy, California
Vice President: Symon Gould, New York*

Church of God Party
President: Homer Aubrey Tomlinson, New York
Vice President: Willie Isaac Bass, North Carolina*

Constitution Party
President: Douglas MacArthur, Wisconsin
Vice President: Harry Flood Byrd, Virginia

Greenback Party
President: Frederick C. Proehl, Washington
Vice President: Edward J. Bedell, Indiana

Poor Man's Party
President: Henry B. Krajewski, New Jersey
Vice President: Frank Jenkins, New Jersey

Election of 1956

Republican Party
President: Dwight David Eisenhower, Pennsylvania
Vice President: Richard Milhous Nixon, California

Democratic Party
President: Adlai Ewing Stevenson, Illinois
Vice President: Estes Kefauver, Tennessee

States' Rights Party
President: Thomas Coleman Andrews, Virginia
Vice President: Thomas Harold Werdel, California
Ticket also favored by Constitution Party.

Prohibition Party
President: Enoch Arden Holtwick, Illinois
Vice President: Edward M. Cooper, California

Socialist Labor Party
President: Eric Hass, New York
Vice President: Georgia Cozzini, Wisconsin

Texas Constitution Party
President: William Ezra Jenner, Indiana*
Vice President: Joseph Bracken Lee, Utah*

Socialist Workers Party
President: Farrell Dobbs, New York
Vice President: Myra Tanner Weiss, New York

American Third Party
President: Henry Krajewski, New Jersey
Vice President: Ann Marie Yezo, New Jersey

Socialist Party
President: Darlington Hoopes, Pennsylvania
Vice President: Samuel Herman Friedman, New York

Pioneer Party
President: William Langer, North Dakota*
Vice President: Burr McCloskey, Illinois*

American Vegetarian Party
President: Herbert M. Shelton, California*
Vice President: Symon Gould, New York*

Greenback Party
President: Frederick C. Proehl, Washington
Vice President: Edward Kirby Meador, Massachusetts*

States' Rights Party of Kentucky
President: Harry Flood Byrd, Virginia
Vice President: William Ezra Jenner, Indiana

South Carolinians for Independent Electors
President: Harry Flood Byrd, Virginia

Christian National Party
President: Gerald Lyman Kenneth Smith
Vice President: Charles I. Robertson

Election of 1960

Democratic Party
President: John Fitzgerald Kennedy, Massachusetts
Vice President: Lyndon Baines Johnson, Texas

Republican Party
President: Richard Milhous Nixon, California
Vice President: Henry Cabot Lodge, Massachusetts

National States' Rights Party
President: Orval Eugene Faubus, Arkansas
Vice President: John Geraerdt Crommelin, Alabama

Socialist Labor Party
President: Eric Hass, New York
Vice President: Georgia Cozzini, Wisconsin

Prohibition Party
President: Rutherford Losey Decker, Missouri
Vice President: Earle Harold Munn, Michigan

Socialist Workers Party
President: Farrell Dobbs, New York
Vice President: Myra Tanner Weiss, New York

Conservative Party of New Jersey
President: Joseph Bracken Lee, Utah
Vice President: Kent H. Courtney, Louisiana

Conservative Party of Virginia
President: C. Benton Coiner, Virginia
Vice President: Edward M. Silverman, Virginia

Constitution Party (Texas)
President: Charles Loten Sullivan, Mississippi
Vice President: Merritt B. Curtis, District of Columbia

Constitution Party (Washington)
President: Merritt B. Curtis, District of Columbia
Vice President: B. N. Miller

Greenback Party
President: Whitney Hart Slocomb, California*
Vice President: Edward Kirby Meador, Massachusetts*

Independent Afro-American Party
President: Clennon King, Georgia
Vice President: Reginald Carter

Tax Cut Party (America First Party; American Party)
President: Lar Daly, Illinois
Vice President: Merritt Barton Curtis, District of Columbia

Theocratic Party
President: Homer Aubrey Tomlinson, New York
Vice President: Raymond L. Teague, Alaska*

Vegetarian Party
President: Symon Gould, New York
Vice President: Christopher Gian-Cursio, Florida

Election of 1964

Democratic Party
President: Lyndon Baines Johnson, Texas
Vice President: Hubert Horatio Humphrey, Minnesota

Republican Party
President: Barry Morris Goldwater, Arizona
Vice President: William Edward Miller, New York

Socialist Labor Party
President: Eric Hass, New York
Vice President: Henning A. Blomen, Massachusetts

Prohibition Party
President: Earle Harold Munn, Michigan
Vice President: Mark Shaw, Massachusetts

Socialist Workers Party
President: Clifton DeBerry, New York
Vice President: Edward Shaw, New York

National States' Rights Party
President: John Kasper, Tennessee
Vice President: J. B. Stoner, Georgia

Constitution Party
President: Joseph B. Lightburn, West Virginia
Vice President: Theodore C. Billings, Colorado

Independent States' Rights Party
President: Thomas Coleman Andrews, Virginia
Vice President: Thomas H. Werdel, California*

Theocratic Party
President: Homer Aubrey Tomlinson, New York
Vice President: William R. Rogers, Missouri*

Universal Party
President: Kirby James Hensley, California
Vice President: John O. Hopkins, Iowa

Election of 1968

Republican Party
President: Richard Milhous Nixon, New York
Vice President: Spiro Theodore Agnew, Maryland
Democratic Party
President: Hubert Horatio Humphrey, Minnesota
Vice President: Edmund Sixtus Muskie, Maine
American Independent Party
President: George Corley Wallace, Alabama
Vice President: Curtis Emerson LeMay, Ohio
LeMay replaced S. Marvin Griffin, who originally had been selected.
Peace and Freedom Party
President: Eldridge Cleaver
Vice President: Judith Mage, New York
Socialist Labor Party
President: Henning A. Blomen, Massachusetts
Vice President: George Sam Taylor, Pennsylvania
Socialist Workers Party
President: Fred Halstead, New York
Vice President: Paul Boutelle, New Jersey
Prohibition Party
President: Earle Harold Munn, Sr., Michigan
Vice President: Rolland E. Fisher, Kansas
Communist Party
President: Charlene Mitchell, California
Vice President: Michael Zagarell, New York
Constitution Party
President: Richard K. Troxell, Texas
Vice President: Merle Thayer, Iowa
Freedom and Peace Party
President: Dick Gregory (Richard Claxton Gregory), Illinois
Patriotic Party
President: George Corley Wallace, Alabama
Vice President: William Penn Patrick, California*
Theocratic Party
President: William R. Rogers, Missouri
Universal Party
President: Kirby James Hensley, California
Vice President: Rcscoe B. MacKenna

Election of 1972

Republican Party
President: Richard Milhous Nixon, California
Vice President: Spiro Theodore Agnew, Maryland
Democratic Party
President: George Stanley McGovern, South Dakota
Vice President: Thomas Francis Eagleton, Missouri
Eagleton resigned and was replaced on August 8, 1972, by Robert Sargent Shriver, Maryland, selected by the Democratic National Committee.
American Independent Party
President: John George Schmitz, California
Vice President: Thomas Jefferson Anderson, Tennessee
Socialist Workers Party
President: Louis Fisher, Illinois
Vice President: Genevieve Gunderson, Minnesota
Socialist Labor Party
President: Linda Jenness, Georgia
Vice President: Andrew Pulley, Illinois
Communist Party
President: Gus Hall, New York
Vice President: Jarvis Tyner

Prohibition Party
President: Earle Harold Munn, Sr., Michigan
Vice President: Marshall Uncapher
Libertarian Party
President: John Hospers, California
Vice President: Theodora Nathan, Oregon
People's Party
President: Benjamin McLane Spock
Vice President: Julius Hobson, District of Columbia
America First Party
President: John V. Mahalchik
Vice President: Irving Homer
Universal Party
President: Gabriel Green
Vice President: Daniel Fry

Election of 1976

Democratic Party
President: Jimmy Carter, Georgia
Vice President: Walter F. Mondale, Minnesota
Republican Party
President: Gerald R. Ford, Michigan
Vice President: Robert Dole, Kansas
Independent Candidate
President: Eugene J. McCarthy, Minnesota
Vice President: none [4]
Libertarian Party
President: Roger MacBride, Virginia
Vice President: David P. Bergland, California
American Independent Party
President: Lester Maddox, Georgia
Vice President: William Dyke, Wisconsin
American Party
President: Thomas J. Anderson, Tennessee
Vice President: Rufus Shackleford, Florida
Socialist Workers Party
President: Peter Camejo, California
Vice President: Willie Mae Reid, California
Communist Party
President: Gus Hall, New York
Vice President: Jarvis Tyner, New York
People's Party
President: Margaret Wright, California
Vice President: Benjamin Spock, New York
U.S. Labor Party
President: Lyndon H. LaRouche, New York
Vice President: R.W. Evans, Michigan
Prohibition Party
President: Benjamin C. Bubar, Maine
Vice President: Earl F. Dodge, Colorado
Socialist Labor Party
President: Jules Levin, New Jersey
Vice President: Constance Blomen, Massachusetts
Socialist Party
President: Frank P. Zeidler, Wisconsin
Vice President: J. Quinn Brisben, Illinois
Restoration Party
President: Ernest L. Miller
Vice President: Roy N. Eddy
United American Party
President: Frank Taylor
Vice President: Henry Swan

---

1. 1912: Schlesinger's History of Presidential Elections lists the Socialist Labor Party vice presidential candidate as Francis. No first name is given for Francis.
2. 1924: Scammon's America at the Polls lists the American Party vice presidential candidate as Leander L. Pickett.
3. 1928: America at the Polls lists the Farmer Labor Party vice presidential candidate as L. R. Tillman.

4. 1976: McCarthy, who ran as an independent with no party designation, had no national running mate, favoring the elimination of the office. But as various state laws required a running mate, he had different ones in different states, amounting to nearly two dozen, all political unknowns.
* Candidate appeared in Kane's Facts About the Presidents but could not be verified in another source; see text p. 115.

Presidential Primaries

Presidential Primaries

Presidential primaries originated as an outgrowth of the progressive movement in the early 20th century. Progressives, populists, and reformers in general at the turn of the century were fighting state and municipal corruption. They objected to the links between political bosses and big business and advocated returning the government to the people.

Part of this "return to the people" was the inauguration of primary elections, wherein candidates for office would be chosen by the voters of their party rather than by what were looked upon as boss-dominated conventions. It was only a matter of time before the idea spread from state and local elections to presidential contests. Since there was no provision for a nationwide primary, state primaries were initiated to choose delegates to the national party conventions (delegate selection primaries), and to register voters' preferences on their parties' eventual presidential nominees (preference primaries).

Florida enacted the first presidential primary law in 1901. The law gave party officials an option of holding a party primary to choose any party candidate for public office, as well as delegates to the national conventions. However, there was no provision for placing names of presidential candidates on the ballot — either in the form of a preference vote or with information indicating the preference of the candidates for convention delegates.

Wisconsin's progressive Republican politician, Gov. Robert M. La Follette, gave a major boost to the presidential primary following the 1904 Republican national convention. It was at that convention that the credentials of La Follette's progressive delegation were rejected and a regular Republican delegation was seated from Wisconsin. Angered by what he considered his unfair treatment, La Follette returned to his home state and began pushing for a presidential primary law. The result was the Wisconsin law of 1905 providing for the mandatory direct election of national convention delegates. The law, however, did not include a provision for indicating delegate preference for presidential candidates.

Pennsylvania closely followed Wisconsin (in 1906) with a statute providing that each candidate for delegate to a national convention could have printed beside his name on the official primary ballot the name of the presidential candidate he would support at the convention. However, no member of either party exercised this option in the 1908 primary.

La Follette's sponsorship of the delegate selection primary helped make the concept part of the progressive political program. The growth of the progressive movement rapidly resulted in the enactment of presidential primary laws in other states.

The next step in presidential primaries — the preferential vote for president — took place in Oregon. There, in 1910, Sen. Jonathan Bourne (R 1907-13), a progressive

Republican colleague of La Follette (then a senator), sponsored a referendum to establish a presidential preference primary, with delegates legally bound to support the winner of the preference primary.

By 1912, with Oregon in the lead, twelve states had enacted presidential primary laws which provided for either direct election of delegates, a preferential vote, or both. Three other states had adopted laws that gave state party committees the option of permitting the voters to elect delegates to the national nominating conventions. The number had expanded to 26 states by 1916.

The first major test of the impact of presidential primary laws — in 1912 — demonstrated that victories in the primaries did not ensure a candidate's nomination at the convention. Former President Theodore Roosevelt, campaigning in twelve Republican primaries, won nine of them, including a defeat of incumbent President William Howard Taft (R) in Taft's home state of Ohio. Roosevelt lost only three — to Taft by a narrow margin in Massachusetts and to La Follette in North Dakota and in La Follette's home state of Wisconsin.

Despite this impressive string of primary victories, however, the Republican national convention rejected Roosevelt in favor of Taft. The Republican National Committee, which organized the convention, and the convention's credentials committee, which ruled on contested delegates, both were dominated by Taft supporters. Moreover, Taft was backed by many state organizations, especially in the South, where most delegates were chosen by caucuses or conventions dominated by party leaders.

On the Democratic side, the primaries were more closely connected with the results of the convention. New Jersey Gov. Woodrow Wilson (D) and Speaker of the House Champ Clark (D) of Missouri were closely matched in total primary votes, with Wilson only 29,632 votes ahead of Clark. Wilson emerged with the nomination after a long struggle with Clark at the convention.

Likewise in 1916, Democratic primary results foreshadowed the winner of the nomination. However, Wilson was then the incumbent president and had no major opposition

Sources

James W. Davis. *Presidential Primaries: Road to the White House.* New York: Thomas Y. Crowell Co., 1967.

Richard M. Scammon. *America Votes 1956-57.* New York: The Macmillan Co., 1958. *America Votes 4,* Pittsburgh: University of Pittsburgh Press, 1962. *America Votes 6, America Votes 8, America Votes 10, America Votes 12.* Washington, D.C.: Congressional Quarterly Inc., 1966, 1970, 1973, 1977.

for renomination. But once again, Republican presidential primaries had little to do with the nominating process at the convention. The eventual nominee, U.S. Supreme Court Justice Charles Evans Hughes, won only two primaries.

In 1920, presidential primaries did not play a major role in determining the winner of either party's nomination. Democrat James M. Cox, the eventual nominee, ran in only one primary, his home state of Ohio. Most of the Democratic primaries featured favorite son candidates or write-in votes. And at the convention, Democrats took 44 ballots to make their choice.

Similarly, the main entrants in the Republican presidential primaries that year failed to capture their party's nomination. Sen. Warren G. Harding (R) of Ohio, the compromise choice, won the primary in his home state but lost badly in Indiana and garnered only a handful of votes elsewhere. The three leaders in the primaries — Sen. Hiram Johnson (R) of California, Gen. Leonard Wood of New Hampshire and Illinois Gov. Frank O. Lowden (R) all lost out in the end.

After the first wave of enthusiasm for presidential primaries in the 1910s, interest waned. By 1935, eight states had repealed their presidential primary laws.

The diminution of reform zeal during the 1920s, and the preoccupation of the country with depression in the 1930s and war in the 1940s appeared to have been leading factors in this decline. Also, party leaders were not enthusiastic about primaries; the cost of conducting primaries was relatively high, both for the candidates and the states; many primaries were ignored by presidential candidates; and there was often low voter participation.

But after World War II, interest picked up again. Some politicians with presidential ambitions, knowing the party leadership was not enthusiastic about their candidacies, entered the primaries to try to generate a bandwagon effect. In 1948, Harold Stassen (R), governor of Minnesota from 1939 to 1943, entered Republican presidential primaries in opposition to the Republican organization and was able to make some dramatic headway before losing to Gov. Thomas E. Dewey (R) of New York in Oregon. And in 1952, Tennessee Sen. Estes Kefauver (D 1949-63), riding a wave of public recognition as head of a Senate Organized Crime Investigating Committee, challenged Democratic party leaders by winning several primaries, including an upset of President Truman in New Hampshire. The Eisenhower-Taft struggle for the Republican Party nomination that year also stimulated interest in the primaries.

John F. Kennedy (D) in 1960, Barry M. Goldwater (R) in 1964, Richard M. Nixon (R) in 1968, George S. McGovern (D) in 1972, and Jimmy Carter (D) in 1976 — all party

1980 Democratic Party Rules for Primaries

In the 1970s, the Democratic Party moved toward a proportional representation system for presidential primaries, in which candidates for president win delegates in proportion to the vote cast for each of them. This replaces the so-called winner-take-all primaries in which the candidate with the most votes won all the delegates.

During 1978, the Democratic Party adopted a series of new rules regarding the delegate selection process, some of which completed the movement to proportional representation.

At a Democratic National Committee meeting in June 1978, the main battle was over the threshold at which presidential candidates would be able to win convention delegates. For the 1976 convention, any candidate who received at least 15 percent of the vote in a caucus or proportional representation primary was guaranteed a share of the delegates. Liberals wished to retain this formula.

The commission drawing up the new rules proposed raising the threshold, arguing that 15 percent was too low, allowing minor candidates to continue hopeless campaigns while delaying the process of party consensus building. The result was a compromise, with a floating figure ranging from 15 to 25 percent depending on a variety of factors, including the number of delegates to be elected in each district.

Other changes adopted at the June meeting included rules to shorten the period when the delegate selection season can take place in every state from six to three months (stretching from the second Tuesday in March to the second Tuesday in June), to require primary states to set candidate filing deadlines 30 to 90 days before the election, to increase the size of state delegations by 10 percent to accommodate state party and elected officials, and to limit participation in the delegate selection process to Democrats only. Banned by this last rule are open, cross-over primaries, such as the one in Wisconsin, where voters have been able to participate in the Democratic election without designating their party affiliation.

No exemption will be permitted for Wisconsin in 1980 as there was in 1976 but states in violation of the other rules may apply for exemptions if they are unsuccessful in changing state laws to bring conformance with the new rules.

In a later decision, taken at their midterm convention in Memphis in December 1978, Democrats decreed an end to winner-take-all primaries, banning the last remaining type, the single-member delegate districts. According to the Memphis rule, every delegate district, no matter how small, will have to elect several delegates and award some of them to any candidate who meets the threshold requirement of the primary vote. As the proportional representation rule applies also to states choosing national convention delegates through caucuses or conventions, the net effect of all the new Democratic rules is that in 1980, for the first time, all 50 states will elect Democratic delegates through a system of proportional representation.

In another decision taken at Memphis, Democrats required state delegations to be equally divided between men and women. Equal division assures that in 1980, women will have greater representation than at any previous nominating convention. Because of the rule adopted earlier to expand the size of the 1980 convention by 10 percent to include state party and elected officials, who are predominantly men, the next convention may not be quite 50 percent female. But the percentage of women will be well above the previous high of 40 percent in 1972 and the 1976 level of 33 percent.

presidential nominees — were able to use the primaries to show their vote-getting and organizational abilities.

With the demand for political reform in the 1960s and early 1970s, the presidential primaries became more popular as a route to the nomination. The revival of the old progressive reformist faith that primaries would allow the people to choose their own leaders made the participation in primaries almost mandatory for anyone seeking a presidential nomination. By 1976, 26 states plus the District of Columbia held some variation of the presidential preference primary. Also, in Alabama, New York and Texas, delegates to the national party conventions were elected in primaries, but none of these states provided for a specific expression statewide of presidential preference by the voter.

Proposals for Reform

Despite the growing use of primaries however, the existing system came under considerable criticism. The critics often cited the length of the primary season (nearly twice as long as the general election campaign), the expense, the physical strain on the candidates and the variations and complexities of state laws as leading problems of presidential primaries.

To deal with these problems, several states in 1974-75 discussed the feasibility of creating regional primaries, in which individual states within a geographical region would hold their primaries on the same day. Supporters of the concept believed it would reduce candidate expenses and strain and would permit concentration on regional issues.

The idea achieved some limited success when two groups of states — one in the West and the other in the South — decided to organize regional primaries in 1976 in each of their areas. However, the two groups both chose the same day, May 25, to hold their primaries, thus defeating one of the main purposes of the plan by continuing to force candidates to shuttle across the country to cover both areas. The western states participating in the grouping were Idaho, Nevada and Oregon; the southern states were Arkansas, Kentucky and Tennessee.

Attempts were also made in New England to construct a regional primary. But jealousy on the part of New Hampshire for its first-in-the-nation primary and hesitancy by the other New England state legislatures defeated the idea. Only Vermont joined Massachusetts, on March 2, in holding a simultaneous presidential primary.

Other approaches to changing the primary system have been attempted at the national level. National reform proposals included a single nationwide primary, standardization of the date of primaries to shorten the campaign season, and a law mandating a regional primary system.

Since 1911, hundreds of bills have been introduced in Congress to reform the presidential primary system. The largest quantities were introduced in sessions after the 1912, 1952 and 1968 nominating campaigns. All three campaigns produced the feeling among many voters that the will of the electorate, as expressed in the primaries, had been thwarted by national conventions. But since 1911 the only legislation enacted by Congress concerned the presidential primary in the District of Columbia. Rarely did primary reform legislation even reach the hearing stage.

Types of Primaries

Presidential primaries consist of two basic types. One is the presidential preference primary in which voters vote directly for the person they wish to be nominated for president. The second type is the delegate selection primary in which voters elect delegates to the national conventions.

States may use various combinations of these methods:

● A state may have a preference vote but choose delegates at party conventions. The preference vote may or may not be binding on the delegates.

● A state may combine the preference and delegate selection primaries by electing delegates pledged or favorable to a candidate named on the ballot. However, under this system, state party organizations may run unpledged slates of delegates.

● A state may have an advisory preference vote and a separate delegate selection vote in which delegates may be listed as either pledged to a candidate, favorable or unpledged.

● A state may have a mandatory preference vote with a separate delegate selection vote. In these cases, the delegates are required to support the preference primary winner.

For those primaries in which the preference vote is binding upon delegates, state laws may vary as to the number of ballots through which delegates at the convention may remain committed.

Primaries may also vary in other ways. In some states only members of a political party may vote in the party's primary (closed primaries); in others, anyone may vote in whichever party's primary he chooses (open primaries). Also, delegate selection may take place on a statewide at-large basis, or by district, or by a combination of the two.

Bibliography

Books

Davis, James W. *The Presidential Primary, 1928-1960.* Minneapolis, Minn.: 1962.

———. *Presidential Primaries: Road to the White House.* New York: Crowell, 1967.

Eisenstein, James. *Presidential Primaries of 1976.* Washington, Conn.: Center for Information on America, 1976.

Eisenstein, Virginia. *Presidential Primaries of 1968.* Washington, Conn.: Center for Information on America, 1968.

———. *Presidential Primaries of 1972.* Washington, Conn.: Center for Information on America, 1971.

Ernst, Harry. *The Primary That Made a President: West Virginia, 1960.* New York: McGraw-Hill, 1962.

Faber, Harold, ed. *The Road to the White House.* New York: McGraw-Hill, 1965.

Hadley, Arthur T. *The Invisible Primary.* Englewood Cliffs, N.J.: Prentice-Hall, 1976.

Herzog, Arthur. *McCarthy for President.* New York: Viking Press, 1969.

Judah, Charles B. *The Presidential Primary.* Albuquerque, N.M.: University of New Mexico Press, 1953.

Link, Arthur. *Wilson: The Road to the White House.* Princeton, N.J.: Princeton University, 1947.

Merriam, Charles E. *Primary Elections.* Chicago: University of Chicago, 1928.

Michelet, Simon. *Presidential Primaries of 1928.* Washington, D.C.: 1928.

Overacker, Louise. *The Presidential Primary.* New York: Macmillan, 1926.

Sait, Edward M. "The Presidential Primary," *American Parties and Elections.* New York: Appleton, Century, 1939, pp. 546-554.

Schram, Martin. *Running for President 1976: The Carter Campaign.* Briarcliff Manor, N.Y.: Stein & Day, 1977.

Stavis, Ben. *We Were the Campaign: New Hampshire to Chicago for McCarthy.* Boston: Beacon Press, 1969.

A Study of the Presidential Primary. Carson City, Nev.: Legislative Counsel Bureau, 1959.

Articles

Allen, C.D. "The Presidential Primary." *Queens Quarterly,* July-September 1912, pp. 92-99.

"Are the Primaries Secondary?" *Society,* July 1976, pp. 7-10.

Aylesworth, L. R. "Presidential Primary Elections: Legislation of 1910-1912." *American Political Science Review,* August 1912, pp. 429-433.

Barnett, E.D. "Presidential Primary in Oregon." *Political Science Quarterly,* March 1916, pp. 81-104.

Beniger, J. R. "Legacy of Carter and Reagan: Political Reality Overtakes the Myth of the Presidential Primaries." *Intellect,* Fall 1977, pp. 234-237.

Bode, Kenneth. "Primary Politics: Presidential Primaries." *New Republic,* Sept. 6, 1975, pp. 8-10.

Boots, R.S. "Presidential Primary: A Comprehensive Examination of the Presidential Primary at Work and Proposals of Reform." *National Municipal Review,* September 1920, pp. 597-617.

Childs, Richard S. "Presidential Primaries Need Overhaul." *National Civic Review,* January 1975, pp. 14-20.

Chilton, W. E. "West Virginia and the Primary." *New Leader,* May 23, 1960, pp. 3-18.

Comer, John. "Another Look at the Effects of the Divisive Primary." *American Politics Quarterly,* January 1976, pp. 121-128.

Dauer, Manning. "Toward a Model State Presidential Primary Law." *American Political Science Review,* March 1956, p. 145.

Davenport, F. M. "Pre-Nomination Campaign: The Failure of the Presidential Primary." *Outlook,* April 5, 1916, pp. 807-810.

Dickey, Francis J. "The Presidential Preference Primary." *American Political Science Review,* August 1915, pp. 467-487.

Harbison, M. C. "The Presidential Preference Primary." *Tennessee Planner,* April 1953, pp. 131-136.

Harris, J. P. "New Primary System." *State Government,* July 1948, p. 140.

Holcombe, John W. "Presidential Preference Vote and the Electoral College." *Forum,* December 1912, pp. 681-686.

Hy, Ronn and Saeger, Richard. "Should We Have a National Presidential Primary?" *Public Administration Survey,* March 1976, pp. 1-5.

Laprade, William T. "Nominating Primary." *North American Review,* August 1914, pp. 235-243.

"Legislative Note on Presidential Primaries." *American Political Science Review,* February 1916, pp. 116-120.

Lundeen, Ernest. "Presidential Primaries." *Congressional Record,* March 15, 1919, pp. 5480-5486.

Marshall, Thomas R. "Delegate Selection in 1976: Evaluating Caucuses and Primaries." *National Civic Review,* September 1977, pp. 391-396.

McNickle, Roma K. "Presidential Primaries, 1952." *Editorial Research Reports,* Jan. 16, 1952, Vol. I, pp. 43-59.

Patch, Buel W. "Presidential Primaries." *Editorial Reseach Reports,* Jan. 14, 1948, Vol. I, pp. 21-32.

Pierson, James E. and Smith, Terry B. "Primary Divisiveness and General Election Success." *Journal of Politics,* May 1975, pp. 555-562.

Potts, C. S. "The Convention System and the Presidential Primary." *American Review of Reviews,* May 1912, pp. 561-566.

"Presidential Primaries, 1960." *Editorial Research Reports,* Jan. 6, 1960, Vol. I, pp. 436-447.

"Presidential Primaries: Proposals for a New System." *Congressional Quarterly Weekly Report,* July 8, 1972, pp. 1650-1655.

"Presidential Primary System." *Congressional Digest,* August 1928, pp. 221-224.

Putney, Bryant. "Nomination by Primary." *Editorial Research Reports,* Aug. 19, 1938, Vol. II, pp. 119-136.

Stoddard, W. L. "Presidential Primary in Oregon." *Political Science Quarterly,* March 1916, pp. 81-104.

"The United States Presidential Elections: Procedures and Prospects, the Primaries and Conventions." *World Today,* July 1952, pp. 278-287.

Sources

The main source for the primary returns from 1912 through 1952 was James W. Davis' *Presidential Primaries: Road to the White House*. Copyright © 1967 by Harper & Row, Publishers, Inc. Reprinted by Permission of the Publisher.

Congressional Quarterly has supplemented Davis' material with the following sources: Louise Overacker's *The Presidential Primary*, the source used by Davis for the 1912-1924 returns; "Presidential Preference Primaries, 1928-1956," a 1960 Library of Congress study by Walter Kravitz; Paul Davis, Malcolm Moos, and Ralph Goldman, *Presidential Nominating Politics in 1952*, the Johns Hopkins Press, 1954; the offices of secretaries of state; state handbooks and newspapers. All statistics and footnotes are from Davis, unless otherwise indicated.

The basic source for the primary returns from 1956 through 1976 was Richard M. Scammon's *America Votes* series. All statistics and footnotes are from Scammon, unless otherwise indicated.

Figures in the following charts represent one of three types of votes:
● Votes cast directly for a presidential candidate.
● Votes cast for delegates whose candidate preference was indicated on the ballot.
● Votes cast for unpledged delegates. (Included in the "unpledged" category were delegates designated on the ballot as "uninstructed" and "no preference.")

For the delegate-at-large vote in 1912-1924 primaries, Overacker listed the average vote for delegates at large. For the 1928-1952 delegate-at-large vote, Davis listed the highest vote received by any one delegate at large. Congressional Quarterly followed Davis' style for subsequent years.

Percentages in the following tables have been calculated to two decimal points and then rounded; 0.05 percent appears as 0.1 percent. Therefore, columns of percentages do not always total 100 percent. Presidential candidates, primary winners, favorite sons, members of Congress and prominent national and state political figures are included in the state-by-state primary results; others receiving votes are listed in the footnotes.

1912 Primaries

	Republican			Democratic		
		Votes	%		Votes	%
March 19	**North Dakota**					
	Robert M. LaFollette (Wis.)	34,123	57.2	John Burke (N.D.)[1]	9,357	100.0
	Theodore Roosevelt (N.Y.)	23,669	39.7			
	William H. Taft (Ohio)	1,876	3.1			
March 26	**New York**[2]					
April 2	**Wisconsin**					
	LaFollette	133,354	73.2	Woodrow Wilson (N.J.)	45,945	55.7
	Taft	47,514	26.1	Champ Clark (Mo.)	36,464	44.2
	Roosevelt	628	.3	Others	148	.2
	Others	643	.4			
April 9	**Illinois**					
	Roosevelt	266,917	61.1	Clark	218,483	74.3
	Taft	127,481	29.2	Wilson	75,527	25.7
	LaFollette	42,692	9.8			
April 13	**Pennsylvania**					
	Roosevelt	282,853[3]	59.7	Wilson	98,000[3]	100.0
	Taft	191,179[3]	40.3			
April 19	**Nebraska**					
	Roosevelt	45,795	58.7	Clark	21,027	41.0
	LaFollette	16,785	21.5	Wilson	14,289	27.9
	Taft	13,341	17.1	Judson Harmon (Ohio)	12,454	24.3
	Others	2,036	2.6	Others	3,499	6.8
April 19	**Oregon**					
	Roosevelt	28,905	40.2	Wilson	9,588	53.0
	LaFollette	22,491	31.3	Clark	7,857	43.4
	Taft	20,517	28.5	Harmon	606	3.3
	Others	14	—	Others	49	.3
April 30	**Massachusetts**					
	Taft	86,722	50.4	Clark	34,575	68.9
	Roosevelt	83,099	48.3	Wilson	15,002	29.9
	LaFollette	2,058	1.2	Others	627	1.2
	Others	99	.1			
May 6	**Maryland**					
	Roosevelt	29,124	52.8	Clark	34,021	54.4
	Taft	25,995	47.2	Wilson	21,490	34.3
				Harmon	7,070	11.3
May 14	**California**					
	Roosevelt	138,563	54.6	Clark	43,163	71.5
	Taft	69,345	27.3	Wilson	17,214	28.5
	LaFollette	45,876	18.1			
May 21	**Ohio**					
	Roosevelt	165,809	55.3	Harmon	96,164	51.7
	Taft	118,362	39.5	Wilson	85,084	45.7
	LaFollette	15,570	5.2	Clark	2,428	1.3
				Others	2,440	1.3

Republican   ## Democratic

	Votes	%		Votes	%
May 28 New Jersey					
Roosevelt	61,297	56.3	Wilson	48,336	98.9
Taft	44,034	40.5	Clark[4]	522	1.1
LaFollette	3,464	3.2			
June 4 South Dakota					
Roosevelt	38,106	55.2	Wilson[5]	4,694	35.2
Taft	19,960	28.9	Clark[5]	4,275	32.0
LaFollette	10,944	15.9	Clark[5]	2,722	20.4
			Others	1,655	12.4
TOTALS					
Roosevelt	1,164,765	51.5	Wilson	435,169	44.6
Taft	766,326	33.9	Clark	405,537	41.6
LaFollette	327,357	14.5	Harmon	116,294	11.9
Others	2,792	.1	Burke	9,357	1.0
			Others	8,418	.9
	2,261,240			974,775	

1. Burke was the "favorite son" candidate, according to the North Dakota secretary of state.
2. Primary law optional in 1912. Republicans elected pledged delegates but figures not available.
3. Unofficial figures.
4. Write-in.

5. No presidential preference. Three sets of delegates ran: one labelled "Wilson-Bryan" which came out openly for Wilson; one "Wilson-Clark-Bryan" which became identified with Clark; one Champ Clark which was accused by the Clark people of being a scheme to split the Clark vote. The "Wilson-Clark-Bryan" list polled 4,275 and the Champ Clark list 2,722. The delegates were given to Wilson by the convention.

1916 Primaries

	Republican			Democratic		
	Votes	%			Votes	%
March 7 Indiana						
Charles W. Fairbanks (Ind.)[1]	176,078	100.0	Woodrow Wilson (N.J.)		160,423	100.0
March 14 Minnesota						
Albert B. Cummins (Iowa)	54,214	76.8	Wilson		45,136	100.0
Others	16,403	23.2				
March 14 New Hampshire						
Unpledged delegates	9,687	100.0	Wilson		5,684	100.0
March 21 North Dakota						
Robert M. LaFollette (Wis.)	23,374[2]	70.4	Wilson		12,341	100.0
Others	9,851[2]	29.6				
April 3 Michigan						
Henry Ford (Mich.)	83,057	47.4	Wilson		84,972	100.0
William A. Smith (Mich.)	77,872	44.4				
William O. Simpson (Mich.)	14,365	8.2				
April 4 New York						
Unpledged delegates	147,038	100.0	Wilson		112,538	100.0
April 4 Wisconsin						
LaFollette[1]	110,052	98.8	Wilson		109,462	99.8
Others	1,347	1.2	Others		231	.2
April 11 Illinois						
Lawrence Y. Sherman (Ill.)[1]	155,945	90.2	Wilson		136,839	99.8
Theodore Roosevelt (N.Y.)[3]	15,348	8.9	Others		219	.2
Others	1,689	1.0				
April 18 Nebraska						
Cummins	29,850	33.7	Wilson		69,506	87.7
Ford	26,884	30.3	Others		9,744	12.3
Charles E. Hughes (N.Y.)[3]	15,837	17.9				
Roosevelt[3]	2,256	2.5				
Others	13,780	15.6				
April 21 Montana						
Cummins	10,415	89.9	Wilson		17,960	100.0
Others	1,173	10.1				
April 25 Iowa						
Cummins	40,257	100.0	Wilson		31,447	100.0
April 25 Massachusetts						
Unpledged delegates at large[4]	60,462	57.3	Wilson		19,580	100.0
Roosevelt[4]	45,117	42.7				
April 25 New Jersey						
Roosevelt[3]	1,076	73.7	Wilson		25,407	100.0
Hughes[3]	383	26.3				

Republican	Votes	%	**Democratic**	Votes	%

April 25 Ohio

Republican	Votes	%	Democratic	Votes	%
Theodore E. Burton (Ohio)[1]	122,165	86.8	Wilson	82,688	97.2
Roosevelt[3]	1,932	1.4	Others	2,415	2.8
Ford[3]	1,683	1.2			
Hughes[3]	469	.3			
Others	14,428	10.3			

May 2 California

Unpledged delegates	236,277	100.0	Wilson	75,085	100.0

May 16 Pennsylvania

Martin G. Brumbaugh (Pa.)[1]	233,095	86.3	Wilson	142,202	98.7
Ford[3]	20,265	7.5	Others	1,839	1.3
Roosevelt[3]	12,359	4.6			
Hughes[3]	1,804	.7			
Others	2,682	1.0			

May 16 Vermont

Hughes[3]	5,480	70.0	Wilson	3,711	99.4
Roosevelt[3]	1,931	24.6	Others	23	.6
Others	423	5.4			

May 19 Oregon

Hughes	56,764	59.8	Wilson	27,898	100.0
Cummins	27,558	29.0			
Others	10,593	11.2			

May 23 South Dakota

Cummins	29,656	100.0	Wilson	10,341	100.0

June 6 West Virginia

[5]   [5]

TOTALS

Unpledged delegates	453,464	23.6	Wilson	1,173,220	98.8
Brumbaugh	233,095	12.1	Others	14,471	1.2
Cummins	191,950	10.0			
Fairbanks	176,078	9.2		1,187,691	
Sherman	155,945	8.1			
LaFollette	133,426	6.9			
Ford	131,889	6.9			
Burton	122,165	6.4			
Hughes	80,737	4.2			
Roosevelt	80,019	4.2			
Smith	77,872	4.0			
Simpson	14,365	.7			
Others[6]	72,369	3.8			
	1,923,374				

1. *Source for names of "favorite son" candidates: The New York Times.*
2. *Source for vote breakdown: North Dakota secretary of state.*
3. *Write-in.*
4. *No presidential preference vote but one set of delegates at large was for Roosevelt and the other set unpledged.*

5. *Figures not available. Republican winner was Sen. Theodore E. Burton (R Ohio) and Democratic winner was Woodrow Wilson, according to The New York Times.*
6. *In addition to scattered votes, "others" includes Robert G. Ross who received 5,-506 votes in the Nebraska primary; Henry D. Estabrook who received 9,851 in the North Dakota primary and 8,132 in the Nebraska primary.*

1920 Primaries

	Republican			Democratic	
	Votes	%		Votes	%

March 9   New Hampshire

Leonard Wood (N.H.)[1]	8,591	53.0	Unpledged delegates[1]	7,103	100.0
Unpledged delegates	5,604	34.6			
Hiram Johnson (Calif.)[1]	2,000	12.3			

March 16   North Dakota

Johnson	30,573	96.1	William G. McAdoo (N.Y.)[2]	49	12.6
Leonard Wood[2]	987	3.1	Others[2]	340	87.4
Frank O. Lowden (Ill.)[2]	265	.8			

March 23   South Dakota

Leonard Wood	31,265	36.5	Others	6,612	100.0
Lowden	26,981	31.5			
Johnson	26,301	30.7			
Others	1,144	1.3			

April 5   Michigan

Johnson	156,939	38.4	McAdoo	18,665	21.1
Leonard Wood	112,568[3]	27.5	Edward I. Edwards (N.J.)	16,642	18.8
Lowden	62,418	15.3	A. Mitchell Palmer (Pa.)	11,187	12.6
Herbert C. Hoover (Calif.)	52,503	12.8	Others	42,000	47.5
Others	24,729	6.0			

April 6   New York

Unpledged delegates	199,149	100.0	Unpledged delegates	113,300	100.0

April 6   Wisconsin [4]

Leonard Wood[2]	4,505	15.0	James M. Cox (Ohio)[2]	76	2.2
Hoover[2]	3,910	13.0	Others	3,391	97.8
Johnson[2]	2,413	8.0			
Lowden[2]	921	3.1			
Others	18,350	60.9			

April 13   Illinois

Lowden	236,802	51.1	Edwards[2]	6,933	32.3
Leonard Wood	156,719	33.8	McAdoo[2]	3,838	17.9
Johnson	64,201	13.8	Cox[2]	266	1.2
Hoover[2]	3,401	.7	Others	10,418	48.6
Others	2,674	.6			

April 20   Nebraska

Johnson	63,161	46.2	Gilbert M. Hitchcock (Neb.)	37,452	67.3
Leonard Wood	42,385	31.0	Others	18,230	32.7
John J. Pershing (Mo.)	27,669	20.3			
Others	3,432	2.5			

April 23   Montana

Johnson	21,034	52.4	Others[2]	2,994	100.0
Leonard Wood	6,804	17.0			
Lowden	6,503	16.2			
Hoover	5,076	12.6			
Warren G. Harding (Ohio)	723	1.8			

April 27   Massachusetts

Unpledged delegates	93,356	100.0	Unpledged delegates	21,226	100.0

Republican	Votes	%	Democratic	Votes	%
April 27	**New Jersey**				
Leonard Wood	52,909	*50.2*	Edwards	4,163	*91.4*
Johnson	51,685	*49.0*	McAdoo[2]	180	*4.0*
Hoover	900	*.9*	Others	213	*4.7*
April 27	**Ohio**				
Harding	123,257	*47.6*	Cox	85,838	*97.8*
Leonard Wood	108,565	*41.9*	McAdoo[2]	292	*.3*
Johnson[2]	16,783	*6.5*	Others	1,647	*1.9*
Hoover[2]	10,467	*4.0*			
May 3	**Maryland**				
Leonard Wood	15,900	*66.4*	[5]		
Johnson	8,059	*33.6*			
May 4	**California**				
Johnson	369,853	*63.9*	Unpledged delegates	23,831	*100.0*
Hoover	209,009	*36.1*			
May 4	**Indiana**				
Leonard Wood	85,708	*37.9*	[5]		
Johnson	79,840	*35.3*			
Lowden	39,627	*17.5*			
Harding	20,782	*9.2*			
May 18	**Pennsylvania**				
Edward R. Wood (Pa.)	257,841	*92.3*	Palmer[6]	80,356	*73.7*
Johnson[2]	10,869	*3.8*	McAdoo	26,875	*24.6*
Leonard Wood[2]	3,878	*1.4*	Edwards[2]	674	*.6*
Hoover[2]	2,825	*1.0*	Others	1,132	*1.0*
Others[2]	4,059	*1.5*			
May 18	**Vermont**				
Leonard Wood	3,451	*66.1*	McAdoo[2]	137	*31.4*
Hoover[2]	564	*10.8*	Edwards[2]	58	*13.3*
Johnson[2]	402	*7.7*	Cox[2]	14	*3.2*
Lowden[2]	29	*.5*	Others	227	*52.1*
Others	777	*14.9*			
May 21	**Oregon**				
Johnson	46,163	*38.4*	McAdoo	24,951	*98.6*
Leonard Wood	43,770	*36.5*	Others	361	*1.4*
Lowden	15,581	*13.0*			
Hoover	14,557	*12.1*			
May 25	**West Virginia**				
Leonard Wood	27,255	*44.6*	[5]		
Others	33,849 [7]	*55.4*			

135

Republican

	Votes	%
June 5 North Carolina		
Johnson	15,375	*73.3*
Leonard Wood	5,603	*26.7*

TOTALS

	Votes	%
Johnson	965,651	*30.3*
Leonard Wood	710,863	*22.3*
Lowden	389,127	*12.2*
Hoover	303,212	*9.5*
Unpledged delegates	298,109	*9.4*
Edward R. Wood	257,841	*8.1*
Harding	144,762	*4.5*
Pershing	27,669	*.9*
Others[8]	89,014	*2.8*
	3,186,248	

Democratic

	Votes	%
(June 5 — North Carolina)		*5*

	Votes	%
Unpledged delegates	165,460	*28.9*
Palmer	91,543	*16.0*
Cox	86,194	*15.0*
McAdoo	74,987	*13.1*
Hitchcock	37,452	*6.6*
Edwards	28,470	*5.0*
Others[9]	87,565	*15.3*
	571,671	

1. Source: Louise Overacker, The Presidential Primaries (1926), p. 238-39. There was no preference vote. In the Republican primary, figures given were for delegates at large favoring Wood and Johnson. In the Democratic primary, although delegates were unpledged, the organization (Robert Charles Murchie) group was understood to be for Hoover. The highest Democratic Hoover delegate received 3,714 votes.

2. Write-in.

3. Source: Overacker, op. cit., p. 238.

4. No names entered for presidential preference in the Republican primary. The real contest lay between two lists of delegates, one headed by Robert M. La Follette and the other by Emanuel L. Philipp.

5. No names entered and no preference vote recorded.

6. Source for name of "favorite son" candidate: The New York Times.

7. Most of these votes were received by Sen. Howard Sutherland (R W.Va.). The figure is unofficial.

8. In addition to scattered votes, "others" includes Robert G. Ross who received 1,698 votes in the Nebraska primary.

9. In addition to scattered votes, "others" includes Robert G. Ross who received 13,179 in the Nebraska primary.

1924 Primaries

	Republican			Democratic		
	Votes	%		Votes	%

March 11   New Hampshire

| Calvin Coolidge (Mass.) | 17,170 | 100.0 | Unpledged delegates | 6,687 | 100.0 |

March 18   North Dakota

Coolidge	52,815	42.1	William G. McAdoo (Calif.)	11,273	100.0
Robert M. LaFollette (Wis.)	40,252	32.1			
Hiram Johnson (Calif.)	32,363	25.8			

March 25   South Dakota

| Johnson | 40,935 | 50.7 | McAdoo[1] | 6,983 | 77.4 |
| Coolidge | 39,791 | 49.3 | Unpledged delegates[1] | 2,040 | 22.6 |

April 1   Wisconsin[2]

LaFollette[3]	40,738	62.5	McAdoo	54,922	68.2
Coolidge[3]	23,324	35.8	Alfred E. Smith (N.Y.)[3]	5,774	7.2
Johnson[3]	411	.6	Others	19,827	24.6
Others	688	1.1			

April 7   Michigan

Coolidge	236,191	67.2	Henry Ford (Mich.)[4]	48,567	53.4
Johnson	103,739	29.5	Woodbridge N. Ferris (Mich.)[4]	42,028	46.2
Others	11,312	3.2	Others	435	.5

April 8   Illinois

Coolidge	533,193	58.0	McAdoo	180,544	98.9
Johnson	385,590	42.0	Smith[3]	235	.1
LaFollette[3]	278	—	Others	1,724	.9
Others	21	—			

April 8   Nebraska

Coolidge	79,676	63.6	McAdoo[3]	9,342	57.3
Johnson	45,032	35.9	Smith[3]	700	4.3
Others	627	.5	Others[3]	6,268	38.4

April 22   New Jersey

Coolidge	111,739	89.1	George S. Silzer (N.J.)[5]	35,601	97.7
Johnson	13,626	10.9	Smith[3]	721	2.0
			McAdoo[3]	69	.2
			Others	38	.1

April 22   Pennsylvania

Coolidge[3]	117,262	87.9	McAdoo[3]	10,376	43.7
Johnson[3]	4,345	3.3	Smith[3]	9,029	38.0
LaFollette[3]	1,224	.9	Others[3]	4,341	18.3
Others	10,523	7.9			

April 29   Massachusetts

| Coolidge | 84,840 | 100.0 | Unpledged delegates at large[6] | 30,341 | 100.0 |

April 29   Ohio

| Coolidge | 173,613 | 86.3 | James M. Cox (Ohio)[5] | 74,183 | 71.7 |
| Johnson | 27,578 | 13.7 | McAdoo | 29,267 | 28.3 |

	Republican			**Democratic**		
	Votes	%			Votes	%

May 5   Maryland

	Votes	%			Votes	%
Coolidge	19,657	93.7	7			
Unpledged delegates	1,326	6.3				
Johnson [3]	3	—				

May 6   California

	Votes	%			Votes	%
Coolidge	310,618	54.3	McAdoo		110,235	85.6
Johnson	261,566	45.7	Unpledged delegates		18,586	14.4

May 6   Indiana

	Votes	%			Votes	%
Coolidge	330,045	84.1	7			
Johnson	62,603	15.9				

May 16   Oregon

	Votes	%			Votes	%
Coolidge	99,187	76.8	McAdoo		33,664	100.0
Johnson	30,042	23.2				

May 27   West Virginia

	Votes	%			Votes	%
Coolidge	162,042	100.0	7			

May 28   Montana

	Votes	%			Votes	%
Coolidge	19,200	100.0	McAdoo		10,058	100.0

TOTALS

	Votes	%		Votes	%
Coolidge	2,410,363	68.4	McAdoo	456,733	59.8
Johnson	1,007,833	28.6	Cox	74,183	9.7
LaFollette	82,492	2.3	Unpledged delegates	57,654	7.5
Unpledged delegates	1,326	—	Ford	48,567	6.4
Others	23,171	.7	Ferris	42,028	5.5
			Silzer	35,601	4.7
	3,525,185		Smith	16,459	2.2
			Others	32,633	4.3
				763,858	

1. No presidential preference vote, as McAdoo's was the only name entered, but a contest developed between "McAdoo" and "anti-McAdoo" lists of delegates. Figures are average votes cast for these lists.

2. In Wisconsin the real contest in the Republican primary was between two lists of delegates, one led by La Follette and one by Emanuel L. Philipp. In the Democratic primary, the real contest was between two lists of delegates, one favoring Smith and one favoring McAdoo.

3. Write-in.

4. Source for names of "favorite son" candidates: Michigan Manual, 1925.

5. Source for names of "favorite son" candidates: The New York Times.

6. No presidential preference vote provided for. There were nine candidates for the eight places as delegates at large, one of whom announced his preference for Smith during the campaign and received the second highest number of votes.

7. No names entered and no presidential preference vote taken.

1928 Primaries

	Republican			Democratic		
	Votes	%		Votes	%	

March 13   New Hampshire

	Votes	%		Votes	%
Unpledged delegates at large[1]	25,603	100.0	Unpledged delegates at large[1]	9,716	100.0

March 20   North Dakota

Frank O. Lowden (Ill.)	95,857	100.0	Alfred E. Smith (N.Y.)	10,822	100.0

April 2   Michigan

Herbert C. Hoover (Calif.)	282,809	97.6	Smith	77,276	98.3
Lowden	5,349	1.8	Thomas Walsh (Mont.)	1,034	1.3
Calvin Coolidge (Mass.)	1,666	.6	James A. Reed (Mo.)	324	.4

April 3   Wisconsin

George W. Norris (Neb.)	162,822	87.1	Reed	61,097	75.0
Hoover	17,659	9.4	Smith	19,781	24.3
Lowden	3,302	1.8	Walsh	541	.7
Coolidge	680	.4			
Charles G. Dawes (Ill.)	505	.3			
Others	1,894	1.0			

April 10   Illinois

Lowden	1,172,278	99.3	Smith	44,212	91.7
Hoover	4,368	.4	Reed	3,786	7.9
Coolidge	2,420	.2	William G. McAdoo (Calif.)	213	.4
Dawes	756	.1			
Others	946	.1			

April 10   Nebraska

Norris	96,726	91.8	Gilbert M. Hitchcock (Neb.)	51,019	91.5
Hoover	6,815	6.5	Smith	4,755	8.5
Lowden	711	.7			
Dawes	679	.7			
Coolidge	452	.4			

April 24   Ohio

Hoover	217,430	68.1	Smith	42,365	65.9
Frank B. Willis (Ohio)	84,461	26.5	Atlee Pomerene (Ohio)	13,957	21.7
Dawes	4,311	1.4	Victor Donahey (Ohio)	7,935	12.3
Lowden	3,676	1.2			
Others	9,190	2.9			

April 24   Pennsylvania

[2]		[2]	

April 28   Massachusetts

Hoover[3]	100,279	85.2	Smith	38,081	98.1
Coolidge[3]	7,767	6.6	Walsh	254	.7
Alvan Fuller (Mass.)	1,686	1.4	Others	478	1.2
Lowden[3]	1,040	.9			
Others	6,950	5.9			

May 1   California

Hoover	567,219	100.0	Smith	134,471	54.1
			Reed	60,004	24.1
			Walsh	46,770	18.8
			Others	7,263	2.9

	Republican Votes	%		Democratic Votes	%
May 7 Indiana					
James E. Watson (Ind.)	228,795	53.0	Evans Woollen (Ind.)	146,934	100.0
Hoover	203,279	47.0			
May 7 Maryland[4]					
Hoover	27,128	83.3	[5]		
Unpledged delegates	5,426	16.7			
May 8 Alabama					
[5]			Unpledged delegates at large[6]	138,957	100.0
May 15 New Jersey					
Hoover	382,907	100.0	Smith[3]	28,506	100.0
May 18 Oregon					
Hoover	101,129	98.7	Smith	17,444	48.5
Lowden	1,322	1.3	Walsh	11,272	31.3
			Reed	6,360	17.7
			Others	881	2.5
May 22 South Dakota					
Unpledged delegates at large[7]	34,264	100.0	Unpledged delegates at large[7]	6,221	100.0
May 29 West Virginia					
Guy D. Goff (W.Va.)	128,429	54.0	Smith	81,739	50.0
Hoover	109,303	46.0	Reed	75,796	46.4
			Others	5,789	3.5
June 5 Florida					
[5]			Unpledged delegates at large[8]	108,167	100.00

TOTALS					
Hoover	2,020,325	49.2	Smith	499,452	39.5
Lowden	1,283,535	31.2	Unpledged delegates	263,061	20.8
Norris	259,548	6.3	Reed	207,367	16.4
Watson	228,795	5.6	Woollen	146,934	11.6
Goff	128,429	3.1	Walsh	59,871	4.7
Willis	84,461	2.1	Hitchcock	51,019	4.0
Unpledged delegates	65,293	1.6	Pomerene	13,957	1.1
Coolidge	12,985	.3	Donahey	7,935	.6
Dawes	6,251	.2	McAdoo	213	—
Fuller	1,686	—	Others[10]	14,411	1.1
Others[9]	18,980	.5			
	4,110,288			1,264,220	

1. Winning Republican delegates were unofficially pledged to Hoover and winning Democratic delegates were unofficially pledged to Smith, according to Walter Kravitz, "Presidential Preferential Primaries: Results 1928-1956" (1960), p. 4.

2. No figures available.

3. Write-in.

4. Source: Kravitz, op. cit., p. 5.

5. No primary.

6. The Montgomery Advertiser of May 3, 1928, described the delegates as independent and anti-Smith.

7. Winning Republican delegates favored Lowden and winning Democratic delegates favored Smith, according to Kravitz, op. cit., p. 5.

8. The Miami Herald of June 6, 1928, described the delegates as unpledged and anti-Smith.

9. In addition to scattered votes, "others" includes Robert G. Ross who received 8,280 votes in the Ohio primary.

10. In addition to scattered votes, "others" includes Poling who received 7,263 votes in the California primary; and Workman who received 881 in the Oregon primary and 5,-789 in the West Virginia primary.

1932 Primaries

	Republican Votes	%		Democratic Votes	%
March 8 New Hampshire					
Unpledged delegates at large[1]	22,903	100.0	Unpledged delegates at large[1]	15,401	100.0
March 15 North Dakota					
Joseph I. France (Md.)	36,000[2]	59.0	Franklin D. Roosevelt (N.Y.)	52,000[2]	61.9
Jacob S. Coxey (Ohio)	25,000[2]	41.0	William H. Murray (Okla.)	32,000[2]	38.1
March 23 Georgia					
[3]			Roosevelt	51,498	90.3
			Others	5,541	9.7
April 5 Wisconsin					
George W. Norris (Neb.)	139,514	95.5	Roosevelt	241,742	98.6
Herbert C. Hoover (Calif.)	6,588	4.5	Alfred E. Smith (N.Y.)[4]	3,502	1.4
April 12 Nebraska					
France	40,481	74.4	Roosevelt	91,393	63.5
Hoover	13,934	25.6	John N. Garner (Texas)	27,359	19.0
			Murray	25,214	17.5
April 13 Illinois					
France	345,498	98.7	James H. Lewis (Ill.)	590,130	99.8
Hoover	4,368	1.2	Roosevelt	1,084	.2
Charles G. Dawes (Ill.)	129	—	Smith	266	—
			Others[4]	72	—
April 26 Massachusetts					
Unpledged delegates at large[5]	57,534	100.0	Smith[5]	153,465	73.1
			Roosevelt[5]	56,454	26.9
April 26 Pennsylvania					
France	352,092	92.9	Roosevelt	133,002	56.6
Hoover	20,662	5.5	Smith	101,227	43.1
Others	6,126	1.6	Others	563	.2
May 2 Maryland					
Hoover	27,324	60.0	[6]		
France	17,008	37.3			
Unpledged delegates	1,236	2.7			
May 3 Alabama					
[3]			Unpledged delegates[7]	134,781	100.0
May 3 California					
Hoover	657,420	100.0	Garner	222,385	41.3
			Roosevelt	175,008	32.5
			Smith	141,517	26.3
May 3 South Dakota					
Johnson[8]	64,464	64.7	Roosevelt	35,370	100.0
Others	35,133	35.3			

	Republican Votes	%		Democratic Votes	%

May 10   Ohio

Coxey	75,844	58.9	Murray	112,512	96.4
France	44,853	34.8	Roosevelt[4]	1,999	1.7
Hoover	8,154	6.3	Smith[4]	951	.8
			George White (Ohio)	834	.7
			Newton D. Baker (Ohio)	289	.2
			Garner[4]	72	—

May 10   West Virginia

France	88,005	100.0	Roosevelt	219,671	90.3
			Murray	19,826	8.2
			Others	3,727	1.5

May 17   New Jersey

| France | 141,330 | 93.3 | Smith | 5,234 | 61.9 |
| Hoover | 10,116 | 6.7 | Roosevelt | 3,219 | 38.1 |

May 20   Oregon

France	72,681	69.0	Roosevelt	48,554	78.6
Hoover	32,599	31.0	Murray	11,993	19.4
			Others	1,214	2.0

June 7   Florida

[3]			Roosevelt	203,372	87.7
			Murray	24,847	10.7
			Others	3,645	1.6

TOTALS

France	1,137,948	48.5	Roosevelt	1,314,366	44.5
Hoover	781,165	33.3	Lewis	590,130	20.0
Norris	139,514	5.9	Smith	406,162	13.8
Coxey	100,844	4.3	Garner	249,816	8.5
Unpledged delegates	81,673	3.5	Murray	226,392	7.7
Johnson	64,464	2.7	Unpledged delegates	150,182	5.1
Dawes	129	—	White	834	—
Others[9]	41,259	1.8	Baker	289	—
			Others[10]	14,762	.5
	2,346,996			2,952,933	

1. Hoover delegates won the Republican primary and Roosevelt delegates won the Democratic primary, according to Kravitz, op. cit., p. 6.

2. Unofficial figures.

3. No primary.

4. Write-in.

5. Delegate-at-large vote in Republican and Democratic primaries. Hoover delegates won the Republican primary, according to Kravitz, op. cit., p. 6. The New York Times of April 28, 1932, also reported that the Republican delegates were pledged to Hoover.

6. No names entered, according to the Maryland Record of Election Returns.

7. These were unpledged delegates who favored Roosevelt, according to Kravitz, op. cit., p. 6.

8. The winning Republican delegation supported Hoover, according to Kravitz, op. cit., p. 7.

9. In addition to scattered votes, "others" includes Bogue who received 35,133 in the South Dakota primary.

10. In addition to scattered votes, "others" includes Leo J. Chassee who received 3,645 in the Florida primary and 3,727 in the West Virginia primary; and Howard who received 5,541 votes in the Georgia primary.

1936 Primaries

	Republican			Democratic		
	Votes	%		Votes	%	

March 10 New Hampshire

	Republican			Democratic		
Unpledged delegates at large[1]	32,992	100.0	Unpledged delegates at large[1]	15,752	100.0	

April 7 Wisconsin

	Republican			Democratic		
William E. Borah (Idaho)	187,334	98.2	Franklin D. Roosevelt (N.Y.)	401,773	100.0	
Alfred M. Landon (Kan.)	3,360	1.8	John N. Garner (Texas)	108	—	
			Alfred E. Smith (N.Y.)	46	—	

April 14 Illinois

	Republican			Democratic		
Frank Knox (Ill.)	491,575	53.7	Roosevelt	1,416,411	100.0	
Borah	419,220	45.8	Others[2]	411	—	
Landon	3,775	.4				
Others[2]	205	—				

April 14 Nebraska

	Republican			Democratic		
Borah	70,240	74.5	Roosevelt	139,743	100.0	
Landon	23,117	24.5				
Others	973	1.0				

April 28 Massachusetts

	Republican			Democratic		
Landon[2]	76,862	80.6	Roosevelt[2]	51,924	85.9	
Herbert C. Hoover (Calif.)[2]	7,276	7.6	Smith[2]	2,928	4.8	
Borah[2]	4,259	4.5	Charles E. Coughlin (Mich.)[2]	2,854	4.7	
Knox[2]	1,987	2.1	Others[2]	2,774	4.6	
Others[2]	5,032	5.3				

April 28 Pennsylvania

	Republican			Democratic		
Borah	459,982	100.0	Roosevelt	720,309	95.3	
			Henry Breckinridge (N.Y.)	35,351	4.7	

May 4 Maryland

	Republican			Democratic		
[3]			Roosevelt	100,269	83.4	
			Breckinridge	18,150	15.1	
			Unpledged delegates	1,739	1.4	

May 5 California

	Republican			Democratic		
Earl Warren (Calif.)	350,917	57.4	Roosevelt	790,235	82.5	
Landon	260,170	42.6	Upton Sinclair (Calif.)	106,068	11.1	
			John S. McGroarty (Calif.)	61,391	6.4	

May 5 South Dakota

	Republican			Democratic		
Warren E. Green[4]	44,518	50.1	Roosevelt	48,262	100.0	
Borah	44,261	49.9				

May 12 Ohio

	Republican			Democratic		
Stephen A. Day (Ohio)	155,732	93.4	Roosevelt	514,366	94.0	
Landon	11,015	6.6	Breckinridge	32,950	6.0	

May 12 West Virginia

	Republican			Democratic		
Borah	105,855	84.8	Roosevelt	288,799	97.3	
Others	18,986	15.2	Others	8,162	2.7	

	Republican			**Democratic**		
	Votes	%			Votes	%

May 15 Oregon

Borah	91,949	90.2	Roosevelt		88,305	99.8
Landon	4,467	4.4	Others		208	.2
Others	5,557	5.4				

May 19 New Jersey

Landon	347,142	79.2	Breckinridge		49,956	81.1
Borah	91,052	20.8	Roosevelt[2]		11,676	18.9

June 6 Florida

[3]			Roosevelt		242,906	89.7
			Others		27,982	10.3

TOTALS

Borah	1,474,152	44.4	Roosevelt	4,814,978	92.9
Landon	729,908	22.0	Breckinridge	136,407	2.6
Knox	493,562	14.9	Sinclair	106,068	2.0
Warren	350,917	10.6	McGroarty	61,391	1.2
Day	155,732	4.7	Unpledged delegates	17,491	.3
Green	44,518	1.3	Smith	2,974	.1
Unpledged delegates	32,992	1.0	Coughlin	2,854	.1
Hoover	7,276	.2	Garner	108	—
Others[5]	30,753	.9	Others[6]	39,537	.8
	3,319,810			5,181,808	

1. Delegates favorable to Knox won the Republican primary and Roosevelt delegates won the Democratic primary, according to Kravitz, op. cit., p. 8.
2. Write-in.
3. No preferential primary held.
4. These delegates were unpledged but favored Landon, according to Kravitz, op. cit., p. 9.

5. In addition to scattered votes, "others" includes Leo J. Chassee who received 18,986 votes in the West Virginia primary.
6. In addition to scattered votes, "others" includes Joseph A. Coutremarsh who received 27,982 votes in the Florida primary and 8,162 votes in the West Virginia primary.

1940 Primaries

Republican	Votes	%	Democratic	Votes	%
March 12 New Hampshire					
Unpledged delegates at large	34,616	100.0	Unpledged delegates at large [1]	10,501	100.0
April 2 Wisconsin					
Thomas E. Dewey (N.Y.)	70,168	72.6	Franklin D. Roosevelt (N.Y.)	322,991	75.4
Arthur Vandenberg (Mich.)	26,182	27.1	John N. Garner (Texas)	105,662	24.6
Robert A. Taft (Ohio)	341	.4			
April 9 Illinois					
Dewey	977,225	99.9	Roosevelt	1,176,531	86.0
Others [2]	552	.1	Garner	190,801	14.0
			Others [2]	35	—
April 9 Nebraska					
Dewey	102,915	58.9	Roosevelt	111,902	100.0
Vandenberg	71,798	41.1			
April 23 Pennsylvania					
Dewey	52,661	66.7	Roosevelt	724,657	100.0
Franklin D. Roosevelt (N.Y.)	8,294	10.5			
Arthur H. James (Pa.)	8,172	10.3			
Taft	5,213	6.6			
Vandenberg	2,384	3.0			
Herbert C. Hoover (Calif.)	1,082	1.4			
Wendell Willkie (N.Y.)	707	.9			
Others	463	.6			
April 30 Massachusetts					
Unpledged delegates at large [3]	98,975	100.0	Unpledged delegates at large [3]	76,919	100.0
May 5 South Dakota					
Unpledged delegates	52,566	100.0	Unpledged delegates	27,636	100.0
May 6 Maryland					
Dewey	54,802	100.0	[4]		
May 7 Alabama					
[4]			Unpledged delegates at large [5]	196,508	100.0
May 7 California					
Jerrold L. Seawell [6]	538,112	100.0	Roosevelt	723,782	74.0
			Garner	114,594	11.7
			Unpledged delegates [6]	139,055	14.2
May 14 Ohio					
Taft	510,025	99.5	Unpledged delegates at large [7]	283,952	100.0
Dewey [2]	2,059	.4			
John W. Bricker (Ohio)	188	—			
Vandenberg [2]	83	—			
Willkie	53	—			
Others	69	—			

Republican	Votes	%	**Democratic**	Votes	%
May 14 West Virginia					
R. N. Davis (W.Va.)	106,123	*100.0*	H. C. Allen (W.Va.)	102,729	*100.0*
May 17 Oregon					
Charles L. McNary (Ore.)	133,488	*95.9*	Roosevelt	109,913	*87.2*
Dewey	5,190	*3.7*	Garner	15,584	*12.4*
Taft	254	*.2*	Others	601	*.5*
Willkie	237	*.2*			
Vandenberg	36	—			
May 21 New Jersey					
Dewey	340,734	*93.9*	Roosevelt[2]	34,278	*100.0*
Willkie[2]	20,143	*5.6*			
Roosevelt[2]	1,202	*.3*			
Taft[2]	595	*.2*			
Vandenberg[2]	168	—			
TOTALS					
Dewey	1,605,754	*49.7*	Roosevelt	3,240,054	*71.7*
Seawell	538,112	*16.7*	Unpledged delegates	734,571	*16.4*
Taft	516,428	*16.0*	Garner	426,641	*9.5*
Unpledged delegates	186,157	*5.8*	Allen	102,729	*2.3*
McNary	133,488	*4.1*	Others	636	—
Davis	106,123	*3.3*			
Vandenberg	100,651	*3.1*		4,468,631	
Willkie	21,140	*.7*			
Roosevelt	9,496	*.3*			
James	8,172	*.3*			
Hoover	1,082	—			
Bricker	188	—			
Others	1,084	—			
	3,227,875				

1. *Roosevelt delegates won, according to Kravitz, op. cit., p. 10.*

2. *Write-in.*

3. *An unpledged Republican slate defeated a slate of delegates pledged to Dewey, according to Kravitz, op. cit., p. 10. Sixty-nine James A. Farley delegates and three unpledged delegates won in the Democratic primary, according to Kravitz, ibid. The New York Times of May 1, 1940, also reported that most Democratic delegates favored Farley.*

4. *No primary.*

5. *Winning delegates were pledged to "favorite son" candidate William B. Bankhead,* then Speaker of the U.S. House of Representatives, according to Kravitz, op. cit., p. 10, and the Montgomery Advertiser of May 8, 1940.

6. *The Los Angeles Times of May 8, 1940, reported that the Republican delegation was unpledged. In the Democratic primary, according to Davis, p. 293, unpledged slates were headed by Willis Allen, head of the California "Ham and Eggs" pension ticket which received 90,718 votes; and by Lt. Gov. Ellis E. Patterson, whose slate, backed by Labor's Non-Partisan League, received 48,337 votes.*

7. *Democratic delegates were pledged to Charles Sawyer (Ohio), according to Ohio Election Statistics, 1940, and Kravitz, op. cit., p. 10.*

1944 Primaries

	Republican			Democratic		
	Votes	%			Votes	%

March 14   New Hampshire

	Votes	%		Votes	%
Unpledged delegates at large[1]	16,723	100.0	Unpledged delegates at large [1]	6,772	100.0

April 5   Wisconsin

	Votes	%		Votes	%
Douglas MacArthur (Wis.)	102,421	72.6	Franklin D. Roosevelt (N.Y.)	49,632	94.3
Thomas E. Dewey (N.Y.)	21,036	14.9	Others	3,014	5.7
Harold E. Stassen (Minn.)	7,928	5.6			
Wendell Willkie (N.Y.)	6,439	4.6			
Others	3,307	2.3			

April 11   Illinois

	Votes	%		Votes	%
MacArthur	550,354	92.0	Roosevelt	47,561	99.3
Dewey	9,192	1.5	Others	343	.7
Everett M. Dirksen (Ill.)	581	.1			
John W. Bricker (Ohio)	148	—			
Stassen	111	—			
Willkie	107	—			
Others	37,575	6.3			

April 11   Nebraska

	Votes	%		Votes	%
Stassen	51,800	65.7	Roosevelt	37,405	99.2
Dewey	18,418	23.3	Others	319	.8
Willkie	8,249	10.5			
Others	432	.5			

April 25   Massachusetts

	Votes	%		Votes	%
Unpledged delegates at large	53,511	100.0	Unpledged delegates at large	57,299	100.0

April 25   Pennsylvania

	Votes	%		Votes	%
Dewey[2]	146,706	83.8	Roosevelt	322,469	99.7
MacArthur[2]	9,032	5.2	Others	961	.3
Franklin D. Roosevelt (N.Y.)	8,815	5.0			
Willkie[2]	3,650	2.1			
Bricker[2]	2,936	1.7			
Edward Martin (Pa.)	2,406	1.4			
Stassen[2]	1,502	.9			

May 1   Maryland

	Votes	%			
Unpledged delegates	17,600	78.9	[3]		
Willkie	4,701	21.1			

May 2   Alabama

				Votes	%
[3]			Unpledged delegates at large[4]	116,922	100.0

May 2   Florida

				Votes	%
[3]			Unpledged delegates at large[5]	118,518	100.0

May 2   South Dakota

	Votes	%		Votes	%
Charles A. Christopherson[6]	33,497	60.2	Fred Hildebrandt (S.D.)[6]	7,414	52.4
Others[6]	22,135	39.8	Others[6]	6,727	47.6

Republican

Democratic

	Votes	%		Votes	%
May 9 Ohio					
Unpledged delegates at large [7]	360,139	*100.0*	Unpledged delegates at large [7]	164,915	*100.0*
May 9 West Virginia					
Unpledged delegates at large	91,602	*100.0*	Claude R. Linger (W.Va.)	59,282	*100.0*
May 16 California					
Earl Warren (Calif.)	594,439	*100.0*	Roosevelt	770,222	*100.0*
May 16 New Jersey					
Dewey	17,393	*86.2*	Roosevelt	16,884	*99.6*
Roosevelt [2]	1,720	*8.5*	Thomas E. Dewey (N.Y.)	60	*.4*
Willkie	618	*3.1*			
Bricker	203	*1.0*			
MacArthur	129	*.6*			
Stassen	106	*.5*			
May 19 Oregon					
Dewey [2]	50,001	*78.2*	Roosevelt	79,833	*98.7*
Stassen [2]	6,061	*9.5*	Others	1,057	*1.3*
Willkie [2]	3,333	*5.2*			
Bricker [2]	3,018	*4.7*			
MacArthur [2]	191	*.3*			
Others	1,340	*2.1*			

TOTALS	Votes	%		Votes	%
MacArthur	662,127	*29.1*	Roosevelt	1,324,006	*70.9*
Warren	594,439	*26.2*	Unpledged delegates	464,426	*24.9*
Unpledged delegates	539,575	*23.8*	Linger	59,282	*3.2*
Dewey	262,746	*11.6*	Hildebrandt	7,414	*.4*
Stassen	67,508	*3.0*	Dewey	60	*—*
Christopherson	33,497	*1.5*	Others [9]	12,421	*.7*
Willkie	27,097	*1.2*			
Roosevelt	10,535	*.5*		1,867,609	
Bricker	6,305	*.3*			
Martin	2,406	*.1*			
Dirksen	581	*—*			
Others [8]	64,789	*2.9*			
	2,271,605				

1. Nine unpledged and two Dewey delegates won the Republican primary, and Roosevelt delegates won the Democratic primary, according to Kravitz, op. cit., p. 12.

2. Write-in.

3. No primary.

4. The Montgomery Advertiser of May 3, 1944, reported that these delegates were pro-Roosevelt but uninstructed.

5. The New York Times of May 3, 1944, reported that a contest for delegates took place between supporters of Roosevelt and supporters of Sen. Harry F. Byrd (D Va.). A vote breakdown showing Roosevelt and Byrd strength is unavailable.

6. The winning Republican slate was pledged to Stassen, the losing Republican slate to Dewey and the two Democratic slates to Roosevelt, according to the office of the South Dakota secretary of state and Kravitz, op. cit., p. 12.

7. Bricker delegates won the Republican primary and Joseph T. Ferguson delegates won the Democratic primary, according to Kravitz, op. cit., p. 13.

8. In addition to scattered votes, "others" includes Riley A. Bender who received 37,575 votes in the Illinois primary and Joe H. Bottum who received 22,135 in the South Dakota primary.

9. In addition to scattered votes, "others" includes Powell who received 6,727 votes in the South Dakota primary.

1948 Primaries

	Republican			Democratic		
	Votes	%		Votes	%

March 9   New Hampshire

	Republican			Democratic	
Unpledged delegates at large[1]	28,854	100.0	Unpledged delegates at large[1]	4,409	100.0

April 6   Wisconsin

	Republican			Democratic	
Harold E. Stassen (Minn.)	64,076	39.4	Harry S Truman (Mo.)	25,415	83.8
Douglas MacArthur (Wis.)	55,302	34.0	Others	4,906	16.2
Thomas E. Dewey (N.Y.)	40,943	25.2			
Others	2,429	1.5			

April 13   Illinois

	Republican			Democratic	
Riley A. Bender (Ill.)	324,029	96.9	Truman	16,299	81.7
MacArthur	6,672	2.0	Dwight D. Eisenhower (N.Y.)	1,709	8.6
Stassen	1,572	.5	Scott Lucas (Ill.)	427	2.1
Dewey	953	.3	Others[2]	1,513	7.6
Robert A. Taft (Ohio)	705	.2			
Others[2]	475	.1			

April 13   Nebraska

	Republican			Democratic	
Stassen	80,979	43.5	Truman	67,672	98.7
Dewey	64,242	34.5	Others	894	1.3
Taft	21,608	11.6			
Arthur Vandenberg (Mich.)	9,590	5.2			
MacArthur	6,893	3.7			
Earl Warren (Calif.)	1,761	.9			
Joseph W. Martin (Mass.)	910	.5			
Others	24	—			

April 20   New Jersey[3]

	Republican			Democratic	
Dewey	3,714	41.4	Truman	1,100	92.5
Stassen	3,123	34.8	Henry A. Wallace (Iowa)	87	7.3
MacArthur	718	8.0	Others	2	.2
Vandenberg	516	5.8			
Taft	495	5.5			
Dwight D. Eisenhower (N.Y.)	288	3.2			
Joseph W. Martin	64	.7			
Alfred E. Driscoll (N.J.)	44	—			
Warren	14	.2			

April 27   Massachusetts

	Republican			Democratic	
Unpledged delegates at large[4]	72,191	100.0	Unpledged delegates at large[4]	51,207	100.0

April 27   Pennsylvania

	Republican			Democratic	
Stassen[2]	81,242	31.5	Truman	328,891	96.0
Dewey[2]	76,988	29.8	Eisenhower	4,502	1.3
Edward Martin (Pa.)	45,072	17.5	Wallace	4,329	1.3
MacArthur[2]	18,254	7.1	Harold E. Stassen (Minn.)	1,301	.4
Taft[2]	15,166	5.9	Douglas MacArthur (Wis.)	1,220	.4
Vandenberg	8,818	3.4	Others	2,409	.7
Harry S Truman (Mo.)	4,907	1.9			
Eisenhower	4,726	1.8			
Henry A. Wallace (Iowa)	1,452	.6			
Others	1,537	.6			

May 4   Alabama

	Republican			Democratic	
[5]			Unpledged delegates at large[6]	161,629	100.0

	Republican				Democratic	
	Votes	%			Votes	%

May 4   Florida

[5]			Others [7]		92,169	100.0

May 4   Ohio

Unpledged delegates at large [8]	426,767	100.0	Unpledged delegates at large [8]		271,146	100.0

May 11   West Virginia

Stassen	110,775	83.2	Unpledged delegates at large		157,102	100.0
Others	22,410	16.8				

May 21   Oregon

Dewey	117,554	51.8	Truman		112,962	93.8
Stassen	107,946	47.6	Others		7,436	6.2
Others	1,474	.6				

June 1   California

Warren	769,520	100.0	Truman		811,920	100.0

June 1   South Dakota

Hitchcock [9]	45,463	100.0	Truman [9]		11,193	58.3
			Unpledged Delegates [9]		8,016	41.7

TOTALS

Warren	771,295	29.1	Truman		1,375,452	63.9
Unpledged delegates	527,812	19.9	Unpledged delegates		653,509	30.4
Stassen	449,713	16.9	Eisenhower		6,211	.3
Bender	324,029	12.2	Wallace		4,416	.2
Dewey	304,394	11.5	Stassen		1,301	.1
MacArthur	87,839	3.3	MacArthur		1,220	.1
Hitchcock	45,463	1.7	Lucas		427	—
Edward Martin	45,072	1.7	Others		109,329	5.1
Taft	37,974	1.4				
Vandenberg	18,924	.7			2,151,865	
Eisenhower	5,014	.2				
Truman	4,907	.2				
Wallace	1,452	.1				
Joseph W. Martin	974	—				
Driscoll	44	—				
Others [10]	28,349	1.1				
	2,653,255					

1. Six unpledged and two Dewey delegates won in the Republican primary, and Truman delegates won in the Democratic primary, according to Kravitz, op. cit., p. 14.

2. Write-in.

3. Source: Kravitz, op. cit., p. 14.

4. The Boston Globe of April 28, 1948, reported that the Republican delegation was "generally unpledged" but was expected to support the "favorite son" candidacy of Sen. Leverett Saltonstall (R Mass.) on the first convention ballot. The Globe reported that Democratic delegates were presumed to favor Truman's nomination.

5. No primary.

6. Unpledged, anti-Truman slate, according to Kravitz, op. cit., p. 15.

7. Unpledged slate, according to Kravitz, ibid.

8. Taft won 44 delegates and Stassen nine in the Republican primary, and W.A. Julian won 55 delegates and Bixler one in the Democratic primary, according to Kravitz., ibid.

9. Republican delegates were unpledged, according to Kravitz, op. cit., p. 15. In the Democratic primary, according to Davis, p. 297, the slate led by South Dakota Democratic Party Chairman Lynn Fellows endorsed Truman and the slate headed by former Rep. Fred Hildebrandt (D S.D.) ran uninstructed.

10. In addition to scattered votes, "others" includes Byer who received 15,675 votes and Vander Pyl who received 6,735 votes in the West Virginia primary.

1952 Primaries

	Republican			Democratic		
		Votes	%		Votes	%
March 11 New Hampshire						
	Dwight D. Eisenhower (N.Y.)	46,661	50.4	Estes Kefauver (Tenn.)	19,800	55.0
	Robert A. Taft (Ohio)	35,838	38.7	Harry S Truman (Mo.)	15,927	44.2
	Harold E. Stassen (Minn.)	6,574	7.1	Douglas MacArthur (Wis.)	151	.4
	Douglas MacArthur (Wis.)[1]	3,227	3.5	James A. Farley (N.Y.)	77	.2
	Others	230	.3	Adlai E. Stevenson (Ill.)	40	.1
March 18 Minnesota						
	Stassen	129,706	44.4	Hubert H. Humphrey (Minn.)	102,527	80.0
	Eisenhower[1]	108,692	37.2	Kefauver[1]	20,182	15.8
	Taft[1]	24,093	8.2	Truman[1]	3,634	2.8
	Earl Warren (Calif.)[1]	5,365	1.8	Dwight D. Eisenhower (N.Y.)	1,753	1.4
	MacArthur[1]	1,369	.5			
	Estes Kefauver (Tenn.)	386	.1			
	Others	22,712	7.8			
April 1 Nebraska						
	Taft[1]	79,357	36.2	Kefauver	64,531	60.3
	Eisenhower[1]	66,078	30.1	Robert S. Kerr (Okla.)	42,467	39.7
	Stassen	53,238	24.3			
	MacArthur[1]	7,478	3.4			
	Warren[1]	1,872	.9			
	Others	11,178	5.1			
April 1 Wisconsin						
	Taft	315,541	40.6	Kefauver	207,520	85.9
	Warren	262,271	33.8	Others	34,005	14.1
	Stassen	169,679	21.8			
	Others	29,133	3.8			
April 8 Illinois						
	Taft	935,867	73.6	Kefauver	526,301	87.7
	Stassen	155,041	12.2	Stevenson	54,336	9.1
	Eisenhower[1]	147,518	11.6	Truman	9,024	1.5
	MacArthur[1]	7,504	.6	Eisenhower	6,655	1.1
	Warren	2,841	.2	Others[1]	3,798	.6
	Others	23,550	1.9			
April 15 New Jersey						
	Eisenhower	390,591	60.7	Kefauver	154,964	100.0
	Taft	228,916	35.6			
	Stassen	23,559	3.7			
April 22 Pennsylvania						
	Eisenhower	863,785	73.6	Kefauver[1]	93,160	53.3
	Taft[1]	178,629	15.2	Eisenhower[1]	28,660	16.4
	Stassen	120,305	10.3	Truman[1]	26,504	15.2
	MacArthur[1]	6,028	.5	Robert A. Taft (Ohio)	8,311	4.8
	Warren	3,158	.3	Averell Harriman (N.Y.)[1]	3,745	2.1
	Harry S Truman (Mo.)	267	—	Stevenson[1]	3,678	2.1
	Others	1,121	.1	Richard B. Russell (Ga.)[1]	1,691	1.0
				Others	9,026	5.2
April 29 Massachusetts						
	Eisenhower[1]	254,898	69.8	Kefauver	29,287	55.7
	Taft[1]	110,188	30.2	Eisenhower	16,007	30.5
				Truman	7,256	13.8

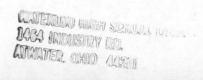

	Republican			Democratic	
	Votes	%		Votes	%

May 5 Maryland[2]

[3]			Kefauver	137,885	74.8
			Unpledged delegates	46,361	25.2

May 6 Florida

[3]			Russell	367,980	54.5
			Kefauver	285,358	42.3
			Others	21,296	3.2

May 6 Ohio

Taft[4]	663,791	78.8	Kefauver [4]	305,992	62.3
Stassen[4]	178,739	21.2	Robert J. Bulkley (Ohio) [4]	184,880	37.7

May 13 West Virginia

Taft	139,812	78.5	Unpledged delegates at large	191,471	100.0
Stassen	38,251	21.5			

May 16 Oregon

Eisenhower	172,486	64.6	Kefauver	142,440	72.3
Warren	44,034	16.5	William O. Douglas (Wash.)	29,532	15.0
MacArthur	18,603	7.0	Stevenson	20,353	10.3
Taft[1]	18,009	6.7	Eisenhower[1]	4,690	2.4
Wayne L. Morse (Ore.)	7,105	2.7			
Stassen	6,610	2.5			
Others	350	.1			

June 3 California

Warren	1,029,495	66.4	Kefauver	1,155,839	70.4
Thomas H. Werdel (Calif.)	521,110	33.6	Edmund G. Brown (Calif.)	485,578	29.6

June 3 South Dakota

Taft	64,695	50.3	Kefauver	22,812	66.0
Eisenhower	63,879	49.7	Others[5]	11,741	34.0

June 17 District of Columbia[6]

[3]			Harriman	14,075	
			Kefauver	3,377	
			Stevenson[1]	176	
			Others[1]	1,153	

TOTALS

Taft	2,794,736	35.8	Kefauver	3,169,448	64.3
Eisenhower	2,114,588	27.1	Brown	485,578	9.9
Warren	1,349,036	17.3	Russell	369,671	7.5
Stassen	881,702	11.3	Unpledged delegates	237,832	4.8
Werdel	521,110	6.7	Bulkley	184,880	3.8
MacArthur	44,209	.6	Humphrey	102,527	2.1
Morse	7,105	.1	Stevenson	78,583	1.6
Kefauver	386	—	Truman	62,345	1.3
Truman	267	—	Eisenhower	57,765	1.2
Others[7]	88,274	1.1	Kerr	42,467	.9
			Douglas	29,532	.6
	7,801,413		Harriman	17,820	.4
			Taft	8,311	.2
			MacArthur	151	—
			Farley	77	—
			Others[8]	81,019	1.6
				4,928,006	

1. Write-in.
2. Source: Kravitz, op. cit., p. 18, and the office of the Maryland secretary of state.
3. No primary.
4. Delegate-at-large vote.
5. These delegates ran on an uninstructed slate, according to Kravitz, op. cit., p. 19.
6. Source: David, Moos, and Goldman, Nominating Politics in 1952, Vol. 2, p. 331-332.
7. In addition to scattered votes, "others" includes Schneider who received 230 votes in the New Hampshire primary and 350 in the Oregon primary; Kenny who received 10,411 in the Nebraska primary; Ritter who received 26,208 and Stearns who received 2,925 in the Wisconsin primary; Slettendahl who received 22,712 in the Minnesota primary and Riley Bender who received 22,321 votes in the Illinois primary.
8. In addition to scattered votes, "others" includes Fox who received 18,322 votes and Charles Broughton who received 15,683 votes in the Wisconsin primary; Compton who received 11,331 and Shaw who received 9,965 in the Florida primary.

1956 Primaries

	Republican			Democratic		
	Votes	%		Votes	%

March 13 New Hampshire

Dwight D. Eisenhower (Pa.)	56,464	98.9	Estes Kefauver (Tenn.)	21,701	84.6
Others	600	1.1	Others	3,945	15.4

March 20 Minnesota

Eisenhower	198,111	98.4	Kefauver	245,885	56.8
William F. Knowland (Calif.)	3,209	1.6	Adlai E. Stevenson (Ill.)	186,723	43.2
Others	51	—	Others	48	—

April 3 Wisconsin

Eisenhower	437,089	95.9	Kefauver	330,665[1]	100.0
Others	18,743	4.1			

April 10 Illinois

Eisenhower	781,710	94.9	Stevenson	717,742	95.3
Knowland	33,534	4.1	Kefauver[2]	34,092	4.5
Others	8,455	1.0	Others	1,640	.2

April 17 New Jersey

Eisenhower	357,066	100.0	Kefauver	117,056	95.7
Others	23	—	Others	5,230	4.3

April 24 Alaska (Territory)

Eisenhower	8,291	94.4	Stevenson	7,123	61.1
Knowland	488	5.6	Kefauver	4,536	38.9

April 24 Massachusetts

Eisenhower[2]	51,951	95.1	John W. McCormack (Mass.)[2]	26,128	47.9
Adlai E. Stevenson (Ill.)[2]	604	1.1	Stevenson[2]	19,024	34.9
Christian A. Herter (Mass.)[2]	550	1.0	Kefauver[2]	4,547	8.3
Richard M. Nixon (N.Y.)[2]	316	.6	Dwight D. Eisenhower (Pa.)[2]	1,850	3.4
John W. McCormack (Mass.)[2]	268	.5	John F. Kennedy (Mass.)[2]	949	1.7
Knowland[2]	250	.5	Averell Harriman (N.Y.)[2]	394	.7
Others[2]	700	1.3	Frank J. Lausche (Ohio)[2]	253	.5
			Others[2]	1,379	2.5

April 24 Pennsylvania

Eisenhower	951,932	95.5	Stevenson	642,172	93.6
Knowland	43,508	4.4	Kefauver[2]	36,552	5.3
Others	976	.1	Others	7,482	1.1

May 1 District of Columbia[3]

Eisenhower	18,101	100.0	Stevenson	17,306	66.2
			Kefauver	8,837	33.8

May 7 Maryland

Eisenhower	66,904	95.5	Kefauver	112,768	65.9
Unpledged delegates	3,131	4.5	Unpledged delegates	58,366	34.1

May 8 Indiana

Eisenhower	351,903	96.4	Kefauver	242,842[1]	100.0
Others	13,320	3.6			

154

	Republican			Democratic	
	Votes	%		Votes	%

May 8 Ohio

John W. Bricker (Ohio)	478,453[1]	100.0	Lausche	276,670[1]	100.0

May 8 West Virginia

Unpledged delegates at large	111,883[1]	100.0	Unpledged delegates at large	112,832[1]	100.0

May 15 Nebraska

Eisenhower	102,576	99.8	Kefauver	55,265	94.0
Others	230	.2	Others	3,556	6.0

May 18 Oregon

Eisenhower	231,418[1]	100.0	Stevenson[2]	98,131	60.2
			Kefauver[2]	62,987	38.6
			Harriman[2]	1,887	1.2

May 29 Florida

Eisenhower	39,690	92.0	Stevenson	230,285	51.5
Knowland	3,457	8.0	Kefauver	216,549	48.5

June 5 California

Eisenhower	1,354,764[1]	100.0	Stevenson	1,139,964	62.6
			Kefauver	680,722	37.4

June 5 Montana

S.C. Arnold[4]	32,732	85.7	Kefauver	77,228[1]	100.0
Others	5,447	14.3			

June 5 South Dakota

Unpledged delegates[5]	59,374[1]	100.0	Kefauver	30,940[1]	100.0

TOTALS

Eisenhower	5,007,970	85.9	Stevenson	3,051,347	52.3
Bricker	478,453	8.2	Kefauver	2,278,636	39.1
Unpledged delegates	174,388	3.0	Lausche	276,923	4.7
Knowland	84,446	1.4	Unpledged delegates	171,198	2.9
S.C. Arnold	32,732	.6	McCormack	26,128	.4
Stevenson	604	—	Harriman	2,281	—
Herter	550	—	Eisenhower	1,850	—
Nixon	316	—	Kennedy	949	—
McCormack	268	—	Others	23,280	.4
Others[6]	48,545	.8			
	5,828,272			5,832,592	

1. Figures obtained from Scammon's office. In America Votes, Scammon did not record vote totals if a candidate was unopposed or if the primary was strictly for delegate selection.
2. Write-in.
3. Source: Davis, op. cit., pp. 300-301.
4. Voters cast their ballots for S. C. Arnold, "stand-in" candidate for Eisenhower.

5. Slate unofficially pledged to Eisenhower but appeared on the ballot as "No preference."
6. In addition to scattered votes, "others" includes Lar Daly who received 8,364 votes in the Illinois primary, 13,320 votes in the Indiana primary and 5,447 votes in the Montana primary; and John Bowman Chapple who received 18,743 votes in the Wisconsin primary.

1960 Primaries

	Republican			Democratic		
		Votes	%		Votes	%

March 8   New Hampshire

Republican	Votes	%	Democratic	Votes	%
Richard M. Nixon (N.Y.)	65,204	89.3	John F. Kennedy (Mass.)	43,372	85.2
Nelson A. Rockefeller (N.Y.)[1]	2,745	3.8	Others	7,527	14.8
John F. Kennedy (Mass.)[1]	2,196	3.0			
Others[1]	2,886	4.0			

April 5   Wisconsin

Republican	Votes	%	Democratic	Votes	%
Nixon	339,383[2]	100.0	Kennedy	476,024	56.5
			Hubert H. Humphrey (Minn.)	366,753	43.5

April 12   Illinois

Republican	Votes	%	Democratic	Votes	%
Nixon	782,849[2]	99.9	Kennedy[1]	34,332	64.6
Others[1]	442[2]	.1	Adlai E. Stevenson (Ill.)[1]	8,029	15.1
			Stuart Symington (Mo.)[1]	5,744	10.8
			Humphrey[1]	4,283	8.1
			Lyndon B. Johnson (Texas)[1]	442	.8
			Others[1]	337	.6

April 19   New Jersey

Republican	Votes	%	Democratic	Votes	%
Unpledged delegates at large	304,766[2]	100.0	Unpledged delegates at large	217,608[2]	100.0

April 26   Massachusetts

Republican	Votes	%	Democratic	Votes	%
Nixon[1]	53,164	86.0	Kennedy[1]	91,607	92.4
Rockefeller[1]	4,068	6.6	Stevenson[1]	4,684	4.7
Kennedy[1]	2,989	4.8	Humphrey[1]	794	.8
Henry Cabot Lodge (Mass.)[1]	373	.6	Richard M. Nixon (Calif.)[1]	646	.7
Adlai E. Stevenson (Ill.)[1]	266	.4	Symington[1]	443	.4
Barry Goldwater (Ariz.)[1]	221	.4	Johnson[1]	268	.3
Dwight D. Eisenhower (Pa.)[1]	172	.3	Others[1]	721	.7
Others[1]	592	1.0			

April 26   Pennsylvania

Republican	Votes	%	Democratic	Votes	%
Nixon	968,538	98.1	Kennedy[1]	183,073	71.3
Rockefeller[1]	12,491	1.3	Stevenson[1]	29,660	11.5
Kennedy[1]	3,886	.4	Nixon[1]	15,136	5.9
Stevenson[1]	428	—	Humphrey[1]	13,860	5.4
Goldwater[1]	286	—	Symington[1]	6,791	2.6
Others[1]	1,202	.1	Johnson[1]	2,918	1.1
			Rockefeller[1]	1,078	.4
			Others[1]	4,297	1.7

May 3   District of Columbia[3]

Republican	Votes	%	Democratic	Votes	%
Unpledged delegates	9,468	100.0	Humphrey	8,239	57.4
			Wayne L. Morse (Ore.)	6,127	42.6

May 3   Indiana

Republican	Votes	%	Democratic	Votes	%
Nixon	408,408	95.4	Kennedy	353,832	81.0
Others	19,677	4.6	Others	82,937	19.0

May 3   Ohio

Republican	Votes	%	Democratic	Votes	%
Nixon	504,072[2]	100.0	Michael V. DiSalle (Ohio)	315,312[2]	100.0

	Republican			Democratic		
	Votes	**%**			**Votes**	**%**
May 10 Nebraska						
Nixon[1]	74,356	93.8	Kennedy		80,408	88.7
Rockefeller[1]	2,028	2.6	Symington[1]		4,083	4.5
Goldwater[1]	1,068	1.3	Humphrey[1]		3,202	3.5
Others[1]	1,805	2.3	Stevenson[1]		1,368	1.5
			Johnson[1]		962	1.1
			Others[1]		669	.7
May 10 West Virginia						
Unpledged delegates at large	123,756[2]	100.0	Kennedy		236,510	60.8
			Humphrey		152,187	39.2
May 17 Maryland						
[4]			Kennedy		201,769	70.3
			Morse		49,420	17.2
			Unpledged delegates		24,350	8.5
			Others		11,417	4.0
May 20 Oregon						
Nixon	211,276	93.1	Kennedy		146,332	51.0
Rockefeller[1]	9,307	4.1	Morse		91,715	31.9
Kennedy[1]	2,864	1.3	Humphrey		16,319	5.7
Goldwater[1]	1,571	.7	Symington		12,496	4.4
Others[1]	2,015	.9	Johnson		11,101	3.9
			Stevenson[1]		7,924	2.8
			Others[1]		1,210	.4
May 24 Florida						
Nixon	51,036[2]	100.0	George A. Smathers (Fla.)		322,235[2]	100.0
June 7 California						
Nixon	1,517,652[2]	100.0	Edmund G. Brown (Calif.)		1,354,031	67.7
			George H. McLain (Calif.)		646,387	32.3
June 7 South Dakota						
Unpledged delegates	48,461[2]	100.0	Humphrey		24,773[2]	100.0
TOTALS						
Nixon	4,975,938	89.9	Kennedy		1,847,259	32.5
Unpledged delegates	486,451	8.8	Brown		1,354,031	23.8
Rockefeller	30,639	.6	McLain		646,387	11.4
Kennedy	11,935	.2	Humphrey		590,410	10.4
Goldwater	3,146	.1	Smathers		322,235	5.7
Stevenson	694	—	DiSalle		315,312	5.5
Lodge	373	—	Unpledged delegates		241,958	4.3
Eisenhower	172	—	Morse		147,262	2.6
Others[5]	28,619	.5	Stevenson		51,665	.9
			Symington		29,557	.5
	5,537,967		Nixon		15,782	.3
			Johnson		15,691	.3
			Others[6]		109,115	1.9
					5,686,664	

1. Write-in.
2. Figures obtained from Scammon's office. In America Votes, Scammon did not record vote totals if a candidate was unopposed or if the primary was strictly for delegate selection.
3. Source: District of Columbia Board of Elections.
4. No primary.
5. In addition to scattered votes, "others" includes Paul C. Fisher who received

2,388 votes in the New Hampshire primary and Frank R. Beckwith who received 19,677 in the Indiana primary.
6. In addition to scattered votes, "others" includes Lar Daly who received 40,853 votes in the Indiana primary and 7,536 in the Maryland primary; Paul C. Fisher who received 6,853 votes in the New Hampshire primary; John H. Latham who received 42,084 in the Indiana primary and Andrew J. Easter who received 3,881 votes in the Maryland primary.

157

1964 Primaries

Republican	Votes	%

Democratic	Votes	%

March 10   New Hampshire

Republican	Votes	%	Democratic	Votes	%
Henry Cabot Lodge (Mass.)[1]	33,007	35.5	Lyndon B. Johnson (Texas)[1]	29,317	95.3
Barry M. Goldwater (Ariz.)	20,692	22.3	Robert F. Kennedy (N.Y.)[1]	487	1.6
Nelson A. Rockefeller (N.Y.)	19,504	21.0	Henry Cabot Lodge (Mass.)[1]	280	.9
Richard M. Nixon (Calif.)[1]	15,587	16.8	Richard M. Nixon (Calif.)[1]	232	.8
Margaret Chase Smith (Maine)	2,120	2.3	Barry M. Goldwater (Ariz.)[1]	193	.6
Harold E. Stassen (Pa.)	1,373	1.5	Nelson A. Rockefeller (N.Y.)[1]	109	.4
William W. Scranton (Pa.)[1]	105	.1	Others[1]	159	.5
Others	465	.5			

April 7   Wisconsin

Republican	Votes	%	Democratic	Votes	%
John W. Byrnes (Wis.)	299,612	99.7	John W. Reynolds (Wis.)	522,405	66.2
Unpledged delegate	816	.3	George C. Wallace (Ala.)	266,136	33.8

April 14   Illinois

Republican	Votes	%	Democratic	Votes	%
Goldwater	512,840	62.0	Johnson[1]	82,027	91.6
Smith	209,521	25.3	Wallace[1]	3,761	4.2
Henry Cabot Lodge[1]	68,122	8.2	Robert F. Kennedy[1]	2,894	3.2
Nixon[1]	30,313	3.7	Others[1]	841	.9
George C. Wallace (Ala.)[1]	2,203	.3			
Rockefeller[1]	2,048	.2			
Scranton[1]	1,842	.2			
George W. Romney (Mich.)[1]	465	.1			
Others[1]	437	.1			

April 21   New Jersey

Republican	Votes	%	Democratic	Votes	%
Henry Cabot Lodge[1]	7,896	41.7	Johnson[1]	4,863	82.3
Goldwater[1]	5,309	28.0	Wallace[1]	491	8.3
Nixon[1]	4,179	22.1	Robert F. Kennedy[1]	431	7.3
Scranton[1]	633	3.3	Others[1]	124	2.1
Rockefeller[1]	612	3.2			
Others[1]	304	1.6			

April 28   Massachusetts

Republican	Votes	%	Democratic	Votes	%
Henry Cabot Lodge[1]	70,809	76.9	Johnson[1]	61,035	73.4
Goldwater[1]	9,338	10.1	Robert F. Kennedy[1]	15,870	19.1
Nixon[1]	5,460	5.9	Lodge[1]	2,269	2.7
Rockefeller[1]	2,454	2.7	Edward M. Kennedy (Mass.)[1]	1,259	1.5
Scranton[1]	1,709	1.9	Wallace[1]	565	.7
Lyndon B. Johnson (Texas)[1]	600	.7	Adlai E. Stevenson (Ill.)[1]	452	.5
Smith[1]	426	.5	Hubert H. Humphrey (Minn.)[1]	323	.4
George C. Lodge (Mass.)[1]	365	.4	Others[1]	1,436	1.7
Romney[1]	262	.3			
Others[1]	711	.8			

April 28   Pennsylvania

Republican	Votes	%	Democratic	Votes	%
Scranton[1]	235,222	51.9	Johnson[1]	209,606	82.8
Henry Cabot Lodge[1]	92,712	20.5	Wallace[1]	12,104	4.8
Nixon[1]	44,396	9.8	Robert F. Kennedy[1]	12,029	4.8
Goldwater[1]	38,669	8.5	William W. Scranton (Pa.)[1]	8,156	3.2
Johnson[1]	22,372	4.9	Lodge[1]	4,895	1.9
Rockefeller[1]	9,123	2.0	Others[1]	6,438	2.5
Wallace[1]	5,105	1.1			
Others[1]	5,269	1.2			

May 2   Texas

Republican	Votes	%
Goldwater	104,137	74.7
Henry Cabot Lodge[1]	12,324	8.8
Rockefeller	6,207	4.5
Nixon[1]	5,390	3.9
Stassen	5,273	3.8
Smith	4,816	3.5
Scranton[1]	803	.6
Others[1]	373	.3

[2]

Republican

Democratic

	Votes	%		Votes	%
May 5 District of Columbia[3]					
[3]			Unpledged delegates	41,095	*100.0*
May 5 Indiana					
Goldwater	267,935	*67.0*	Matthew E. Welsh (Ind.)	376,023	*64.9*
Stassen	107,157	*26.8*	Wallace	172,646	*29.8*
Others	24,588	*6.2*	Others	30,367	*5.2*
May 5 Ohio					
James A. Rhodes (Ohio)	615,754[4]	*100.0*	Albert S. Porter (Ohio)	493,619[4]	*100.0*
May 12 Nebraska					
Goldwater	68,050	*49.1*	Johnson[1]	54,713	*89.3*
Nixon[1]	43,613	*31.5*	Robert F. Kennedy[1]	2,099	*3.4*
Henry Cabot Lodge[1]	22,622	*16.3*	Wallace[1]	1,067	*1.7*
Rockefeller[1]	2,333	*1.7*	Lodge[1]	1,051	*1.7*
Scranton[1]	578	*.4*	Nixon[1]	833	*1.4*
Johnson[1]	316	*.2*	Goldwater[1]	603	*1.0*
Others[1]	1,010	*.7*	Others[1]	904	*1.5*
May 12 West Virginia					
Rockefeller	115,680[4]	*100.0*	Unpledged delegates at large	131,432[4]	*100.0*
May 15 Oregon					
Rockefeller	94,190	*33.0*	Johnson	272,099[4]	*99.5*
Henry Cabot Lodge	79,169	*27.7*	Wallace[1]	1,365[4]	*.5*
Goldwater	50,105	*17.6*			
Nixon	48,274	*16.9*			
Smith	8,087	*2.8*			
Scranton	4,509	*1.6*			
Others	1,152	*.4*			
May 19 Maryland					
Unpledged delegates	57,004	*58.2*	Daniel B. Brewster (Md.)	267,106	*53.1*
Others	40,994	*41.8*	Wallace	214,849	*42.7*
			Unpledged delegates	12,377	*2.5*
			Others	8,275	*1.6*
May 26 Florida					
Unpledged delegates	58,179	*57.8*	Johnson	393,339[4]	*100.0*
Goldwater	42,525	*42.2*			
June 2 California					
Goldwater	1,120,403	*51.6*	Unpledged delegates[5]	1,693,813	*68.0*
Rockefeller	1,052,053	*48.4*	Unpledged delegates[5]	798,431	*32.0*
June 2 South Dakota					
Unpledged delegates	57,653	*68.0*	Unpledged delegates	28,142[4]	*100.0*
Goldwater	27,076	*32.0*			

Republican

TOTALS	Votes	%
Goldwater	2,267,079	38.2
Rockefeller	1,304,204	22.0
Rhodes	615,754	10.4
Henry Cabot Lodge	386,661	6.5
Byrnes	299,612	5.0
Scranton	245,401	4.1
Smith	224,970	3.8
Nixon	197,212	3.3
Unpledged delegates	173,652	2.9
Stassen	113,803	1.9
Johnson	23,288	.4
Wallace	7,308	.1
Romney	727	—
George C. Lodge	365	—
Others6	75,303	1.3
	5,935,339	

Democratic

	Votes	%
Unpledged delegates	2,705,290	43.3
Johnson	1,106,999	17.7
Wallace	672,984	10.8
Reynolds	522,405	8.4
Porter	493,619	7.9
Welsh	376,023	6.0
Brewster	267,106	4.3
Robert F. Kennedy	33,810	.5
Henry Cabot Lodge	8,495	.1
Scranton	8,156	.1
Edward M. Kennedy	1,259	—
Nixon	1,065	—
Goldwater	796	—
Stevenson	452	—
Humphrey	323	—
Rockefeller	109	—
Others7	48,544	.8
	6,247,435	

1. Write-in.

2. No primary authorized.

3. Source: District of Columbia Board of Elections. No figures available for vote for delegates to Republican convention.

4. Figures obtained from Scammon's office. In America Votes, Scammon did not record vote totals if a candidate was unopposed or if the primary was strictly for delegate selection.

5. Gov. Edmund G. Brown (D Calif.) headed the winning slate of delegates and Mayor Sam Yorty of Los Angeles headed the losing slate.

6. In addition to scattered votes, "others" includes Norman LePage who received 82 votes in the New Hampshire primary; Frank R. Beckwith who received 17,884 votes and Joseph G. Ettl who received 6,704 votes in the Indiana primary; John W. Steffey who received 22,135 votes and Robert E. Ennis who received 18,859 votes in the Maryland primary.

7. In addition to scattered votes, "others" includes Lar Daly who received 15,160 votes, John H. Latham who received 8,067 votes and Fay T. Carpenter Swain who received 7,140 votes in the Indiana primary; and Andrew J. Easter who received 8,275 votes in the Maryland primary.

1968 Primaries*

Republican

	Votes	%

Democratic

	Votes	%

March 12 New Hampshire

Republican	Votes	%	Democratic	Votes	%
Richard M. Nixon (N.Y.)	80,666	77.6	Lyndon B. Johnson (Texas)[1]	27,520	49.6
Nelson A. Rockefeller (N.Y.)[1]	11,241	10.8	Eugene J. McCarthy (Minn.)	23,263	41.9
Eugene J. McCarthy (Minn.)[1]	5,511	5.3	Richard M. Nixon (N.Y.)[1]	2,532	4.6
Lyndon B. Johnson (Texas)[1]	1,778	1.7	Others	2,149	3.9
George W. Romney (Mich.)	1,743	1.7			
Harold E. Stassen (Pa.)	429	.4			
Others	2,570	2.5			

April 2 Wisconsin

Republican	Votes	%	Democratic	Votes	%
Nixon	390,368	79.7	McCarthy	412,160	56.2
Ronald Reagan (Calif.)	50,727	10.4	Johnson	253,696	34.6
Stassen	28,531	5.8	Robert F. Kennedy (N.Y.)[1]	46,507	6.3
Rockefeller[1]	7,995	1.6	Unpledged delegates	11,861	1.6
Unpledged delegates	6,763	1.4	George C. Wallace (Ala.)[1]	4,031	.5
Romney[1]	2,087	.4	Hubert H. Humphrey (Minn.)[1]	3,605	.5
Others	3,382	.7	Others	1,142	.2

April 23 Pennsylvania

Republican	Votes	%	Democratic	Votes	%
Nixon[1]	171,815	59.7	McCarthy	428,259	71.7
Rockefeller[1]	52,915	18.4	Robert F. Kennedy[1]	65,430	11.0
McCarthy[1]	18,800	6.5	Humphrey[1]	51,998	8.7
George C. Wallace (Ala.)[1]	13,290	4.6	Wallace[1]	24,147	4.0
Robert F. Kennedy (N.Y.)[1]	10,431	3.6	Johnson[1]	21,265	3.6
Reagan[1]	7,934	2.8	Nixon[1]	3,434	.6
Hubert H. Humphrey (Minn.)[1]	4,651	1.6	Others[1]	2,556	.4
Johnson[1]	3,027	1.1			
Raymond P. Shafer (Pa.)[1]	1,223	.4			
Others[1]	3,487	1.2			

April 30 Massachusetts

Republican	Votes	%	Democratic	Votes	%
Rockefeller[1]	31,964	30.0	McCarthy	122,697	49.3
John A. Volpe (Mass.)	31,465	29.5	Robert F. Kennedy[1]	68,604	27.6
Nixon[1]	27,447	25.8	Humphrey[1]	44,156	17.7
McCarthy[1]	9,758	9.2	Johnson[1]	6,890	2.8
Reagan[1]	1,770	1.7	Nelson A. Rockefeller (N.Y.)[1]	2,275	1.0
Kennedy[1]	1,184	1.1	Wallace[1]	1,688	.7
Others[1]	2,933	2.8	Others[1]	2,593	1.0

May 7 District of Columbia

Republican	Votes	%	Democratic	Votes	%
Nixon-Rockefeller[2]	12,102	90.1	Robert F. Kennedy[3]	57,555	62.5
Unpledged delegates[2]	1,328	9.9	Humphrey[3]	32,309	35.1
			Humphrey[3]	2,250	2.4

May 7 Indiana

Republican	Votes	%	Democratic	Votes	%
Nixon	508,362[4]	100.0	Robert F. Kennedy	328,118	42.3
			Roger D. Branigin (Ind.)	238,700	30.7
			McCarthy	209,695	27.0

May 7 Ohio

Republican	Votes	%	Democratic	Votes	%
James A. Rhodes (Ohio)	614,492[4]	100.0	Stephen M. Young (Ohio)	549,140[4]	100.0

Republican   ## Democratic

	Votes	%		Votes	%

May 14   Nebraska[5]

	Votes	%		Votes	%
Nixon	140,336	70.0	Robert F. Kennedy	84,102	51.7
Reagan	42,703	21.3	McCarthy	50,655	31.2
Rockefeller[1]	10,225	5.1	Humphrey[1]	12,087	7.4
Stassen	2,638	1.3	Johnson	9,187	5.6
McCarthy[1]	1,544	.8	Nixon[1]	2,731	1.7
Others	3,030	1.5	Ronald Reagan (Calif.)[1]	1,905	1.2
			Wallace[1]	1,298	.8
			Others	646	.4

May 14   West Virginia

	Votes	%		Votes	%
Unpledged delegates at large	81,039[4]	100.0	Unpledged delegates at large	149,282[4]	100.0

May 28   Florida

	Votes	%		Votes	%
Unpledged delegates	51,509[4]	100.0	George A. Smathers (Fla.)	236,242	46.1
			McCarthy	147,216	28.7
			Unpledged delegates	128,899	25.2

May 28   Oregon

	Votes	%		Votes	%
Nixon	203,037	65.0	McCarthy	163,990	44.0
Reagan	63,707	20.4	Robert F. Kennedy	141,631	38.0
Rockefeller[1]	36,305	11.6	Johnson	45,174	12.1
McCarthy[1]	7,387	2.4	Humphrey[1]	12,421	3.3
Kennedy[1]	1,723	.6	Reagan[1]	3,082	.8
			Nixon[1]	2,974	.8
			Rockefeller[1]	2,841	.8
			Wallace[1]	957	.3

June 4   California

	Votes	%		Votes	%
Reagan	1,525,091[4]	100.0	Robert F. Kennedy	1,472,166	46.3
			McCarthy	1,329,301	41.8
			Unpledged delegates	380,286	12.0

June 4   New Jersey

	Votes	%		Votes	%
Nixon[1]	71,809	81.1	McCarthy[1]	9,906	36.1
Rockefeller[1]	11,530	13.0	Robert F. Kennedy[1]	8,603	31.3
Reagan[1]	2,737	3.1	Humphrey[1]	5,578	20.3
McCarthy[1]	1,358	1.5	Wallace[1]	1,399	5.1
Others[1]	1,158	1.3	Nixon[1]	1,364	5.0
			Others[1]	596	2.2

June 4   South Dakota

	Votes	%		Votes	%
Nixon	68,113[4]	100.0	Robert F. Kennedy	31,826	49.5
			Johnson	19,316	30.0
			McCarthy	13,145	20.4

June 11   Illinois

	Votes	%		Votes	%
Nixon[1]	17,490	78.1	McCarthy[1]	4,646	38.6
Rockefeller[1]	2,165	9.7	Edward M. Kennedy (Mass.)[1]	4,052	33.7
Reagan[1]	1,601	7.1	Humphrey[1]	2,059	17.1
Others[1]	1,147	5.1	Others[1]	1,281	10.6

Republican

TOTALS	Votes	%
Reagan	1,696,270	37.9
Nixon	1,679,443	37.5
Rhodes	614,492	13.7
Rockefeller	164,340	3.7
Unpledged delegates	140,639	3.1
McCarthy	44,358	1.0
Stassen	31,598	.7
Volpe	31,465	.7
Robert F. Kennedy	13,338	.3
Wallace	13,290	.3
Nixon-Rockefeller[2]	12,102	.3
Johnson	4,805	.1
Humphrey	4,651	.1
Romney	3,830	.1
Shafer	1,223	—
Others[6]	17,707	.4
	4,473,551	

Democratic

	Votes	%
McCarthy	2,914,933	38.7
Robert F. Kennedy	2,304,542	30.6
Unpledged delegates	670,328	8.9
Young	549,140	7.3
Johnson	383,048	5.1
Branigin	238,700	3.2
Smathers	236,242	3.1
Humphrey	166,463	2.2
Wallace	33,520	.4
Nixon	13,035	.2
Rockefeller	5,116	.1
Reagan	4,987	.1
Edward M. Kennedy	4,052	.1
Others[7]	10,963	.1
	7,535,069	

---

* Delegate selection primaries were held in Alabama and New York. In America Votes, Scammon did not record vote totals if the primary was strictly for delegate selection and there was no presidential preference voting.

1. Write-in.

2. Prior to the primary, the District Republican organization agreed to divide the nine delegate votes, with six going to Nixon and three going to Rockefeller, according to the 1968 Congressional Quarterly Almanac, Vol. XXIV. Figures obtained from Scammon's office.

3. Figures obtained from Scammon's office. Two slates favored Humphrey; a member of an "independent" Humphrey slate received 2,250 votes.

4. Figures obtained from Scammon's office. In America Votes, Scammon did not record vote totals if a candidate was unopposed or if the primary was strictly for delegate selection.

5. In the American Party presidential primary, Wallace received 493 of the 504 votes cast, or 97.8% of the vote, according to the office of the Nebraska secretary of state.

6. In addition to scattered votes, "others includes Willis E. Stone who received 527 votes, Herbert F. Hoover who received 247 votes, David Watumull who received 161 votes, William W. Evans who received 151 votes, Elmer W. Coy who received 73 votes and Don DuMont who received 39 votes in the New Hampshire primary; and Americus Liberator who received 1,302 votes in the Nebraska primary.

7. In addition to scattered votes, "others" includes John G. Crommelin who received 186 votes, Richard E. Lee who received 170 votes and Jacob J. Gordon who received 77 votes in the New Hampshire primary.

1972 Primaries*

Republican	Votes	%	Democratic	Votes	%

March 7 New Hampshire

Republican	Votes	%	Democratic	Votes	%
Richard M. Nixon (Calif.)	79,239	67.6	Edmund S. Muskie (Maine)	41,235	46.4
Paul N. McCloskey (Calif.)	23,190	19.8	George S. McGovern (S.D.)	33,007	37.1
John M. Ashbrook (Ohio)	11,362	9.7	Sam Yorty (Calif.)	5,401	6.1
Others	3,417	2.9	Wilbur D. Mills (Ark.)[1]	3,563	4.0
			Vance Hartke (Ind.)	2,417	2.7
			Edward M. Kennedy (Mass.)[1]	954	1.1
			Hubert H. Humphrey (Minn.)[1]	348	.4
			Henry M. Jackson (Wash.)[1]	197	.2
			George C. Wallace (Ala.)[1]	175	.2
			Others	1,557	1.8

March 14 Florida

Republican	Votes	%	Democratic	Votes	%
Nixon	360,278	87.0	Wallace	526,651	41.6
Ashbrook	36,617	8.8	Humphrey	234,658	18.6
McCloskey	17,312	4.2	Jackson	170,156	13.5
			Muskie	112,523	8.9
			John V. Lindsay (N.Y.)	82,386	6.5
			McGovern	78,232	6.2
			Shirley Chisholm (N.Y.)	43,989	3.5
			Eugene J. McCarthy (Minn.)	5,847	.5
			Mills	4,539	.4
			Hartke	3,009	.2
			Yorty	2,564	.2

March 21 Illinois

Republican	Votes	%	Democratic	Votes	%
Nixon[1]	32,550	97.0	Muskie	766,914	62.6
Ashbrook[1]	170	.5	McCarthy	444,260	36.3
McCloskey[1]	47	.1	Wallace[1]	7,017	.6
Others[1]	802	2.4	McGovern[1]	3,687	.3
			Humphrey[1]	1,476	.1
			Chisholm[1]	777	.1
			Jackson[1]	442	—
			Kennedy[1]	242	—
			Lindsay[1]	118	—
			Others	211	—

April 4 Wisconsin

Republican	Votes	%	Democratic	Votes	%
Nixon	277,601	96.9	McGovern	333,528	29.6
McCloskey	3,651	1.3	Wallace	248,676	22.0
Ashbrook	2,604	.9	Humphrey	233,748	20.7
None of the names shown	2,315	.8	Muskie	115,811	10.3
Others	273	.1	Jackson	88,068	7.8
			Lindsay	75,579	6.7
			McCarthy	15,543	1.4
			Chisholm	9,198	.8
			None of the names shown	2,450	.2
			Yorty	2,349	.2
			Patsy T. Mink (Hawaii)	1,213	.1
			Mills	913	.1
			Hartke	766	.1
			Kennedy[1]	183	—
			Others	559	—

Republican

	Votes	%

Democratic

	Votes	%

April 25 **Massachusetts**

Republican	Votes	%	Democratic	Votes	%
Nixon	99,150	81.2	McGovern	325,673	52.7
McCloskey	16,435	13.5	Muskie	131,709	21.3
Ashbrook	4,864	4.0	Humphrey	48,929	7.9
Others	1,690	1.4	Wallace	45,807	7.4
			Chisholm	22,398	3.6
			Mills	19,441	3.1
			McCarthy	8,736	1.4
			Jackson	8,499	1.4
			Kennedy[1]	2,348	.4
			Lindsay	2,107	.3
			Hartke	874	.1
			Yorty	646	.1
			Others	1,349	.2

April 25 **Pennsylvania**

Republican	Votes	%	Democratic	Votes	%
Nixon[1]	153,886	83.3	Humphrey	481,900	35.1
George C. Wallace (Ala.)[1]	20,472	11.1	Wallace	292,437	21.3
Others[1]	10,443	5.7	McGovern	280,861	20.4
			Muskie	279,983	20.4
			Jackson	38,767	2.8
			Chisholm[1]	306	—
			Others	585	—

May 2 **District of Columbia**

[2]

Democratic	Votes	%
Walter E. Fauntroy (D.C.)	21,217	71.8
Unpledged delegates	8,343	28.2

May 2 **Indiana**

Republican	Votes	%	Democratic	Votes	%
Nixon	417,069	100.0	Humphrey	354,244	47.1
			Wallace	309,495	41.2
			Muskie	87,719	11.7

May 2 **Ohio**

Republican	Votes	%	Democratic	Votes	%
Nixon	692,828	100.0	Humphrey	499,680	41.2
			McGovern	480,320	39.6
			Muskie	107,806	8.9
			Jackson	98,498	8.1
			McCarthy	26,026	2.1

May 4 **Tennessee**

Republican	Votes	%	Democratic	Votes	%
Nixon	109,696	95.8	Wallace	335,858	68.2
Ashbrook	2,419	2.1	Humphrey	78,350	15.9
McCloskey	2,370	2.1	McGovern	35,551	7.2
Others	4	—	Chisholm	18,809	3.8
			Muskie	9,634	2.0
			Jackson	5,896	1.2
			Mills	2,543	.5
			McCarthy	2,267	.5
			Hartke	1,621	.3
			Lindsay	1,476	.3
			Yorty	692	.1
			Others	24	—

Republican

Democratic

	Votes	%		Votes	%
May 6 North Carolina					
Nixon	159,167	*94.8*	Wallace	413,518	*50.3*
McCloskey	8,732	*5.2*	Terry Sanford (N.C.)	306,014	*37.3*
			Chisholm	61,723	*7.5*
			Muskie	30,739	*3.7*
			Jackson	9,416	*1.1*
May 9 Nebraska					
Nixon	179,464	*92.4*	McGovern	79,309	*41.3*
McCloskey	9,011	*4.6*	Humphrey	65,968	*34.3*
Ashbrook	4,996	*2.6*	Wallace	23,912	*12.4*
Others	801	*.4*	Muskie	6,886	*3.6*
			Jackson	5,276	*2.7*
			Yorty	3,459	*1.8*
			McCarthy	3,194	*1.7*
			Chisholm	1,763	*.9*
			Lindsay	1,244	*.6*
			Mills	377	*.2*
			Kennedy[1]	293	*.2*
			Hartke	249	*.1*
			Others	207	*.1*
May 9 West Virginia					
Unpledged delegates at large	95,813[3]	*100.0*	Humphrey	246,596	*66.9*
			Wallace	121,888	*33.1*
May 16 Maryland					
Nixon	99,308	*86.2*	Wallace	219,687	*38.7*
McCloskey	9,223	*8.0*	Humphrey	151,981	*26.8*
Ashbrook	6,718	*5.8*	McGovern	126,978	*22.4*
			Jackson	17,728	*3.1*
			Yorty	13,584	*2.4*
			Muskie	13,363	*2.4*
			Chisholm	12,602	*2.2*
			Mills	4,776	*.8*
			McCarthy	4,691	*.8*
			Lindsay	2,168	*.4*
			Mink	573	*.1*
May 16 Michigan					
Nixon	321,652	*95.5*	Wallace	809,239	*51.0*
McCloskey	9,691	*2.9*	McGovern	425,694	*26.8*
Unpledged delegates	5,370	*1.6*	Humphrey	249,798	*15.7*
Others	30	*—*	Chisholm	44,090	*2.8*
			Muskie	38,701	*2.4*
			Unpledged delegates	10,700	*.7*
			Jackson	6,938	*.4*
			Hartke	2,862	*.2*
			Others	51	*—*
May 23 Oregon					
Nixon	231,151	*82.0*	McGovern	205,328	*50.2*
McCloskey	29,365	*10.4*	Wallace	81,868	*20.0*
Ashbrook	16,696	*5.9*	Humphrey	51,163	*12.5*
Others	4,798	*1.7*	Jackson	22,042	*5.4*
			Kennedy	12,673	*3.1*
			Muskie	10,244	*2.5*
			McCarthy	8,943	*2.2*
			Mink	6,500	*1.6*
			Lindsay	5,082	*1.2*
			Chisholm	2,975	*.7*
			Mills	1,208	*.3*
			Others	618	*.2*

Republican | Democratic

May 23 **Rhode Island**	Votes	%		Votes	%
Nixon	4,953	88.3	McGovern	15,603	41.2
McCloskey	337	6.0	Muskie	7,838	20.7
Ashbrook	175	3.1	Humphrey	7,701	20.3
Unpledged delegates	146	2.6	Wallace	5,802	15.3
			Unpledged delegates	490	1.3
			McCarthy	245	.6
			Jackson	138	.4
			Mills	41	.1
			Yorty	6	—
June 6 California					
Nixon	2,058,825	90.1	McGovern	1,550,652	43.5
Ashbrook	224,922	9.8	Humphrey	1,375,064	38.6
Others	175	—	Wallace[1]	268,551	7.5
			Chisholm	157,435	4.4
			Muskie	72,701	2.0
			Yorty	50,745	1.4
			McCarthy	34,203	1.0
			Jackson	28,901	.8
			Lindsay	26,246	.7
			Others	20	—
June 6 New Jersey					
Unpledged delegates at large	215,719[3]	100.0	Chisholm	51,433	66.9
			Sanford	25,401	33.1
June 6 New Mexico					
Nixon	49,067	88.5	McGovern	51,011	33.3
McCloskey	3,367	6.1	Wallace	44,843	29.3
None of the names shown	3,035	5.5	Humphrey	39,768	25.9
			Muskie	6,411	4.2
			Jackson	4,236	2.8
			None of the names shown	3,819	2.5
			Chisholm	3,205	2.1
June 6 South Dakota					
Nixon	52,820	100.0	McGovern	28,017	100.0
TOTALS					
Nixon	5,378,704	86.9	Humphrey	4,121,372	25.8
Unpledged delegates	317,048	5.1	McGovern	4,053,451	25.3
Ashbrook	311,543	5.0	Wallace	3,755,424	23.5
McCloskey	132,731	2.1	Muskie	1,840,217	11.5
Wallace	20,472	.3	McCarthy	553,955	3.5
None of the names shown	5,350	.1	Jackson	505,198	3.2
Others[4]	22,433	.4	Chisholm	430,703	2.7
			Sanford	331,415	2.1
	6,188,281		Lindsay	196,406	1.2
			Yorty	79,446	.5
			Mills	37,401	.2
			Fauntroy	21,217	.1
			Unpledged delegates	19,533	.1
			Kennedy	16,693	.1
			Hartke	11,798	.1
			Mink	8,286	.1
			None of the names shown	6,269	—
			Others[5]	5,181	—
				15,993,965	

* Delegate selection primaries were held in Alabama and New York. In America Votes, Scammon did not record vote totals if the primary was strictly for delegate selection and there was no presidential preference voting.

1. Write-in.
2. No Republican primary in 1972.

3. Figures obtained from Scammon's office. In America Votes, Scammon did not record vote totals if the primary was strictly for delegate selection.
4. In addition to scattered votes, "others" includes Patrick Paulsen, who received 1,211 votes in the New Hampshire primary.
5. In addition to scattered votes, "others" includes Edward T. Coll, who received 280 votes in the New Hampshire primary and 589 votes in the Massachusetts primary.

1976 Primaries*

	Republican			Democratic	
	Votes	%		Votes	%

February 24   New Hampshire

Gerald R. Ford (Mich.)	55,156	49.4	Jimmy Carter (Ga.)	23,373	28.4
Ronald Reagan (Calif.)	53,569	48.0	Morris K. Udall (Ariz.)	18,710	22.7
Others[1]	2,949	2.6	Birch Bayh (Ind.)	12,510	15.2
			Fred R. Harris (Okla.)	8,863	10.8
			Sargent Shriver (Md.)	6,743	8.2
			Hubert H. Humphrey (Minn.)[1]	4,596	5.6
			Henry M. Jackson (Wash.)[1]	1,857	2.3
			George C. Wallace (Ala.)[1]	1,061	1.3
			Ellen McCormack(N.Y.)	1,007	1.2
			Others	3,661	4.8

March 2   Massachusetts

Ford	115,375	61.2	Jackson	164,393	22.3
Reagan	63,555	33.7	Udall	130,440	17.7
None of the names shown	6,000	3.2	Wallace	123,112	16.7
Others[1]	3,519	1.8	Carter	101,948	13.9
			Harris	55,701	7.6
			Shriver	53,252	7.2
			Bayh	34,963	4.8
			McCormack	25,772	3.5
			Milton J. Shapp (Pa.)	21,693	2.9
			None of the names shown	9,804	1.3
			Humphrey[1]	7,851	1.1
			Edward M. Kennedy (Mass.)[1]	1,623	0.2
			Lloyd Bentsen (Texas)	364	—
			Others	4,905	0.7

March 2   Vermont

Ford	27,014	84.0	Carter	16,335	42.2
Reagan[1]	4,892	15.2	Shriver	10,699	27.6
Others[1]	251	—	Harris	4,893	12.6
			McCormack	3,324	8.6
			Others	3,463	9.0

March 9   Florida

Ford	321,982	52.8	Carter	448,844	34.5
Reagan	287,837	47.2	Wallace	396,820	30.5
			Jackson	310,944	23.9
			None of the names shown	37,626	2.9
			Shapp	32,198	2.5
			Udall	27,235	2.1
			Bayh	8,750	.7
			McCormack	7,595	.6
			Shriver	7,084	.5
			Harris	5,397	.4
			Robert C. Byrd (W.Va.)	5,042	.4
			Frank Church (Idaho)	4,906	.4
			Others	7,889	.6

March 16   Illinois

Ford	456,750	58.9	Carter	630,915	48.1
Reagan	311,295	40.1	Wallace	361,798	27.6
Lar Daly (Ill.)	7,582	1.0	Shriver	214,024	16.3
Others[1]	266	—	Harris	98,862	7.5
			Others[1]	6,315	.5

Republican			Democratic		
	Votes	%		Votes	%

March 23 North Carolina

Republican	Votes	%	Democratic	Votes	%
Reagan	101,468	52.4	Carter	324,437	53.6
Ford	88,897	45.9	Wallace	210,166	34.7
None of the names shown	3,362	1.7	Jackson	25,749	4.3
			None of the names shown	22,850	3.8
			Udall	14,032	2.3
			Harris	5,923	1.0
			Bentsen	1,675	.3

April Wisconsin

Republican	Votes	%	Democratic	Votes	%
Ford	326,869	55.2	Carter	271,220	36.6
Reagan	262,126	44.3	Udall	263,771	35.6
None of the names shown	2,234	.3	Wallace	92,460	12.5
Others[1]	583	—	Jackson	47,605	6.4
			McCormack	26,982	3.6
			Harris	8,185	1.1
			None of the names shown	7,154	1.0
			Shriver	5,097	.7
			Bentsen	1,730	.2
			Bayh	1,255	.2
			Shapp	596	.1
			Others[1]	14,473	2.0

April 27 Pennsylvania

Republican	Votes	%	Democratic	Votes	%
Ford	733,472	92.1	Carter	511,905	37.0
Reagan[1]	40,510	5.1	Jackson	340,340	24.6
Others[1]	22,678	2.8	Udall	259,166	18.7
			Wallace	155,902	11.3
			McCormack	38,800	2.8
			Shapp	32,947	2.4
			Bayh	15,320	1.1
			Harris	13,067	.9
			Humphrey[1]	12,563	.9
			Others	5,032	.3

May 4 District of Columbia

Republican	Votes	%	Democratic	Votes	%
[2]			Carter	10,521	31.6
			Walter E. Fauntroy (unpledged delegates)	10,149	30.5
			Udall	6,999	21.0
			Walter E. Washington (unpledged delegates)	5,161	15.5
			Harris	461	1.4

May 4 Georgia

Republican	Votes	%	Democratic	Votes	%
Reagan	128,671	68.3	Carter	419,272	83.4
Ford	59,801	31.7	Wallace	57,594	11.5
			Udall	9,755	1.9
			Byrd	3,628	.7
			Jackson	3,358	.7
			Church	2,477	.5
			Shriver	1,378	.3
			Bayh	824	.2
			Harris	699	.1
			McCormack	635	.1
			Bentsen	277	.1
			Shapp	181	—
			Others	2,393	.5

Republican			Democratic		

May 4   Indiana

Republican	Votes	%	Democratic	Votes	%
Reagan	323,779	51.3	Carter	417,480	68.0
Ford	307,513	48.7	Wallace	93,121	15.2
			Jackson	72,080	11.7
			McCormack	31,708	5.2

May 11   Nebraska

Republican	Votes	%	Democratic	Votes	%
Reagan	113,493	54.5	Church	67,297	38.5
Ford	94,542	45.4	Carter	65,833	37.6
Others	379	.1	Humphrey	12,685	7.2
			Kennedy	7,199	4.1
			McCormack	6,033	3.4
			Wallace	5,567	3.2
			Udall	4,688	2.7
			Jackson	2,642	1.5
			Harris	811	.5
			Bayh	407	.2
			Shriver	384	.2
			Others[1]	1,467	.8

May 11   West Virginia

Republican	Votes	%	Democratic	Votes	%
Ford	88,386	56.8	Byrd	331,639	89.0
Reagan	67,306	43.2	Wallace	40,938	11.0

May 18   Maryland

Republican	Votes	%	Democratic	Votes	%
Ford	96,291	58.0	Edmund G. Brown Jr. (Calif.)	286,672	48.4
Reagan	69,680	42.0	Carter	219,404	37.1
			Udall	32,790	5.5
			Wallace	24,176	4.1
			Jackson	13,956	2.4
			McCormack	7,907	1.3
			Harris	6,841	1.2

May 18   Michigan

Republican	Votes	%	Democratic	Votes	%
Ford	690,180	64.9	Carter	307,559	43.4
Reagan	364,052	34.3	Udall	305,134	43.1
Unpledged delegates	8,473	.8	Wallace	49,204	6.9
Others[1]	109	—	Unpledged delegates	15,853	2.2
			Jackson	10,332	1.5
			McCormack	7,623	1.1
			Shriver	5,738	.8
			Harris	4,081	.6
			Others[1]	3,142	.4

May 25   Arkansas

Republican	Votes	%	Democratic	Votes	%
Reagan	20,628	63.4	Carter	314,306	62.6
Ford	11,430	35.1	Wallace	83,005	16.5
Unpledged delegates	483	1.5	Unpledged delegates	57,152	11.4
			Udall	37,783	7.5
			Jackson	9,554	1.9

May 25   Idaho

Republican	Votes	%	Democratic	Votes	%
Reagan	66,743	74.3	Church	58,570	78.7
Ford	22,323	24.9	Carter	8,818	11.9
Unpledged delegates	727	.8	Humphrey	1,700	2.3
			Brown[1]	1,453	2.0
			Wallace	1,115	1.5
			Udall	981	1.3
			Unpledged delegates	964	1.3
			Jackson	485	.7
			Harris	319	.4

Republican				**Democratic**		

May 25 **Kentucky**	Votes	%			Votes	%
Ford	67,976	50.9		Carter	181,690	59.4
Reagan	62,683	46.9		Wallace	51,540	16.8
Unpledged delegates	1,781	1.3		Udall	33,262	10.9
Others	1,088	.8		McCormack	17,061	5.6
				Unpledged delegates	11,962	3.9
				Jackson	8,186	2.7
				Others	2,305	.8

May 25 **Nevada**						
Reagan	31,637	66.3		Brown	39,671	52.7
Ford	13,747	28.8		Carter	17,567	23.3
None of the names shown	2,365	5.0		Church	6,778	9.0
				None of the names shown	4,603	6.1
				Wallace	2,490	3.3
				Udall	2,237	3.0
				Jackson	1,896	2.5

May 25 **Oregon**						
Ford	150,181	50.3		Church	145,394	33.6
Reagan	136,691	45.8		Carter	115,310	26.7
Others[1]	11,663	3.9		Brown[1]	106,812	24.7
				Humphrey	22,488	5.2
				Udall	11,747	2.7
				Kennedy	10,983	2.5
				Wallace	5,797	1.3
				Jackson	5,298	1.2
				McCormack	3,753	.9
				Harris	1,344	.3
				Bayh	743	.2
				Others[1]	2,963	.7

May 25 **Tennessee**						
Ford	120,685	49.8		Carter	259,243	77.6
Reagan	118,997	49.1		Wallace	36,495	10.9
Unpledged delegates	2,756	1.1		Udall	12,420	3.7
Others[1]	97	—		Church	8,026	2.4
				Unpledged delegates	6,148	1.8
				Jackson	5,672	1.7
				McCormack	1,782	.5
				Harris	1,628	.5
				Brown[1]	1,556	.5
				Shapp	507	.2
				Humphrey[1]	109	—
June 1 **Montana**				Others[1]	492	.1

June 1 **Montana**						
Reagan	56,683	63.1		Church	63,448	59.4
Ford	31,100	34.6		Carter	26,329	24.6
None of the names shown	1,996	2.2		Udall	6,708	6.3
				None of the names shown	3,820	3.6
				Wallace	3,680	3.4
June 1 **Rhode Island**				Jackson	2,856	2.7

June 1 **Rhode Island**						
Ford	9,365	65.3		Unpledged delegates	19,035	31.5
Reagan	4,480	31.2		Carter	18,237	30.2
Unpledged delegates	507	3.5		Church	16,423	27.2
				Udall	2,543	4.2
				McCormack	2,468	4.1
				Jackson	756	1.3
				Wallace	507	.8
				Bayh	247	.4
				Shapp	132	.2

# Republican	Votes	%	# Democratic	Votes	%

June 1   South Dakota

Republican	Votes	%	Democratic	Votes	%
Reagan	43,068	51.2	Carter	24,186	41.2
Ford	36,976	44.0	Udall	19,510	33.3
None of the names shown	4,033	4.8	None of the names shown	7,871	13.4
			McCormack	4,561	7.8
			Wallace	1,412	2.4
			Harris	573	1.0
			Jackson	558	1.0

June 8   California

Republican	Votes	%	Democratic	Votes	%
Reagan	1,604,836	65.5	Brown	2,013,210	59.0
Ford	845,655	34.5	Carter	697,092	20.4
Others[1]	20	—	Church	250,581	7.3
			Udall	171,501	5.0
			Wallace	102,292	3.0
			Unpledged delegates	78,595	2.3
			Jackson	38,634	1.1
			McCormack	29,242	.9
			Harris	16,920	.5
			Bayh	11,419	.3
			Others[1]	215	—

June 8   New Jersey

Republican	Votes	%	Democratic	Votes	%
Ford	242,122	100.00	Carter	210,655	58.4
			Church	49,034	13.6
			Jackson	31,820	8.8
			Wallace	31,183	8.6
			McCormack	21,774	6.0
			Others	16,373	4.5

June 8   Ohio

Republican	Votes	%	Democratic	Votes	%
Ford	516,111	55.2	Carter	593,130	52.3
Reagan	419,646	44.8	Udall	240,342	21.2
			Church	157,884	13.9
			Wallace	63,953	5.6
			Gertrude W. Donahey (unpledged delegates)	43,661	3.9
			Jackson	35,404	3.1

TOTALS

Republican	Votes	%	Democratic	Votes	%
Ford	5,529,899	53.3	Carter	6,235,609	38.8
Reagan	4,758,325	45.9	Brown	2,449,374	15.3
None of the names shown	19,990	0.2	Wallace	1,995,388	12.4
Unpledged delegates	14,727	0.1	Udall	1,611,754	10.0
Daly	7,582	0.1	Jackson	1,134,375	7.1
Others[3]	43,602	0.4	Church	830,818	5.2
			Byrd	340,309	2.1
	10,374,125		Shriver	304,399	1.9
			Unpledged delegates	248,680	1.5
			McCormack	238,027	1.5
			Harris	234,568	1.5
			None of the names shown	93,728	0.6
			Shapp	88,254	0.5
			Bayh	86,438	0.5
			Humphrey	61,992	0.4
			Kennedy	19,805	0.1
			Bentsen	4,046	—
			Others[4]	75,088	0.5
				16,052,652	

* Delegate selection primaries were held in Alabama, New York and Texas. In **America Votes**, Scammon did not record vote totals if the primary was strictly for delegate selection and there was no presidential preference voting.

1. Write-in.

2. Ford unopposed. No primary held.

3. In addition to scattered write-in votes, "others" include Tommy Klein, who received 1,088 votes in Kentucky.

4. In addition to scattered write-in votes, "others" include Frank Ahern who received 1,487 votes in Georgia; Stanley Arnold, 371 votes in New Hampshire; Arthur O. Blessitt, 828 votes in New Hampshire and 7,889 in Georgia; Frank Bona, 135 votes in New Hampshire and 263 in Georgia; Billy Joe Clegg, 174 votes in New Hampshire; Abram Eisenman, 351 votes in Georgia; John S. Gonas, 2,288 votes in New Jersey; Jesse Gray, 3,574 votes in New Jersey; Robert L. Kelleher, 87 votes in New Hampshire, 1,603 in Massachusetts and 139 in Georgia; Rick Loewenherz, 49 votes in New Hampshire; Frank Lomento, 3,555 votes in New Jersey, Floyd L. Lunger, 3,935 votes in New Jersey; H. R. H. "Fifi" Rockefeller, 2,305 votes in Kentucky; George Roden, 153 votes in Georgia; Ray Rollinson, 3,021 votes in New Jersey; Terry Sanford, 53 votes in New Hampshire and 351 votes in Massachusetts; Bernard B. Schechter, 173 votes in New Hampshire.

Biographical Directory of Candidates

CQ

Biographical Directory of Presidential and Vice Presidential Candidates

The names in the directory include all persons who have received electoral votes for president or vice president since 1789. Also included are a number of prominent third party candidates who received popular votes but no electoral votes. The material is organized as follows: Name, State(s) in the year(s) the individual received electoral votes, Party or Parties with which the individual was identified at the time(s) they received electoral votes, dates of birth and death (where applicable), major offices held, and the year(s) in which the person received electoral votes. For third party candidates who received no electoral votes, the dates indicate the year(s) in which they were candidates.

For the elections of 1789, 1792, 1796 and 1800 presidential electors did not vote separately for president and vice president (See text, p. 19). It was, therefore, difficult in many cases to determine whether an individual receiving electoral votes in these elections was a candidate for president or vice president. Where no determination could be made from the sources consulted by Congressional Quarterly, the year(s) in which the individual received electoral votes is given with no specification as to whether the individual was a candidate for president or vice president.

The following sources were used: *Biographical Directory of the American Congress, 1774-1971*, U.S. Government Printing Office, 1971; *Dictionary of American Biography*, Charles Scribner's Sons, New York, 1928-36; *Encyclopedia of American Biography*, John A. Garraty editor, Harper and Row, New York, 1974; *Who's Who in American Politics*, 6th edition, 1977-78, edited by Jaques Cattell Press, R. R. Bowker Co., New York, 1977; *Who Was Who in America, 1607-1968*, Marquis Co., Chicago, 1943-68; Petersen, Svend, *A Statistical History of the American Presidential Elections*, Frederick Ungar Publishing Co., New York, 1968; Scammon, Richard M., *America Votes 10* (1972), Governmental Affairs Institute, Congressional Quarterly, Washington, 1973; *America Votes 12* (1976), Governmental Affairs Institute, Congressional Quarterly, Washington, 1977.

ADAMS, Charles Francis - Mass. (Free Soil) Aug. 18, 1807 - Nov. 21, 1886; House, 1859-61; Minister to Great Britain, 1861-68; Candidacy: VP - 1848.

ADAMS, John - Mass. (Federalist) Oct. 30, 1735 - July 4, 1826; Continental Congress, 1774; signer of Declaration of Independence, 1776; Minister to Great Britain, 1785; Vice President, 1789-97; President, 1797-1801; Candidacies: VP - 1789, 1792; P - 1796, 1800.

ADAMS, John Quincy - Mass. (Democratic-Republican, National Republican) July 11, 1767 - Feb. 23, 1848; Senate, 1803-08; Minister to Russia, 1809-14; Minister to Great Britain, 1815-17; Secretary of State, 1817-25; President, 1825-29; House, 1831-48; Candidacies: P - 1820, 1824, 1828.

ADAMS, Samuel - Mass. (Federalist) Sept. 27, 1722 - Oct. 2, 1803; Continental Congress, 1774-82; signer of Declaration of Independence; Governor, 1794-97; Candidacy: 1796.

AGNEW, Spiro Theodore - Md. (Republican) Nov. 9, 1918—; Governor, 1967-69; Vice President, 1969-73 (resigned Oct. 10, 1973); Candidacies: VP - 1968, 1972.

ARMSTRONG, James - Pa. (Federalist) Aug. 29, 1748 - May 6, 1828; House, 1793-95; Candidacy: 1789.

ARTHUR, Chester Alan - N.Y. (Republican) Oct. 5, 1830 - Nov. 18, 1886; Collector, Port of N.Y., 1871-78; Vice President, 1881; President (succeeded James A. Garfield, who was assassinated) 1881-85; Candidacy: VP - 1880.

BANKS, Nathaniel Prentice - Mass. (Liberal Republican) Jan. 30, 1816 - Sept. 1, 1894; House, 1853-57, 1865-73, 1875-79, 1889-91; Governor, 1858-61; Candidacy: VP - 1872.

BARKLEY, Alben William - Ky. (Democratic) Nov. 24, 1877 - April 30, 1956; House, 1913-27; Senate, 1927-49, 1955-56; Senate majority leader, 1937-47; Senate minority leader, 1947-49; Vice President, 1949-53; Candidacy: VP - 1948.

BELL, John - Tenn. (Constitutional Union) Feb. 15, 1797 - Sept. 10, 1869; House, 1827-41; House Speaker, 1834-35; Secretary of War, 1841; Senate, 1847-59; Candidacy: P - 1860.

BENSON, Allan Louis - N.Y. (Socialist) Nov. 6, 1871 - Aug. 19, 1940; Writer, editor; founder of *Reconstruction Magazine*, 1918; Candidacy: P - 1916.

BIDWELL, John - Calif. (Prohibition) Aug. 5, 1819 - April 4, 1900; California pioneer; Major in Mexican War; House, 1865-67; Candidacy: P - 1892.

BIRNEY, James Gillespie - N.Y. (Liberty) Feb. 4, 1792 - Nov. 25, 1857; Kentucky state legislature, 1816-17; Alabama state legislature, 1819-20; Candidacies: P - 1840, 1844.

BLAINE, James Gillespie - Maine (Republican) Jan. 31, 1830 - Jan. 27, 1893; House, 1863-76; House speaker, 1869-75; Senate, 1876-81; Secretary of State, 1881, 1889-92; President, first Pan American Congress, 1889; Candidacy: P - 1884.

BLAIR, Francis Preston Jr. - Mo. (Democratic) Feb. 19, 1821 - July 8, 1875; House, 1857-59, 1860, 1861-62, 1863-64; Senate, 1871-73; Candidacy: VP - 1868.

BRAMLETTE, Thomas E. - Ky. (Democratic) Jan. 3, 1817 - Jan. 12, 1875; Governor, 1863-67; Candidacies: VP - 1872.

BRECKINRIDGE, John Cabell - Ky. (Democratic, Southern Democratic) Jan. 21, 1821 - May 17, 1875; House, 1851-55; Vice President, 1857-61; Senate, 1861; major general, Confederacy, 1861-65; Secretary of War, Confederacy, 1865; Candidacies: VP - 1856; P - 1860.

BRICKER, John William - Ohio (Republican) Sept. 6, 1893—; Attorney General of Ohio, 1933-37; Governor, 1939-45; Senate, 1947-59; Candidacy: VP - 1944.

BROWN, Benjamin Gratz - Mo. (Democratic) May 28, 1826 - Dec. 13, 1885; Senate, 1863-67; Governor, 1871-73; Candidacy: VP- 1872.

BRYAN, Charles Wayland - Neb. (Democratic) Feb. 10, 1867 - March 4,

1945; Governor, 1923-25, 1931-35; Candidacy: VP- 1924.

BRYAN, William Jennings - Neb. (Democratic, Populist) March 19, 1860 - July 26, 1925; House, 1891-95; Secretary of State, 1913-15; Candidacies: P - 1896, 1900, 1908.

BUCHANAN, James - Pa. (Democratic) April 23, 1791 - June 1, 1868; House, 1821-31; Minister to Russia, 1832-34; Senate, 1834-45; Secretary of State, 1845-49; Minister to Great Britain, 1853-56; President, 1857-61; Candidacy: P - 1856.

BURR, Aaron - N.Y. (Democratic-Republican) Feb. 6, 1756 - Sept. 14, 1836; Attorney General of N.Y., 1789-90; Senate, 1791-97; Vice President, 1801-05; Candidacies: 1792, 1796, 1800.

BUTLER, Benjamin Franklin - Mass. (Greenback, Anti-Monopoly) Nov. 5, 1818 - Jan. 11, 1893; House, 1867-75, 1877-79; Governor, 1883-84; Candidacy: P - 1884.

BUTLER, Nicholas Murray - N.Y. (Republican) April 2, 1862 - Dec. 7, 1947; president, Columbia University, 1901-45; president, Carnegie Endowment for International Peace, 1925-45; Candidacy: VP - 1912 (Substituted as candidate after Oct. 30, 1912, death of nominee James S. Sherman.)

BUTLER, William Orlando - Ky. (Democratic) April 19, 1791 - Aug. 6, 1880; House, 1839-43; Candidacy: VP- 1848.

BYRD, Harry Flood - Va. (States' Rights Democratic, Independent Democratic) June 10, 1887 - Oct. 20, 1966; Governor, 1926-30; Senate, 1933-65; Candidacies: P - 1956, 1960.

CALHOUN, John Caldwell - S.C. (Democratic-Republican, Democratic) March 18, 1782-March 31, 1850; House, 1811-17; Secretary of War, 1817-25; Vice President, 1825-32; Senate, 1832-43, 1845-50; Secretary of State, 1844-45; Candidacies: VP - 1824, 1828.

CARTER, James Earl Jr. - Ga. (Democratic) Oct. 1, 1924—; state senate, 1963-67; Governor, 1971-75; President, 1977—; Candidacy: P - 1976.

CASS, Lewis - Mich. (Democratic) Oct. 9, 1782 - June 17, 1866; Military and civil governor of Michigan Territory, 1813-31; Secretary of War, 1831-36; Minister to France, 1836-42; Senate, 1845-48, 1849-57; Secretary of State, 1857-60; Candidacy: P - 1848.

CLAY, Henry - Ky. (Democratic-Republican, National Republican, Whig) April 12, 1777-June 29, 1852;

Senate, 1806-07, 1810-11, 1831-42, 1849-52; House, 1811-14, 1815-21, 1823-25; House Speaker, 1811-14, 1815-20, 1823-25; Secretary of State, 1825-29; Candidacies: P - 1824, 1832, 1844.

CLEVELAND, Stephen Grover - N.Y. (Democratic) March 18, 1837 - June 24, 1908; Mayor of Buffalo, 1882; Governor, 1883-85; President, 1885-89, 1893-97; Candidacies: P - 1884, 1888, 1892.

CLINTON, De Witt - N.Y. (Independent Democratic-Republican, Federalist) March 2, 1769 - Feb. 11, 1828; Senate, 802-03; Mayor of New York, 1803-07, 1810, 1811, 1813, 1814; Governor, 1817-23, 1825-28; Candidacy: P - 1812.

CLINTON, George - N.Y. (Democratic-Republican) July 26, 1739 - April 20, 1812; Continental Congress, 1775-76; Governor, 1777-95, 1801-04; Vice President, 1805-12; Candidacies: VP- 1789, 1792, 1796, 1804, 1808.

COLFAX, Schuyler - Ind. (Republican) March 23, 1823 - Jan. 13, 1885; House, 1855-69; Speaker of the House, 1863-69; Vice President, 1869-73; Candidacy: VP - 1868.

COLQUITT, Alfred Holt - Ga. (Democratic) April 20, 1824 - March 26, 1894; House, 1853-55; Governor, 1877-82; Senate, 1883-94; Candidacy: VP - 1872.

COOLIDGE, Calvin - Mass. (Republican) July 4, 1872 - Jan. 5, 1933; Governor, 1919-21; Vice President, 1921-23; President, 1923-29; Candidacies: VP - 1920; P - 1924.

COX, James Middleton - Ohio (Democratic) March 31, 1870 - July 15, 1957; House, 1909-13; Governor, 1913-15, 1917-21; Candidacy: P - 1920.

CRAWFORD, William Harris - Ga. (Democratic-Republican) Feb. 24, 1772 - Sept. 15, 1834; Senate, 1807-13; President pro tempore of the Senate, 1812-13; Secretary of War, 1815-16; Secretary of the Treasury, 1816-25; Candidacy: P - 1824.

CURTIS, Charles - Kan. (Republican) Jan. 25, 1860 - Feb. 8, 1936; House, 1893-1907; Senate, 1907-13, 1915-29; President pro tempore, 1911; Vice President, 1929-33; Candidacies: VP - 1928, 1932.

DALLAS, George Mifflin - Pa. (Democratic) July 10, 1792 - Dec. 31, 1864; Senate, 1831-33; Minister to Russia, 1837-39; Vice President, 1845-49; Minister to Great Britain, 1856-61; Candidacy: VP - 1844.

DAVIS, David - Ill. (Democratic) March 9, 1815 - June 26, 1886; Associate Justice

of the Supreme Court, 1862-77; Senate, 1877-83; Candidacy: P - 1872.

DAVIS, Henry Gassaway - W.Va. (Democratic) Nov. 16, 1823 - March 11, 1916; Senate, 1871-83; Chairman of Pan American Railway Committee, 1901-16; Candidacy: VP - 1904.

DAVIS, John William - W. Va. (Democratic) April 13, 1873 - March 24, 1955; House, 1911-13; Solicitor General, 1913-18; Ambassador to Great Britain, 1918-21; Candidacy: P - 1924.

DAWES, Charles Gates - Ill. (Republican) Aug. 27, 1865 - Apr. 23, 1951; U.S. Comptroller of the Currency, 1898-1901; first Director of the Bureau of the Budget, 1921-22; Vice President, 1925-29; Ambassador to Great Britain, 1929-32; Candidacy: VP - 1924.

DAYTON, William Lewis - N.J. (Republican) Feb. 17, 1807 - Dec. 1, 1864; Senate, 1842-51; Minister to France, 1861-64; Candidacy: VP - 1856.

DEBS, Eugene Victor - Ind. (Socialist) Nov. 5, 1855 - Oct. 20, 1926; Indiana legislature, 1885; president, American Railway Union, 1893-97; Candidacies: P - 1900, 1904, 1908, 1912, 1920.

DEWEY, Thomas Edmund - N.Y. (Republican) March 24, 1902 - March 16, 1971; District Attorney, New York County, 1937-41; Governor, 1943-55; Candidacies: P - 1944, 1948.

DOLE, Robert Joseph - Kan. (Republican) July 22, 1923—; House, 1961-69; Senate, 1969—; Candidacy: VP - 1976.

DONELSON, Andrew Jackson - Tenn. (American "Know-Nothing") Aug. 25, 1799 - June 26, 1871; Minister to Prussia, 1846-48; Minister to Germany, 1848-49; Candidacy: VP - 1856.

DOUGLAS, Stephen Arnold - Ill. (Democratic) April 23, 1813 - June 3, 1861; House, 1843-47; Senate, 1847-61; Candidacy: P - 1860.

EAGLETON, Thomas Francis - Mo. (Democratic) Sept. 4, 1929—; Attorney General of Missouri, 1961-65; Lieutenant Governor, 1965-68; Senate, 1968—; Candidacy: VP - 1972 (resigned from Democratic ticket July 31, replaced by R. Sargent Shriver Jr.)

EISENHOWER, Dwight David - N.Y., Pa. (Republican) Oct. 14, 1890 - March 28, 1969; General of U.S. Army, 1943-48; Army chief of staff, 1945-48; president of Columbia University, 1948-51; Commander of North Atlantic Treaty Organization, 1951-52; President, 1953-61; Candidacies: P - 1952, 1956.

ELLMAKER, Amos - Pa. (Anti-Masonic) Feb. 2, 1787 - Nov. 28, 1851; House, 1815; Attorney General of Pennsylvania, 1816-19, 1828-29; Candidacy: VP - 1832.

ELLSWORTH, Oliver - Conn. (Federalist) April 29, 1745 - Nov. 26, 1807; Continental Congress, 1777-84; Senate, 1789-96; Chief Justice of U.S. Supreme Court, 1796-1800; Minister to France, 1799; Candidacy: 1796.

ENGLISH, William Hayden - Ind. (Democratic) Aug. 27, 1822 - Feb. 7, 1896; House, 1853-61; Candidacy: VP - 1880.

EVERETT, Edward - Mass. (Constitutional Union) April 11, 1794 - Jan. 15, 1865; House, 1825-35; Governor, 1836-40; Minister to Great Britain, 1841-45; President of Harvard University, 1846-49; Secretary of State, 1852-53; Senate, 1853-54; Candidacy: VP- 1860.

FAIRBANKS, Charles Warren - Ind. (Republican) May 11, 1852 - June 4, 1918; Senate, 1897-1905; Vice President, 1905-09; Candidacies: VP - 1904, 1916.

FIELD, James Gaven - Va. (Populist) Feb. 24, 1826 - Oct. 12, 1901; major in the Confederate Army, 1861-65; Attorney General of Virginia, 1877-82; Candidacy: VP- 1892.

FILLMORE, Millard - N.Y. (Whig, (American "Know-Nothing") Jan. 7, 1800 - March 8, 1874; House, 1833-35, 1837-43; N.Y. Comptroller, 1847-49; Vice President, 1849-50; President, 1850-53; Candidates: VP - 1848; P - 1856.

FISK, Clinton Bowen - N.J. (Prohibition) Dec. 8, 1828 - July 9, 1890; Civil War brevet major general; founder Fisk University, 1866; member Board of Indian Commissioners, 1874, president, 1881-90; Candidacy: P - 1888.

FLOYD, John - Va. (Independent Democratic) April 24, 1783 - Aug. 17, 1837; House, 1817-29; Governor, 1830-34; Candidacy: P - 1832.

FORD, Gerald Rudolph Jr. - Mich. (Republican) July 14, 1913—; House, 1949-73; Vice President, 1973-74; President, 1974-77; Candidacy: P - 1976.

FRELINGHUYSEN, Theodore - N.J. (Whig) March 28, 1787 - April 12, 1862; Attorney General of New Jersey, 1817-29; Senate, 1829-35; president of Rutgers College, 1850-62; Candidacy: VP - 1844.

FREMONT, John Charles - Calif. (Republican) Jan. 21, 1813 - July 13, 1890; explorer and Army officer in West before 1847; Senate, 1850-51; Gover-

nor of Arizona Territory, 1878-81; Candidacy: P - 1856.

GARFIELD, James Abram - Ohio (Republican) Nov. 19, 1831 - Sept. 19, 1881; Major General in Union Army during Civil War; House, 1863-80; President, Mar. 4-Sept. 19, 1881; Candidacy: P - 1880.

GARNER, John Nance - Texas (Democratic) Nov. 22, 1868 - Nov. 7, 1967; House, 1903-33; Speaker of the House, 1931-33; Vice President, 1933-41; Candidacies: VP- 1932, 1936.

GERRY, Elbridge - Mass. (Democratic-Republican) July 17, 1744 - Nov. 23, 1814; Continental Congress, 1776-81, 1782-85; signer of Declaration of Independence; Constitutional Convention, 1787; House, 1789-93; Governor, 1810-12; Vice President, 1813-14; Candidacy: VP - 1812.

GOLDWATER, Barry Morris - Ariz. (Republican) Jan. 1, 1909—; Senate, 1953-65, 1969—; Candidacies: VP - 1960; P - 1964.

GRAHAM, William Alexander - N.C. (Whig) Sept. 5, 1804 - Aug. 11, 1875; Senate, 1840-43; Governor, 1845-49; Secretary of the Navy, 1850-52; Confederate Senate, 1864; Candidacy: VP - 1852.

GRANGER, Francis - N.Y. (Whig) Dec. 1, 1792 - Aug. 31, 1868; House, 1835-37, 1839-41, 1841-43; Postmaster General, 1841; Candidacy: VP - 1836.

GRANT, Ulysses Simpson - Ill. (Republican) April 27, 1822 - July 23, 1885; commander-in-chief, Union Army during Civil War; Secretary of War, 1867; President, 1869-77; Candidacies: P - 1868, 1872.

GREELEY, Horace - N.Y. (Liberal Republican, Democratic) Feb. 3, 1811 - Nov. 29, 1872; founder and editor, *New York Tribune*, 1841-72; House, 1848-49; Candidacy: P - 1872.

GRIFFIN, S. Marvin - Ga. (American Independent) Sept. 4, 1907—; Governor, 1955-59; Candidacy: VP - 1968.

GROESBECK, William Slocum - Ohio (Democratic) July 24, 1815 - July 7, 1897; House, 1857-59; delegate to International Monetary Conference in Paris, 1878; Candidacy: VP - 1872.

HALE, John Parker - N.H. (Free Soil) Mar. 31, 1806 - Nov. 19, 1873; House, 1843-45; Senate, 1847-53, 1855-65; Minister to Spain, 1865-69; Candidacy: P - 1852.

HAMLIN, Hannibal - Maine (Republican) Aug. 27, 1809 - July 4, 1891; House, 1843-47; Senate, 1848-57, 1857-61, 1869-81; Governor, Jan. 8-Feb. 20,

1857; Vice President, 1861-65; Candidacy: VP - 1860.

HANCOCK, John - Mass. (Federalist) Jan. 12, 1737 - Oct. 8, 1793; Continental Congress, 1775-80, 1785-86; president of Continental Congress, 1775-77; Governor, 1780-85, 1787-93; Candidacy: 1789.

HANCOCK, Winfield Scott - Pa. (Democratic) Feb. 14, 1824 - Feb. 9, 1886; Brigadier General, commander of II Army Corps, Civil War; Candidacy: P - 1880.

HARDING, Warren Gamaliel - Ohio (Republican) Nov. 2, 1865 - Aug. 2, 1923; Lieutenant Governor, 1904-05; Senate, 1915-21; President, 1921-23; Candidacy: P - 1920.

HARPER, Robert Goodloe - Md. (Federalist) Jan. 1765 - Jan. 14, 1825; House, 1795-1801; Senate, 1816; Candidacy: VP- 1816, 1820.

HARRISON, Benjamin - Ind. (Republican) Aug. 20, 1833-March 13, 1901; Union officer in Civil War; Senate, 1881-87; President, 1889-93; Candidacies: P - 1888, 1892.

HARRISON, Robert H. - Md. 1745 - 1790; chief justice General Court of Maryland, 1781; Candidacy: 1789.

HARRISON, William Henry - Ohio (Whig) Feb. 9, 1773 - April 4, 1841; delegate to Congress from the Northwest Territory, 1799-1800; Territorial Governor of Indiana, 1801-13; House, 1816-19; Senate, 1825-28; President, Mar. 4 - April 4, 1841; Candidacies: P - 1836, 1840.

HAYES, Rutherford Birchard - Ohio (Republican) Oct. 4, 1822 - Jan. 17, 1893; Major General in Union Army during Civil War; House, 1865-67; Governor, 1868-72, 1876-77; President, 1877-81; Candidacy: P - 1876.

HENDRICKS, Thomas Andrews - Ind. (Democratic) Sept. 7, 1819 - Nov. 25, 1885; House, 1851-55; Senate, 1863-69; Governor, 1873-77; Vice President, 1885; Candidacies: P - 1872; VP - 1876, 1884.

HENRY, John - Md. (Democratic-Republican) Nov. 1750 - Dec. 16, 1798; Continental Congress, 1778-81, 1784-87; Senate, 1789-97; Governor, 1797-98; Candidacy: 1796.

HOBART, Garret Augustus - N.J. (Republican) June 3, 1844 - Nov. 21, 1899; New Jersey senate, 1876-82; president of New Jersey senate, 1881-82; Republican National Committee, 1884-

96; Vice President, 1897-99; Candidacy: VP - 1896.

HOOVER, Herbert Clark - Calif. (Republican) Aug. 10, 1874 - Oct. 20, 1964; U.S. Food Administrator, 1917-19; Secretary of Commerce, 1921-28; President, 1929-33; chairman, Commission on Organization of the Executive Branch of Government, 1947-49, 1953-55; Candidacies: P - 1928, 1932.

HOSPERS, John - Calif. (Libertarian) June 9, 1918—; director of school of philosophy at University of Southern California; Candidacy: P - 1972.

HOWARD, John Eager - Md. (Federalist) June 4, 1752 - Oct. 12, 1827; Continental Congress, 1784-88; Governor, 1788-91; Senate, 1796-1803; Candidacy: VP-1816.

HUGHES, Charles Evans - N.Y. (Republican) April 11, 1862 - Aug. 27, 1948; Governor, 1907-10; Associate Justice of U.S. Supreme Court, 1910-16; Secretary of State, 1921-25; Chief Justice of U.S. Supreme Court, 1930-41; Candidacy: P - 1916.

HUMPHREY, Hubert Horatio Jr. - Minn. (Democratic) May 27, 1911 - Jan. 13, 1978; mayor of Minneapolis, 1945-48; Senate, 1949-64, 1971-78; Vice President, 1965-69; Candidacies: VP - 1964; P - 1968.

HUNTINGTON, Samuel - Conn., July 3, 1731 - Jan. 5, 1796; Continental Congress, 1776-84; president of Continental Congress, 1779-81, 1783; Governor, 1786-96; Candidacy: 1789.

INGERSOLL, Jared - Pa. (Federalist) Oct. 24, 1749 - Oct. 31, 1822; Continental Congress, 1780-81; Constitutional Convention, 1787; Candidacy: VP - 1812.

IREDELL, James - N.C. (Federalist) Oct. 5, 1751 - Oct. 20, 1799; Associate Justice of U.S. Supreme Court, 1790-99; Candidacy: 1796.

JACKSON, Andrew - Tenn. (Democratic-Republican, Democratic) March 15, 1767 - June 8, 1845; House, 1796-97; Senate, 1797-98; 1823-25; Territorial Governor of Florida, 1821; President, 1829-37; Candidacies: P - 1824, 1828, 1832.

JAY, John - N.Y.(Federalist) Dec. 12, 1745 - May 17, 1829; Continental Congress, 1774-77, 1778-79; president of Continental Congress, 1778-79; Minister to Spain, 1779; Chief Justice of U.S. Supreme Court, 1789-95; Governor, 1795-1801; Candidacies: 1789, 1796, 1800.

JEFFERSON, Thomas - Va. (Democratic-Republican) April 13, 1743 - July 4, 1826; Continental Congress, 1775-76, 1783-85; author and signer of Declaration of Independence, 1776; Governor, 1779-81; Minister to France, 1784-89, Secretary of State, 1789-93; Vice President, 1797-1801; President, 1801-09; Candidacies: VP - 1792; P - 1796, 1800, 1804.

JENKINS, Charles Jones - Ga. (Democratic) Jan. 6, 1805 - June 14, 1883; Governor, 1865-68; Candidacy: P - 1872.

JOHNSON, Andrew - Tenn. (Republican) Dec. 29, 1808 - July 31, 1875; House, 1843-53; Governor, 1853-57; Senate, 1857-62, 1875; Vice President, 1865; President, 1865-69; Candidacy: VP - 1864.

JOHNSON, Herschel Vespasian - Ga. (Democratic) Sept. 18, 1812 - Aug. 16, 1880; Senate, 1848-49; Governor, 1853-57; Senator in Confederate Congress, 1862-65; Candidacy: VP-1860.

JOHNSON, Hiram Warren - Calif. (Progressive) Sept. 2, 1866 - Aug. 6, 1945; Governor, 1911-17; Senate, 1917-45; Candidacy: VP- 1912.

JOHNSON, Lyndon Baines - Texas (Democratic) Aug. 27, 1908 - Jan. 22, 1973; House, 1937-49; Senate, 1949-61; Vice President, 1961-63; President, 1963-69; Candidacies: VP - 1960; P - 1964.

JOHNSON, Richard Mentor - Ky. (Democratic) Oct. 17, 1781 - Nov. 19, 1850; House, 1807-19, 1829-37; Senate, 1819-29; Vice President, 1837-41; Candidacies: VP - 1836, 1840.

JOHNSTON, Samuel - N.C. (Federalist) Dec. 15, 1733 - Aug. 18, 1816; Continental Congress, 1780-82; Senate, 1789-93; Candidacy: 1796.

JONES, Walter Burgwyn - Ala. (Independent Democratic) Oct. 16, 1888 - Aug. 1, 1963; Alabama legislature, 1919-20; Alabama circuit court judge, 1920-35; Presiding judge, 1935-63; Candidacy: P - 1956.

JULIAN, George Washington - Ind. (Free Soil, Liberal Republican) May 5, 1817 - July 7, 1899; House, 1849-51, 1861-71; Candidacies: VP - 1852, 1872.

KEFAUVER, Estes - Tenn. (Democratic) July 26, 1903 - Aug. 10, 1963; House, 1939-49; Senate, 1949-63; Candidacy: VP - 1956.

KENNEDY, John Fitzgerald - Mass. (Democratic) May 29, 1917 - Nov. 22, 1963; House, 1947-53; Senate, 1953-60; President, 1961-63; Candidacy: P - 1960.

KERN, John Worth - Ind. (Democratic) Dec. 20, 1849 - Aug. 17, 1917; Senate, 1911-17; Candidacy: VP - 1908.

KING, Rufus - N.Y. (Federalist) March 24, 1755 - April 29, 1827; Continental Congress, 1784-87; Constitutional Convention, 1787; Senate, 1789-96, 1813-25; Minister to Great Britain, 1796-1803, 1825-26; Candidacies: VP - 1804, 1808; P - 1816.

KING, William Rufus de Vane - Ala. (Democratic) April 7, 1786 - April 18, 1853; House, 1811-16; Senate, 1819-44, 1848-52; Minister to France, 1844-46; Vice President, March 4 - April 18, 1853; Candidacy: VP - 1852.

KNOX, Franklin - Ill. (Republican) Jan. 1, 1874 - April 28, 1944; Secretary of Navy, 1940-44; Candidacy: VP - 1936.

LA FOLLETTE, Robert Marion - Wis. (Progressive) June 14, 1855 - June 18, 1925; House, 1885-91; Governor, 1901-06; Senate, 1906-25; Candidacy: P - 1924.

LANDON, Alfred Mossman - Kan. (Republican) Sept. 9, 1887—; Governor, 1933-37; Candidacy: P - 1936.

LANE, Joseph - Ore. (Southern Democratic) Dec. 14, 1801 - April 19, 1881; Governor of Oregon Territory, 1849-50, May 16-19, 1853; House (Territorial Delegate), 1851-59; Senate, 1859-61; Candidacy: VP - 1860.

LANGDON, John - N.H. (Democratic-Republican) June 25, 1741 - Sept. 18, 1819; Continental Congress, 1775-1776, 1783; Governor, 1788-89; 1805-09, 1810-12; Senate, 1789-1801; first president pro tempore of Senate, 1789; Candidacies: VP - 1808.

LEE, Henry - Mass. (Independent Democratic) Feb. 4, 1782 - Feb. 6, 1867; Merchant and publicist; Candidacy: VP - 1832.

LeMAY, Curtis Emerson - Ohio (American Independent) Nov. 15, 1906—; Air Force Chief of Staff, 1961-65; Candidacy: VP - 1968.

LEMKE, William - N.D. (Union) Aug. 13, 1878 - May 30, 1950; House, 1933-41, 1943-50; Candidacy: P - 1936.

LINCOLN, Abraham - Ill. (Republican) Feb. 12, 1809 - April 15, 1865; House, 1847-49; President, 1861-65; Candidacies: P - 1860, 1864.

LINCOLN, Benjamin - Mass. (Federalist) Jan. 24, 1733 - May 9, 1810; Major

General in Continental Army, 1777-81; Secretary of War, 1781-83; Candidacy: 1789.

LODGE, Henry Cabot Jr. - Mass. (Republican) July 5, 1902—; Senate, 1937-44, 1947-53; Ambassador to United Nations, 1953-60; Ambassador to Republic of Vietnam, 1963-64, 1965-67; Candidacy: VP - 1960.

LOGAN, John Alexander - Ill. (Republican) Feb. 9, 1826 - Dec. 26, 1886; House, 1859-62, 1867-71; Senate, 1871-77, 1879-86; Candidacy: VP- 1884.

MACHEN, Willis Benson - Ky. (Democratic) April 10, 1810 - Sept. 29, 1893; Confederate Congress, 1861-65; Senate, 1872-73; Candidacy: VP- 1872.

MACON, Nathaniel - N.C. (Democratic-Republican) Dec. 17, 1757 - June 29, 1837; House, 1791-1815; Speaker of the House, 1801-07; Senate, 1815-28; Candidacy: VP- 1824.

MADISON, James - Va. (Democratic-Republican) March 16, 1751 - June 28, 1836; Continental Congress, 1780-83, 1786-88; Constitutional Convention, 1787; House, 1789-97; Secretary of State, 1801-09; President, 1809-17; Candidacies: P - 1808, 1812.

MANGUM, Willie Person - N.C. (Independent Democrat) May 10, 1792 - Sept. 7, 1861; House, 1823-26; Senate, 1831-36, 1840-53; Candidacy: P - 1836.

MARSHALL, John - Va. (Federalist) Sept. 24, 1755 - July 6, 1835; House 1799-1800; Secretary of State, 1800-01; Chief Justice of U.S. Supreme Court, 1801-35; Candidacy: VP - 1816.

MARSHALL, Thomas Riley - Ind. (Democratic) March 14, 1854 - June 1, 1925; Governor, 1909-13; Vice President, 1913-21; Candidacies: VP - 1912, 1916.

McCARTHY, Eugene Joseph - Minn. (Independent) March 29, 1916—; House, 1949-59; Senate, 1959-71; Candidacy: P - 1976.

McCLELLAN, George Brinton - N.J. (Democratic) Dec. 3, 1826 - Oct. 29, 1885; General-in-Chief of Army of the Potomac, 1861; Governor, 1878-81; Candidacy: P - 1864.

McGOVERN, George Stanley - S.D. (Democratic) July 19, 1922—; House, 1957-61; Senate, 1963—; Candidacy: P - 1972.

McKINLEY, William Jr. - Ohio (Republican) Jan. 29, 1843 - Sept. 14, 1901; House, 1877 - May 27, 1884, 1885-91; Governor, 1892-96; President,

1897 - Sept. 14, 1901; Candidacies: P - 1896, 1900.

McNARY, Charles Linza - Ore. (Republican) June 12, 1874 - Feb. 25, 1944; state supreme court judge, 1913-15; Senate, 1917 - Nov. 5, 1918, Dec. 18, 1918 - 1944; Candidacy: VP - 1940.

MILLER, William Edward - N.Y. (Republican) March 22, 1914—; House, 1951-65; chairman of Republican National Committee, 1961-64; Candidacy: VP- 1964.

MILTON, John - Ga. ca. 1740 - ca. 1804, Secretary of State, Georgia, ca. 1778, 1781, 1783; Candidacy: 1789.

MONDALE, Walter Frederick - Minn. (Democratic) Jan. 5, 1928—; Senate, 1964-76; Vice President, 1977—; Candidacy: VP - 1976.

MONROE, James - Va. (Democratic-Republican) April 28, 1758 - July 4, 1831; Senate, 1790-94; Minister to France, 1794-96, 1803; Minister to England, 1803-07; Governor, 1799-1802, 1811; Secretary of State, 1811-17; President, 1817-25; Candidacies: VP - 1808; P - 1816, 1820.

MORTON, Levi Parsons - N.Y. (Republican) May 16, 1824 - May 16, 1920; House, 1879-81; Minister to France, 1881-85; Vice President, 1889-93; Governor, 1895-97; Candidacy: VP - 1888.

MUSKIE, Edmund Sixtus - Maine (Democratic) March 28, 1914—; Governor, 1955-59; Senate, 1959—; Candidacy: VP - 1968.

NATHAN, Theodora Nathalia - Ore. (Libertarian) Feb. 9, 1923—; Broadcast journalist; National Judiciary Committee, Libertarian Party, 1972-75; Vice-chairperson, Oregon state Libertarian party, 1974-75; Candidacy: VP- 1972.

NIXON, Richard Milhous - Calif., N.Y. (Republican) Jan. 9, 1913—; House, 1947-50; Senate, 1950-53; Vice President, 1953-61; President, 1969-74; Candidacies: VP - 1952, 1956; P - 1960, 1968, 1972.

PALMER, John McAuley - Ill. (Democratic, National Democratic) Sept. 13, 1817 - Sept. 25, 1900; Governor, 1869-73; Senate, 1891-97; Candidacies: VP- 1872; P - 1896.

PARKER, Alton Brooks - N.Y. (Democratic) May 14, 1852 - May 10, 1926; Chief Justice of New York Court of Appeals,1898-1904; Candidacy: P - 1904.

PENDLETON, George Hunt - Ohio (Democratic) July 19, 1825 - Nov. 24,

1889; House, 1857-65; Senate, 1879-85; Minister to Germany, 1885-89; Candidacy: VP - 1864.

PIERCE, Franklin - N.H. (Democratic) Nov. 23, 1804 - Oct. 8, 1869; House, 1833-37; Senate, 1837-42; President, 1853-57; Candidacy: P - 1852.

PINCKNEY, Charles Cotesworth - S.C. (Federalist) Feb. 25, 1746 - Aug. 16, 1825; president, state senate, 1779, Minister to France, 1796; Candidacies: VP - 1800; P - 1804, 1808.

PINCKNEY, Thomas - S.C. (Federalist) Oct. 23, 1750 - Nov. 2, 1828; Governor, 1787-89; Minister to Great Britain, 1792-96; Envoy to Spain, 1794-95; House, 1797-1801; Candidacy: 1796.

POLK, James Knox - Tenn. (Democratic) Nov. 2, 1795 - June 15, 1849; House, 1825-39; Speaker of the House, 1835-39; Governor, 1839-41; President, 1845-49; Candidacies: VP - 1840; P - 1844.

REAGAN, Ronald Wilson - Calif. (Republican) Feb. 6, 1911—; Governor, 1967-75; Candidacy: P - 1976.

REID, Whitelaw - N.Y. (Republican) Oct. 27, 1837 - Dec. 15, 1912; Minister to France, 1889-92; Editor-in-chief, *New York Tribune,* 1872-1905; Candidacy: VP - 1892.

ROBINSON, Joseph Taylor - Ark. (Democratic) Aug. 26, 1872 - July 14, 1937; House, 1903-13; Governor, Jan. 16 - March 8, 1913; Senate, 1913-37; Senate minority leader, 1923-33; Senate majority leader, 1933-37; Candidacy: VP - 1928.

RODNEY, Daniel - Del. (Federalist) Sept. 10, 1764 - Sept. 2, 1846; Governor, 1814-17; House, 1822-23; Senate, 1826-27; Candidacy: VP - 1820.

ROOSEVELT, Franklin Delano - N.Y. (Democratic) Jan. 30, 1882 - April 12, 1945; Assistant Secretary of Navy, 1913-20; Governor, 1929-33; President, 1933-45; Candidacies: VP - 1920; P - 1932, 1936, 1940, 1944.

ROOSEVELT, Theodore - N.Y. (Republican, Progressive) Oct. 27, 1858 - Jan. 6, 1919; Governor, 1899-1901; Assistant Secretary of Navy, 1897-98; Vice President, March 4 - Sept. 14, 1901; President, 1901-09; Candidacies: VP - 1900; P - 1904, 1912.

ROSS, James - Pa. (Federalist) July 12, 1762 - Nov. 27, 1847; Senate, 1794-1803; Candidacy: VP- 1816.

RUSH, Richard - Pa. (Democratic-Republican, National-Republican) Aug.

29, 1780 - July 30, 1859; Attorney General, 1814-17; Minister to Great Britain, 1817-24; Secretary of Treasury, 1825-28; Candidacy: VP- 1820, 1828.

RUTLEDGE, John - S.C. (Federalist) Sept. 1739 - July 23, 1800; Continental Congress, 1774-76, 1782-83; Governor, 1779-82; Constitutional Convention, 1787; Associate Justice of U.S. Supreme Court, 1789-91; Candidacy: 1789.

SANFORD, Nathan - N.Y.(Democratic-Republican) Nov. 5, 1777 - Oct. 17, 1838; Senate, 1815-21, 1826-31; Candidacy: VP- 1824.

SCHMITZ, John George - Calif. (American Independent) Aug. 12, 1930—; House, 1970-73; Candidacy: P - 1972.

SCOTT, Winfield - N.J.(Whig) June 13, 1786 - May 29, 1866; General-in-chief of U.S. Army, 1841-61; Candidacy: P- 1852.

SERGEANT, John - Pa. (National-Republican) Dec. 5, 1779 - Nov. 23, 1852; House, 1815-23, 1827-29, 1837-41; Candidacy: VP - 1832.

SEWALL, Arthur - Maine (Democratic) Nov. 25, 1835 - Sept. 5, 1900; Democratic National Committee member, 1888-96; Candidacy: VP - 1896.

SEYMOUR, Horatio - N.Y. (Democratic) May 31, 1810 - Feb. 12, 1886; Governor, 1853-55, 1863-65; Candidacy: P - 1868.

SHERMAN, James Schoolcraft - N.Y. (Republican) Oct. 24, 1855 - Oct. 30, 1912; House, 1887-91, 1893-1909; Vice President, 1909-12; Candidacies: VP - 1908, 1912 (Died during 1912 campaign; Nicholas Murray Butler replaced Sherman on the Republican ticket.)

SHRIVER, Robert Sargent Jr. - Md. (Democratic) Nov. 9, 1915—; Director, Peace Corps, 1961-66; Director, Office of Economic Opportunity, 1964-68; Ambassador to France, 1968-70; Candidacy: VP - 1972 (Replaced Thomas F. Eagleton on Democratic ticket Aug. 8.)

SMITH, Alfred Emanuel - N.Y. (Democratic) Dec. 30, 1873 - Oct. 4, 1944; Governor, 1919-21, 1923-29; Candidacy: P - 1928.

SMITH, William - S.C., Ala. (Independent Democratic-Republican) Sept. 6, 1762 - June 26, 1840; Senate, 1816-23, 1826-31; Candidacies: VP - 1828, 1836.

SPARKMAN, John Jackson - Ala. (Democratic) Dec. 20, 1899—; House, 1937-46; Senate, 1946-79; Candidacy: VP - 1952.

STEVENSON, Adlai Ewing - Ill. (Democratic) Oct. 23, 1835 - June 14, 1914; House, 1875-77, 1879-81; Assistant Postmaster General, 1885-89; Vice President, 1893-97; Candidacies: VP - 1892, 1900.

STEVENSON, Adlai Ewing II - Ill. (Democratic) Feb. 5, 1900 - July 14, 1965; Assistant to the Secretary of Navy, 1941-44; Assistant to the Secretary of State, 1945; Governor, 1949-53; Ambassador to United Nations, 1961-65; Candidacies: P - 1952, 1956.

STOCKTON, Richard (Federalist) - N.J. April 17, 1764 - March 7, 1828; Senate, 1796-99; House, 1813-15; Candidacy: VP- 1820.

TAFT, William Howard - Ohio (Republican) Sept. 15, 1857 - March 8, 1930; Secretary of War, 1904-08; President, 1909-13; Chief Justice of U.S. Supreme Court, 1921-30; Candidacies: P - 1908, 1912.

TALMADGE, Herman Eugene - Ga. (Independent Democratic) Aug. 9, 1913—; Governor, 1947, 1948-55; Senate, 1957—; Candidacy: VP - 1956.

TAYLOR, Glen Hearst - Idaho (Progressive) April 12, 1904—; Senate, 1945-51; Candidacy: VP- 1948.

TAYLOR, Zachary - La. (Whig) Nov. 24, 1784 - July 9, 1850; Major General, U.S. Army; President, 1849-50; Candidacy: P - 1848.

TAZEWELL, Littleton Waller - Va. (Democratic) Dec. 17, 1774 - May 6, 1860; House, 1800-01; Senate, 1824-32; Governor, 1834-36; Candidacy: VP - 1840.

TELFAIR, Edward - Ga.; 1735 - Sept. 17, 1807; Continental Congress, 1778-82, 1784-85, 1788-89; Governor, 1786, 1790-93; Candidacy: 1789.

THOMAS, Norman Mattoon - N.Y. (Socialist) Nov. 20, 1884 - Dec. 19, 1968; Presbyterian minister, 1911-31; author and editor; Candidacies: P - 1928, 1932, 1936, 1940, 1944, 1948.

THURMAN, Allen Granberry - Ohio (Democratic) Nov. 13, 1813 - Dec. 12, 1895; House, 1845-47; Ohio state supreme court, 1851-56; Senate, 1869-81; Candidacy: VP - 1888.

THURMOND, James Strom - S.C. (States' Rights Democrat, Democratic) Dec. 5, 1902—; Governor, 1947-51; Senate, 1954-56, 1956—; Candidacies: P - 1948; VP - 1960.

TILDEN, Samuel Jones - N.Y.(Democratic) Feb. 9, 1814 - Aug. 4, 1886; Governor, 1875-77; Candidacy: P - 1876.

TOMPKINS, Daniel D. - N.Y.(Democratic-Republican) June 21, 1774 - June 11, 1825; Governor, 1807-17; Vice President, 1817-25; Candidacies: VP - 1816, 1820.

TRUMAN, Harry S - Mo. (Democratic) May 8, 1884 - Dec. 26, 1972; Senate, 1935-45; Vice President, Jan. 20 - April 12, 1945; President, 1945-53; Candidacies: VP - 1944; P - 1948.

TYLER, John - Va. (Whig) March 29, 1790 - Jan. 18, 1862; Governor, 1825-27; Senate, 1827-36; Vice President, March 4 - April 4, 1841; President, 1841-45; Candidacies: VP - 1836, 1840.

VAN BUREN, Martin - N.Y. (Democratic, Free Soil) Dec. 5, 1782 - July 24, 1862; Senate, 1821-28; Governor, Jan. - March, 1829; Secretary of State, 1829-31; Vice President, 1833-37; President, 1837-41; Candidacies: VP - 1824, 1832; P - 1836, 1840, 1848.

WALLACE, George Corley - Ala. (American Independent) Aug. 25, 1919—; Governor, 1963-67, 1971-79; Candidacy: P - 1968.

WALLACE, Henry Agard - Iowa (Democratic, Progressive) Oct. 7, 1888 - Nov. 18, 1965; Secretary of Agriculture, 1933-40; Vice President, 1941-45; Secretary of Commerce, 1945-46; Candidacies: VP - 1940; P - 1948.

WARREN, Earl - Calif. (Republican) March 19, 1891 - July 9, 1974; Governor, 1943-53; Chief Justice of U.S. Supreme Court, 1953-69; Candidacy: VP- 1948.

WASHINGTON, George - Va. (Federalist) Feb. 22, 1732 - Dec. 14, 1799; First and Second Continental Congresses, 1774, 1775; Commander-in-chief of armed forces, 1775-83; president of Constitutional Convention, 1787; President, 1789-97; Candidacies: P - 1789, 1792, 1796.

WATSON, Thomas Edward - Ga. (Populist) Sept. 5, 1856 - Sept. 26, 1922; House, 1891-93; Senate, 1921-22; Candidacies: VP - 1896; P - 1904, 1908.

WEAVER, James Baird - Iowa (Greenback, Populist) June 12, 1833 - Feb. 6, 1912; House, 1879-81, 1885-89; Candidacies: P - 1880, 1892.

WEBSTER, Daniel - Mass. (Whig) Jan. 18, 1782 - Oct. 24, 1852; House, 1813-17, 1823-27; Senate, 1827-41, 1845-50; Secretary of State, 1841-43, 1850-52; Candidacy: P - 1836.

WHEELER, Burton Kendall - Mont. (Progressive) Feb. 27, 1882 - Jan. 6,

1975; Senate, 1923-47; Candidacy: VP-1924.

WHEELER, William Almon - N.Y. (Republican) June 19, 1819 - June 4, 1887; House, 1861-63, 1869-77; Vice President, 1877-81; Candidacy: VP - 1876.

WHITE, Hugh Lawson - Tenn. (Whig) Oct. 30, 1773 - April 10, 1840; Senate, 1825-March 3, 1835, Oct. 6, 1835-1840; Candidacy: P - 1836.

WILKINS, William - Pa. (Democratic) Dec. 20, 1779 - June 23, 1865; Senate, 1831-34; Minister to Russia, 1834-35; House, 1843-44; Secretary of War, 1844-45; Candidacy: VP - 1832.

WILLKIE, Wendell Lewis - N.Y. (Republican) Feb. 18, 1892 - Oct. 8, 1944; Utility executive, 1933-40; Candidacy: P - 1940.

WILSON, Henry - Mass. (Republican) Feb. 16, 1812 - Nov. 22, 1875; Senate, 1855-73; Vice President, 1873-75; Candidacy: VP - 1872.

WILSON, Woodrow - N.J. (Democratic) Dec. 28, 1856 - Feb. 3, 1924; Governor, 1911-13; President, 1913-21; Candidacies: P - 1912, 1916.

WIRT, William - Md. (Anti-Masonic) Nov. 8, 1772 - Feb. 18, 1834; Attorney General, 1817-29; Candidacy: P - 1832.

WRIGHT, Fielding Lewis - Miss. (States' Rights Democratic) May 16, 1895 - May 4, 1956; Governor, 1946-52; Candidacy: VP - 1948.

Index of Candidates' Popular Vote Returns

The following index lists all individuals receiving popular votes for President from 1824 to 1976. The index indicates the year(s) in which popular votes were cast for the individual.

The popular vote returns for major candidates appear in chronological order on pages 67 to 102. The returns for the minor candidates are listed in chronological order on pages 103 to 111.

General Index

The following General Index covers all sections of this book with the exception of popular votes for president. For a complete index of all individuals receiving popular votes for president from 1824 to 1976, see page 185.

A

Adams, Charles Francis
  Biography - 177
  Party VP nominee - (1848) 115
Adams, John
  Biography - 177
  Electoral votes, Pres. - (1789) 19; (1792) 20; (1796) 21; (1800) 22
Adams, John Quincy
  Biography - 177
  Election by House, 1825 - 7
  Electoral votes, Pres. - (1820) 25; (1824) 25; (1828) 26
  Popular and electoral votes, 1824 - 5
Adams, John Quincy (II)
  Party VP nominee - (1872) 116
Adams, Samuel
  Biography - 177
  Electoral votes - (1796) 21
Agnew, Spiro Theodore
  Biography - 177
  Electoral votes, VP - (1968) 63; (1972) 63
  Party VP nominee - (1968, 1972) 121
Ahern, Frank
  Presidential primaries - (1976) 173
Aiken, John W.
  Party Pres. nominee - (1936, 1940) 119
  Party VP nominee - (1932) 119
Albaugh, Arla A.
  Party VP nominee - (1944) 119
Allen, H. C.
  Presidential primaries - (1940) 146
Allen, Seymour E.
  Party Pres. nominee - (1932) 119
Allen, Willis
  Presidential primaries - (1940) 146
Amendments. See Constitution, U.S.
America First Party. See also Tax Cut Party.
  Nominees - 119, 121
American Independent Party
  Nominees - 121
American (Know-Nothing) Party
  Nominees - 116
American Labor Party
  Nominees - 120
American National Party
  Nominees - 116
American Party. See also Tax Cut Party.
  Nominees - 116-118, 121
American Prohibition Party
  Nominees - 117
American Third Party
  Nominees - 113
American Vegetarian Party
  Nominees - 120
Anderson, Thomas Jefferson
  Party Pres. nominee - (1976) 121
  Party VP nominee - (1972) 121
Andrews, Thomas Coleman
  Party Pres. nominee - (1956, 1964) 120
Anti-Masonic Party
  Nominees - 115
Anti-Monopoly Party
  Nominees - 116
Armstrong, James
  Biography - 177
  Electoral votes - (1789) 19
Arnold, S. C.
  Presidential primaries - (1956) 155
Arnold, Stanley
  Presidential primaries - (1976) 173

Arthur, Chester Alan
  Biography - 177
  Electoral votes, VP - (1880) 63
  Party VP nominee - (1880) 116
Ashbrook, John M.
  Presidential primaries - (1972) 164-167

B

Babson, Roger Ward
  Party Pres. nominee - (1940) 119
Bailey, Lloyd W.
  North Carolina elector challenge, 1968 - 11
Baker, Newton D.
  Presidential primaries - (1932) 142
Bankhead, William B.
  Presidential primaries - (1940) 146
Banks, Nathaniel Prentice
  Biography - 177
  Electoral votes, VP - (1872) 63
  Party Pres. nominee - (1856) 116
Barker, Wharton
  Party Pres. nominee - (1900) 117
Barkley, Alben William
  Biography - 177
  Electoral votes, VP - (1948) 63
  Party VP nominee - (1948) 119
Barnburners. See Free Soil Party.
Barnum, R. G.
  Party VP nominee - (1920) 118
Bass, Charlotta A.
  Party VP nominee - (1952) 119, 120
Bass, Willie Isaac
  Party VP nominee - (1952) 120
Bayh, Birch
  Electoral College reform - 13
  Presidential primaries - (1976) 168-173
Beckwith, Frank R.
  Presidential primaries - (1960) 157; (1964) 160
Bedell, Edward J.
  Party VP nominee - (1952) 120
Bell, John
  Biography - 177
  Electoral votes, Pres. - (1860) 32
  Party Pres. nominee - (1860) 116
Bender, Riley A.
  Presidential primaries - (1944) 148; (1948) 149, 150; (1952) 153
Bennington, Wesley Henry
  Party VP nominee - (1928) 118
Benson, Allan Louis
  Biography - 177
  Party Pres. nominee - (1916) 118
Bentley, Charles Eugene
  Party Pres. nominee - (1896) 117
Bentsen, Lloyd
  Presidential primaries - (1976) 168-169, 172-173
Bergland, David P.
  Party VP nominee - (1976) 121
Bidwell, John
  Biography - 177
  Party Pres. nominee - (1892) 117
Billings, Theodore C.
  Party VP nominee - (1964) 120
Bi-Metallic League. See National Silver Party.

Biographies
  Pres., V.P. candidates - 177-183
Birney, James Gillespie
  Biography - 177
  Party Pres. nominee - (1840, 1844) 115
Bixler, —
  Presidential primaries - (1948) 150
Black, James
  Party Pres. nominee - (1872) 116
Blaine, James Gillespie
  Biography - 177
  Electoral vote, Pres. - (1884) 38
  Party Pres. nominee - (1884) 116
Blair, Francis Preston Jr.
  Biography - 177
  Electoral votes, VP - (1868) 62
  Party VP nominee - (1868) 116
Blessitt, Arthur O.
  Presidential primaries - (1976) 173
Blomen, Constance
  Party VP nominee - (1976) 121
Blomen, Henning A.
  Party Pres. nominee - (1968) 121
  Party VP nominee - (1964) 120
Bogue, —
  Presidential primaries - (1932) 142
Bona, Frank
  Presidential primaries - (1976) 173
Borah, William E.
  Presidential primaries - (1936) 143, 144
Bottum, Joe H.
  Presidential primaries - (1944) 148
Bouck, William
  Party VP nominee - (1924) 118
Bourne, Jonathan
  Presidential preference primary - 125
Boutelle, Paul
  Party VP nominee - (1968) 121
Bradley, Joseph P.
  Hayes-Tilden contest - 11
Bramlette, Thomas E.
  Biography - 177
  Electoral votes, VP - (1872) 62
Branigin, Roger D.
  Presidential primaries - (1968) 161, 163
Breckinridge, Henry
  Presidential primaries - (1936) 143, 144
Breckinridge, John Cabell
  Biography - 177
  Electoral votes, Pres. - (1860) 32
  Electoral votes, VP - (1856) 62
  Party Pres. nominee - (1860) 116
  Party VP nominee - (1856) 116
Brehm, Marie Caroline
  Party VP nominee - (1924) 118
Brewster, Daniel B.
  Presidential primaries - (1964) 159, 160
Bricker, John William
  Biography - 177
  Electoral votes, VP - (1944) 63
  Party VP nominee - (1944) 119
  Presidential primaries - (1940) 145, 146; (1944) 147, 148; (1956) 155
Brisben, J, Quinn
  Party VP nominee - (1976) 121
Brooks, John Anderson
  Party Pres. nominee - (1888) 117
Broughton, Charles
  Presidential primaries - (1952) 153

Browder, Earl Russell
  Party Pres. nominee - (1936, 1940) 119
Brown, Benjamin Gratz
  Biography - 177
  Democratic elector vote, 1872 - 5
  Electoral votes, Pres. - (1872) 35
  Electoral votes, VP - (1872) 62
  Party VP nominee - (1872) 116
Brown, Edmund G.
  Presidential primaries - (1952) 152; (1960) 157; (1964) 160
Brown, Edmund G. Jr.
  Presidential primaries - (1976) 170-173
Brumbaugh, Martin G.
  Presidential primaries - (1916) 133
Bryan, Charles Wayland
  Biography - 177
  Electoral votes, VP - (1924) 63
  Party VP nominee - (1924) 118
Bryan, William Jennings
  Biography - 178
  Electoral votes, Pres. - (1896) 41; (1900) 42; (1908) 44
  Party Pres. nominee - (1896, 1900, 1908) 117
  Presidential primaries - (1912) 131
Bubar, Benjamin C.
  Party Pres. nominee - (1976) 121
Buchanan, James
  Biography - 178
  Electoral votes, Pres. - (1856) 31
  Party Pres. nominee - (1856) 116
Buckner, Simon Bolivar
  Party VP nominee - (1896) 117
Bulkley, Robert J.
  Presidential primaries - (1952) 152
"Bull Moose." See Progressive Party ("Bull Moose").
Burke, John
  Presidential primaries - (1912) 130, 131
Burr, Aaron
  Biography - 178
  Electoral votes - (1792) 20; (1796) 21; (1800) 22
  Jefferson-Burr deadlock, 1800 - 6
Burton, Theodore E.
  Presidential primaries - (1916) 133
Butler, Benjamin Franklin
  Biography - 178
  Party Pres. nominee - (1884) 109
Butler, Nicholas Murray
  Biography - 178
  Electoral votes, VP - (1912) 63
Butler, William Orlando
  Biography - 178
  Electoral votes, VP - (1848) 62
  Party VP nominee - (1848) 115
Byer, —
  Presidential primaries - (1948) 150
Byrd, Harry Flood
  Biography - 178
  Electoral votes, Pres. - (1960) 57
  Party Pres. nominee - (1956) 120
  Party VP nominee - (1952) 119, 120
  Presidential primaries - (1944) 148
Byrd, Robert C.
  Presidential primaries - (1976) 168-169, 172-173
Byrnes, John W.
  Presidential primaries - (1964) 158, 160

U

V

W

Y

Z